TAXATION (TX – UK)
FA 2021

Practice & Revision Kit

For exams in June 2022, September 2022, December 2022 and March 2023

First edition 2008
Sixteenth edition October 2021

ISBN 9781 5097 4204 2
(previous ISBN 9781 5097 3491 7)
e-ISBN 9781 5097 4257 8

British Library Cataloguing-in-Publication Data
A catalogue record for this book
is available from the British Library

Published by

BPP Learning Media Ltd
BPP House, Aldine Place
London W12 8AA

www.bpp.com/learningmedia

Printed in the United Kingdom

Your learning materials, published by BPP Learning Media Ltd, are printed on paper obtained from traceable, sustainable sources.

We are grateful to the Association of Chartered Certified Accountants for permission to reproduce past examination questions. The suggested solutions in the Practice & Revision Kit have been prepared by BPP Learning Media Ltd, except where otherwise stated.

About this Practice & Revision Kit

It will only be possible (for exams in June 2019 onwards) for candidates to sit TX – UK as a computer-based exam (CBE). Paper-based exams are no longer available for this exam.

This Practice & Revision Kit is valid for exams from the June 2022 sitting through to the March 2023 sitting and in this Practice & Revision Kit you will find questions in both multiple choice question (MCQ) and objective testing question (OTQ) format. OTQs include a wider variety of questions types including MCQ as well as number entry, multiple response and drag and drop. More information on these question types will be available on the ACCA website.

More information on the exam formats can be found on page **xvii**.

The TX exam is 3 hours in duration and the timings of the questions are based on this time allocation. Prior to the start of each exam there will be time allocated for students to be informed of the exam instructions.

These materials are reviewed by the ACCA examining team. The objective of the review is to ensure that the material properly covers the syllabus and study guide outcomes, used by the examining team in setting the exams, in the appropriate breadth and depth. The review does not ensure that every eventuality, combination or application of examinable topics is addressed by the ACCA Approved Content. Nor does the review comprise a detailed technical check of the content as the Approved Content Provider has its own quality assurance processes in place in this respect.

BPP Learning Media do everything possible to ensure the material is accurate and up to date when sending to print. In the event that any errors are found after the print date, they are uploaded to the following website: www.bpp.com/learningmedia/Errata.

Contents

Question index

The headings in this checklist/index indicate the main topics of questions, but questions may cover several different topics.

Questions set under the old F6 Taxation (UK) exam format are included in this Kit because their style and content are similar to those that may appear in the Taxation (TX – UK) exams from 1 September 2016. Some of these questions have been amended to reflect the new exam format and this is shown by (amended) in the title of the question.

Topic index

Listed below are the key Taxation (TX – UK) syllabus topics and the numbers of the questions of this Kit (excluding the Mock exams) covering those topics.

If you need to concentrate your practice and revision on certain topics, or if you want to attempt all available questions that refer to a particular subject, you will find this index useful.

Syllabus topic	Question numbers
UK tax system	1, 2, 3, 8, 16, 31, 32, 41
Computing taxable income and the income tax liability	43, 44, 45, 46, 48, 49, 53, 75, 76, 86, 87, 93, 102, 107, 108, 109, 110, 111, 112, 113, 114, 115, 116, 117, 118, 237, 238, 239, 315
Employment income	47, 50, 51, 52, 54, 98, 101, 102, 103, 104, 105, 106, 109, 111, 112, 113, 114, 115, 117, 118, 315
Pensions	55, 73, 74, 77, 83, 84, 85, 98, 109, 110, 113, 114, 115
Property income for individuals	56, 57, 58, 101, 109, 113, 116, 117, 118, 239
Computing trading income for individuals	59, 60, 90, 95, 96, 101, 102, 107, 108, 110, 116, 117
Capital allowances for individuals	61, 62, 63, 81, 110, 113, 116
Assessable trading income for individuals	64, 65, 66, 78, 79, 80, 82, 88, 89, 108, 113, 116
Trading losses for individuals	67, 68, 91, 92, 99, 100, 103, 115, 116
Partnerships	69, 70, 98, 103, 114, 116, 117
National insurance contributions	71, 72, 94, 102, 104, 106, 107, 113, 237, 238, 243, 315
Computing chargeable gains for individuals	87, 107, 119, 120, 121, 122, 129, 130, 131, 136, 138, 143, 147, 148, 149, 153, 154, 155, 157, 158, 159, 160, 161, 162, 239
Chargeable gains for individuals: chattels and PPR exemption	123, 124, 125, 137, 152, 159
Chargeable gains for individuals: business reliefs	126, 127, 132, 133, 139, 140, 142, 146, 150, 151, 156, 162, 161, 162, 315
Chargeable gains for individuals: shares and securities	128, 134, 135, 144, 145, 161, 162
Self-assessment and payment of tax by individuals	4, 5, 9, 10, 11, 12, 17, 18, 19, 20, 24, 25, 26, 27, 28, 29, 30, 33, 34, 35, 41, 101, 117, 141, 315
Inheritance tax	163 – 207
Computing taxable total profits (including property income and capital allowances for companies) and the corporation tax liability	106, 208, 209, 210, 211, 235, 237, 238, 239, 240, 241, 242, 243, 244, 245, 246, 247, 248, 249

BPP LEARNING MEDIA

Syllabus topic	Question numbers
Chargeable gains for companies	212, 218, 219, 220, 221, 222, 223, 224, 225, 226, 227, 233, 239, 245, 246, 247, 248, 249
Losses for companies	213, 214, 234, 240, 242, 245, 246, 247, 248, 249
Groups of companies	215, 216, 217, 228, 229, 230, 231, 232, 236, 241, 244, 246, 248, 249
Self-assessment and payment of tax by companies	6, 7, 13, 14, 15, 21, 22, 23, 36, 37, 38, 39, 40, 42, 245
Value added tax	250 – 301, 312 – 315

Revising Taxation (TX – UK)

Topics to revise

All questions are compulsory so you must revise the **whole** syllabus. Since the exam includes 15 objective test questions in Section A and 15 objective test questions in Section B, you should expect questions to cover a large part of the syllabus. Selective revision **will limit** the number of questions you can answer and hence reduce your chances of passing. It is better to go into the exam knowing a reasonable amount about most of the syllabus rather than concentrating on a few topics to the exclusion of the rest.

Passing the Taxation (TX – UK) exam

Displaying the right qualities

- You will be required to identify the requirements of objective test questions quickly, so that you can make your answers confidently within the available time.

- In constructed response questions you will be required to carry out calculations, with clear workings and a logical structure. If your numbers are not perfect you will not necessarily lose too many marks so long as your method is correct and you have stated any assumptions you have made.

- You will also be expected to apply your tax knowledge to the facts of each particular question and also to identify the compliance issues for your client.

- You may also be required to describe rules and conditions, so take care to practise the descriptive elements of the answers.

Avoiding weaknesses

- There is no choice in this exam, all questions have to be answered. You must therefore study the entire syllabus, there are no short-cuts.

- Ability to answer objective test questions and cases improves with practice. Try to get as much practice with these questions as you can.

- The constructed response questions will be based on simple scenarios and answers must be focused and specific to the requirement of the question.

- Answer all parts of the constructed response questions. Even if you cannot do all the calculation elements, you will still be able to gain marks in the descriptive parts.

Gaining the easy marks

Easy marks in this exam tend to fall into three categories.

Objective test questions (OTQs)

Some OTQs are easier than others. Answer those that you feel fairly confident about as quickly as you can. Come back later to those you find more difficult. This could be a way of making use of the time in the examination most efficiently and effectively. Some OTQs will not involve calculations. Make sure that you understand the wording of 'written' OTQs before selecting your answer.

Calculations in Section C questions

There will always be basic marks available for straightforward tasks such as putting easy figures into proformas, for example putting the cost figure for an addition into a capital allowances proforma. Do not miss out on these easy marks by not learning your proformas properly.

Discussions in Section C questions

A constructed response question may separate descriptive requirements from calculations, so that you do not need to do the calculations first in order to answer the descriptive parts. This means that you should be able to gain marks from the descriptive parts without having to complete the calculations.

Descriptive requirements may focus on administrative, or compliance, details such as filing deadlines and tax payment dates. Make your points concisely, bearing in mind that one mark usually equates to one point to be made.

Read the question carefully and more than once, to ensure you are actually answering the specific requirements. Don't write about matters which are not specifically required – even if these are technically correct, you will not gain any marks and will waste valuable time.

Tackling Objective Test Case Questions

First, read the whole case scenario. Highlight any specific instructions or assumptions, such as 'Ignore the annual exempt amount' in a capital gains tax question. Then skim through the requirements of the five questions. If you are sitting your exam in-centre you can make notes either on the on-screen scratchpad or on the scrap paper available to you in the exam. If you are sitting your exam via remote invigilation only the on-screen scratchpad can be used. You can familiarise yourself with the on-screen scratchpad by testing it on the Practice Platform.

The questions are independent of each other and can be answered in any order. Some of the OTQs will be easier than others. For example, you may be asked to identify the filing date for a tax return and the penalty for late filing. Answer these OTQs quickly.

Other OTQs will be more difficult and/or complex. There are two types of OTQ that may take you longer to answer.

The first more time-consuming OTQ will involve doing a computation. For example, you may be asked to calculate the personal allowance available to a taxpayer whose adjusted net income exceeds £100,000. You will probably need to use a quick pro-forma to answer a computational question like this.

If the OTQ is a multiple choice question, remember that the wrong answers will usually involve common errors, so don't assume that because you have the same answer as one of the options that your answer is necessarily correct! Double check to make sure you haven't made any silly mistakes, such as deducting the whole of the excess of adjusted net income over the £100,000 threshold (instead of half of it) when working out the restriction for the personal allowance. If you haven't got the same answer as any of the options, rework your computation, thinking carefully about what errors you could have made. If you still haven't got one of the options, choose the one which is nearest to your answer.

The second more time-consuming OTQ is one where you are asked to consider a number of statements and identify which one (or more) of them is correct. Make sure that you read each statement at least twice before making your selection. Be careful to follow the requirements of the OTQ exactly, for example if you are asked to identify **TWO** correct statements.

Exam information

Computer-based exams

Applied Skills exams are all computer-based exams.

Format of the exam

The exam format will comprise 3 exam sections.

Section	Style of question type	Description	Proportion of exam, %
A	Objective test (OT)	15 questions × 2 marks	30
B	Objective test (OT) case	3 questions × 10 marks Each question will contain 5 subparts each worth 2 marks	30
C	Constructed Response (Long questions)	1 question × 10 marks 2 questions × 15 marks	40
Total			100

Section A and B questions will be selected from the entire syllabus. The responses to each question or subpart in the case of OT cases are marked automatically as either correct or incorrect by computer.

The 10-mark Section C question can come from any part of the syllabus. The 15-mark Section C questions will mainly focus on the following syllabus areas but a minority of marks can be drawn from any other area of the syllabus:

- Income tax (syllabus area B)
- Corporation tax (syllabus area E)

The responses to these questions are human marked.

CBE practice platform

Practising as many exam-style questions as possible in the ACCA CBE practice platform will be the key to passing this exam. You must do questions under timed conditions and ensure you produce full answers to the discussion parts as well as doing the calculations.

Also ensure that you attempt all mock exams under exam conditions.

ACCA have launched a free on-demand resource designed to mirror the live exam experience helping you to become more familiar with the exam format. You can access the platform via the Study Support Resources section of the ACCA website navigating to the CBE question practice section and logging in with your myACCA credentials.

Additional information

The study guide provides more detailed guidance on the syllabus and can be found by visiting the exam resource finder on the ACCA website.

Useful websites

The websites below provide additional sources of information of relevance to your studies for *Taxation (TX – UK)*.

- www.accaglobal.com

  ACCA's website. The students' section of the website is invaluable for detailed information about the qualification, past issues of *Student Accountant* (including technical articles) and a free downloadable Student Planner App.

- www.bpp.com

  Our website provides information about BPP products and services, with a link to the ACCA website.

Helping you with your revision

BPP Learning Media – Approved Content Provider

As an ACCA **Approved Content Provider**, BPP Learning Media gives you the **opportunity** to use revision materials reviewed by the ACCA examining team. By incorporating the ACCA examining team's comments and suggestions regarding the depth and breadth of syllabus coverage, the BPP Learning Media Practice & Revision Kit provides excellent **ACCA approved** support for your revision.

Tackling revision and the exam

Using feedback obtained from the ACCA examining team review:

- We look at the dos and don'ts of revising for, and taking, ACCA exams

- We focus on Taxation (TX – UK); we discuss revising the syllabus, what to do (and what not to do) in the exam, how to approach different types of question and ways of obtaining easy marks

Selecting questions

We provide signposts to help you plan your revision.

- A full question index

- A topic index listing all the questions that cover key topics, so that you can locate the questions that provide practice on these topics, and see the different ways in which they might be examined

Making the most of question practice

At BPP Learning Media we realise that you need more than just questions and model answers to get the most from your question practice.

- Our **Top tips** included for certain questions provide essential advice on tackling questions, presenting answers and the key points that answers need to include.

- We show you how you can pick up **easy marks** on some questions, as we know that picking up all readily available marks often can make the difference between passing and failing.

- We include **marking guides** to show you what the examining team rewards.

- We include **comments from the examining team** to show you where students struggled or performed well in the actual exam.

- We refer to the **FA 2021 Workbook** (for exams in June 2021, September 2021, December 2021 and March 2022) for detailed coverage of the topics covered in questions.

Attempting mock exams

There are four mock exams that provide practice at coping with the pressures of the exam day. We strongly recommend that you attempt them under exam conditions.

Mock exam 1 is the September 2016 exam, **Mock exam 2** is the Specimen exam, **Mock exam 3** is the December 2016 exam and **Mock exam 4** is the March/June 2021 exam.

BPP LEARNING MEDIA

Essential skills areas to be successful in Taxation (TX UK)

We think there are three areas you should develop in order to achieve exam success in TX:

(1)   Knowledge application
(2)   Specific Taxation skills
(3)   Exam success skills

These are shown in the diagram below.

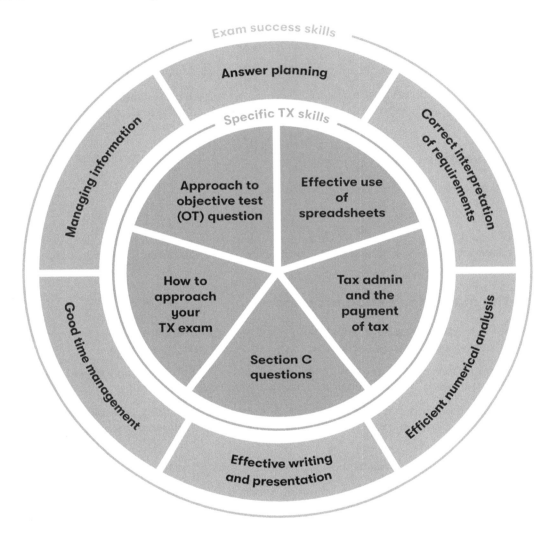

Specific TX skills

These are the skills specific to TX that we think you need to develop in order to pass the exam.

In the Workbook, there are five **Skills Checkpoints** which define each skill and show how it is applied in answering a question. A brief summary of each skill is given below.

Skill 1: Approach to objective test (OT) questions

Section A of the exam will include 15 OT questions worth two marks each. Section B of the exam will include three OT cases, worth 10 marks each. Each OT case contains a group of five OT questions based around a single scenario. 60% of your TX exam is therefore made up of OT questions. It is essential that you have a good approach to answering these questions. OT questions are auto-marked; your workings will therefore not be considered; you have to answer the whole question correctly to earn their two marks.

A step-by-step technique for tackling OT questions is outlined below:

General guidance for approaching OT questions

STEP 1: Answer the questions you know first.

If you're having difficulty answering a question, move on and come back to tackle it once you've answered all the questions you know. It is often quicker to answer discursive style OT questions first, leaving more time for calculations.

General guidance for approaching OT questions

STEP 2: Answer all questions.

There is no penalty for an incorrect answer in ACCA exams; there is nothing to be gained by leaving an OT question unanswered. If you are stuck on a question, as a last resort, it is worth selecting the option you consider most likely to be correct and moving on. Make a note of the question, so if you have time after you have answered the of the questions, you can revisit it.

Guidance for answering specific OT questions

STEP 3: Read the requirement first!

The requirement will be stated in bold text in the exam. Identify what you are being asked to do, any technical knowledge required and **what type of OT question** you are dealing with. Look for key words in the requirement such as 'which **TWO** of the following,' 'which of the following is **NOT**'

Guidance for answering specific OT questions

STEP 4: Apply you technical knowledge to the data presented in the question.

Take your time working through questions, and make sure to read through each answer option with care. OT questions are designed so that each answer option is plausible. Work through each response option and eliminate those you know are incorrect.

Skills Checkpoint 1 covers this technique in detail through application of an OT case question.

Skill 2: Effective use of spreadsheets

It is very likely that you will be required to use the spreadsheet response option in the constructed workspace for Section C questions. It is imperative that you know how to use the spreadsheet functions to prepare accurate and easy to follow calculations.

The key steps are outlined below.

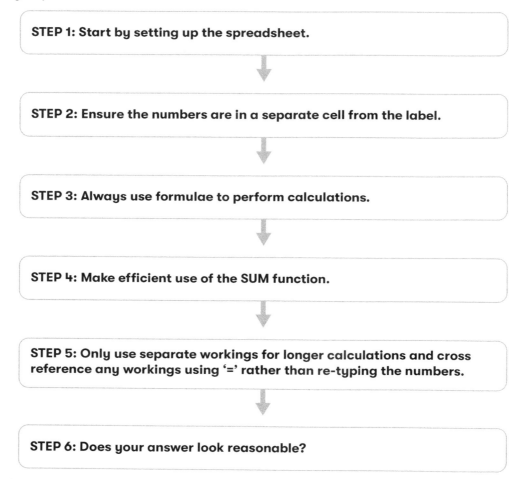

STEP 1: Start by setting up the spreadsheet.

STEP 2: Ensure the numbers are in a separate cell from the label.

STEP 3: Always use formulae to perform calculations.

STEP 4: Make efficient use of the SUM function.

STEP 5: Only use separate workings for longer calculations and cross reference any workings using '=' rather than re-typing the numbers.

STEP 6: Does your answer look reasonable?

Skills Checkpoint 2 covers this technique in detail through application to a question.

Skill 3: The UK tax system and its administration

You must study the whole syllabus in order to pass the TX exam, but having the administration knowledge at your fingertips will give you extra time in the exam to answer the more difficult questions.

This skills checkpoint gives you a list of quickfire questions to help you learn the basic information.

Skill 4: Section C questions

Section C questions contain one 10-mark question and two 15-mark questions. One 15-mark question will focus on income tax and the other one will focus on corporation tax. This means that you know roughly what to expect and you can use proformas where relevant to help with the long calculations. Discursive elements will be relatively short. 10-mark questions often cover more than one tax and are designed to act as a bridge question between TX and the higher level exam, ATX.

A step-by-step technique for attempting these questions is outlined below.

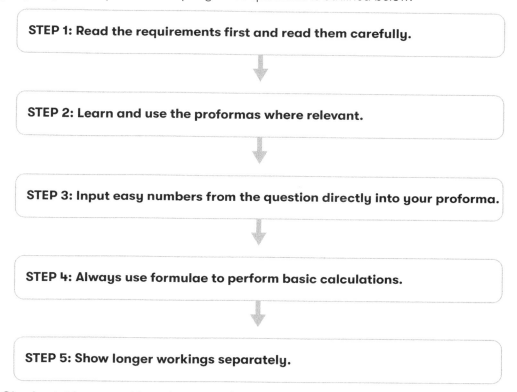

STEP 1: Read the requirements first and read them carefully.

STEP 2: Learn and use the proformas where relevant.

STEP 3: Input easy numbers from the question directly into your proforma.

STEP 4: Always use formulae to perform basic calculations.

STEP 5: Show longer workings separately.

Skills Checkpoint 4 covers this technique in detail through application to a question.

Skill 5: How to approach your TX exam

You can answer your TX exam in whatever order you prefer. It is important that you adopt a strategy that works best for you. We would suggest that you decide on your preferred approach and practice it by doing a timed mock exam before your real exam.

A suggested approach to tackling your TX exam is outlined below.

Complete Section A first - allocated time 54 minutes

Tackle any easier OT questions first. Often discursive style questions can be answered quickly, saving more time for calculations. Do not leave any questions unanswered. Even if you are unsure make a reasoned guess.

Complete Section B next - allocated time 54 minutes

You will have 18 mins of exam time to allocate to each of the three OT case questions in Section B. Use the same approach to OT questions as discussed for Section A.

There will normally be discursive and numerical questions within each case. Again, it is better to tackle the discursive type questions first and make a reasoned guess for any questions you are unsure on.

Finally, complete Section C - allocated time 72 minutes

Start with the question you feel most confident with.

Skills checkpoint 5 covers this technique in more detail.

Exam success skills

Passing the TX exam requires more than applying syllabus knowledge and demonstrating the specific TX skills; it also requires the development of excellent exam technique through question practice.

We consider the following six skills to be vital for exam success. The Skills Checkpoints show how each of these skills can be applied in the exam.

Exam success skill 1

Managing information

Questions in the exam will present you with a lot of information. The skill is how you handle this information to make the best use of your time. The key is determining how you will approach the exam and then actively reading the questions.

Advice on developing Managing information

Approach

The exam is 3 hours long. There is no designated 'reading' time at the start of the exam, however, one approach that can work well is to start the exam by spending 10–15 minutes carefully reading through all of the questions to familiarise yourself with the exam.

Once you feel familiar with the exam, consider the order in which you will attempt the questions; always attempt them in your order of preference. For example, you may want to leave to last the question you consider to be the most difficult.

If you do take this approach, remember to adjust the time available for each question appropriately – see Exam success skill 6: Good time management.

If you find that this approach doesn't work for you, don't worry – you can develop your own technique.

Active reading

You must take an active approach to reading each question. Focus on the requirement first, underlining/highlighting key verbs such as 'prepare', 'comment', 'explain', 'discuss', to ensure you answer the question properly. Then read the rest of the question, underlining/highlighting and annotating important and relevant information, and making notes of any relevant technical information you think you will need.

Exam success skill 2

Correct interpretation of the requirements

The active verb used often dictates the approach that written answers should take (eg 'explain', 'discuss', 'evaluate'). It is important you identify and use the verb to define your approach. The **correct interpretation of the requirements** skill means correctly producing only what is being asked for by a requirement. Anything not required will not earn marks.

Advice on developing correct interpretation of the requirements

This skill can be developed by analysing question requirements and applying this process:

Step 1	**Read the requirement**
	Firstly, read the requirement a couple of times slowly and carefully and highlight the active verbs. Use the active verbs to define what you plan to do. Make sure you identify any sub-requirements and any topics which you are specifically told you do not need to cover in your answer. Also note the number of marks available for each requirement or sub-requirement, as this will indicate the time available and hence the level of depth required in your answer.
Step 2	**Read the rest of the question**
	By reading the requirement first, you will have an idea of what you are looking out for as you read through the scenario. This is a great time saver and means you don't end up having to read the whole question in full twice. You should do this in an active way – see Exam success skill 1: Managing Information.
Step 3	**Read the requirement again**
	Read the requirement again to remind yourself of the exact wording before starting your answer. This will capture any misinterpretation of the requirements or any missed requirements entirely. This should become a habit in your approach and, with repeated practice, you will find the focus, relevance and depth of your answer plan will improve.

Exam success skill 3

Answer planning: Priorities, structure and logic

This skill requires the planning of the key aspects of an answer which accurately and completely responds to the requirement.

Advice on developing Answer planning: Priorities, structure and logic

Everyone will have a preferred style for an answer plan. For example, it may be a mind map, bullet-pointed lists or simply making some notes. Choose the approach that you feel most comfortable with, or, if you are not sure, try out different approaches for different questions until you have found your preferred style.

For 10 mark Section C questions, it can be useful to draw up a separate answer plan in the format of your choosing (eg a mind map or bullet-pointed lists). You will want to remind yourself of key facts from the scenario to avoid having to re-read the question – you should at the very least make a few notes including vital information such as the following key factors:

- Nature of the taxpayer: is it an individual or a company?

- For individuals: their age, any family relationships, their residence and domicile status, whether they're a basic, higher or additional rate taxpayer, and whether they've used their CGT annual exempt amount/IHT exemptions

- For companies: their ownership structure and group relationships

- Relevant dates: the year end(s) of businesses, dates of actual or proposed transactions, the date that a business started, dates of gifts (or death!) for IHT

Exam success skill 4

Efficient numerical analysis

This skill aims to maximise the marks awarded by making clear to the marker the process of arriving at your answer. This is achieved by laying out an answer such that, even if you make a few errors, you can still score subsequent marks for follow-on calculations. It is vital that you do not lose marks purely because the marker cannot follow what you have done.

Advice on developing Efficient numerical analysis

This skill can be developed by applying the following process:

Step 1   **Use a standard proforma working where relevant**

If answers can be laid out in a standard proforma then always plan to do so. This will help the marker to understand your working and allocate the marks easily. It will also help you to work through the figures in a methodical and time-efficient way.

Step 2   **Show your workings**

Keep your workings as clear and simple as possible and ensure they are cross-referenced to the main part of your answer.

Step 3   **Keep moving!**

It is important to remember that, in an exam situation, it is difficult to get every number 100% correct. The key is therefore ensuring you do not spend too long on any single calculation. If you are struggling with a solution then make a sensible assumption, state it and move on.

Exam success skill 5

Effective writing and presentation

Written answers should be presented so that the marker can clearly see the points you are making, presented in the format specified in the question. The skill is to provide efficient written answers with sufficient breadth of points that answer the question, in the right depth, in the time available.

Advice on developing Effective writing and presentation

Step 1   **Use headings**

Using the headings and sub-headings from your answer plan will give your answer structure, order and logic. This will ensure your answer links back to the requirement and is clearly signposted, making it easier for the marker to understand the different points you are making. Underlining your headings will also help the marker.

Step 2   **Write your answer in short, but full, sentences**

Use short, punchy sentences with the aim that every sentence should say something different and generate marks. Write in full sentences, ensuring your style is professional.

Step 3   **Do your calculations first and explanation second**

Questions sometimes ask for an explanation with supporting calculations. The best approach is to prepare the calculation first then add the explanation. Performing the calculation first should enable you to explain what you have done.

Exam success skill 6

Good time management

This skill means planning your time across all the requirements so that all tasks have been attempted at the end of the 3 hours available and actively checking on time during your exam. This is so that you can flex your approach and prioritise requirements which, in your judgement, will generate the maximum marks in the available time remaining.

Advice on developing Good time management

The exam is 3 hours long, which translates to 1.8 minutes per mark. At the beginning of a question, work out the amount of time you should be spending on each requirement. If you take the approach of spending 10–15 minutes reading and planning at the start of the exam, adjust the time allocated to each question accordingly.

Keep an eye on the clock

Aim to attempt all requirements, but be ready to be ruthless and move on if your answer is not going as planned. The challenge for many is sticking to planned timings. Be aware this is difficult to achieve in the early stages of your studies and be ready to let this skill develop over time.

Questions

Part A The UK tax system and its administration
Questions 1 to 42 cover the UK tax system and its administration, the subject of Chapters 1, 17 and 23 of the BPP Workbook for Taxation (TX – UK).

OTQ bank – The UK tax system and its administration 1
36 mins

1 Which TWO of the following statements are true about inheritance tax?

☐ It is an indirect tax.

☐ It is a progressive tax.

☐ It is an environmental tax.

☐ It is a redistributive tax. (2 marks)

2 Which TWO of the following have legal force?

☐ Revenue and Customs Brief

☐ A Statutory Instrument

☐ An Act of Parliament

☐ An Extra Statutory Concession (2 marks)

3 Fare plc wishes to appeal against the assessment of £10,000,000 of corporation tax by HM Revenue & Customs (HMRC).

By whom is Fare plc's appeal most likely to be heard?

○ By the First Tier Tribunal

○ By the Upper Tribunal

○ By the Supreme Court

○ By the Court of Appeal (2 marks)

4 Daren made a chargeable gain of £50,000 on the sale of a painting on 30 June 2021. This was Daren's only disposal in the tax year 2021/22. He had previously paid his income tax through deduction at source so has not had to submit a self-assessment tax return.

By what date must Daren notify HM Revenue & Customs (HMRC) of his chargeability to capital gains tax in relation to the gain made on 30 June 2021 and by what date must he pay the capital gains tax liability?

	Notification	Payment
○	31 January 2023	31 January 2023
○	5 October 2022	31 January 2023
○	5 October 2022	31 July 2023
○	31 January 2023	31 July 2023 (2 marks)

BPP
LEARNING
MEDIA

5   Sarah received NS&I investment account interest of £5,300 in the tax year 2021/22 which she deliberately omitted from her self-assessment tax return for that tax year. She did not attempt to conceal the omission. HM Revenue & Customs (HMRC) discovered the error from records collected from NS&I and Sarah then made a prompted disclosure of the error. Sarah is a higher rate taxpayer and she had already used her savings income nil rate band on other income.

What is the minimum penalty that HMRC may impose on Sarah in respect of this error?

○   £742

○   £1,484

○   £424

○   £1,855   (2 marks)

---

6   For the year ended 30 June 2021, Forgetful Ltd had a corporation tax liability of £166,250, which it did not pay until 31 July 2022. Forgetful Ltd is not a large company.

How much interest will Forgetful Ltd be charged by HM Revenue & Customs (HMRC) in respect of the late payment of its corporation tax liability for the year ended 30 June 2021?

○   £360

○   £2,161

○   £4,323

○   £1,441   (2 marks)

---

7   Mammoth Ltd commenced trading on 1 January 2022. The company's profits have been as follows:

Period	£
Year ended 31 December 2022	524,000
Year ended 31 December 2023	867,000
Year ended 31 December 2024	912,000

Throughout all of these periods, Mammoth Ltd had one related 51% group company.

What is the first year for which Mammoth Ltd will be required to pay its corporation tax liability by quarterly instalments?

○   Year ended 31 December 2023

○   None of the years ended 31 December 2022, 2023 or 2024

○   Year ended 31 December 2024

○   Year ended 31 December 2022   (2 marks)

8   Taxes can be either capital taxes or revenue taxes, although some taxes are neither type of tax.

Identify, by clicking on the relevant boxes in the table below, the correct classification for the following three taxes.

Value added tax	NEITHER TYPE	CAPITAL TAX	REVENUE TAX
Inheritance tax	NEITHER TYPE	CAPITAL TAX	REVENUE TAX
National insurance contributions	NEITHER TYPE	CAPITAL TAX	REVENUE TAX

(2 marks)

9   In the year ended 31 March 2022, Luck Ltd had taxable total profits of £400,000 and received the following dividends:

	£
From unconnected companies	5,200
From a company in which Luck Ltd has an 80% shareholding	4,300
From a company in which Luck Ltd has a 45% shareholding	1,400

What is the value of Luck Ltd's profits for the year ended 31 March 2022 for the purposes of determining whether it should pay corporation tax in instalments?

[▼]

Pull down list:

£406,600

£410,900

£405,700

£405,200   (2 marks)

10   **For the tax year 2021/22, what are the latest dates by which a taxpayer, who is an individual and who does not wish to incur a penalty, should file a self-assessment tax return on paper or online?**

	Paper tax return	*Online tax return*
○	31 October 2022	31 January 2024
○	31 October 2022	31 January 2023
○	31 October 2023	31 January 2023
○	31 October 2023	31 January 2024

(2 marks)

(Total = 20 marks)

11   HM Revenue & Customs (HMRC) issued Lenny with a notice to file his self-assessment tax return for the tax year 2021/22 on 30 April 2022. Lenny submitted the return online on 15 March 2023.

Match the due date for submission of the online return and the date by which HMRC will have to notify Lenny of a compliance check into this return.

31 October 2022	31 January 2023
15 March 2024	30 April 2024

Submission	
Notification	

(2 marks)

12   Gareth's tax payable for 2020/21 and 2021/22 is as follows:

	2020/21 £	2021/22 £
Income tax	10,000	12,500
Class 2 NIC	159	159
Class 4 NIC	2,000	2,500
Capital gains tax	1,000	2,000

Gareth always pays the correct amount of tax on each due date.

What is the amount payable by Gareth to HM Revenue & Customs (HMRC) on 31 January 2023 in respect of the tax year 2021/22?

Pull down list:

£5,000

£5,159

£4,000

£4,159

(2 marks)

13   For the year to 31 March 2022 Key Ltd, which is not a large company, had a corporation tax liability of £22,400. It paid £10,000 of this liability on 1 December 2022 and the remaining £12,400 on 1 February 2023.

What is the interest payable by Key Ltd on late paid tax?

£

(2 marks)

14 Jess plc is required to pay corporation tax by instalments. It had prepared accounts to 31 March each year but decided to prepare accounts for the ten month period to 31 January 2022. Jess plc's corporation tax liability for the period to 31 January 2022 was £500,000.

What is the amount of the final instalment of corporation tax for the period ended 31 January 2022 and when is it due?

○   £125,000 due on 1 November 2022

○   £166,667 due on 14 January 2022

○   £50,000 due on 14 May 2022

○   £150,000 due on 14 May 2022

(2 marks)

15 More Ltd prepares accounts to 30 September each year. It was given notice by HM Revenue & Customs (HMRC) to submit its corporation tax return for the year to 30 September 2021 on 30 November 2021. The return was submitted on 1 December 2022. This was the first late return for the company.

What is the maximum penalty payable by More Ltd as a result of its late submission?

£ [   ]

(2 marks)

16 Mick has already realised a capital gain on the disposal of Asset 1 but is proposing to pretend that the disposal date actually falls into next tax year.

Mick is also planning to dispose of Asset 2 but is proposing to delay the actual sale until after 5 April.

In relation to which disposal(s) is Mick committing tax evasion?

○   Both disposals

○   Neither disposal

○   Asset 1 only

○   Asset 2 only

(2 marks)

17 Quinn will not make the balancing payment in respect of her tax liability for the tax year 2020/21 until 17 October 2022.

What is the total percentage penalty which Quinn will be charged by HM Revenue & Customs (HMRC) in respect of the late balancing payment for the tax year 2020/21?

[▼]

Pull down list:

15%

10%

5%

30%

(2 marks)

18 Dennis has made a deliberate error in his self-assessment tax return for the tax year 2021/22.

What is the time limit for HM Revenue & Customs (HMRC) to issue a discovery assessment?

○ 5 April 2023

○ 5 April 2026

○ 5 April 2028

○ 5 April 2042   (2 marks)

---

19 Daljit received a notice from HM Revenue & Customs (HMRC) to submit his self-assessment tax return for the tax year 2021/22. He did not submit the return by the due date.

What can HMRC do to collect any tax owing in respect of Daljit's unfiled return?

▼

Pull down list:

Start a compliance check enquiry into the return

Make a determination

Raise a discovery assessment

Offer an internal review   (2 marks)

---

20 Based on her income tax liability of £15,600 for the tax year 2020/21, Sarah was liable to make two payments on account for the tax year 2021/22 of £7,800 each.

In May 2022, Sarah made a claim to reduce her second payment on account to £6,000. This reduced payment was made on 30 September 2022.

Sarah's actual income tax liability for the tax year 2021/22 was £16,000, and she paid the full balance outstanding on 31 January 2023.

How much interest is payable by Sarah to HM Revenue & Customs (HMRC) in respect of her second payment on account for the tax year 2021/22?

○ £49

○ £52

○ £24

○ £16   (2 marks)

(Total = 20 marks)

21   Little Fence Ltd has made up accounts for the 15-month period ended 31 March 2022.

By which date(s) must Little Fence Ltd file its corporation tax self-assessment tax return(s) for the 15-month period ended 31 March 2022?

○   The return for the year ended 31 December 2021 must be filed by 31 October 2022. The return for the period ended 31 March 2022 must be filed by 31 December 2022.

○   One return for the 15-month period ended 31 March 2022 must be filed by 31 March 2023.

○   The return for the year ended 31 December 2021 must be filed by 31 December 2022. The return for the period ended 31 March 2022 must be filed by 31 March 2023.

○   The returns for the year ended 31 December 2021 and the period ended 31 March 2022 must both be filed by 31 March 2023.

(2 marks)

22   Dayfis Ltd was incorporated on 1 October 2021. The company started to trade on 1 December 2021 and made up its first accounts for the period to 30 June 2022.

By which date must Dayfis Ltd notify HM Revenue & Customs (HMRC) of its first accounting period?

○   1 December 2021

○   1 January 2022

○   1 March 2022

○   30 June 2023

(2 marks)

23   Dee Ltd has been late in filing its last two self-assessment corporation tax returns. The company's self-assessment corporation tax return for the year ended 31 December 2021 shows corporation tax due of £7,000.

If Dee Ltd files its self-assessment tax return for the year ended 31 December 2021 on 31 August 2023, what amount of penalty will be charged by HM Revenue & Customs (HMRC)?

○   £1,200

○   £700

○   £1,000

○   £1,700

(2 marks)

24 Petula filed her self-assessment tax return for the tax year 2020/21 on 20 September 2021. She subsequently amended the return on 29 March 2022.

What is the latest date by which HM Revenue & Customs (HMRC) can give written notice of its intention to commence a compliance check into items changed by the amended tax return?

- ○ 31 January 2023
- ○ 20 September 2022
- ○ 29 March 2023
- ○ 30 April 2023   (2 marks)

---

25 Certain individuals are required to complete a self-assessment tax return. The taxpayer must sign a declaration that the information given on the tax return and any supplementary pages is correct and complete to the best of the taxpayer's knowledge.

Which of the following statements is FALSE?

- ○ The tax return comprises a main return form, together with supplementary pages for particular sources of income
- ○ Partnerships must file a separate return and account for each partner's tax through this return
- ○ If HM Revenue & Customs (HMRC) calculates the tax for the taxpayer, it merely does so based on the information provided and does not judge the accuracy of it
- ○ An employee who only has employment income, with the tax collected under PAYE, is not required to complete a tax return   (2 marks)

(Total = 10 marks)

OT case – Domingo and Fargo (June 2009) (amended)

18 mins

The following scenario relates to questions 26 to 30.

Domingo and Fargo are brothers. In the tax year 2021/22 Domingo is employed and Fargo is self-employed. Fargo is required to make a balancing payment of £1,800 in respect of his income tax liability for the tax year 2021/22 and payments on account for the tax year 2022/23.

For the tax year 2021/22 Domingo wants to file a paper self-assessment tax return. Fargo wants to file his tax return online. Both notices to file returns were issued by HM Revenue & Customs (HMRC) to Domingo and Fargo on 1 July 2022.

26   What are the latest dates for Domingo and Fargo to submit their respective self-assessment tax returns for the tax year 2021/22 given their stated filing preferences?

	Domingo	Fargo
○	31 October 2022	31 October 2022
○	31 October 2022	31 January 2023
○	31 January 2023	31 October 2022
○	31 January 2023	31 January 2023

(2 marks)

27   How long must Domingo and Fargo retain the records used in preparing their respective tax returns for the tax year 2020/21?

	Domingo	Fargo
○	31 January 2028	31 January 2023
○	31 January 2028	31 January 2025
○	31 January 2024	31 January 2024
○	31 January 2024	31 January 2028

(2 marks)

28   What is the maximum penalty that may be imposed on Domingo and Fargo for not retaining their records for the required period?

- ○   £100
- ○   £500
- ○   £1,500
- ○   £3,000

(2 marks)

29   What are the dates by which Fargo should make the balancing payment for the tax year
     2021/22 and the first payment on account for the tax year 2022/23, and the second
     payment on account for the tax year 2022/23?

     Balancing payment 2021/22

     and first POA 2022/23   *Second POA 2022/23*

     ○   31 July 2022   31 July 2023

     ○   31 July 2022   31 January 2024

     ○   31 January 2023   31 July 2023

     ○   31 January 2023   31 January 2024   (2 marks)

---

30   What are the interest payable and maximum penalty payable if Fargo makes the
     balancing payment for the tax year 2021/22 exactly four months late?

     ○   Interest £16, penalty £90

     ○   Interest £47, penalty £90

     ○   Interest £16, penalty £180

     ○   Interest £47, penalty £180   (2 marks)

                                                                        (Total = 10 marks)

OT case – Ernest (June 2010) (amended)

18 mins

The following scenario relates to Questions 31 to 35.

You should assume that today's date is 30 June 2022.

You are a trainee Chartered Certified Accountant and your firm is dealing with the tax affairs of Ernest.

Ernest's self-assessment tax return for the tax year 2020/21 was submitted to HM Revenue & Customs (HMRC) on 15 May 2021 and Ernest paid the resulting income tax liability by the due date. However, you have just discovered that during the tax year 2020/21 Ernest disposed of a freehold non-residential property, the details of which were omitted from his self-assessment tax return. The capital gains tax liability in respect of this disposal is £18,000 and this amount has not been paid.

Ernest has suggested that since HMRC's right to make a compliance check enquiry into his self-assessment tax return for the tax year 2020/21 expired on 15 May 2022, no disclosure should be made to HMRC of the capital gain.

31 Identify, by clicking on the relevant boxes in the table below, whether each of the following statements concerning tax evasion and tax avoidance is true or false.

Tax evasion is illegal.	TRUE	FALSE
Both tax evasion and tax avoidance are illegal.	TRUE	FALSE
Tax avoidance is legal but may fail if challenged in the courts by HMRC.	TRUE	FALSE
Tax evasion always involves providing HM Revenue & Customs with false information.	TRUE	FALSE

(2 marks)

32 Which TWO of the following statements are correct about how your firm should deal with the suggestion from Ernest that no disclosure is made to HMRC of his capital gain?

☐ Ernest should be advised to disclose details of the capital gain to HMRC.

☐ If Ernest does not disclose the gain to HMRC, your firm can definitely still continue to act for him.

☐ If your firm ceases to act for Ernest, it must disclose this to HMRC and provide detailed reasons why it has ceased to act.

☐ If Ernest does not disclose the gain to HMRC, your firm would be obliged to report under the money laundering regulations.

(2 marks)

33 What is the maximum penalty that could be imposed on Ernest for the error by omission in his tax return in relation to the capital gain, assuming that it is considered to be deliberate but not concealed?

○ £18,000

○ £12,600

○ £9,000

○ £5,400

(2 marks)

34   Assuming that HMRC discovers the capital gain and Ernest then makes a disclosure of it, what is the minimum penalty that could be imposed on Ernest for the error if it is considered to be deliberate but not concealed?

[▼]

Pull down list:

£0

£2,700

£6,300

£9,000   (2 marks)

---

35   If Ernest pays the capital gains tax liability on 31 July 2022, what is the interest that will be charged on this late payment?

○   £468

○   £405

○   £234

○   £203   (2 marks)

                                                             (Total = 10 marks)

OT case – Thai Curry Ltd

18 mins

The following scenario relates to Questions 36 to 40.

Thai Curry Ltd prepares accounts for the year ended 31 March 2022 and has taxable total profits of £171,705, resulting in a corporation tax liability of £32,624.

Thai Curry Ltd has previously always submitted its corporation tax returns on time and had a corporation tax liability for the year to 31 March 2021 of £22,000.

The company is in dispute with HM Revenue & Customs (HMRC) in relation to its corporation tax return for the year ended 31 March 2021 and has been offered an internal review of the case. The case is likely to be allocated to either the complex track or the standard track if it instead chooses to go to a formal appeal.

36   **What is the date by which Thai Curry Ltd's self-assessment corporation tax return for the year ended 31 March 2022 should be submitted?**

31 December 2022   31 January 2023   31 March 2023   31 July 2023

(2 marks)

---

37   **What is the total amount of late filing penalties that will be charged on Thai Curry Ltd if it submits its return for the year ended 31 March 2022 and pays the corporation tax due eight months late?**

▼

Pull down list:

£3,262

£6,525

£6,725

£3,462

(2 marks)

---

38   **How should Thai Curry Ltd's corporation tax liability for the year ended 31 March 2022 be paid?**

○   £32,624 on 1 January 2023

○   £11,000 on 31 January 2022 and 31 July 2022, £10,624 on 31 January 2023

○   £8,156 on 14 October 2021, 14 January 2022, 14 April 2022 and 14 July 2022

○   £5,500 on 14 October 2021, 14 January 2022 and 14 April 2022, £16,124 on 14 July 2022

(2 marks)

---

39 Which TWO of the following statements are correct about the internal review procedure?

☐ An internal review is a less costly and more effective way to resolve disputes informally than a formal appeal.

☐ The review is carried out by the HMRC officer who has previously dealt with the case.

☐ HMRC must usually carry out the review within 45 days.

☐ After the review conclusion is notified, the company cannot make a further appeal.

(2 marks)

40 Match what body is initially likely to hear Thai Curry Ltd's appeal if it does not take up the offer of an internal review.

First tier

Upper tier

Complex track	

Standard track	

(2 marks)

(Total = 10 marks)

41 John

(a)   **You should assume today's date is 30 November 2021.**

John is a new client whom you met today. On 6 April 2020, he commenced in self-employment and prepared his first set of accounts to 5 April 2021. John had not previously filed a self-assessment tax return and has not received any communication from HM Revenue & Customs (HMRC) about his tax affairs.

As this will be his first self-assessment tax return, John is also concerned that HMRC might carry out a compliance check.

Required

(i)   Advise John of the latest date by which he should have notified HMRC of his chargeability to income tax for the tax year 2020/21 and the maximum and minimum penalties for late notification if he immediately notifies HMRC of his chargeability and is deemed to have been careless.   **(3 marks)**

(ii)   State the period during which HMRC will have to notify John if it intends to carry out a compliance check in respect of his self-assessment tax return for the tax year 2020/21, and the possible reasons why such a check would be made.

Note. You should assume for part (ii) that John will file his tax return by the due filing date.   **(3 marks)**

(b)   The UK Government uses tax policies to encourage certain types of activity.

Required

Briefly explain how the UK Government's tax policies encourage:

(i)   Individuals to save   **(1 mark)**

(ii)   Individuals to support charities   **(1 mark)**

(iii) Entrepreneurs to build their own businesses and to invest in plant and machinery   **(2 marks)**

(Total = 10 marks)

42 Sugar plc   18 mins

Sugar plc has been in business for many years. It owns 45% of the ordinary shares of Honey plc and 75% of the ordinary shares of Molasses plc. Molasses plc owns 70% of the ordinary shares of Treacle plc. This structure has existed for many years.

In the year to 31 March 2022, Sugar plc had taxable total profits of £470,000. It also received dividends of £50,000 from Honey plc. In the year to 31 March 2023, Sugar plc will have taxable total profits of £600,000. It will not receive any dividends in that year.

Required

(a)   Define what is meant by a related 51% group company and explain which companies are related 51% group companies of Sugar plc.   **(3 marks)**

(b)   Explain whether or not Sugar plc is a large company for the purposes of payment of corporation tax for the years ended 31 March 2022 and 31 March 2023.   **(3 marks)**

(c)   Assuming that Sugar plc is a large company in both years but was not a large company for any previous year, calculate Sugar plc's corporation tax liabilities for the years ended 31 March 2022 and 31 March 2023 and explain when these will be paid.   **(4 marks)**

_____

(Total = 10 marks)

PART B INCOME TAX AND NIC LIABILITIES

Questions 43 to 118 cover income tax and NIC liabilities, the subject of Chapters 2 to 12 of the BPP Workbook for Taxation (TX – UK).

OTQ bank – Income tax and NIC liabilities 1   36 mins

43   Hana was UK resident in the tax year 2020/21. He worked full-time in Egypt throughout the tax year 2021/22.

What is the maximum number of days which Hana can spend in the UK and be treated as automatically not resident in the UK for the tax year 2021/22?

○   15

○   45

○   90

○   182   (2 marks)

44   **Which TWO of the following types of income are exempt from income tax?**

☐   Interest on an NS&I Investment account

☐   Premium bond prizes

☐   Interest on UK government stocks ('gilts')

☐   Dividends on shares held in an Individual Savings Account   (2 marks)

45   In the tax year 2021/22 Claudio has taxable income (after deduction of his personal allowance) consisting of £3,000 of non-savings income and £12,500 of savings income.

What is Claudio's income tax liability for the tax year 2021/22?

○   £2,500

○   £2,900

○   £2,700

○   £3,100   (2 marks)

46   Mike and Delia are a married couple. In the tax year 2021/22, Mike has taxable non-savings income (after deducting his personal allowance) of £13,500. Delia has no income in the tax year 2021/22. Delia has made an election in relation to her personal allowance for the tax year 2021/22.

What is Mike's income tax liability for the tax year 2021/22?

○   £186

○   £2,448

○   £1,440

○   £2,700   (2 marks)

47   John is employed by Zebra plc. He was provided with a computer for private use on 6 November 2020. The market value of the computer when first provided to an employee for private use was £3,600 and the computer had a market value of £2,000 when first provided to John for private use. Zebra plc gave the computer to John on 5 April 2022 when it had a market value of £1,000.

   What are the total taxable benefits for John in respect of the computer for the tax year 2021/22?

   ○   £2,880

   ○   £3,300

   ○   £1,720

   ○   £1,833   (2 marks)

---

48   In the tax year 2021/22 Susie receives employment income of £170,000. She made a gross gift aid donation of £10,000 in January 2022.

   What is Susie's income tax liability for the tax year 2021/22?

   ○   £59,460

   ○   £61,460

   ○   £58,960

   ○   £53,432   (2 marks)

---

49   Petunia is a single parent with a two-year old son. She receives child benefit of £1,095 in the tax year 2021/22. Petunia has net income of £57,000 in 2021/22 and she made gross personal pension contributions of £2,000 during 2021/22.

   What is Petunia's child benefit income tax charge for the tax year 2021/22?

   ○   £1,095

   ○   £438

   ○   £548

   ○   £767   (2 marks)

---

50   Judith works for Sabre Ltd for an annual salary of £18,000. On 30 September 2021, she received a bonus of £4,000 in respect of Sabre Ltd's trading results for the year ended 31 March 2021. She expects to receive a bonus of £4,800 on 30 September 2022 in respect of Sabre Ltd's results for the year ended 31 March 2022. Judith also received £500 from a customer on 1 December 2021 as a gratuity for good service.

   What is Judith's employment income for the tax year 2021/22?

   ○   £22,000

   ○   £22,800

   ○   £22,500

   ○   £23,300   (2 marks)

---

51 **Which TWO of the following are qualifying travel expenses?**

☐ Travel from employer's office to visit a client

☐ Travel from home to a workplace to which an employee has been seconded for 36 months

☐ Travel from home to a permanent place of work

☐ Travel from home to visit a trade fair relevant to the employer's business 100 miles away from permanent place of work **(2 marks)**

---

52 Since 2017, Sergey has lived in job-related accommodation provided by his employer for Sergey's personal security. He has an annual gross salary of £60,000 for the tax year 2021/22.

Throughout the tax year 2021/22, Sergey's employer paid for heating, cleaning and lighting the accommodation at a cost of £7,000. His employer also provided Sergey with furniture on 6 April 2021 at a cost of £10,000.

What is the amount assessable on Sergey in the tax year 2021/22 in relation to the furniture, heating, cleaning and lighting costs?

○ £6,000

○ £9,000

○ £7,000

○ £8,000 **(2 marks)**

(Total = 20 marks)

OTQ bank – Income tax and NIC liabilities 2   36 mins

53   Marion bought £20,000 (nominal value) 5% UK Government Loan Stock on 1 July 2021. Interest is payable on 30 June and 31 December each year. Marion sold the loan stock to Gerald on 31 October 2021 including interest.

Match the amounts amount of savings income taxable on Marion and Gerald in respect of the loan stock for the tax year 2021/22.

£0	£500

£333	£167

Marion	

Gerald		(2 marks)

---

54   Trevor is employed by Cress plc. He is provided with a brand new car available for private use for the tax year 2021/22. The car has CO_2 emissions of 107 g/km and a list price of £20,000 although Cress plc actually paid £18,000 for the car as the result of a dealer discount. The car has a diesel engine which does not meet the RDE2 standard. No private fuel is provided.

What is Trevor's taxable car benefit for the tax year 2021/22 ?

- ○   £4,500
- ○   £5,220
- ○   £5,000
- ○   £5,800   (2 marks)

---

55   Troy is a sole trader who had trading income of £60,000 in the tax year 2020/21 and £80,000 in the tax year 2021/22. He has no other income. He joined a personal pension scheme on 6 April 2020 and made gross contributions of £25,000 in 2020/21. This was the first pension provision that Troy had made.

What gross amount can Troy contribute to his personal pension scheme in March 2022 without incurring an annual allowance charge?

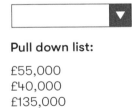

Pull down list:

£55,000
£40,000
£135,000
£25,000   (2 marks)

---

56   Luke rents out a room in his own residence throughout 2021/22. The rent is £150 a week. Luke's expenses of the letting are £20 per week, none of which is loan interest on the property.

What is the amount of property business income taxable on Luke for 2021/22 if he makes any relevant election?

○   £6,760

○   £0

○   £7,800

○   £300   **(2 marks)**

---

57   Susie rents out a furnished house. The house does not qualify as a furnished holiday letting. The furnishings include a new sofa which was bought in the tax year 2021/22 to replace an old one which was disposed of at the same time. The old sofa cost £3,000 in 2009 and was disposed of in January 2022 for proceeds of £200. The new sofa was bought in January 2022 for £5,500 and was larger than the old one. If Susie had bought a newer sofa of the same model as the old one it would have cost £4,000.

What deduction against property business income can Susie claim for the cost of the sofa bought in 2021/22?

○   £5,500

○   £3,800

○   £5,300

○   £4,000   **(2 marks)**

---

58   Amrul bought a house on 1 September 2021 and immediately let it out on a quarterly tenancy with rent of £900 being payable in advance on 1 September, 1 December, 1 March and 1 June each year. The tenant also paid a security deposit of £500. The tenant was still in the property on 5 April 2022.

Amrul paid a buildings insurance premium of £150 on 1 September 2021 for a 12-month period from that date.

Amrul drove 178 miles in his own car in relation to the letting during the period 1 September 2021 to 5 April 2022. He wishes to use approved mileage allowances to calculate his motoring expenses.

What is Amrul's property business income for the tax year 2021/22?

[▼]

Pull down list:

£1,932
£2,970
£2,470
£2,505   **(2 marks)**

59 Harry is a sole trader. He prepares accounts for the year ended 5 April 2022 and has deducted the following items of expenditure in the statement of profit or loss:

	£
Depreciation	3,000
Accountancy fees for preparing accounts	1,000
Entertainment of: staff (party at £300 per person for 6 employees)	1,800
customers	2,400

How much should be added back to Harry's net profit to arrive at his adjusted taxable profit?

£ [   ]   (2 marks)

---

60 Rose is a sole trader who prepares accounts to 5 April each year using the cash basis of accounting. Her results for the period of account to 5 April 2022 show the following:

	£
Cash sales	41,000
Invoice sales	4,000
Cash expenses	20,200

The figure for invoice sales includes an invoice for £1,500 which was paid on 10 April 2022. In addition to the cash expenses of £20,200, Rose incurred motoring expenses of £2,800 for driving 8,000 miles of which 6,500 miles were for business purposes. Rose wishes to use approved mileage allowances for motoring.

What is Rose's taxable trading income for the tax year 2021/22?

£ [   ]   (2 marks)

---

61 Olive is self-employed, preparing her accounts to 5 April each year. She claims capital allowances on a motor car used in her business. The motor car has a CO_2 emission rate of 145 grams per kilometre, with 40% of Olive's mileage for private purposes. The motor car had a tax written down value of £12,000 at 6 April 2021. Olive sold the motor car for £6,000 on 1 November 2021.

What amount of capital allowances can Olive claim in respect of the motor car for the tax year 2021/22?

○ £3,600

○ £648

○ £2,400

○ £216   (2 marks)

---

62   Ella started in business as a sole trader on 6 November 2021 and prepared her first set of accounts to 5 April 2022. On 6 December 2021 she acquired plant at a cost of £430,000.

What are the maximum capital allowances that Ella can claim for the period of account to 5 April 2022?

[▼]

Pull down list:

£339,133
£419,067
£417,667
£430,000

(2 marks)

(Total = 20 marks)

OTQ bank – Income tax and NIC liabilities 3 — 36 mins

63 Joe has been in business for many years preparing accounts to 5 April each year. The tax written down value of his main pool at 6 April 2021 was £12,000. Joe sold machinery on 10 June 2021 for £11,900 which had originally cost £11,600. He made no acquisitions during the year ended 5 April 2022.

What is the maximum capital allowance that Joe can claim for the period of account to 5 April 2022?

- ○ £1,000
- ○ £400
- ○ £100
- ○ £72

(2 marks)

---

64 Alexandra started in business as a sole trader on 1 August 2020 and prepared her first set of accounts to 30 April 2022.

Match the start date and the end date of Alexandra's basis period for the tax year 2021/22, her second tax year of trading.

1 August 2020	6 April 2021	1 May 2021
31 July 2021	5 April 2022	30 April 2022

Start date	
End date	

(2 marks)

---

65 Timothy started in business as a sole trader on 1 February 2020. He prepared his first set of accounts to 30 November 2020 and his second set of accounts to 30 November 2021. His taxable trading profits were as follows:

p/e 30 November 2020	£30,000
y/e 30 November 2021	£42,000

What are Timothy's overlap profits?

£ _____

(2 marks)

---

66 Walter had been in business as a sole trader for many years preparing accounts to 31 December each year. He ceased trading on 31 March 2022. Walter had overlap profits of £2,000 on commencement. His taxable trading profits were as follows:

y/e 31 December 2021	£18,000
p/e 31 March 2022	£3,000

What is Walter's taxable trading income for the final year of trading?

£ _____

(2 marks)

---

67   Joyce started in business as a sole trader on 1 January 2021 and prepared her first set of accounts to 30 September 2021 and her second set of accounts to 30 September 2022. She made the following losses in her first two periods of trading:

	£
p/e 30 September 2021	(9,000)
y/e 30 September 2022	(14,400)

Match the amounts of the trading losses with the tax years.

£3,000	£9,000	£9,600

£11,400	£12,600	£14,400

2020/21	

2021/22		(2 marks)

---

68   Humphrey is a sole trader who has been trading for a number of years.

Humphrey incurred a trading loss in the tax year 2021/22. He wishes to make a claim to offset this loss against his total income of the tax year 2020/21.

What is the deadline for Humphrey to claim this relief?

- ○   31 January 2023
- ○   31 January 2024
- ○   5 April 2025
- ○   5 April 2026   (2 marks)

---

69   Peter and Jane have been in partnership for many years preparing accounts to 31 July each year and sharing profits equally. On 1 September 2020, they changed their profit sharing agreement so that Peter was entitled to a salary of £9,000 each year and the remaining profits were then split two parts to Peter and three parts to Jane. The partnership made a trading profit of £96,000 in the year to 31 July 2021.

What is Peter's taxable trading profit for the tax year 2021/22?

£	

(2 marks)

70   Robin and Stuart had been in partnership for many years preparing accounts to 31 December each year and sharing profits equally. On 1 January 2022, Tania joined the partnership and profits were then split 2:2:1. The partnership made a profit of £96,000 in the year to 31 December 2021 and £112,000 in the year to 31 December 2022.

Match the taxable trading profits of the partners for 2021/22.

£5,600	£11,200	£22,400

£47,200	£48,000

Robin and Stuart each	

| Tania | | (2 marks)
|---|---|

---

71   Shona started in business on 1 January 2022 as a sole trader and prepared her first set of accounts for the 14 weeks to 5 April 2022. Her taxable trading profit for that period was £10,600.

What are Shona's total national insurance contributions for the tax year 2021/22?

£ [   ]   (2 marks)

---

72   Mark has been in business as a sole trader for many years preparing accounts to 5 April. He made a trading loss of £(2,000) in the year to 5 April 2021 and has not made any claim in respect of this loss. In the year to 5 April 2022, he made a trading profit of £14,700.

What are Mark's Class 4 national insurance contributions for the tax year 2021/22?

£ [   ]   (2 marks)

(Total = 20 marks)

OT case – Ann, Basil and Chloe (December 2008) (amended)

18 mins

The following scenario relates to Questions 73 to 77.

Ann

Ann is self-employed. Her taxable income for the tax year 2021/22 was £76,000 which was all trading income. Ann made contributions of £49,000 (gross) into a personal pension scheme between September 2021 and March 2022. This was the second year that she had been a member of a pension scheme and she had an unused annual allowance of £20,000 brought forward from 2020/21.

Basil

Basil is employed. During the tax year 2021/22 Basil had taxable income of £250,000 which was all employment income. Basil made contributions of £50,000 (gross) into a personal pension scheme during the tax year 2021/22. This was the first year that he had been a member of a pension scheme. In future, his employer may contribute to Basil's personal pension scheme.

Chloe

Chloe lets out an unfurnished property. For the tax year 2021/22 her taxable income was £16,630 which was all property business income. Chloe made contributions of £8,200 (gross) into a personal pension scheme during the tax year 2021/22. This was the first year that she had been a member of a pension scheme. Chloe does not have any interest payable on her buy-to-let property.

73 **Which TWO of the following statements about relevant earnings are correct?**

- ☐ Individuals can always make gross pension contributions of £3,600 in 2021/22 even if they do not have any relevant earnings in that tax year.

- ☐ Relevant earnings relate both to contributions to personal pension schemes and to occupational pension schemes.

- ☐ If an individual makes pension contributions less than relevant earnings in a tax year, the excess can be carried forward for three years and used to cover pension contributions.

- ☐ Relevant earnings do not include income from furnished holiday lettings. **(2 marks)**

74 **Identify, by clicking on the relevant boxes in the table below, whether each of the following statements about the annual allowance is true or false.**

Employer contributions do not count towards the annual allowance.	TRUE	FALSE
The annual allowance can be carried forward for three years to the extent that it is unused in the tax year.	TRUE	FALSE
The annual allowance is available even if the individual is not a member of a pension scheme in a tax year and so can be carried forward.	TRUE	FALSE
If tax-relievable pension contributions exceed the annual allowance, there is a charge to income tax.	TRUE	FALSE

(2 marks)

75   What is Ann's income tax liability for the tax year 2021/22?

£ [   ]   (2 marks)

76   What is Basil's annual allowance charge for the tax year 2021/22?

£ [   ]   (2 marks)

77   What is Chloe's tax relief on her pension contribution for the tax year 2021/22?

   ○   £0
   ○   £1,640
   ○   £900
   ○   £720   (2 marks)

(Total = 10 marks)

OT case – Ae, Bee, Cae, and Eu (December 2008) (amended)

18 mins

The following scenario relates to Questions 78 to 82.

Ae, Bee and Cae

Ae and Bee commenced in partnership on 1 July 2019 preparing accounts to 30 April. Cae joined as a partner on 1 July 2021. Profits were always shared equally. The partnership's trading profits since the commencement of trading have been as follows:

	£
Period ended 30 April 2020	54,000
Year ended 30 April 2021	66,000
Year ended 30 April 2022	87,000

Eu

Eu ceased trading on 30 September 2023, having been self-employed since 1 July 2012.

(1) Eu's trading profits for the final three periods of trading were as follows:

	£
Year ended 30 June 2022	62,775
Year ended 30 June 2023	57,600
Three-month period ended 30 September 2023	14,400

These figures are before taking account of capital allowances.

(2) Eu's capital allowances in the year to 30 June 2022 were £1,575 and in the year to 30 June 2023 were £1,292.

(3) The tax written down value of the capital allowances main pool at 1 July 2023 was £5,883. On 15 September 2023 Eu purchased office furniture for £2,400. All of the items included in the main pool were sold for £5,175 (all for less than cost) on 30 September 2023.

(4) Until the final period of trading Eu had always prepared accounts to 30 June. Her overlap profits for the period 1 July 2012 to 5 April 2013 were £9,800.

78 What is Ae's trading income assessment for the tax year 2020/21?

- ○ £27,000
- ○ £24,300
- ○ £32,500
- ○ £33,000

(2 marks)

79 What is Cae's trading income assessment for the tax year 2021/22?

- ○ £26,583
- ○ £24,167
- ○ £29,000
- ○ £21,750

(2 marks)

BPP LEARNING MEDIA

80   What is Eu's trading income assessment for the tax year 2022/23?

     ○   £56,025

     ○   £62,775

     ○   £57,600

     ○   £61,200   (2 marks)

---

81   What are Eu's capital allowances for the three-month period ended 30 September 2023?

     ○   £3,108

     ○   £1,491

     ○   £2,775

     ○   £559   (2 marks)

---

82   Assuming that the capital allowances for the three-month period ended 30 September 2023 were £3,000, what is Eu's trading income assessment for the tax year 2023/24?

     ○   £1,600

     ○   £57,908

     ○   £62,200

     ○   £67,708   (2 marks)

(Total = 10 marks)

OT case – Rosie and Sam (December 2012) (amended)

18 mins

The following scenario relates to Questions 83 to 87.

You should assume that today's date is 15 February 2022.

Rosie

Rosie has recently been promoted to managing director at Hornburg plc. During the tax year 2021/22 Rosie will be paid gross director's remuneration of £260,000 and she has received dividend income of £500,000. She had income of £130,000 in 2018/19, 2019/20 and 2020/21. She has made the following gross personal pension contributions:

Tax year	Pension contribution
	£
2019/20	26,000
2020/21	Nil

Rosie has been a member of a pension scheme since the tax year 2019/20 and Hornburg plc makes an employer's contribution of £10,000 per year.

Sam

In September 2019 Sam invested £7,000 in a flexible cash ISA. In May 2021 he invested a further £6,000 in that cash ISA. He withdrew £5,000 from the cash ISA in October 2021. Sam is now considering investing more cash into the cash ISA before 5 April 2022. He also invested £4,000 in premium bonds and government securities ('gilts') in the tax year 2021/22.

83   **What is the total pension scheme annual allowance that Rosie has available for the tax year 2021/22?**

   ○   £74,000

   ○   £38,000

   ○   £114,000

   ○   £78,000

   (2 marks)

---

84   **Use ONE of the following to complete the sentence below:**

20	25
45	55

   If Rosie makes pension contributions in excess of her available annual allowances there will be a charge to income tax at

   ☐ %

   on the excess contributions.

   (2 marks)

---

85   What are the tax consequences for Rosie if she takes pension benefits under flexible access drawdown?

	Lump sum	Rest of pension fund
○	Up to 10% of fund can be taken tax free	Taxable as pension income when received
○	Up to 10% of fund can be taken as tax-free lump sum	5% of fund taxable as pension income each year whether or not received
○	Up to 25% of fund can be taken as tax-free lump sum	Taxable as pension income when received
○	Up to 25% of fund can be taken as tax-free lump sum	5% of fund taxable as pension income each year whether or not received

(2 marks)

86   What is the maximum amount that Sam can invest into the cash ISA for the tax year 2021/22 in addition to his investments already made?

[　　　　　　▼]

Pull down list:

£14,000
£19,000
£12,000
£15,000

(2 marks)

87   Match the income tax and capital gains tax treatments of Sam's investments in premium bonds and government securities.

Exempt from income tax, chargeable to capital gains tax		Chargeable to income tax and capital gains tax

Exempt from both income tax and capital gains tax		Chargeable to income tax, exempt from capital gains tax

Premium bonds	

Government securities	

(2 marks)

(Total = 10 marks)

OT case – Fang and Hong (December 2013) (amended)

18 mins

The following scenario relates to Questions 88 to 92.

Fang

Fang commenced self-employment on 1 August 2019. She has a trading profit of £45,960 for the year ended 31 July 2020, and a trading profit of £39,360 for the year ended 31 July 2021. Fang has overlap profits on commencement.

Hong

Hong has been in self-employment since 2007, preparing accounts to 5 April. For the year ended 5 April 2022 she made a trading loss of £45,800, and has claimed this against her total income for the tax year 2020/21.

For the year ended 5 April 2021 Hong made a trading profit of £29,700. She also has a property business profit of £3,900 for the tax year 2020/21. Hong has an unused trading loss of £2,600 brought forward from the tax year 2019/20.

During the tax year 2020/21 Hong disposed of an investment property and this resulted in a chargeable gain. As Hong has claimed relief against total income of this tax year, she may include a further claim to set the trading loss against her chargeable gain for the year.

88 **Match the amount of trading profit which will have been assessed on Fang for each of the tax years 2019/20 and 2020/21.**

£30,640		£39,360

£45,960		£48,000

2019/20	

2020/21		(2 marks)

---

89 **In which ONE of the following ways can overlap profits be relieved?**

○ Against first available current year basis profits

○ Against trading income on cessation

○ Against general income of the tax year of commencement and/or the preceding tax year

○ Against general income in the three tax years preceding the year of commencement

(2 marks)

BPP
LEARNING
MEDIA

90   How could Fang have obtained relief for trading expenditure incurred prior to
      1 August 2019 and for computer equipment which Fang already owned which was
      brought into business use on 1 August 2019?

	Trading expenditure	Computer equipment
○	Added to overlap profit and relieved on cessation	Addition for capital allowances purposes based on its original cost
○	Treated as incurred on 1 August 2019	Addition for capital allowances purposes based on its original cost
○	Added to overlap profit and relieved on cessation	Addition for capital allowances purposes based on its market value at 1 August 2019
○	Treated as incurred on 1 August 2019	Addition for capital allowances purposes based on its market value at 1 August 2019

(2 marks)

91   What was the amount of loss for the year ended 5 April 2022 which was relieved against
      Hong's income for the tax year 2020/21?

[▼]

Pull down list:

£2,600
£31,000
£33,600
£18,430

(2 marks)

92   Which TWO of the following statements about the further claim to set Hong's trading loss
      against her chargeable gain for the tax year 2020/21 are correct?

☐   The trading loss is first set against general income of the tax year 2020/21 and only
     any excess loss is set against chargeable gains of that year.

☐   The amount of chargeable gains for the tax year 2020/21 is computed ignoring the
     annual exempt amount for the purposes of this relief.

☐   Capital losses of the tax year 2020/21 are taken into account, but not brought
     forward losses, for the purposes of this relief.

☐   Hong can specify the amount to be set against chargeable gains, so her annual
     exempt amount for the tax year 2020/21 is not wasted.   (2 marks)

(Total = 10 marks)

OT case – Chi (June 2014) (amended)   18 mins

The following scenario relates to Questions 93 to 97.

Chi commenced self-employment on 6 April 2021, and for the year ended 5 April 2022 her trading profit using the normal accruals basis was £53,000, calculated as follows:

	Note	£	£
Revenue	1		72,500
Expenses			
Motor expenses	2	4,400	
Other expenses	3	8,200	
Capital allowances	4	6,900	
			(19,500)
Trading profit			53,000

Notes

1   *Revenue*

   The revenue figure of £72,500 includes receivables of £1,600 which were owed as at 5 April 2022.

2   *Motor expenses*

   The total motor expenses for the year ended 5 April 2022 were £5,500, of which 20% was for private journeys. This proportion has been disallowed in calculating the trading profit. During the year ended 5 April 2022, Chi drove 13,200 business miles.

3   *Other expenses*

   The other expenses figure of £8,200 includes payables of £900 which were owed as at 5 April 2022.

4   *Capital allowances*

   Capital allowances consist of an annual investment allowance claim of £4,020 in respect of office equipment purchased on 6 April 2021, and a writing down allowance of £2,880 claimed in respect of Chi's motor car. The motor car had cost £20,000 on 6 April 2021.

93   **Based on the trading profit of £53,000 for the year ended 5 April 2022, what is Chi's income tax liability for the tax year 2021/22?**

   £ [   ]   (2 marks)

94   **Based on the trading profit of £53,000 for the year ended 5 April 2022, what are the Class 4 national insurance contributions payable by Chi for the tax year 2021/22?**

   £ [   ]   (2 marks)

95 Which TWO of the following statements about the cash basis of assessment are correct?

- ☐ The trader must prepare accounts to 5 April each year.
- ☐ The trader can deduct capital expenditure on plant and machinery (other than motor cars) as business expenses rather than using capital allowances.
- ☐ A trader can start to use the cash basis if his receipts for the tax year do not exceed £150,000.
- ☐ Under the cash basis, a trader can offset losses against other income or gains.

(2 marks)

96 If Chi uses the cash basis and claims approved mileage allowances, what is the amount of motor expenses (Note 2) which are allowable?

- ○ £4,400
- ○ £5,300
- ○ £5,940
- ○ £8,180

(2 marks)

97 If Chi uses the cash basis, what is the amount of revenue which is chargeable (Note 1) and the other expenses (Note 3) which are allowable for the year ended 5 April 2022?

- ○ Revenue £72,500, other expenses £8,200
- ○ Revenue £70,900, other expenses £8,200
- ○ Revenue £72,500, other expenses £7,300
- ○ Revenue £70,900, other expenses £7,300

(2 marks)

(Total = 10 marks)

98 Kagan (September/December 2019)

This scenario relates to four requirements.

You should assume that today's date is 4 April 2021.

On 2 April 2021, Kagan inherited some quoted ordinary shares valued at £510,000 following the death of his aunt. Kagan is unsure whether to retain the shares or sell some of them in order to make some alternative investments.

Kagan is aged 61 and is an additional rate taxpayer. Prior to the inheritance, his taxable income, consisting entirely of employment income, for the tax year 2021/22 would have been £400,000. The income tax liability on this income for the tax year 2021/22 would have been £165,000.

Prior to receiving the inheritance, Kagan's chargeable estate for inheritance tax (IHT) purposes was valued at £1,700,000. IHT of £550,000 would be payable were he to die in the near future.

Retain the inherited shares

If Kagan simply retains the inherited shares, then he will receive dividend income of £15,300 during the tax year 2021/22. This is in addition to his employment income of £400,000.

Sell some inherited shares and make four alternative investments

Kagan is considering selling some of his inherited shares (for which there has only been a minimal increase in value since he inherited them) to fund the following four investments, all of which will be made at the start of the tax year 2021/22:

(1) Kagan will make a gross personal pension contribution of £100,000. Kagan is a member of a pension scheme but has not made any contributions in recent years because his income has been substantially lower than it is for the tax year 2021/22. Kagan will immediately withdraw £25,000 of the pension fund tax free. This is the permitted 25% tax-free lump sum. However, no pension will be taken during the tax year 2021/22.

(2) Kagan will invest £50,000 in premium bonds. The expected amount of premium bond prizes which will be received during the tax year 2021/22 is £700.

(3) Kagan will invest the maximum permitted amount of £20,000 in a cash individual savings account (ISA). This ISA will pay interest of £400 during the tax year 2021/22.

(4) Kagan will purchase a freehold property for £295,000 (including all costs of purchase). The property will be let out unfurnished, with Kagan receiving property income of £9,600 during the tax year 2021/22.

After making these four investments, Kagan will be left with £65,000 of inherited shares, on which he will receive dividend income of £1,950 during the tax year 2021/22. He will also have his employment income of £400,000.

Kagan will not make any other disposals during the tax year 2021/22.

Required

(a) Calculate Kagan's revised income tax liability for the tax year 2021/22 if he retains the inherited shares. **(1 mark)**

(b) (i) Explain why little or no capital gains tax (CGT) will be payable if Kagan sells some of his inherited shares. **(1 mark)**

(ii) Calculate Kagan's revised income tax liability for the tax year 2021/22 if he sells some of his inherited shares and makes the four alternative investments.

Notes

1 For this part of the question, you are expected to produce a full income tax computation.

2 You should indicate by use of zero (0) any items which are not taxable. **(6 marks)**

(c) For each of the four alternative investments (pension contribution, premium bonds, ISA and freehold property) state whether the investment will reduce Kagan's potential IHT liability compared to him retaining the inherited shares.

Note. For this part of the question, no computations are required. **(2 marks)**

(Total = 10 marks)

99 Michael and Sean (June 2012) (amended)   18 mins

You are a trainee Chartered Certified Accountant and your manager has asked for your help regarding two taxpayers who have both made trading losses.

Michael

Michael commenced in self-employment on 1 July 2020, preparing accounts to 5 April. His results for the first two periods of trading were as follows:

		£
Nine-month period ended 5 April 2021	– Trading loss	(26,230)
Year ended 5 April 2022	– Trading profit	9,665

For the tax years 2016/17 to 2018/19 Michael had the following income from employment:

	£
2016/17	45,100
2017/18	20,365
2018/19	57,095

Michael did not have any income during the period 6 April 2019 to 30 June 2020.

Sean

Sean has been in self-employment since 2009, but ceased trading on 31 December 2021. He has always prepared accounts to 31 December. His results for the final five years of trading were as follows:

		£
Year ended 31 December 2017	– Trading profit	21,300
Year ended 31 December 2018	– Trading profit	14,400
Year ended 31 December 2019	– Trading profit	18,900
Year ended 31 December 2020	– Trading profit	3,700
Year ended 31 December 2021	– Trading loss	(23,100)

For each of the tax years 2017/18 to 2021/22 Sean has property business profits of £12,600.

Sean has unused overlap profits brought forward of £3,600.

Required

For each of the two taxpayers, Michael and Sean, identify the loss relief claims that are available to them, and explain which of the available claims would be the most beneficial.

Notes

1   You should clearly state the amount of any reliefs claimed and the rates of income tax saved. However, you are not expected to calculate any income tax liabilities.

2   You should assume that the tax rates and allowances for the tax year 2021/22 apply throughout.

3   The following mark allocation is provided as guidance for this requirement:

   Michael, 4½ marks

   Sean, 5½ marks   (10 marks)

_____

(Total = 10 marks)

100 Samantha (December 2007)

Samantha has been self-employed since 2006. She has the following income and chargeable gains for the tax years 2019/20 to 2022/23:

	2019/20	2020/21	2021/22	2022/23
	£	£	£	£
Trading profit/(loss)	7,290	42,600	(79,000)	19,285
Building society interest	–	6,100	3,800	2,130
Chargeable gains/(loss)	21,800	23,300	(3,400)	14,800

The chargeable gains are stated **before** taking account of loss relief and the annual exempt amount.

Required

(a) State the factors that will influence an individual's choice of loss relief claims.   **(3 marks)**

(b) Calculate Samantha's taxable income and taxable gains for each of the tax years 2019/20, 2020/21, 2021/22 and 2022/23 on the assumption that she relieves the trading loss of £79,000 for the tax year 2021/22 on the most favourable basis.

You should assume that the tax rules and the tax rates and allowances for the tax year 2021/22 apply throughout.   **(7 marks)**

(Total = 10 marks)

101 Robinette (September/December 2019)

27 mins

This scenario relates to three requirements.

Robinette ceased self-employment on 30 June 2021. She was then employed by Bird plc for the six-month period from 1 August 2021 to 31 January 2022. Robinette commenced self-employment again, in a new business, on 1 February 2022.

Self-employment ceasing on 30 June 2021

(1) Robinette's trading profit for the final 14-month period of trading from 1 May 2020 to 30 June 2021 was £106,900. This figure is **before** taking account of capital allowances.

(2) The tax written down value of the capital allowances main pool at 1 May 2020 was £15,300. On 11 June 2020 Robinette purchased a laptop computer for £2,600.

On the cessation of trading, Robinette personally retained the laptop computer. Its value on 30 June 2021 was £1,750. The remaining items included in the main pool were sold for £7,300 on 30 June 2021.

(3) Robinette had unused overlap profits brought forward of £22,700.

Employment from 1 August 2021 to 31 January 2022

(1) During the six-month period from 1 August 2021 to 31 January 2022, Robinette was paid a gross monthly salary of £10,600 in respect of her employment with Bird plc.

(2) Throughout the period from 1 August 2021 to 31 January 2022, Bird plc provided Robinette with living accommodation. The property was rented by Bird plc at a cost of £690 per month (this is higher than the annual value of the property). Bird plc also paid for the running costs relating to the property, and for the period 1 August 2021 to 31 January 2022 these amounted to £1,440.

(3) Throughout the period from 1 August 2021 to 31 January 2022, Robinette's two-year old son was provided with a place at Bird plc's workplace nursery. The total cost to the company of providing this nursery place was £4,800 (120 days at £40 per day).

(4) Robinette used her private motor car for business purposes. During the period from 1 August 2021 to 31 January 2022, she drove 5,200 miles in the performance of her duties for Bird plc, for which the company paid an allowance of 35 pence per mile.

Self-employment from 1 February 2022

(1) Robinette's trading profit for the first five-month period of trading from 1 February to 30 June 2022 was £55,700. This figure is **before** taking account of capital allowances.

(2) The only item of plant and machinery owned by Robinette, and used in this business, is office equipment which was purchased for £26,200 on 1 February 2022.

Property income

(1) During the period 1 August 2021 to 31 January 2022, Robinette let out her main residence at a monthly rent of £1,100. Robinette lived in this property up to 31 July 2021 and then again from 1 February 2022 onwards.

(2) The only expenditure incurred by Robinette in respect of the letting was property insurance, which cost £624 for the year ended 5 April 2022.

(3) Robinette has opted to calculate her property income using the accruals basis. Rent-a-room relief is not available in respect of the letting.

Self-assessment tax return

Robinette filed for her self-assessment tax return for the tax year 2021/22 on 14 August 2022. She is quite confident that all of her income for the tax year 2021/22 was correctly declared and that no deductions were incorrectly claimed.

Required

(a)   Calculate Robinette's taxable income for the tax year 2021/22.   (12 marks)

Note. You should indicate by the use of zero (0) any items which are not taxable or deductible.

(b)   (i)   State the period during which HM Revenue and Customs (HMRC) will have to notify Robinette if they intend to carry out a compliance check in respect of her self-assessment tax return for the tax year 2021/22, and the likely reason why such a check would be made.   (2 marks)

      (ii)   Advise Robinette as to how long she must retain the records used in preparing her self-assessment tax return for the tax year 2021/22.   (1 mark)

(Total = 15 marks)

102 Lucy

18 mins

Assume that it is 1 March 2021.

Lucy is considering two work arrangements. She will start her chosen arrangement on 6 April 2021 and will continue with that arrangement for the whole of the tax year 2021/22.

Employment with Red plc

Lucy has been offered employment with Red plc. She would be paid a salary of £36,000 and would be required to work at Red plc's offices.

Lucy would travel from home to Red plc's offices by train and would buy an annual season ticket costing £1,500.

Self-employment

Lucy would work for a number of clients at their offices. She would receive fees of £36,000 from her clients in the year to 5 April 2022.

Lucy would travel from home to client offices in her own car. Her business mileage would be 4,600 miles during the year and she estimates this would actually cost 40p per mile.

Lucy would prepare accounts to 5 April 2022 and elect to use the cash basis and approved mileage allowances.

Required

Determine which of the work arrangements would result in Lucy having a higher amount of disposable income after deducting income tax, national insurance contributions and travel costs.

Note. You are expected to calculate the income tax and NIC liability for Lucy for each arrangement and then calculate her disposable income in each case, taking into account her travel costs.

(10 marks)

(Total = 10 marks)

103 Daniel, Francine and Gregor (September/December 2015)

18 mins

(a) Amanda, Beatrice and Claude have been in partnership since 1 November 2013, preparing accounts to 31 October annually. Daniel joined as a partner on 1 May 2021. Profits have always been shared equally. The partnership's recent tax adjusted trading profits are as follows:

	£
Year ended 31 October 2020	147,000
Year ended 31 October 2021	96,000
Year ended 31 October 2022 (forecast)	180,000

Required

Calculate Daniel's trading income assessment for the tax year 2021/22. (3 marks)

(b) Francine is employed by Fringe plc. On 1 August 2021, Fringe plc provided Francine with a loan of £96,000 to help her purchase a holiday cottage. On 1 October 2021, the loan was increased by a further £14,000 so that Francine could renovate the cottage. Francine pays interest at an annual rate of 1.5% on this loan.

The taxable benefit in respect of this loan is calculated using the average method.

Required

Calculate Francine's taxable benefit for the tax year 2021/22 in respect of the loan from Fringe plc. (3 marks)

(c) Gregor has been self-employed since 6 April 2005. He has the following income and chargeable gains for the tax years 2020/21 and 2021/22:

	2020/21	2021/22
	£	£
Trading profit/(loss)	14,700	(68,800)
Business property profit/(loss)	4,600	(2,300)
Building society interest (gross)	1,300	900
Chargeable gain/(loss)	(2,900)	17,400

Required

On the assumption that Gregor relieves his trading loss of £68,800 as early as possible, calculate the amount of trading loss carried forward to the tax year 2022/23.

Note. You should assume that the tax allowances for the tax year 2021/22 apply throughout.

(4 marks)

(Total = 10 marks)

104 George (March/June 2016)

18 mins

You should assume that today's date is 1 March 2021.

George is a software developer. He has accepted a one-year contract to update software for Xpee plc.

(1)   The contract will run from 6 April 2021 to 5 April 2022, with a fee of £40,000 payable for the entire year of the contract. A condition of the contract is that George will have to do the work personally and not be permitted to sub-contract the work to anyone else.

(2)   George will work from home, but will have to attend weekly meetings at Xpee plc's offices to receive instructions regarding the work to be performed during the following week.

(3)   George will not incur any significant expenses in respect of the contract apart from the purchase of a new laptop computer for £3,600 on 6 April 2021. This laptop will be used 100% for business purposes.

(4)   During the term of the contract, George will not be permitted to work for any other clients. He will therefore not have any other income during the tax year 2021/22.

(5)   George's tax liability for the tax year 2020/21 was collected through PAYE, so he will not be required to make any payments on account in respect of the tax year 2021/22.

George has several friends who are also software developers. He understands that his employment status is not clear cut but that his income tax liability for the tax year 2021/22 will be the same regardless of whether he is treated as employed or as self-employed. However, George appreciates that there are advantages to being classed as self-employed.

Required

(a)   List **FOUR** factors which are indicators of George being treated as an employee in relation to his contract with Xpee plc rather than as self-employed.

        Note. You should confine your answer to the information given in the question.   **(2 marks)**

(b)   Calculate George's income tax liability and national insurance contributions for the tax year 2021/22 if he is treated as self-employed in respect of his contract with Xpee plc.

        (4 marks)

(c)   If George is treated as being an employee of Xpee plc instead of self-employed:

        (i)   Explain why his income tax liability will be payable earlier   **(2 marks)**

        (ii)   Calculate the additional amount of national insurance contributions which he personally will suffer for the tax year 2021/22   **(2 marks)**

(Total = 10 marks)

105 Joe (December 2010) (amended)

27 mins

On 31 December 2021 Joe resigned as an employee of Firstly plc, and on 1 January 2022 commenced employment with Secondly plc. The following information is available for the tax year 2021/22:

Employment with Firstly plc

(1)　From 6 April 2021 to 31 December 2021 Joe was paid a salary of £6,360 per month. In addition to his salary, Joe was paid a bonus of £12,000 on 12 May 2021. He had become entitled to this bonus on 22 March 2021.

(2)　Joe contributed 6% of his monthly gross salary of £6,360 into Firstly plc's occupational pension scheme. Firstly plc contributed 3%.

(3)　On 1 May 2021 Firstly plc provided Joe with an interest-free loan of £120,000 so that he could purchase a holiday cottage. Joe repaid £50,000 of the loan on 31 July 2021, and repaid the balance of the loan of £70,000 when he ceased employment with Firstly plc on 31 December 2021.

(4)　During the period from 6 April 2021 to 31 December 2021 Joe's three year old daughter was provided with a place at Firstly plc's workplace nursery. The total cost to the company of providing this nursery place was £11,400 (190 days at £60 per day).

(5)　Firstly plc provided Joe with a home entertainment system for his personal use costing £4,400 on 6 April 2021. The company gave the home entertainment system to Joe for free when he left the company on 31 December 2021, although its market value at that time was £3,860.

Employment with Secondly plc

(1)　From 1 January 2022 to 5 April 2022 Joe was paid a salary of £6,565 per month. He worked one day a week at home and the remainder at Secondly plc's offices.

(2)　During the period 1 January 2022 to 5 April 2022 Joe contributed a total of £3,000 (gross) into a personal pension scheme.

(3)　From 1 January 2022 to 5 April 2022 Secondly plc provided Joe with living accommodation. The property has an annual value of £10,400 and is rented by Secondly plc at a cost of £2,250 per month. On 1 January 2022 Secondly plc purchased furniture for the property at a cost of £16,320.

(4)　From 1 January 2022 to 5 April 2022 Secondly plc paid Joe £15 per month to cover additional household costs incurred when he worked at home.

Required

Calculate Joe's employment income for the tax year 2021/22.

(15 marks)

(Total = 15 marks)

106 Sammi (December 2010)

You should assume that today's date is 20 March 2021.

Sammi is a director of Smark Ltd, a profitable company. The company has given her the choice of being provided with a leased company motor car or alternatively being paid additional director's remuneration and then privately leasing the same motor car herself.

Company motor car

The motor car will be provided throughout the tax year 2021/22, and will be leased by Smark Ltd at an annual cost of £27,630. The motor car will be petrol powered, will have a list price of £80,000, and will have an official CO_2 emission rate of 185 grams per kilometre.

The lease payments will cover all the costs of running the motor car except for fuel. Smark Ltd will not provide Sammi with any fuel for private journeys.

Additional director's remuneration

As an alternative to having a company motor car, Sammi will be paid additional gross director's remuneration of £27,000 during the tax year 2021/22. She will then privately lease the motor car at an annual cost of £27,630.

Other information

The amount of business journeys that will be driven by Sammi will be immaterial and can therefore be ignored.

Sammi's current level of director's remuneration is over £150,000 which means that she will pay income tax at the additional rate of 45% in 2021/22. Smark Ltd prepares its accounts to 5 April. The lease of the motor car will commence on 6 April 2021.

Required

(a) Advise Sammi of the income tax and national insurance contribution implications for the tax year 2021/22 if she (1) is provided with the company motor car, and (2) receives additional director's remuneration of £27,000. **(5 marks)**

(b) Advise Smark Ltd of the corporation tax and national insurance contribution implications for the year ended 5 April 2022 if the company (1) provides Sammi with the company motor car, and (2) pays Sammi additional director's remuneration of £27,000.

   Note. You should ignore value added tax (VAT). **(5 marks)**

(c) Determine which of the two alternatives is the more beneficial from each of the respective points of view of Sammi and Smark Ltd. **(5 marks)**

(Total = 15 marks)

107 Simon (December 2009)   **27 mins**

On 19 April 2021 Simon purchased a derelict freehold house for £127,000. Legal fees of £1,800 were paid in respect of the purchase.

Simon then renovated the house at a cost of £50,000, with the renovation being completed on 6 August 2021. He immediately put the house up for sale, and it was sold on 27 August 2021 for £260,000. Legal fees of £2,600 were paid in respect of the sale.

Simon financed the transaction by a bank loan of £150,000 that was taken out on 19 April 2021 at an annual interest rate of 6%. The bank loan was repaid on 28 August 2021.

Simon had no other income or capital gains for the tax year 2021/22 except as indicated above.

Simon has been advised that whether or not he is treated as carrying on a trade will be determined according to the six following 'badges of trade':

(1)   Subject matter of the transaction
(2)   Length of ownership
(3)   Frequency of similar transactions
(4)   Work done on the property
(5)   Circumstances responsible for the realisation
(6)   Motive

Required

(a)   Briefly explain the meaning of each of the six 'badges of trade' listed in the question.

   Note. You are not expected to quote from decided cases.   (3 marks)

(b)   Calculate Simon's income tax liability and his Class 2 and Class 4 national insurance contributions for the tax year 2021/22, if he is treated as carrying on a trade in respect of the disposal of the freehold house.   (8 marks)

(c)   Calculate Simon's capital gains tax liability for the tax year 2021/22, if he is not treated as carrying on a trade in respect of the disposal of the freehold house.   (4 marks)

───

                                                          (Total = 15 marks)

BPP
LEARNING
MEDIA

108 Na (December 2009) (amended)   27 mins

Na commenced self-employment as a hairdresser on 1 January 2019. She had tax adjusted trading profits of £25,200 for the six-month period ended 30 June 2019 and £21,600 for the year ended 30 June 2020.

The following information is available for the tax year 2021/22:

Trading profit for the year ended 30 June 2021

(1) Na's statement of profit or loss for the year ended 30 June 2021 is as follows:

	Note	£	£
Income			63,635
Expenses			
Depreciation		2,635	
Motor expenses	2	2,200	
Professional fees	3	1,650	
Property expenses	4	12,900	
Purchases	5	4,700	
Other expenses	6	16,550	
			(40,635)
Net profit			23,000

(2) Na charges all the running expenses for her motor car to the business. During the year ended 30 June 2021 Na drove a total of 8,000 miles, of which 7,000 were for private journeys.

(3) The figure for professional fees includes £1,260 for legal fees in connection with the grant of a new five-year lease of parking spaces for customers' motor cars.

(4) Na lives in a flat that is situated above her hairdressing studio, and one-third of the total property expenses of £12,900 relate to this flat.

(5) During the year ended 30 June 2021 Na took goods out of the hairdressing business for her personal use without paying for them, and no entry has been made in the accounts to record this. The goods cost £250 (an amount that has been deducted under 'purchases') and had a selling price of £450.

(6) The figure for other expenses of £16,550 includes £480 for a fine in respect of health and safety regulations and £160 for a trade subscription to the Guild of Small Hairdressers.

(7) Na uses her private telephone to make business telephone calls. The total cost of the private telephone for the year ended 30 June 2021 was £1,200, and 20% of this related to business telephone calls. The cost of the private telephone is not included in the statement of profit or loss expenses of £40,635.

(8) Capital allowances for the year ended 30 June 2021 are £810.

Other information

(9) During the tax year 2021/22 Na received interest of £310 from an individual savings account (ISA) and dividends of £1,200 from quoted company shareholdings.

Required

(a) Calculate the amount of trading profits that will have been assessed on Na for the tax years 2018/19, 2019/20 and 2020/21 respectively, clearly identifying the amount of any overlap profits.   (5 marks)

(b) Calculate Na's tax adjusted trading profit for the year ended 30 June 2021.

Note. Your computation should commence with the net profit figure of £23,000, and should list all of the items referred to in notes (1) to (8) indicating by the use of zero (0) any items that do not require adjustment.   (7 marks)

(c) Calculate Na's income tax liability for the tax year 2021/22.   (3 marks)

(Total = 15 marks)

109 John (June 2013) (amended)

27 mins

John is employed by Surf plc. The following information is available for the tax year 2021/22:

(1) During the tax year 2021/22, John was promoted and paid gross remuneration of £328,318. In each of the tax years 2018/19, 2019/20 and 2020/21 his adjusted income was below £150,000.

(2) During the tax year 2021/22, John contributed £18,000 into Surf plc's occupational pension scheme. The company contributed a further £12,000 on his behalf. Both John and Surf plc have made exactly the same contributions for the previous five tax years.

(3) During 2018 Surf plc provided John with a loan which was used to purchase a yacht. The amount of loan outstanding at 6 April 2021 was £84,000. John repaid £12,000 of the loan on 31 July 2021, and then repaid a further £12,000 on 31 December 2021. He paid loan interest of £90 to Surf plc during the tax year 2021/22. The taxable benefit in respect of this loan is calculated using the average method.

(4) During the tax year 2021/22, John made personal pension contributions up to the maximum amount of available annual allowances, including any unused amounts brought forward from previous years. These contributions were in addition to the contributions he made to Surf plc's occupational pension scheme (see note (2)). John has not made any personal pension contributions in previous tax years.

(5) John owns a holiday cottage which is let out as a furnished holiday letting, although the letting does not qualify as a trade under the furnished holiday letting rules. The property business profit for the year ended 5 April 2022 was £14,855 before taking into account interest and £1,875 paid to a letting agent. John paid loan interest of £7,500 for the year in respect of a loan to buy this property.

Required

(a) Calculate John's income tax liability for the tax year 2021/22. **(12 marks)**

(b) State THREE tax advantages of a rental property qualifying as a trade under the furnished holiday letting rules. **(3 marks)**

(Total = 15 marks)

110 Ronald (June 2014) (amended) 27 mins

Ronald is employed and also self-employed. Ronald has tried to prepare his own income tax computation for the tax year 2021/22, but he has found it more difficult than expected. Although the sections which Ronald has completed are correct, there are a significant number of omissions. The omissions are marked as outstanding (O/S). The partly completed income tax computation is as follows:

RONALD – INCOME TAX COMPUTATION 2021/22

	Note	£
Trading income	1	O/S
Employment income		70,065
Property business profit	2	O/S
Building society interest		1,260
Dividends		O/S
		O/S
Personal allowance		(12,570)
Taxable income		O/S

	Note	£
Income tax		
Non-savings income: £37,700 @ 20%		7,540
Non-savings income: O/S @ 40%		O/S
Savings income: £500 @ 0%		0
Savings income: O/S @ 40%		O/S
Dividend income: O/S @ 0%		0
Dividend income: £800 @ 32.5%		260
O/S		
Income tax liability		O/S
Tax suffered at source		
PAYE		(11,513)
Income tax payable		O/S

Notes

1   *Trading profit*

Ronald commenced self-employment on 1 January 2021. He had a tax adjusted trading profit of £3,840 for the four-month period ended 30 April 2021, and £12,060 for the year ended 30 April 2022. These figures are **before** taking account of capital allowances.

The only item of plant and machinery owned by Ronald is his motor car, which cost £24,000 on 1 September 2021.

The motor car has a CO_2 emission rate of 122 grams per kilometre, and 70% of the mileage driven by Ronald is for private journeys.

2   *Property business profit*

Ronald owns a freehold shop. The 10-year old shop was purchased on 1 October 2021, and during October 2021 Ronald spent £8,400 replacing the building's roof. The shop was not usable until this work was carried out, and this fact was represented by a reduced purchase price.

On 1 December 2021, the property was let to a tenant, with Ronald receiving a premium of £12,000 for the grant of a 30-year lease. The monthly rent is £768 payable in advance, and during the period 1 December 2021 to 5 April 2022 Ronald received five rental payments.

Due to a fire, £8,600 was spent on replacing the roof of the shop during February 2022. Only £8,200 of this was paid for by Ronald's property insurance.

Ronald paid insurance of £156 in respect of the property. This was paid on 1 October 2021 and is for the year ended 30 September 2022.

Other information

Ronald did not make any personal pension contributions during the tax year 2021/22. He has never been a member of a pension scheme.

Required

(a)   Calculate the income tax payable by Ronald for the tax year 2021/22.   **(11 marks)**

(b)   Advise Ronald why the maximum gross amount of tax relievable personal pension scheme contribution which he could have made for the tax year 2021/22 is £40,000, and the method by which tax relief would have been given if he had made this amount of contribution.   **(4 marks)**

(Total = 15 marks)

111 Wai (June 2015)

Wai is employed as a sales manager by Qaz plc, and the following information is available in respect of the tax year 2021/22:

(1)   During the tax year 2021/22, Wai was paid a gross monthly salary of £10,200.

(2)   In addition to her salary, Wai has been paid the following bonuses:

Amount	Date of payment	Date of entitlement	In respect of the six-month period ended
£			
4,600	25 April 2021	31 March 2021	31 December 2020
8,100	20 August 2021	3 July 2021	30 June 2021
2,900	3 May 2022	15 April 2022	31 December 2021

(3)   During the period 6 April to 31 August 2021, Wai used her private motor car for both private and business journeys. She was reimbursed by Qaz plc at the rate of 55p per mile for the following mileage:

	Miles
Normal daily travel between home and Qaz plc's offices	2,420
Travel between home and the premises of Qaz plc's clients (none of the clients' premises were located near the offices of Qaz plc)	8,580
Travel between home and a temporary workplace (the assignment was for ten weeks)	2,860
Total mileage reimbursed by Qaz plc	13,860

(4)   During the period 1 September 2021 to 5 April 2022, Qaz plc provided Wai with a brand new diesel powered motor car which meets the RDE2 standard. The car has a list price of £10,013 and an official CO_2 emission rate of 91 grams per kilometre. Qaz plc does not provide Wai with any fuel for private journeys.

(5)   During January 2022, Wai spent ten nights overseas on company business. Qaz plc paid Wai a daily allowance of £10 to cover the cost of personal incidental expenses, such as telephone calls to her family.

(6)   Throughout the tax year 2021/22, Qaz plc allowed Wai the use of two mobile telephones. The telephones had each cost £400 when purchased by the company in March 2021.

(7)   Throughout the tax year 2021/22, Qaz plc provided Wai with living accommodation. The company had purchased the property on 1 June 2018 for £142,000, and it has been provided to Wai since 1 February 2020. Improvements costing £24,200 were made to the property during October 2018, and further improvements costing £9,800 were made during August 2021. The annual value of the property is £4,828.

Qaz plc does not payroll employee benefits.

Required

(a)   Calculate Wai's taxable income for the tax year 2021/22.   (12 marks)

(b)   Briefly outline the information to be included in PAYE forms P60 and P11D, and state the dates by which they should have been provided to Wai for the tax year 2021/22.

   Note. Your answer should be confined to the details which are relevant to Wai, although no figures are required.   (3 marks)

(Total = 15 marks)

112 Samson and Delilah (September/December 2015) (amended)

27 mins

Samson and Delilah are a married couple. They are both employed by Rope plc, and Delilah is also a partner in a partnership. The following information is available in respect of the tax year 2021/22:

Samson

During the tax year 2021/22, Samson was paid a gross annual salary of £112,000 in respect of his employment with Rope plc.

Delilah

(1) During the tax year 2021/22, Delilah was paid a gross annual salary of £184,000 in respect of her employment with Rope plc.

(2) Throughout the tax year 2021/22, Rope plc provided Delilah with a petrol powered motor car which has a list price of £67,200, and an official CO_2 emission rate of 152 grams per kilometre. Rope plc does not provide Delilah with any fuel for private journeys. Delilah was unable to drive her motor car for a period during the tax year 2021/22 because of a skiing accident, and during this period Rope plc provided her with a chauffeur at a total cost of £9,400.

(3) Rope plc provided all its employees with a hamper of groceries costing £42 each in December 2021.

(4) Delilah spent £70 in July 2021 on travelling by train to visit a customer of Rope plc. This amount was reimbursed by Rope plc in August 2021.

(5) During the tax year 2021/22, Delilah donated £250 (gross) per month to charity under the payroll deduction scheme operated by Rope plc.

(6) Delilah has been in partnership with Esther and Felix for a number of years. The partnership's tax adjusted trading profit for the year ended 31 December 2021 was £93,600. Esther is paid an annual salary of £8,000, with the balance of profits being shared 40% to Delilah, 30% to Esther and 30% to Felix.

(7) During the tax year 2021/22, Delilah paid interest of £6,200 (gross) on a personal loan taken out to purchase her share in the partnership.

(8) During the tax year 2021/22, Delilah made charitable gift aid donations totalling £4,864 (net).

Joint income – Building society deposit account

Samson and Delilah have savings in a building society deposit account which is in their joint names. During the tax year 2021/22, they received building society interest totalling £9,600 from this joint account.

Required

(a) Calculate Samson and Delilah's respective income tax liabilities for the tax year 2021/22.

Note. The following mark allocation is provided as guidance for this requirement:

Samson (4 marks)

Delilah (9 marks)   (13 marks)

(b) Calculate Samson's income tax saving for the tax year 2021/22 if the building society deposit account had been in Delilah's sole name instead of in joint names for the entire year.   (2 marks)

_____

(Total = 15 marks)

113 Patience (March/June 2016)

Patience retired on 31 December 2021, and on that date ceased employment and self-employment. The following information is available in respect of the tax year 2021/22:

Employment

(1) Patience was employed by a private school as a teacher. From 6 April to 31 December 2021, she was paid a salary of £3,750 per month.

(2) During the period 6 April to 31 December 2021, Patience contributed 6% of her monthly gross salary of £3,750 into her employer's occupational pension scheme. Patience's employer contributed a further 10% on her behalf.

(3) During the period 6 April to 30 June 2021, Patience's granddaughter was provided with a free place at the private school run by Patience's employer. The normal fee payable would have been £4,600. The additional marginal expense of providing the place for the grandchild was £540.

(4) On 25 June 2021, Patience was given a clock valued at £600 as an award for her 25 years of teaching at her employer's school. She has not previously received any similar awards.

(5) Patience's employer provided her with an interest-free loan so that she could purchase a season ticket for the train to work. The balance of the loan outstanding at 6 April 2021 was £8,000, and Patience repaid the loan in full on 31 December 2021.

Self-employment

(1) Patience was self-employed as a private tutor. Her trading profit for the year ended 31 July 2021 was £14,800. This figure is **after** taking account of capital allowances.

(2) Patience's trading profit for the final five-month period of trading from 1 August to 31 December 2021 was £6,900. This figure is **before** taking account of capital allowances.

(3) The tax written down value of the capital allowances main pool at 1 August 2021 was £2,200. On 10 August 2021, Patience purchased a laptop computer for £1,700.

   On the cessation of trading, Patience personally retained the laptop computer. Its value on 31 December 2021 was £1,200. The remainder of the items included in the main pool were sold for £800 on 31 December 2021.

(4) Patience has unused overlap profits brought forward of £3,700.

Personal pension contributions

During the period 6 April to 31 December 2021, Patience contributed a total of £3,600 (net) into a personal pension scheme.

Pension income

During the period 1 January to 5 April 2022, Patience received the state pension of £1,450, a pension of £7,000 from her employer's occupational pension scheme, and a private pension of £3,650. These were the total gross amounts received.

Property

Patience owned two properties which were let out unfurnished until both properties were sold on 31 December 2021. The following information is available in respect of the two properties:

	Property one £	Property two £
Rent received during the tax year 2021/22	3,600	7,200
Sale proceeds on 31 December 2021	122,000	98,000
Allowable revenue expenditure paid during the tax year 2021/22 (no finance costs)	(4,700)	(2,600)
Purchase cost	(81,000)	(103,700)

Patience has never occupied either of the two properties as her main residence.

Required

Calculate Patience's income tax and capital gains tax liabilities for the tax year **2021/22**.

Notes

1   You should indicate by the use of zero (0) any items which are not taxable or deductible.

2   The following mark allocation is provided as guidance for this question:

Income tax (13 marks)
Capital gains tax (2 marks)   **(15 marks)**

(Total = 15 marks)

114 Petula (March/June 2017)

Petula has been employed as a sales manager by Downtown plc since 6 April 2012. The following information is available in respect of the tax year 2021/22:

(1) During the tax year 2021/22, Petula was paid a gross annual salary of £260,000.

(2) In addition to her salary, Petula has been paid the following bonuses by Downtown plc:

Amount £	Date of payment	Date of entitlement	In respect of the six-month period ended
21,200	30 April 2021	1 April 2021	31 December 2020
18,600	31 October 2021	1 October 2021	30 June 2021
22,400	30 April 2022	1 April 2022	31 December 2021

(3) During the tax year 2021/22, Petula used her private motor car for both private and business journeys. The total mileage driven by Petula throughout the tax year was 26,000 miles, with all of this mileage reimbursed by Downtown plc at the rate of 60p per mile. However, only 21,000 miles were in the performance of Petula's duties for Downtown plc.

(4) Petula pays an annual professional subscription of £630 which is relevant to her employment with Downtown plc. Petula also pays an annual subscription membership fee of £1,840 to a golf club which she uses to entertain Downtown plc's clients. Downtown plc does not reimburse Petula for either of these costs.

(5) During the tax year 2021/22, Petula paid interest of £140 on a personal loan taken out on 6 April 2021 to purchase a computer for sole use in her employment with Downtown plc.

(6) Each tax year since 6 April 2014 (including the tax year 2021/22), Downtown plc has contributed £25,000 into the company's occupational pension scheme on Petula's behalf. Petula has never personally made any pension contributions. Petula's adjusted income for 2018/19, 2019/20 and 2020/21 was below £150,000.

(7) Petula owns a freehold house which was let out furnished throughout the tax year 2021/22. The total amount of rent received during the tax year was £12,000.

During August 2021, Petula purchased a new washer-dryer for the property at a cost of £730. This was a replacement for an old washing machine which was scrapped, with nil proceeds. The cost of a similar washing machine would have been £420.

During November 2021, Petula purchased a new dishwasher for the property at a cost of £580. The property did not previously have a dishwasher.

The other expenditure on the property paid in the tax year 2021/22 amounted to £1,640, none of which is loan interest, and all of this is allowable.

(8) During the tax year 2021/22, Petula rented out one furnished room of her main residence. During the year, she received rent of £8,900 and incurred allowable expenditure of £2,890 in respect of the room. Petula always uses the most favourable basis as regards the tax treatment of the furnished room.

(9) On 1 July 2021, Petula purchased £250,000 (nominal value) of gilts paying interest at the rate of 3% for £300,000. Interest is paid half-yearly on 30 June and 31 December based on the nominal value. Petula sold the gilts on 31 October 2021 for £302,500 (including accrued interest).

Required

(a) Calculate Petula's taxable income for the tax year 2021/22.

Note. Your computation should list all of the items referred to in notes (1) to (9), indicating with the use of zero (0) any items which are not taxable or deductible.   **(12 marks)**

(b) Advise Petula of the total amount of her unused pension annual allowances which are available to carry forward to the tax year 2022/23.   **(3 marks)**

(Total = 15 marks)

115 Dill (September/December 2017)

Up to and including the tax year 2019/20, Dill was always resident in the United Kingdom (UK), being in the UK for more than 300 days each tax year. She was also resident in the UK for the tax year 2021/22. However, during the tax year 2020/21, Dill was overseas for 305 days, spending just 60 days in the UK. Dill has a house in the UK and stayed there on the 60 days which she spent in the UK. She also has a house overseas. For the tax year 2020/21, Dill did not have any close family in the UK, did not do any work in the UK and was not treated as working full-time overseas.

On 6 April 2021, Dill returned to the UK and commenced employment with Herb plc as the IT manager. She also set up a small technology business which she ran on a self-employed basis, but this business failed and Dill ceased self-employment on 5 April 2022. The following information is available for the tax year 2021/22:

Employment

(1) During the tax year 2021/22, Dill was paid a gross annual salary of £430,000.

(2) In addition to her salary, Dill has been paid the following bonuses by Herb plc:

Amount £	Date of payment	Date of entitlement	In respect of the four-month period
16,200	31 December 2021	1 November 2021	31 July 2021
29,100	30 April 2022	1 March 2022	30 November 2021

(3) Throughout the tax year 2021/22, Dill had the use of Herb plc's company gym which is only open to employees of the company. The cost to Herb plc of providing this benefit was £780.

(4) Throughout the tax year 2021/22, Herb plc provided Dill with a home entertainment system for her personal use. The home entertainment system cost Herb plc £5,900 on 6 April 2021.

(5) During the tax year 2021/22, Dill's three-year-old son was provided with a place at Herb plc's workplace nursery. The total cost to the company of providing this nursery place was £7,200 (240 days at £30 per day).

(6) On 1 June 2021, Herb plc provided Dill with an interest-free loan of £96,000 which she used to renovate her main residence. No loan repayments were made before 5 April 2022.

(7) On 25 January 2022, Herb plc paid a health club membership fee of £990 for the benefit of Dill.

(8) During the tax year 2021/22, Dill used her private motor car for both private and business journeys. The total mileage driven by Dill throughout the tax year was 16,000 miles, with all of this mileage reimbursed by Herb plc at the rate of 25p per mile. However, only 14,500 miles were in the performance of Dill's duties for Herb plc.

(9) During the tax year 2021/22, Dill paid an annual professional subscription of £560 which is relevant to her employment with Herb plc. She also paid an annual membership fee of £1,620 to a golf club which she uses to entertain Herb plc's suppliers. Herb plc did not reimburse Dill for either of these costs.

(10) During the tax year 2021/22, Dill contributed the maximum possible tax relievable amount into Herb plc's occupational pension scheme. The company did not make any contributions on her behalf. Dill has never previously been a member of a pension scheme.

Self-employment

For the tax year 2021/22, Dill's self-employed business made a tax adjusted trading loss of £58,000. Dill will claim relief for this loss against her total income for the tax year 2021/22.

Other information

(1)   On 1 November 2021, Dill received a premium bond prize of £1,000.

(2)   On 28 February 2022, Dill received interest of £1,840 on the maturity of savings certificates from NS&I (National Savings and Investments).

Required

(a)   Explain why Dill was treated as not resident in the United Kingdom for the tax year 2020/21.   (3 marks)

(b)   Calculate Dill's taxable income for the tax year 2021/22.

        Note. You should indicate by the use of zero (0) any items which are not taxable or deductible.   (12 marks)

(Total = 15 marks)

116 Danh (March/June 2018)

Up to and including the tax year 2018/19, Danh was always automatically treated as not resident in the UK, spending fewer than 46 days in the UK each year. Danh knows that for the tax year 2021/22, he will automatically be treated as resident in the UK, but is unsure of his residence status for the tax years 2019/20 and 2020/21. For these two tax years, Danh was neither automatically not resident in the UK nor automatically resident. For both of these tax years, Danh spent 100 days in the UK, with the remainder of each tax year spent in the same overseas country. Throughout both tax years, Danh had a property in the UK and stayed there on the 100 days which he spent in the UK. Danh also did substantive work in the UK during both tax years. He does not have any close family in the UK.

On 6 August 2021, Danh commenced self-employment as a sole trader. In addition, on 6 September 2021, Danh joined an existing partnership run by Ebele and Fai. The following information is available for the tax year 2021/22:

Self-employment

(1)   Danh's statement of profit or loss for the eight-month period ended 5 April 2022 is:

	Note	£
Income		96,400
Expenses		
Depreciation		(2,300)
Motor expenses	2	(3,300)
Professional fees	3	(1,800)
Other expenses (all allowable)		(18,800)
Net profit		70,200

(2)   During the eight-month period ended 5 April 2022, Danh drove a total of 12,000 miles, of which 4,000 were for private journeys.

(3)   The figure for professional fees consists of £340 for accountancy and £1,460 for legal fees in connection with the grant of a new five-year lease for business premises.

(4)   Danh runs his business using one of the six rooms in his private house as an office. The total running costs of the house for the eight-month period ended 5 April 2022 were £4,200. No deduction has been made for the cost of using the office in calculating the net profit of £70,200.

(5)   The only item of plant and machinery owned by Danh is his motor car. This was purchased on 6 August 2021 for £14,800, and has a CO_2 emission rate of 40 grams per kilometre.

Partnership loss

(1)   For the year ended 5 April 2022, the partnership made a tax-adjusted trading loss of £12,600. Until 5 September 2021, profits and losses were shared 60% to Ebele and 40% to Fai. Since 6 September 2021, profits and losses have been shared 20% to Danh, 50% to Ebele and 30% to Fai.

(2)   Danh will claim to relieve his share of the partnership's loss against his total income for the tax year 2021/22.

(3)   During the tax year 2021/22, Danh paid interest of £875 (gross) on a personal loan taken out to purchase his share in the partnership.

Property income

(1)   On 6 April 2021, Danh purchased a freehold house which was then let out. The total amount of rent received during the tax year 2021/22 was £14,400.

(2)   Danh partly financed the purchase of the property with a repayment mortgage, paying mortgage interest of £10,000 during the tax year 2021/22.

(3)   The other expenditure on the property for the tax year 2021/22 amounted to £3,980, and this is all allowable.

Required

(a)   Explain whether Danh was treated as resident or not resident in the UK for each of the tax years 2019/20 and 2020/21.
                                                                                                                    (3 marks)

(b)   Calculate Danh's income tax liability for the tax year 2021/22.

        Note. When calculating Danh's trading profit from self-employment for the eight-month period ended 5 April 2022, your computation should commence with the net profit figure of £70,200, indicating by the use of zero (0) any items which do not require adjustment.
                                                                                                                    (12 marks)

                                                                                                      (Total = 15 marks)

117 Martin (September/December 2018)   27 mins

Martin is employed by Global plc and he is also a member of a partnership. The following information is available in respect of the tax year 2021/22.

Employment

(1) During the tax year 2021/22, Martin was paid a gross annual salary of £144,000 in respect of his employment with Global plc.

(2) In addition to his salary, Martin was paid the following bonuses by Global plc:

Amount	In respect of the six-month period ended	Date of payment	Date of entitlement
£			
18,200	28 February 2021	31 March 2021	20 March 2021
21,400	31 August 2021	31 August 2021	20 September 2021
13,700	28 February 2022	30 April 2022	20 March 2022

(3) During the tax year 2021/22, Global plc provided Martin with the following brand new petrol powered motor cars:

Period provided	List price	CO_2 emission date
	£	
6 April to 31 December 2021	18,450	62 grams per kilometre
1 January to 5 April 2022	24,905	77 grams per kilometre

Martin was not provided with any fuel for private use.

(4) On 6 April 2021, Global plc provided Martin with an interest free loan of £8,000 which he used to purchase a motor bike. No loan repayments were made during the year.

(5) Throughout the tax year 2021/22, Global plc allowed Martin private use of a home entertainment system owned by the company. The home entertainment system cost Global plc £7,400 on 6 April 2021.

(6) During the tax year 2021/22, Martin donated a total of £1,000 (gross) to charity under the payroll deduction scheme operated by Global plc.

(7) Martin paid an annual professional subscription of £560 which is relevant to his employment with Global plc. Martin also paid an annual membership fee of £1,240 to a health club which he used to entertain Global plc's clients. Global plc did not reimburse Martin for either of these costs.

Partnership

(1) Martin has been in partnership with Norma and Oprah since 1 January 2008. The partnership's trading profit for the year ended 31 December 2021 was £54,600.

(2) Until 30 September 2021, profits were shared 40% to Martin, 30% to Norma and 30% to Oprah. Since 1 October 2021, profits have been shared equally.

Other income

(1) During the tax year 2021/22, Martin rented out one furnished room of his main residence, receiving rent of £9,200 for the year. No additional expenditure was incurred as a result of the letting.

(2) During the tax year 2021/22, Martin received dividends of £440.

(3) On 30 November 2021, Martin received interest of £1,330 on the maturity of savings certificates from NS&I (National Savings and Investments).

Self-assessment tax return

Martin always files his self-assessment tax return online on 26 December, so his tax return for the tax year 2021/22 will be filed on 26 December 2022.

Because more than 80% of Martin's tax liability is paid under PAYE, he is not required to make self-assessment payments on account.

Required

(a) Calculate Martin's taxable income for the tax year 2021/22.

  Note. You should indicate by the use of zero (0) any items which are not taxable or deductible. (11 marks)

(b) (i) Advise Martin of the deadline for making an amendment to his self-assessment tax return for the tax year 2021/22, and state how HM Revenue and Customs (HMRC) will calculate interest if such an amendment results in additional tax becoming payable. (2 marks)

  (ii) State the latest date by which HMRC will have to notify Martin if they intend to carry out a compliance check in respect of his self-assessment tax return for the tax year 2021/22, and (assuming the check is not made on a completely random basis) the possible reasons why such a check would be made. (2 marks)

(Total = 15 marks)

118 Tonie (March/June 2019)

Up to and including the tax year 2019/20, Tonie was resident in the UK for tax purposes, spending more than 300 days in the UK each year. Tonie understands that for the tax year 2021/22, she will again automatically be treated as resident in the UK, but is unsure of her residence status for the tax year 2020/21. For this tax year, Tonie was neither automatically resident in the UK nor automatically not resident. Throughout the tax year 2020/21, Tonie was travelling around the world and did not stay in any one country for longer than 30 days, although she did spend a total of 50 days in the UK. Tonie has a house in the UK, but it was let out throughout the tax year 2020/21. She is single, has no children, and stayed with a friend on the 50 days which she spent in the UK. Tonie did not do any substantive work in the UK during the 2020/21.

The following information is available for the tax year 2021/22:

Employment

On 6 April 2021, Tonie, who is a software developer, accepted a one-year contract to maintain websites for Droid plc. Droid plc treated the contract as one of employment, with the payments to Tonie being subject to PAYE. However, Tonie thought that, because she was working from home, her employment status should instead have been one of self-employment.

(1)   For the term of the contract, from 6 April 2021 to 5 April 2022, Tonie was paid a fixed gross amount of £6,200 a month. During the term of the contract, Tonie was not permitted to work for any other clients. She was required to do the work personally, not being permitted to sub-contract the work to anyone else.

(2)   During the term of the contract, Tonie worked from home, but had to attend weekly meetings at Droid plc's offices to receive instructions regarding the work to be performed during the following week. During the period 6 April 2021 to 5 April 2022, Tonie used her private motor car for business visits to Droid plc's clients. She drove 2,300 miles, for which Droid plc paid an allowance of 60 pence per mile.

(3)   During the term of the contract, Tonie leased computer equipment at a cost of £180 a month. This was used 100% for business purposes.

Property income

(1)   Tonie owns a freehold house which is let out (this is not a furnished holiday letting). The total amount of rent received during the tax year 2021/22 was £10,080.

(2)   Tonie partly financed the purchase of the property with a repayment mortgage, paying mortgage interest of £8,400 during the tax year 2021/22.

(3)   During May 2021, Tonie purchased a new washer-dryer for the property at a cost of £640. This was a replacement for an old washing machine which was scrapped, with nil proceeds. The cost of a similar washing machine would have been £380.

(4)   During November 2021, Tonie purchased a new dishwasher for the property at a cost of £560. The property did not previously have a dishwasher.

(5)   The other expenditure on the property for the tax year 2021/22 amounted to £3,210, and this is all allowable.

(6)   During the tax year 2021/22, Tonie rented out one furnished room of her main residence. During the year, she received rent of £8,580 and incurred allowable expenditure of £870 in respect of the room. Tonie always uses the most favourable basis as regards the tax treatment of the furnished room.

Other income

(1)   On 1 July 2021, Tonie inherited £100,000 (nominal value) of gilts paying interest at the rate of 3%. The inheritance was valued at £120,000. Interest is paid half-yearly on 30 June and 31 December based on the nominal value. Tonie sold the gilts on 30 November 2021 for £121,250 (including accrued interest).

(2)   On 31 January 2022, Tonie received a premium bond prize of £100.

(3)   On 31 March 2022, Tonie received interest of £520 on the maturity of savings certificates from NS&I (National Savings and Investments).

BPP
LEARNING
MEDIA

Required

(a)   Explain why Tonie was treated as not resident in the UK for the tax year 2020/21.

(2 marks)

(b)   List FOUR factors which are indicators of Tonie being treated as employed in relation to her contract with Droid plc rather than as self-employed.

Note. You should confine your answer to the information given in the question.   (2 marks)

(c)   On the basis that Tonie is treated as employed in relation to her contract with Droid plc, calculate her taxable income for the tax year 2021/22.

Note. You should indicate by the use of zero (0) any items which are not taxable or deductible.   (11 marks)

(Total = 15 marks)

PART C CHARGEABLE GAINS FOR INDIVIDUALS

Questions 119 to 162 cover chargeable gains for individuals, the subject of Chapters 13 to 16 of the BPP Workbook for Taxation (TX – UK).

OTQ bank – Chargeable gains for individuals 1   18 mins

119   **Which of the following gifts made by an individual is exempt from capital gains tax?**

☐   Gift of a motor boat valued at £10,000 (cost £5,000) to his aunt

☐   Gift of unquoted shares in a United Kingdom company valued at £2,500 (cost £1,800) to his brother

☐   Gift of antique jewellery valued at £6,800 (cost £3,200) to his sister

☐   Gift of a sculpture valued at £3,000 (cost £10,000) to his nephew   **(2 marks)**

---

120   Trudy sold a house in November 2021. She had never lived in the house. Her chargeable gain on the sale was £26,300. Trudy has taxable income of £25,620 in the tax year 2021/22. The house does not qualify for business asset disposal relief.

What is Trudy's capital gains tax liability for the tax year 2021/22 assuming that she has no other disposals in that year?

○   £2,712

○   £3,920

○   £6,156

○   £1,592   **(2 marks)**

---

121   Clive purchased a ten hectare plot of land in May 2011 for £80,000. In January 2022, Clive sold three of the hectares for £36,000 with expenses of sale amounting to £1,000. The market value of the remaining seven hectares of land in January 2022 was £90,000.

What is Clive's chargeable gain on the disposal of the three hectares of land in the tax year 2021/22?

[▼]

Pull down list:

£12,600
£13,143
£11,000
£12,143   **(2 marks)**

---

122 James has the following gains and losses arising from disposals of chargeable assets:

Tax year	2019/20 £	2020/21 £	2021/22 £
Gains	2,000	4,000	14,900
Losses	(14,000)	(2,000)	(2,000)

The allowable loss carried forward to 2022/23 will be:

○ £0

○ £2,000

○ £11,400

○ £100 (2 marks)

123 Ellen purchased an antique vase for £1,500. In October 2021 she sold the vase for £7,000.

What is Ellen's chargeable gain on the sale of the vase?

○ £0

○ £1,000

○ £1,667

○ £5,500 (2 marks)

(Total = 10 marks)

OTQ bank – Chargeable gains for individuals 2   36 mins

124   Harold bought a painting for £8,500. In December 2021 he sold the painting for £5,000.

What is Harold's allowable loss on the sale of the painting?

£ [   ]

(2 marks)

125   Angela purchased a house and lived in it for three years. The house was then unoccupied for five years because Angela was seconded to an overseas office. She then lived in the house for two years. Angela then went to live with her sister and the house was unoccupied for four years. Angela then lived in the house for the last year of ownership.

How many years of Angela's 15-year period of ownership of the house will be exempt for the purposes of private residence relief?

[▼]

Pull down list:

14½ years
14 years
11 years
15 years

(2 marks)

126   Sascha owned a factory which had always been used in her business. She sold the factory on 14 May 2021 and realised a gain of £60,000. On 12 August 2021, she purchased a 20-year lease on a warehouse using all the proceeds from the sale of the factory. A claim for relief for replacement of business assets was made. The warehouse will continue to be used in Sascha's trade until it is sold on 14 October 2031.

When will the deferred gain of £60,000 become chargeable to capital gains tax?

12 August 2021	14 May 2031	12 August 2031	14 October 2031

(2 marks)

127   Louise has two chargeable gains from the disposal of shares in the tax year 2021/22:

£8,000 – claim made for business asset disposal relief

£14,100 – claim not made for business asset disposal relief

Louise has taxable income of £38,000 in the tax year 2021/22.

What is Louise's capital gains tax liability for the tax year 2021/22?

£ [   ]

(2 marks)

128 Neil bought 1,000 shares in Garden plc for £1,500 in October 2004. In November 2006, there was a 1 for 2 bonus issue when the shares had a market value of £2.40 each. In July 2011, there was a 3 for 1 rights issue when the shares had a market value of £3 but were offered to existing shareholders for £2.70 each. Neil took up his full entitlement to shares under the rights issue. Neil sold all of his shares in Garden plc in February 2022.

What is the cost of the shares sold in February 2022?

£ _____   (2 marks)

---

129 On 10 January 2022, a freehold property owned by Winifred was damaged by a fire. The property had been purchased on 29 May 2004 for £73,000. Winifred received insurance proceeds of £37,200 on 23 February 2022, and she spent a total of £41,700 during March 2022 restoring the property. Winifred has elected to disregard the part disposal.

What is the base cost of the restored freehold property for capital gains tax purposes?

○   £68,500

○   £77,500

○   £114,700

○   £35,800   (2 marks)

---

130 On 31 March 2022, Jessica sold a copyright for £28,800. The copyright had been purchased on 1 April 2016 for £21,000 when it had an unexpired life of 15 years.

What is Jessica's chargeable gain in respect of the disposal of the copyright?

○   £0

○   £20,400

○   £16,200

○   £7,800   (2 marks)

---

131 For the tax year 2021/22, Nog has a chargeable gain of £24,400 and a capital loss of £10,000. She has unused capital losses of £6,100 brought forward from the tax year 2020/21.

What amount of capital losses can Nog carry forward to the tax year 2022/23?

£ _____   (2 marks)

---

132 Alice is in business as a sole trader. On 13 May 2021, she sold a freehold warehouse for £184,000, and this resulted in a chargeable gain of £38,600. Alice purchased a replacement freehold warehouse on 20 May 2021 for £143,000. Where possible, Alice always makes a claim to roll over gains against the cost of replacement assets. Both buildings have been, or will be, used for business purposes by Alice.

What is the base cost of the replacement warehouse for capital gains tax purposes?

£ _____   (2 marks)

---

133   Larry is a sole trader who made a disposal of a factory on 31 July 2021.

Match the earliest date and the latest date that Larry can make an acquisition of a new qualifying business asset and claim replacement of business asset (rollover) relief.

1 August 2018		31 July 2022

1 August 2020		31 July 2024

Earliest date	

Latest date		(2 marks)

_____

(Total = 20 marks)

OT case – Nim (June 2009) (amended) **18 mins**

The following scenario relates to Questions 134 to 138.

Nim disposed of the following assets during the tax year 2021/22:

(1)   On 20 July 2021 Nim made a gift of 10,000 £1 ordinary shares in Kapook plc to his daughter. On that date the shares were quoted on the stock exchange at £3.70–£3.80. Nim has made the following purchases of shares in Kapook plc:

19 February 2004	8,000 shares for £16,200
6 June 2009	1 for 2 rights issue at £3.65 per share
24 July 2021	2,000 shares for £5,800

Nim's total shareholding was less than 5% of Kapook plc, and so holdover relief is not available.

(2)   On 13 August 2021 Nim transferred his entire shareholding of 5,000 £1 ordinary shares in Jooba Ltd, an unquoted company, to his wife. On that date the shares were valued at £28,200. Nim's shareholding had been purchased on 11 January 2010 for £16,000.

(3)   On 26 November 2021 Nim sold an antique table for net proceeds of £8,700 after deducting the sale costs of £300. The antique table had been purchased for £5,200.

Other information

Nim has unused capital losses of £15,800 brought forward from the tax year 2020/21.

134   **What are the deemed proceeds of the shares in Kapook plc sold on 20 July 2021?**

   ○   £37,000

   ○   £37,250

   ○   £37,500

   ○   £38,000   (2 marks)

---

135   **What is the total cost of the shares in Kapook plc sold on 20 July 2021?**

   ○   £26,333

   ○   £28,500

   ○   £25,667

   ○   £20,533   (2 marks)

---

136   **Which TWO of the following statements about capital gains tax for Nim and his wife are correct?**

   ☐   Nim's wife will take the Jooba Ltd shares at market value at the date of the transfer.

   ☐   Nim will have deemed proceeds on the transfer of the Jooba Ltd shares to his wife so that neither a gain nor a loss will arise.

   ☐   The transfer of the Jooba Ltd shares is exempt from capital gains tax because it is between spouses.

   ☐   Nim's wife will not be able to transfer her annual exempt amount to Nim.   (2 marks)

---

137   What is the gain on the sale of the antique table on 26 November 2021?

[▼]

Pull down list:

£4,500
£5,000
£3,500
£800

(2 marks)

138   Assuming that Nim had chargeable gains of £21,000 in the tax year 2021/22, what is the amount of the loss brought forward from 2020/21 which will be carried forward to 2022/23?

£ [   ]

(2 marks)

(Total = 10 marks)

OT case – Aloi, Bon and Dinah (June 2011) (amended)

18 mins

The following scenario relates to Questions 139 to 143.

On 15 October 2021 Alphabet Ltd, an unquoted trading company, was taken over by XYZ plc. Prior to the takeover Alphabet Ltd's share capital consisted of 100,000 £1 ordinary shares, and under the terms of the takeover the shareholders received for each £1 ordinary share in Alphabet Ltd either cash of £6 per share or one £1 ordinary share in XYZ plc worth £6.50. The following information is available regarding three of the shareholders of Alphabet Ltd:

Aloi

Aloi has been the managing director of Alphabet Ltd since the company's incorporation on 1 January 2012, and she accepted XYZ plc's cash alternative of £6 per share in respect of her shareholding of 60,000 £1 ordinary shares in Alphabet Ltd. Aloi had originally subscribed for 50,000 shares in Alphabet Ltd on 1 January 2012 at their par value, and purchased a further 10,000 shares on 20 May 2013 for £18,600.

On 6 February 2022 Aloi sold an investment non-residential property, and this disposal resulted in a chargeable gain against which her annual exempt amount will be set.

For the tax year 2021/22 Aloi has taxable income of £60,000. All her income tax has previously been collected under PAYE so she has not received a notice to file a return for the tax year 2021/22 and so is required to give notice of her chargeability to capital gains tax to HMRC.

Bon

Bon has been the sales director of Alphabet Ltd since 1 February 2020, having not previously been an employee of the company, although she had been a shareholder since 1 March 2019. She accepted XYZ plc's share alternative of one £1 ordinary share for each of her 25,000 £1 ordinary shares in Alphabet Ltd. Bon had purchased her shareholding on 1 March 2019 for £92,200.

On 4 March 2022 Bon made a gift of 10,000 of her £1 ordinary shares in XYZ plc to her brother. On that date the shares were quoted on the stock exchange at £7.10 – £7.14. Gift holdover relief is not available in respect of this disposal.

Dinah

Dinah has been an employee of Alphabet Ltd since 1 May 2019. She accepted XYZ plc's share alternative of one £1 ordinary share for each of her 3,000 £1 ordinary shares in Alphabet Ltd. Dinah had purchased her shareholding on 20 June 2018 for £4,800.

On 13 November 2021 Dinah sold 1,000 of her £1 ordinary shares in XYZ plc for £6,600.

Dinah died on 5 April 2022, and her remaining 2,000 £1 ordinary shares in XYZ plc were inherited by her daughter. On that date these shares were valued at £16,000.

For the tax year 2021/22 Dinah had taxable income of £12,000.

139 Which TWO of the following statements are correct about Bon and Dinah's entitlement to business asset disposal relief in relation to their shares in Alphabet Ltd if they had accepted the cash alternative on the takeover by XYZ plc?

- ☐ Alphabet Ltd was not Bon's personal company for the requisite time before disposal.
- ☐ Bon was not an officer or employee of Alphabet Ltd for the requisite time before disposal.
- ☐ Dinah was not an officer or employee of Alphabet Ltd for the requisite time before disposal.
- ☐ Alphabet Ltd was not Dinah's personal company for the requisite time before disposal. **(2 marks)**

140 **What is Aloi's capital gains tax liability on the disposal of her shares in Alphabet Ltd assuming that the gain qualifies for business asset disposal relief?**

○   £31,000

○   £52,452

○   £29,140

○   £81,592   (2 marks)

---

141 **Match the the latest dates by which Aloi must:**

(1)   Give notice of her chargeability to capital gains tax for the tax year 2021/22 to HMRC.

(2)   Pay her capital gains liability for the tax year 2021/22 in order to avoid interest and penalties.

5 October 2022	31 January 2023

31 December 2022	31 July 2023

Notification	

| Payment | | (2 marks)
|---|---|

---

142 **What is the chargeable gain arising on Bon's gift of her shares in XYZ plc to her brother?**

○   £34,320

○   £6,200

○   £34,220

○   £61,200   (2 marks)

---

143 **What is Dinah's capital gains tax liability for the tax year 2021/22?**

○   £610

○   £0

○   £900

○   £1,090   (2 marks)

(Total = 10 marks)

The following scenario relates to Questions 144 to 148.

You should assume that today's date is 1 March 2022.

Ginger

Ginger has a holding of 10,000 £1 ordinary shares in Nutmeg Ltd, an unquoted trading company, which she had purchased on 13 February 2005 for £2.40 per share. The current market value of the shares is £6.40 per share, but Ginger intends to sell some of the holding to her daughter at £4.00 per share during March 2022. Ginger and her daughter will elect to use gift holdover relief to hold over any gain.

For the tax year 2021/22, Ginger will not make any other disposals, and has therefore not utilised her annual exempt amount. She has a loss brought forward from 2020/21 of £(800).

Innocent and Nigel

Innocent and Nigel, a married couple, both have shareholdings in Cinnamon Ltd, an unquoted trading company with a share capital of 100,000 £1 ordinary shares.

Innocent has been the managing director of Cinnamon Ltd since the company's incorporation on 1 July 2008, and she currently holds 20,000 shares (with matching voting rights) in the company. These shares were subscribed for on 1 July 2008 at their par value.

Nigel has never been an employee or a director of Cinnamon Ltd, and he currently holds 3,000 shares (with matching voting rights) in the company. These shares were purchased on 23 April 2012 for £46,200.

Either Innocent or Nigel will sell 2,000 of their shares in Cinnamon Ltd during March 2022 for £65,000, but are not sure which of them should make the disposal. For the tax year 2021/22, both Innocent and Nigel have already made disposals which will fully utilise their annual exempt amounts, and they will each have taxable income of £80,000.

144   **What is the chargeable gain per share that Ginger will make on her disposal of shares in Nutmeg Ltd to her daughter?**

○   £4.00

○   £1.60

○   £2.40

○   £0

(2 marks)

145   **If the chargeable gain per share on Ginger's disposal of shares in Nutmeg Ltd had been £1.54 per share, what would be the maximum number of shares that Ginger could have sold to her daughter without incurring a charge to capital gains tax?**

○   2,046

○   7,207

○   8,506

○   3,275

(2 marks)

146 **Which TWO of the following statements about business asset disposal relief are correct?**

☐ Business asset disposal relief is only available on shareholdings owned by a director.

☐ There is a lifetime limit of £1,000,000 for business asset disposal relief.

☐ Business asset disposal relief is only available on shareholdings if they are held in a trading company.

☐ The conditions for business asset disposal relief in relation to a shareholding must be satisfied for five years before the disposal. **(2 marks)**

147 **What would Innocent's capital gains tax liability be if she sold her shares in Cinnamon Ltd during March 2022?**

£ [   ] **(2 marks)**

148 **What would Nigel's capital gains tax liability be if he sold his shares in Cinnamon Ltd during March 2022?**

£ [   ] **(2 marks)**

(Total = 10 marks)

OT case – Jerome (March/June 2016) (amended) 18 mins

The following scenario relates to Questions 149 to 153.

Jerome made the following disposals of assets to family members during the tax year 2021/22:

(1) On 28 May 2021, Jerome sold a house to his wife for £140,000. The value of the house at that date was £187,000. Jerome's uncle had originally purchased the house on 14 July 1995 for £45,900. The uncle died on 12 June 2005, and the house was inherited by Jerome. On that date, the house was valued at £112,800. Jerome has never occupied the house as his main residence.

(2) On 24 June 2021, Jerome made a gift of his entire 12% holding of 12,000 £1 ordinary shares in Reward Ltd, an unquoted trading company, to his son. The market value of the shares on that date was £98,400. The shares had been purchased on 15 March 2006 for £39,000. On 24 June 2021, the market value of Reward Ltd's chargeable assets was £540,000, of which £460,000 was in respect of chargeable business assets. Jerome and his son will elect to use gift holdover relief to hold over the gain on this gift of a business asset.

(3) On 7 November 2021, Jerome made a gift of an antique bracelet valued at £12,200 to his granddaughter. The antique bracelet had been purchased on 1 September 2001 for £2,100.

(4) On 29 January 2022, Jerome made a gift of nine hectares of land valued at £78,400 to his brother. He had originally purchased ten hectares of land on 3 November 2005 for £37,800. The market value of the unsold hectare of land as at 29 January 2022 was £33,600. The land has never been used for business purposes.

149 **What is the base cost of the house for capital gains tax purposes for Jerome's wife?**

○ £45,900

○ £187,000

○ £112,800

○ £140,000 (2 marks)

---

150 **What is the amount of gift holdover relief that can be claimed on the gift of the Reward Ltd shares?**

£ ⬚ (2 marks)

---

151 **Match the latest date for submission of the election for gift holdover relief on the gift of the Reward Ltd shares and person(s) who must make the election.**

31 January 2023		Jerome

5 April 2026		Jerome and his son

Latest date for election	

Person(s) making election		(2 marks)

152   What is the amount of the chargeable gain on the disposal of the antique bracelet?

[▼]

Pull down list:

£10,100
£3,900
£10,333
£10,000   (2 marks)

153   What is the amount of the chargeable gain on the disposal of the nine hectares of land?

    ○   £66,200

    ○   £40,600

    ○   £44,380

    ○   £51,940   (2 marks)

(Total = 10 marks)

OT case – Hali and Goma (March/June 2019)   18 mins

The following scenario relates to Questions 154–158.

You should assume that the tax allowances for the tax year 2021/22 applied in previous tax years.

Hali and Goma are a married couple.

Capital losses brought forward

Hali had capital losses of £39,300 for the tax year 2019/20. He had chargeable gains of £16,300 for the tax year 2020/21.

Goma had capital losses of £9,100 and chargeable gains of £6,900 for the tax year 2020/21. She did not have any capital losses for the tax year 2019/20.

Ordinary shares in Lima Ltd

On 24 July 2021, Hali sold 5,000 £1 ordinary shares in Lima Ltd, for £4.95 per share. Lima Ltd's shares have recently been selling for £5.30 per share, but Hali sold them at the lower price because he needed a quick sale.

Goma, had originally subscribed for 30,000 ordinary shares in Lima Ltd at their par value of £1 per share on 28 July 2008. On 18 August 2017, she gave 8,000 ordinary shares to Hali. On that date, the market value for 8,000 shares was £23,200.

Hali and Goma will both dispose of their remaining shareholdings in Lima Ltd during the tax year 2022/23. However, they are unsure as to whether these disposals will qualify for business asset disposal relief.

Antique table

On 11 October 2021, an antique table owned by Hali was destroyed in a fire. The table had been purchased on 3 June 2010 for £44,000. Hali received insurance proceeds of £62,000 on 12 December 2021, and on 6 January 2022, he purchased a replacement antique table for £63,600. Hali will make a claim to roll over the gain arising from the receipt of the insurance proceeds.

Disposals by Goma during the tax year 2021/22

Goma disposed of the following assets during the tax year 2021/22, all of which resulted in gains:

(1)   Qualifying corporate bonds sold for £38,300

(2)   A motor car (suitable for private use) sold for £11,600

(3)   An antique vase sold for £6,200

(4)   A copyright (with an unexpired life of eight years when purchased) sold for £5,400

(5)   Quoted shares held within an individual savings account (ISA) sold for £24,700

154   **What amount of unused capital losses do Hali and Goma have brought forward to the tax year 2021/22?**

Option	Hali	Goma
1	£23,000	£9,100
2	£23,000	£2,200
3	£35,300	£9,100
4	£35,300	£2,200

○   Option 1

○   Option 2

○   Option 3

○   Option 4   (2 marks)

155 What cost figure and what value per share (disposal value) will be used in calculating the chargeable gain on Hali's sale of 5,000 ordinary shares in Lima Ltd?

Option	Cost figure	Value per share
1	£5,000	£4.95
2	£14,500	£4.95
3	£14,500	£5.30
4	£5,000	£5.30

○ Option 1

○ Option 2

○ Option 3

○ Option 4 (2 marks)

156 In deciding whether Hali and Goma's future disposals of their shareholdings in Lima Ltd will qualify for business asset disposal relief, which ONE of the following statements is correct?

○ Hali and Goma must be directors of Lima Ltd

○ Lima Ltd must be a trading company

○ Hali and Goma must have shareholdings of at least 10% each in Lima Ltd

○ The qualifying conditions must be met for a period of three years prior to the date of disposal (2 marks)

157 What is the base cost of Hali's replacement antique table for capital gains tax (CGT) purposes?

○ £62,000

○ £63,600

○ £45,600

○ £44,000 (2 marks)

158 How many of the five assets disposed of by Goma during the tax year 2021/22 are exempt assets for the purposes of capital gains tax (CGT)?

○ Three

○ Five

○ Two

○ Four (2 marks)

(Total = 10 marks)

159 Jorge (December 2011) (amended)   18 mins

Jorge disposed of the following assets during the tax year 2021/22:

(1)   On 30 June 2021 Jorge sold a house for £308,000. The house had been purchased on 1 January 2004 for £93,000. On 10 June 2010, Jorge had incurred legal fees of £5,000 in relation to a boundary dispute with his neighbour. Throughout the 210 months of ownership the house had been occupied by Jorge as follows:

Months
34	Occupied
18	Unoccupied – Travelling overseas
24	Unoccupied – Required to work overseas by his employer
11	Occupied
30	Unoccupied – Required to work elsewhere in the United Kingdom by his employer
22	Unoccupied – Travelling overseas
26	Unoccupied – Required to work elsewhere in the United Kingdom by his employer
17	Occupied
12	Unoccupied – Required to work overseas by his employer
13	Unoccupied – Travelling overseas
3	Unoccupied – Lived with sister
210	

Jorge let the house out during all of the periods when he did not occupy it personally. Throughout the period 1 January 2004 to 30 June 2021 Jorge did not have any other main residence.

(2)   On 30 September 2021 Jorge sold a copyright for £80,300. The copyright had been purchased on 1 October 2019 for £70,000 when it had an unexpired life of ten years.

(3)   On 6 October 2021 Jorge sold a painting for £5,400. The painting had been purchased on 18 May 2013 for £2,200.

(4)   On 29 October 2021 Jorge sold a motor car for £10,700. The motor car had been purchased on 21 December 2016 for £14,600.

Jorge has capital losses brought forward of £25,000.

Required

Calculate Jorge's taxable gains for the tax year 2021/22.   (10 marks)

(Total = 10 marks)

160 Winston (June 2012) (amended)

18 mins

(a) On 19 May 2021 Winston disposed of a painting, and this resulted in a chargeable gain of £47,560. For the tax year 2021/22 Winston has taxable income of £25,100 after the deduction of the personal allowance.

Winston is considering the sale of a business that he has run as a sole trader since 1 July 2009. The business will be sold for £260,000, and this figure, along with the respective cost of each asset, is made up as follows:

	Sale proceeds £	Cost £
Freehold shop	140,000	80,000
Freehold warehouse	88,000	102,000
Net current assets	32,000	32,000
	260,000	

The freehold warehouse has never been used by Winston for business purposes.

Required

(i) Assuming that Winston does not sell his sole trader business, calculate his capital gains tax liability for the tax year 2021/22. **(3 marks)**

(ii) Calculate Winston's capital gains tax liability for the tax year 2021/22 if he sold his sole trader business on 25 March 2022. **(4 marks)**

(b) On 3 December 2021 Renaldo sold two hectares of land at auction for gross proceeds of £92,000. The auctioneers' commission was 5% of the sale price.

Renaldo's wife's father had originally purchased three hectares of land on 4 August 2002 for £19,500. He died on 17 June 2009, and the land was inherited by Renaldo's wife. On that date the three hectares of land were valued at £28,600.

Renaldo's wife transferred the land to Renaldo on 14 November 2012. On that date the three hectares of land were valued at £39,000. The market value of the unsold hectare of land as at 3 December 2021 was £38,000.

Required

Compute Renaldo's chargeable gain in respect of the disposal on 3 December 2021.

(3 marks)

(Total = 10 marks)

161 Mick (June 2014) (amended)

Mick disposed of the following assets during the tax year 2021/22:

(1) On 19 May 2021, Mick sold a freehold warehouse for £522,000. The warehouse was purchased on 6 August 2003 for £258,000, and was extended at a cost of £99,000 during April 2005. In January 2009, the floor of the warehouse was damaged by flooding and had to be replaced at a cost of £63,000. The warehouse was sold because it was surplus to the business's requirements as a result of Mick purchasing a newly built warehouse during 2020. Both warehouses have always been used for business purposes in a wholesale business run by Mick as a sole trader.

(2) On 24 September 2021, Mick sold 700,000 £1 ordinary shares in Rolling Ltd, an unquoted trading company, for £3,675,000. He had originally purchased 500,000 shares in Rolling Ltd on 2 June 2007 for £960,000. On 1 December 2012, Rolling Ltd made a 3 for 2 bonus issue. Mick has been a director of Rolling Ltd since 1 January 2007.

Required

(a) Assuming that no reliefs are available, calculate the chargeable gain arising from each of Mick's asset disposals during the tax year 2021/22.

Note. You are not required to calculate the taxable gains or the amount of tax payable.

(4 marks)

(b) State which capital gains tax reliefs might be available to Mick in respect of each of his disposals during the tax year 2021/22, and what further information you would require in order to establish if the reliefs are actually available and to establish any restrictions as regards the amount of relief.

Note. For this part of the question you are not expected to perform any calculations.

(6 marks)

(Total = 10 marks)

162 Ruby (September/December 2015) (amended)

18 mins

You should assume that today's date is 1 March 2022.

(a)   On 27 August 2021, Ruby disposed of a residential investment property and this resulted in a chargeable gain of £47,000.

For the tax year 2021/22 Ruby has taxable income of £23,515.

Required

Calculate Ruby's capital gains tax liability for the tax year 2021/22 if this is her only disposal in that tax year.

(2 marks)

(b)   In addition to the disposal already made on 27 August 2021, Ruby is going to make one further disposal during the tax year 2021/22. The disposal will be of either Ruby's holding of £1 ordinary shares in Pola Ltd, or her holding of 50p ordinary shares in Aplo plc.

Shareholding in Pola Ltd

Pola Ltd is an unlisted trading company. The shareholding was subscribed for by Ruby on 14 July 2018 for £23,700 and could be sold for £61,000. Ruby has never been an officer nor an employee of Pola Ltd.

Shareholding in Aplo plc

Aplo plc is a trading company listed on a recognised stock exchange in which Ruby has a shareholding of 40,000 50p ordinary shares. Ruby received the shareholding as a gift from her father on 27 May 2011. On that date, the shares were quoted on the stock exchange at £2.12–£2.18. The shareholding could be sold for £59,000.

No reliefs are available in respect of this disposal.

Required

Calculate Ruby's revised capital gains tax liability for the tax year 2021/22, if she also disposes of either (1) her shareholding in Pola Ltd; or alternatively (2) her shareholding in Aplo plc.

Note. The following mark allocation is provided as guidance for this requirement:

Pola Ltd (4½ marks)

Aplo plc (3½ marks)

(8 marks)

(Total = 10 marks)

PART D INHERITANCE TAX

Questions 163 to 207 cover inheritance tax, the subject of Chapter 18 of the BPP Workbook for Taxation (TX – UK).

OTQ bank – Inheritance tax 1   18 mins

163   Gillian owned a 70% shareholding in Rose Ltd, an unquoted investment company. On 23 July 2021, she gave a 20% shareholding in Rose Ltd to her son. The values of shareholdings in Rose Ltd on 23 July 2021 were as follows:

	£
100% shareholding	600,000
70% shareholding	350,000
50% shareholding	200,000
20% shareholding	80,000

What is the diminution in value of Gillian's estate as a result of her gift on 23 July 2021?

£ [   ]   (2 marks)

---

164   Joel and Sunita were a married couple. Sunita died in July 2008 and 65% of her nil rate band of £312,000 (2008/09) was unused. Joel died in May 2021. He had made a potentially exempt transfer (after all available exemptions) of £75,000 in August 2017. Joel left his estate to his sister. Any relevant elections were made.

What is the nil rate band available to set against Joel's death estate?

Pull down list:

£325,000
£452,800
£461,250
£536,250   (2 marks)

---

165   On 7 July 2016, Paul made a gross chargeable transfer (after all exemptions) of £260,000. On 19 December 2021 he gave £190,000 to a trust. Paul agreed to pay any lifetime inheritance tax (IHT) due.

How much IHT will be payable by Paul on the December 2021 transfer of value?

○   £28,250

○   £31,250

○   £29,750

○   £23,800   (2 marks)

---

166   Donald made the following transactions in the tax year 2021/22:

(1)   A gift of £2,000 to his granddaughter on the occasion of her marriage.

(2)   A sale of a vase to his friend, Alan, for £1,000 which both Donald and Alan believed to be the market value of the vase. The vase was later valued by an auction house as worth £20,000 at the date of the sale.

Ignoring the annual exemption, what is the total value of potentially exempt transfers made by Donald as a result of these gifts?

○   £21,000

○   £0

○   £2,000

○   £19,000   (2 marks)

---

167   Kirstin made a gross chargeable transfer of £150,000 to a trust on 15 September 2012 and gifted shares worth £600,000 to her brother on 10 July 2018. The nil rate band in 2012/13 and 2018/19 was £325,000. Kirstin died on 23 October 2021.

Ignoring the annual exemption, what is the inheritance tax payable on Kirstin's death in relation to her lifetime transfers?

○   £170,000

○   £88,000

○   £136,000

○   £134,080   (2 marks)

                                                                              (Total = 10 marks)

168   Mary made the following gifts in the tax year 2021/22:

(1)   £1,000 on the first day of each month for nine months to her grandson to pay university living expenses. Mary used income surplus to her living requirements to make these payments and had made such payments to her grandson throughout his four-year university course.

(2)   £100 to her grandnephew on his birthday and a further £250 to the same grandnephew as a Christmas gift.

Ignoring the annual exemption, what is the total value of potentially exempt transfers made by Mary as a result of these gifts?

  ○   £9,350

  ○   £100

  ○   £9,000

  ○   £350   (2 marks)

---

169   Daniel owned all 1,000 shares in Q Ltd, an unquoted investment company. On 10 October 2021, Daniel gave 300 of his shares in Q Ltd to his daughter. The values of the shares on 10 October 2021 were as follows:

% shareholding	Value per share
	£
76–100	150
51–75	120
26–50	90
1–25	30

What is the diminution in value of Daniel's estate as a result of his gift on 10 October 2021?

Pull down list:

£123,000
£27,000
£66,000
£18,000   (2 marks)

---

170   Susanna died on 19 November 2021. Her estate consisted of her main residence worth £300,000 (on which there was secured a repayment mortgage of £195,000) and investments and cash totalling £385,000. Susanna left her estate equally to her son and daughter. Susanna had not made any lifetime transfers of value.

How much inheritance tax will be payable on Susanna's estate?

£ _____   (2 marks)

---

171   Rodney died on 13 August 2021. In his will he left £200 in cash to each of his five nephews, investments held in ISAs valued at £350,000 to his daughter, and the residue of his estate, which amounted to £520,000, to his wife.

What is the chargeable estate for inheritance tax purposes?

£ [   ]   (2 marks)

---

172   Sandeep made a gift of £425,000 to a trust on 10 November 2021. No agreement has been made about who will pay the inheritance tax (IHT) in respect of this gift.

What is the due date for payment of the IHT and who is primarily liable for its payment?

○   The trustees are liable to make the payment by 31 May 2022

○   The trustees are liable to make the payment by 30 April 2022

○   Sandeep is liable to make the payment by 31 May 2022

○   Sandeep is liable to make the payment by 30 April 2022   (2 marks)

---

173   Benjamin died on 30 November 2021 leaving an estate valued at £890,000. Inheritance tax of £276,000 was paid in respect of the estate. Under the terms of his will, Benjamin left £260,000 to his wife, a specific legacy of £120,000 (free of tax) to his brother, and the residue of the estate to his grandchildren.

What is the amount of inheritance received by Benjamin's grandchildren?

[▼]

Pull down list:

£614,000
£510,000
£354,000
£234,000   (2 marks)

---

174   Heng is a wealthy 45 year old who would like to reduce the potential inheritance tax liability on her estate when she dies.

Which of the following actions will or will not achieve Heng's aim of reducing the potential inheritance tax liability on her estate when she dies?

Changing the terms of her will so that the residue of her estate goes to her grandchildren rather than her children	WILL ACHIEVE	WILL NOT ACHIEVE
Making lifetime gifts to trusts up to the value of the nil rate band every seven years	WILL ACHIEVE	WILL NOT ACHIEVE
Changing the terms of her will so that the residue of her estate goes to her husband rather than her children	WILL ACHIEVE	WILL NOT ACHIEVE
Making lifetime gifts to her grandchildren early in life	WILL ACHIEVE	WILL NOT ACHIEVE

(2 marks)

175 Chan died on 8 December 2021, having made a lifetime cash gift of £500,000 to a trust on 16 October 2020. Chan paid the inheritance tax arising from this gift.

Match the due date payment of the additional inheritance tax arising from the gift made to the trustees and the persons who are responsible for paying this tax.

8 June 2022		30 June 2022

The trustees		The personal representatives of Chan's estate

Due date	

Persons responsible		(2 marks)

176 Nadia died on 6 December 2021. Her death estate included her main residence which was valued at £360,000 on which there was secured an outstanding repayment mortgage of £140,000. Nadia will leave her entire estate to her three children.

Nadia is a widow. Her husband died in 2009 leaving his entire estate to Nadia.

What amount of residence nil rate band will be available in computing inheritance tax on Nadia's death estate?

- ○ £175,000
- ○ £220,000
- ○ £350,000
- ○ £360,000

(2 marks)

177 Rachel is aged 85 and in poor health. She is keen to minimise the inheritance tax due on her death estate which is likely to have a value of about £1.2 million. Her will currently leaves her main residence (valued at £300,000) to her brother and the residue of her estate to her son. Rachel has never been married.

Complete the following sentence by matching the correct response in each space.

The inheritance tax liability on Rachel's estate will _____ by

_____ if she leaves her main residence to her son rather than her brother.

Increase		£70,000

Decrease		£175,000

(2 marks)

(Total = 20 marks)

OT case – Ning (June 2012) (amended) 18 mins

The following scenario relates to Questions 178 to 182.

You should assume that today's date is 19 March 2022.

Ning owns the following assets:

(1) Two investment properties respectively valued at £674,000 and £442,000. The first property has an outstanding repayment mortgage of £160,000, and the second property is owned outright with no mortgage.

(2) Vintage motor cars valued at £172,000.

(3) Investments in Individual Savings Accounts valued at £47,000, National Savings & Investments savings certificates valued at £36,000, and government stocks (gilts) valued at £69,000.

Ning owes £22,400 in respect of a personal loan from a bank, and she has also verbally promised to pay legal fees of £4,600 incurred by her nephew. Her reasonable funeral expenses will amount to £5,500.

Ning's husband died on 12 March 2007, and 70% of his inheritance tax nil rate band was not used.

On 14 August 2010 Ning had made a gift of £90,000 to her daughter, and on 7 November 2020 she made a gift of her main residence, worth £220,000, to her son. These amounts are after taking account of any available exemptions.

The nil rate band for the tax year 2006/07 is £285,000.

178   What is the net value for the two properties in (1) which will be included in the calculation of Ning's chargeable estate were she to die on 20 March 2022?

   ○   £1,024,000

   ○   £956,000

   ○   £856,000

   ○   £864,000   (2 marks)

---

179   What is the value of the assets in (2) and (3) which will be included in the calculation of Ning's chargeable estate were she to die on 20 March 2022?

   ○   £172,000

   ○   £0

   ○   £324,000

   ○   £152,000   (2 marks)

---

180   What is the total amount of deductions (ignoring mortgage debts) which will be taken into account in the calculation of Ning's chargeable estate were she to die on 20 March 2022?

   ○   £5,500

   ○   £32,500

   ○   £10,100

   ○   £27,900   (2 marks)

---

181   What is the amount of Ning's own nil rate band for calculating the inheritance tax payable in respect of her estate were she to die on 20 March 2022?

    ○   £325,000

    ○   £105,000

    ○   £15,000

    ○   £205,000

(2 marks)

182   What is the amount of Ning's husband's nil rate band that Ning's personal representatives could claim were she to die on 20 March 2022 and by when should the claim be made?

	Amount	Claim
○	£227,500	By 31 March 2024
○	£227,500	By 30 September 2022
○	£199,500	By 31 March 2024
○	£199,500	By 30 September 2022

(2 marks)

(Total = 10 marks)

OT case – Jimmy (June 2011) (amended)

18 mins

The following scenario relates to Questions 183 to 187.

Jimmy died on 14 February 2022. He had used up his nil rate band at the date of his death by making the following gifts during his lifetime:

(1) On 2 August 2020 Jimmy made a cash gift of £10,000 to his grandson as a wedding gift when he got married.

(2) On 9 September 2020 Jimmy gave 200 shares valued at £5 each in J Ltd, an unquoted investment company, to his daughter. Before the gift, Jimmy owned 5,100 shares valued at £30 each in J Ltd. After the gift Jimmy owned 4,900 shares valued at £20 each in J Ltd.

(3) On 14 November 2020 Jimmy made a cash gift of £800,000 to a trust. Jimmy paid the inheritance tax arising from this gift. Additional inheritance tax was payable on this transfer as a result of Jimmy's death.

At the date of his death Jimmy owned assets valued at £980,000. He did not own a main residence at his death. Under the terms of his will Jimmy left £200,000 to his wife and the residue of his estate to his son.

The nil rate band for the tax year 2020/21 was £325,000.

183 **What was the total amount of the exemptions that were deducted in computing the potentially exempt transfer made on 2 August 2020?**

- ○ £3,000
- ○ £8,500
- ○ £6,000
- ○ £11,000

(2 marks)

184 **What is the diminution in value in Jimmy's estate as a result of his gift on 9 September 2020?**

[▼]

Pull down list:

£55,000
£4,000
£6,000
£1,000

(2 marks)

185 **What was the amount of the inheritance tax paid by Jimmy as a result of his gift made on 14 November 2020?**

£ [   ]

(2 marks)

186   Match the due date for payment of the additional inheritance tax on the gift made on 14 November 2020 as a result of Jimmy's death and by whom should it be paid.

| 14 August 2022 | | Trustees of trust |

| 31 August 2022 | | Executors of Jimmy's estate |

| Due date | |

| By whom paid | | (2 marks)

187   What is the inheritance tax chargeable on Jimmy's death estate as a result of his death on 14 February 2022?

£ [   ]   (2 marks)

                                                           (Total = 10 marks)

OT case – Zoe and Luke (June 2015) (amended)   18 mins

The following scenario relates to Questions 188 to 192.

Zoe and Luke are brother and sister; they died within a few months of each other.

Zoe

Zoe died on 17 February 2022.

She had always used her annual exemption in April each year and had made the following additional gifts during her lifetime:

(1)   On 21 March 2015, Zoe made a cash gift of £633,000 to a trust. Zoe paid the inheritance tax (IHT) arising from this gift. The nil rate band for the tax year 2014/15 is £325,000.

(2)   On 17 August 2018, Zoe made a further cash gift of £200,000 to the trust. The trustees paid the IHT arising from the gift. The nil rate band for the tax year 2018/19 is £325,000.

Luke

Luke died on 10 October 2021. He was survived by two adult children, a son and a daughter. Luke's wife had died on 25 July 2008.

On 7 March 2020, Luke had made a cash gift of £270,000 to his daughter as a wedding gift when she got married.

Luke had also paid his son's university tuition fees in each of September 2019, 2020 and 2021, making the payments directly to the university. He was advised that these payments were exempt from inheritance tax under the normal expenditure out of income exemption.

On her death, Luke's wife had left £240,000 to their daughter and the remainder of her estate to Luke. She made no lifetime transfers. The nil rate band for the tax year 2008/09 was £312,000.

188   Which TWO of the following statements about Luke's payment of his son's university tuition fees are correct?

☐   The payments could be exempt without any cash limit under the normal expenditure out of income exemption.

☐   The payments could not be exempt under the normal expenditure out of income exemption because they were paid directly to the university and not to his son.

☐   The payments must have been reported each tax year to HM Revenue & Customs in Luke's income tax return to qualify for the normal expenditure out of income exemption.

☐   The payments must have left Luke with sufficient income to maintain his usual standard of living to qualify for the normal expenditure out of income exemption.

(2 marks)

189   What is the amount of the gross chargeable transfer made by Zoe on 21 March 2015?

○   £702,500

○   £710,000

○   £694,600

○   £756,200

(2 marks)

190 What is the additional IHT which will be payable, as a result of Zoe's death, in respect of the transfer made on 17 August 2018, assuming that the nil rate band has been completely used by the gross chargeable transfer made by Zoe on 21 March 2015?

[▼]

Pull down list:

£40,000
£80,000
£24,000
£64,000

(2 marks)

191 What is the value of the potentially exempt transfer made by Luke on 7 March 2020?

£ [   ]

(2 marks)

192 What is the amount of Luke's wife's nil rate band which could be transferred and used in calculating the IHT on Luke's death?

○   £75,000

○   £72,000

○   £312,000

○   £325,000

(2 marks)

(Total = 10 marks)

OT case – Marcus (September/December 2015) (amended)

18 mins

The following scenario relates to Questions 193 to 197.

Marcus died on 10 March 2022. He had been married to his wife, Barbara, for many years. He had made the following gifts during his lifetime:

(1)   On 14 January 2011, Marcus made a chargeable lifetime transfer of £328,000 to a trust. The trustees paid the lifetime inheritance tax which arose in respect of this gift.

(2)   On 3 January 2018, Marcus made a chargeable lifetime transfer to another trust. In addition to the gift, Marcus paid the related lifetime inheritance tax on this gift. The gross chargeable lifetime transfer amounted to £491,250.

(3)   On 17 March 2018, Marcus made a gift (a potentially exempt transfer) of 30,000 £1 ordinary shares in Scarum Ltd, an unquoted investment company, to his daughter.

   Before the transfer, Marcus owned all of Scarum Ltd's issued share capital of 100,000 £1 ordinary shares. On 17 March 2018, Scarum Ltd's shares were worth £5 each for a holding of 30%, £9 each for a holding of 70%, and £12 each for a holding of 100%.

(4)   On 29 June 2019, Marcus gave a plot of land worth £100,000 to Barbara. Marcus had bought the land in 2008 for £80,000.

The nil rate band for the tax years 2010/11 and 2017/18 was £325,000.

Under the terms of his will, Marcus left his entire estate to Barbara. Barbara has not made any gifts during her lifetime. She is intending to remarry.

Ignore the inheritance tax annual exemption.

193   **What was the amount of the lifetime inheritance tax paid by the trustees (if any) as a result of the gift made on 14 January 2011?**

£ [   ]

(2 marks)

194   **What was the amount of the lifetime inheritance tax paid by Marcus as a result of the gift made on 3 January 2018?**

○   £122,812

○   £33,250

○   £98,250

○   £41,562

(2 marks)

195   **What was the amount of the taper relief deductible from the additional inheritance tax due as a result of the death of Marcus on the gift made on 3 January 2018?**

[▼]

Pull down list:

£117,900
£78,600
£39,900
£26,600

(2 marks)

196   What was the amount of the potentially exempt transfer made by Marcus on
       17 March 2018?

       ○   £360,000

       ○   £270,000

       ○   £150,000

       ○   £570,000   (2 marks)

_____

197   Which TWO of the following statements about Marcus and Barbara for inheritance
       tax purposes are correct?

       ☐   There is no liability for inheritance tax on the transfer of Marcus's estate to Barbara
            because they are treated together as a single chargeable person for inheritance tax.

       ☐   If Barbara remarries, any unused nil rate band on her death can be transferred to
            her spouse if they survive her.

       ☐   The gift of the land on 29 June 2019 by Marcus to Barbara is a potentially exempt
            transfer of £80,000.

       ☐   The transfer of Marcus's estate to Barbara on his death is an exempt transfer.

                                                                              (2 marks)

_____

                                                                       (Total = 10 marks)

OT case – Lebna and Lulu (March/June 2019)   18 mins

The following scenario relates to Questions 198–202.

You should assume that today's date is 1 March 2022.

Lebna and Lulu were a married couple, but Lulu died on 24 January 2017.

Lulu

Lulu left an estate valued at £210,000 for inheritance tax (IHT) purposes. The estate did not include a main residence. Under the terms of her will, Lulu left a specific legacy of £40,000 to her brother, with the residue of the estate to her husband, Lebna. Lulu had made the following lifetime transfers:

Date	Type of transfer	Amount
		£
13 February 2009	Chargeable lifetime transfer	50,000
21 June 2015	Potentially exempt transfer	80,000

Both of these transfers are after taking account of all available exemptions.

The nil rate band for the tax year 2016/17 is £325,000.

Lebna's chargeable estate

Lebna has a chargeable estate valued at £980,000. His estate includes a main residence valued at £340,000 on which there is an outstanding interest-only mortgage of £152,000.

Under the terms of his will, Lebna has left his entire estate to his son.

Gift to son on 22 February 2017

On 22 February 2017, Lebna made a gift of 60,000 £1 ordinary shares in Blean Ltd, an unquoted investment company, to his son. Before the transfer, Lebna owned all of Blean Ltd's share capital of 100,000 ordinary shares. The market value of Blean Ltd's ordinary shares on 22 February 2017 was as follows:

Holding	Market value per share
40%	£4.20
60%	£6.30
100%	£7.10

Lebna had not made any previous lifetime gifts.

Gifts to friends during October 2021

Lebna made cash gifts of £85, £225, £190 and £490 to various friends during October 2021. The gifts of £85 and £190 were to the same friend.

198   **If Lebna were to die today, 1 March 2022, how much of Lulu's nil rate band will the personal representatives of Lebna's estate be able to claim when calculating the IHT payable on his chargeable estate?**

   ○   £155,000

   ○   £205,000

   ○   £35,000

   ○   £285,000   (2 marks)

---

199   If Lebna were to die today, 1 March 2022, what is the total amount of residence nil rate band which will be available when calculating the IHT payable on his chargeable estate?

  ○ £175,000

  ○ £350,000

  ○ £340,000

  ○ £188,000

                       (2 marks)

200   What is the amount of the potentially exempt transfer which Lebna has made to his son on 22 February 2017 (the gift of 60,000 shares in Blean Ltd) after deducting any available exemptions?

  ○ £542,000

  ○ £536,000

  ○ £372,000

  ○ £378,000

                       (2 marks)

201   If Lebna were to die today, 1 March 2022, what taper relief percentage reduction would be available when calculating the IHT payable on the potentially exempt transfer which he made to his son on 22 February 2017 (the gift of 60,000 shares in Blean Ltd), and when would this IHT be due?

Option	Taper relief reduction	Due date
1	60%	30 September 2022
2	60%	1 September 2022
3	40%	1 September 2022
4	40%	30 September 2022

  ○ Option 1

  ○ Option 2

  ○ Option 3

  ○ Option 4

                       (2 marks)

202   What amount of the cash gifts made by Lebna to his friends during October 2021 is covered by the small gifts exemption?

  ○ £500

  ○ £990

  ○ £225

  ○ £275

                       (2 marks)

                    (Total = 10 marks)

203 Pere and Phil (June 2013) (amended)   18 mins

On 23 August 2015, Pere made a gift of a house valued at £420,000 to his son, Phil. This was a wedding gift when Phil got married. The nil rate band for the tax year 2015/16 is £325,000.

Pere

Pere died on 20 March 2022 at which time his estate was valued at £880,000. Under the terms of his will, Pere divided his estate equally, before inheritance tax, between his wife and his son, Phil. Pere had not made any gifts during his lifetime except for the gift of the house to Phil. Pere did not own a main residence.

Phil

Phil sold the house which he received as a wedding gift from Pere, his father, on 5 April 2022. The following information relates to the property:

	£
Net sale proceeds after costs of disposal	496,700
Cost of new boundary wall around the property (there was previously no boundary wall)	(5,200)
Cost of replacing the property's chimney	(2,800)

Phil has taxable income (after deduction of the personal allowance) of £14,150 in 2021/22. The house was never occupied by Phil.

Required

(a)   Calculate the inheritance tax that will be payable as a result of Pere's death.   **(6 marks)**

(b)   Calculate Phil's capital gains tax liability for the tax year 2021/22.   **(4 marks)**

(Total = 10 marks)

204 Afiya (December 2013) (amended)   18 mins

Afiya died on 29 November 2021. She had made the following gifts during her lifetime:

(1)   On 14 September 2020, Afiya made a gift of 6,500 £1 ordinary shares in Cassava Ltd, an unquoted investment company, to her daughter.

   Before the transfer Afiya owned 8,000 shares out of Cassava Ltd's issued share capital of 10,000 £1 ordinary shares. On 14 September 2020, Cassava Ltd's shares were worth £3 each for a holding of 15%, £7 each for a holding of 65%, and £8 each for a holding of 80%.

(2)   On 27 January 2021, Afiya made a cash gift of £400,000 to a trust. Afiya paid the inheritance tax arising from this gift.

On 29 November 2021, Afiya's estate was valued at £623,000 including her main residence which was valued at £90,000. Her executors paid funeral expenses of £3,000 on 12 January 2022. Under the terms of her will Afiya left £150,000 cash to her husband, a specific legacy of £40,000 to her sister, and the residue of the estate to her children.

The nil rate band for the tax year 2020/21 is £325,000.

Required

(a)   Calculate the inheritance tax which will be payable as a result of Afiya's death.   **(9 marks)**

(b)   Calculate the amount of the inheritance which will be received by Afiya's children. **(1 mark)**

(Total = 10 marks)

205 Kendra (June 2014) (amended) 18 mins

You should assume that today's date is 1 January 2022.

Kendra, aged 93, is in poor health with just a few months left to live. She has made no lifetime gifts.

Kendra owns the following assets:

(1) An investment residential property valued at £970,000. The property has never been occupied by Kendra, and if it were disposed of during the tax year 2021/22 the disposal would result in a chargeable gain of £174,000.

(2) Building society deposits of £387,000.

(3) Investments in Individual Savings Accounts (ISAs) valued at £39,000 and savings certificates from National Savings & Investments (NS&I) valued at £17,000.

(4) A life assurance policy on her own life. The policy has an open market value of £210,000, and proceeds of £225,000 will be received following Kendra's death.

None of the above valuations are expected to change in the near future. Kendra has income tax outstanding at her death of £12,800. She also has an outstanding unsecured loan of £1,200 which is due to be repaid on her death.

Under the terms of her will, Kendra has left her entire estate to her children.

The nil rate band of Kendra's husband was fully utilised when he died ten years ago.

For the tax year 2021/22, Kendra will pay income tax at the higher rate.

Required

(a) Calculate the inheritance tax which would be payable if Kendra were to die on 31 March 2022. **(5 marks)**

(b) Advise Kendra why it would not be beneficial to make an immediate lifetime gift of the property valued at £970,000 to her children.

Notes

1 Your answer should take account of both the capital gains tax and the inheritance tax implications of making the gift.

2 For this part of the question you should ignore the capital gains tax annual exempt amount and inheritance tax annual exemptions. **(3 marks)**

(c) Advise Kendra why it might be beneficial for inheritance tax purposes to change the terms of her will so that part of her estate was instead left to her grandchildren rather than her children. **(2 marks)**

(Total = 10 marks)

206 James (March/June 2016)   **18 mins**

James died on 22 January 2022. He had made the following gifts during his lifetime:

(1) On 9 October 2014, a cash gift of £35,000 to a trust. No lifetime inheritance tax was payable in respect of this gift.

(2) On 14 May 2020, a cash gift of £420,000 to his daughter.

(3) On 2 August 2020, a gift of a property valued at £260,000 to a trust. No lifetime inheritance tax was payable in respect of this gift because it was covered by the nil rate band. By the time of James's death on 22 January 2022, the property had increased in value to £310,000.

On 22 January 2022, James's estate was valued at £870,000. James did not own a main residence. Under the terms of his will, James left his entire estate to his children.

The nil rate band of James's wife was fully utilised when she died ten years ago.

The nil rate band for the tax years 2014/15 and 2020/21 is £325,000.

Required

(a) Calculate the inheritance tax which will be payable as a result of James's death, and state who will be responsible for paying the tax.   **(6 marks)**

(b) Explain why it might have been beneficial for inheritance tax purposes if James had left a portion of his estate to his grandchildren rather than to his children.   **(2 marks)**

(c) Explain why it might be advantageous for inheritance tax purposes for a person to make lifetime gifts even when such gifts are made within seven years of death.

Notes

1   Your answer should include a calculation of James's inheritance tax saving from making the gift of property to the trust on 2 August 2020 rather than retaining the property until his death.

2   You are not expected to consider lifetime exemptions in this part of the question.
                                                                              (2 marks)

(Total = 10 marks)

207 Dembe (March/June 2019)

18 mins

You should assume that today's date is 15 February 2022.

You are a trainee chartered certified accountant dealing with the tax affairs of Dembe and her husband Kato.

Personal pension contribution

Dembe is self-employed and her trading profit for the year ended 31 December 2021 is £130,000. She will not have any other income or outgoings for the tax year 2021/22.

Dembe is planning to make a personal pension contribution of £32,000 (net) before 5 April 2022, and would like to know the amount of income tax and national insurance contributions (NICs) which she will save as a result of making the pension contribution.

Sale of residential property

During March 2022, Dembe is going to sell a residential property and this will result in a chargeable gain of £67,000 if she makes the disposal.

Dembe wants to know whether it would be beneficial to transfer the property to Kato, her husband, as a no gain/no loss transfer prior to it being sold during March 2022. The transfer from Dembe to Kato will cost £2,000 in additional legal fees, and this cost will reduce the chargeable gain to £65,000 if the disposal is made by Kato.

Dembe has already made other disposals during the tax year 2021/22 which have utilised her annual exempt amount. Kato, however, has not yet made any disposals.

Kato's taxable income for the tax year 2021/22 is £21,350.

Inheritance tax

Dembe, who knows nothing about inheritance tax (IHT), is concerned about the amount of IHT which will be payable when she and Kato die. The couple's combined chargeable estate is valued at £950,000 for IHT purposes. The estate includes a main residence valued at £360,000.

Under the terms of their wills, Dembe and Kato have initially left their entire estates to each other. Then when the second of them dies, the total estate of £950,000 will be left to the couple's children.

The couple are not sure whether to change the terms of their wills so that assets worth £325,000 are left to their children when the first of them dies.

Neither Dembe nor Kato have made any lifetime gifts.

Required

(a) Calculate the reduction in Dembe's income tax liability and NICs for the tax year 2021/22 if she makes the personal pension contribution of £32,000 (net) before 5 April 2022.

   Note. You are not expected to prepare full tax computations. (4 marks)

(b) Calculate the couple's overall saving for the tax year 2021/22, after taking account of the additional legal fees of £2,000, if the residential property is transferred to Kato and sold by him, rather than the property being sold by Dembe. (3 marks)

(c) Calculate the amount of IHT payable, if any, were Dembe and Kato to both die in the near future, and explain whether or not it might be beneficial to leave assets worth £325,000 to their children when the first of them dies.

   Note. You should assume that the IHT rates and thresholds remain unchanged. (3 marks)

(Total = 10 marks)

PART E CORPORATION TAX LIABILITIES

Questions 208 to 249 cover corporation tax liabilities, the subject of Chapters 19 to 23 of the BPP Workbook for Taxation (TX – UK).

OTQ bank – Corporation tax liabilities   36 mins

208   Jet Ltd has deducted some items in its statement of profit or loss for the year ended 31 December 2020.

Identify, by clicking on the relevant boxes in the table below, whether each of the following items of expenditure are allowable or not allowable for computing Jet Ltd's taxable trading profit.

Legal expenses relating to the acquisition of a new 40-year lease on its factory	ALLOWABLE	NOT ALLOWABLE
Cost of arranging a new bank loan to purchase machinery for trade	ALLOWABLE	NOT ALLOWABLE
Write off of an irrecoverable loan to a former employee	ALLOWABLE	NOT ALLOWABLE
Donation to local charity with mention of Jet Ltd's support in programme for fundraising concert (not a qualifying charitable donation)	ALLOWABLE	NOT ALLOWABLE

(2 marks)

209   Rat Ltd started trading on 1 December 2020 and prepared its first set of accounts to 31 March 2022.

What will Rat Ltd's accounting periods be for the period of account to 31 March 2022?

○   4 months to 31 March 2021, 12 months to 31 March 2022

○   4 months to 5 April 2021, nearly 12 months to 31 March 2022

○   12 months to 30 November 2021, 4 months to 31 March 2022

○   16 months to 31 March 2022   (2 marks)

210   Xeon Ltd purchases a newly-constructed office building from a developer for £1,875,000 on 1 March 2021 and starts using it on 1 April 2021. The purchase price includes acquisition costs of £75,000. Xeon Ltd has a 31 December year end.

What are the maximum SBAs available to Xeon Ltd in the year ended 31 December 2021?

£ [   ]   (2 marks)

211 Kit Ltd was incorporated and started trading on 1 July 2021 and prepared its first set of accounts to 31 December 2021. During the six-month accounting period to 31 December 2021, it purchased two vehicles:

		£
28 November 2021	Motor car [1] (CO_2 emissions 126 g/km)	15,400
2 December 2021	Motor car [2] (CO_2 emissions 41 g/km)	30,400

Motor car [1] is used 20% for private purposes by a director of Kit Ltd.

What are the capital allowances to which Kit Ltd is entitled for the period to 31 December 2021?

[▼]

Pull down list:

£4,122
£3,198
£6,396
£3,106

(2 marks)

212 Eminal Ltd purchased 50,000 shares in Vesterama Ltd for £3.50 a share on 6 June 2002. On 6 June 2021, Eminal Ltd sold 15,000 shares in Vesterama Ltd for £70,000. Eminal Ltd prepares accounts to 31 December each year. Indexation factor: June 2002 to December 2017 = 0.578.

What is Eminal Ltd's chargeable gain or capital loss for the year ended 31 December 2021?

○ £12,845 loss

○ £105,000 loss

○ £0

○ £17,500 gain

(2 marks)

213 Crane plc started trading on 1 January 2021. In the year ended 31 December 2021 the company made an adjusted trading loss of £40,000. In the year ended 31 December 2022 the company will have trading income of £30,000, other taxable income of £6,000 and will make a qualifying charitable donation of £2,700. Crane plc wishes to use carry forward trading loss relief.

What is the most beneficial carry forward trading loss relief claim that Crane plc can make for the year ended 31 December 2022?

£ [   ]

(2 marks)

214   Deal Ltd has the following results:

	12 months to 31 March 2021	9 months to 31 December 2021	12 months to 31 December 2022
	£	£	£
Trading profits/(losses)	45,000	40,000	(160,000)
Property business profits	18,000	15,500	5,000

The company wishes to claim relief for its loss as early as possible.

What is the unused loss carried forward at 31 December 2022?

£ _____   (2 marks)

---

215   Bab Ltd has owned 80% of the ordinary share capital of Boon Ltd for many years. The two companies' results for the year ended 31 December 2021 are as follows:

	Bab Ltd	Boon Ltd
	£	
Trading profit/(loss)	(38,000)	36,000
Chargeable gains	7,000	4,000

What is the maximum amount of current period group relief which Boon Ltd can claim from Bab Ltd for the year ended 31 December 2021?

○   £38,000

○   £31,000

○   £36,000

○   £32,000   (2 marks)

---

216   The Daffodil plc group of companies has the following structure.

All companies are resident in the UK except Geranium Inc.

Identify, by clicking on the relevant boxes in the table below, the companies to which Erica Ltd could surrender a trading loss.

Daffodil plc	Geranium Inc
Flora Ltd	Hellebore Ltd

(2 marks)

217   The Pine plc group of companies has the following structure.

All companies are resident in the UK except Lime Inc.

Identify, by clicking on the relevant boxes in the table below, the companies to which Maple Ltd could transfer a capital loss.

Pine plc	Willow Ltd
Juniper Ltd	Lime Inc

(2 marks)

(Total = 20 marks)

OT case – Luna Ltd (June 2015) (amended)   18 mins

The following scenario relates to Questions 218 to 222.

Luna Ltd had the following transactions in shares during the year ended 31 March 2022:

(1)   On 29 November 2021, Luna Ltd sold its entire shareholding of £1 ordinary shares in Pluto plc for £53,400. Luna Ltd had originally purchased these shares in Pluto plc on 14 June 2008 for £36,800.

(2)   On 30 November 2021, Luna Ltd sold 10,000 of its shares in Neptune plc for £26,000. Luna Ltd had originally purchased 16,000 shares in Neptune plc on 10 May 2010 for £32,000.

(3)   On 10 December 2021, Luna Ltd acquired shares under a rights issue in Saturn plc. Luna Ltd had originally purchased 5,000 £1 ordinary shares in Saturn plc for £7,500 in August 2011. There was a 1 for 1 bonus issue in July 2013 when the shares were worth £1.75 each. The December 2021 rights issue was on a 1 for 4 basis and the cost of the rights issue shares was £2.25 per share.

(4)   On 12 February 2022, Luna Ltd's shareholding in Asteroid plc was taken over by Comet plc. Luna Ltd had originally purchased 10,000 £1 ordinary shares in Asteroid plc and their indexed cost on 12 February 2022 was £33,000.

Under the terms of the takeover, for each of its £1 ordinary shares in Asteroid plc, Luna Ltd received £6.50 in cash plus one £1 ordinary share in Comet plc. Immediately after the takeover, Comet plc's £1 ordinary shares were quoted at £4.50.

Indexation factors are as follows:

June 2008–December 2017 = 0.283
May 2010–December 2017 = 0.244

218   Identify, by clicking on the relevant boxes in the table below, whether each of the following statements concerning the indexation allowance is true or false.

Indexation allowance can reduce a gain to nil but not create a loss	TRUE	FALSE
Indexation allowance can increase an unindexed loss	TRUE	FALSE

(2 marks)

219   What is Luna Ltd's chargeable gain on the sale of Pluto plc shares on 29 November 2021?

£ [   ]

(2 marks)

220   What is the indexed cost of Luna Ltd's holding in Neptune Ltd immediately after the sale on 30 November 2021?

- ○   £12,000
- ○   £39,808
- ○   £24,880
- ○   £14,928

(2 marks)

221 What is the unindexed cost of Luna Ltd's holding in Saturn plc immediately after the rights issue on 10 December 2021?

    ○   £13,125

    ○   £11,875

    ○   £10,313

    ○   £21,875   (2 marks)

222 What is the cost that was used to compute Luna Ltd's chargeable gain on the takeover of Asteroid plc on 12 February 2022?

£ [   ]   (2 marks)

(Total = 10 marks)

OT case – Tay Ltd   18 mins

The following scenario relates to Questions 223 to 227.

Tay Ltd prepares accounts to 31 March each year. In the year to 31 March 2022, it had the following events relating to chargeable assets:

(1)   Received insurance proceeds of £180,000 in December 2021 as the result of the destruction of a freehold warehouse in a flood in that month. The warehouse originally cost £140,000 and had an indexed cost in December 2021 of £155,000. Tay Ltd purchased a new warehouse for £162,000 in March 2022.

(2)   Received shares and cash on the takeover of Grey Ltd. Tay Ltd had acquired 20,000 shares in Grey Ltd. The shares had an indexed cost in September 2021 of £96,000 when Grey Ltd was taken over by Kline plc. On the takeover, Tay Ltd received one £1 ordinary share in Kline plc worth £4 per share and £2 in cash for each one share held in Grey Ltd.

(3)   Sold a piece of machinery which it had used in its trade for £9,000 in July 2021. The machinery had an indexed base cost in July 2021 of £3,500. Capital allowances had been claimed on the machinery.

(4)   Sold a plot of land, which it had held as an investment, for £45,000 in October 2021. The land had been acquired in June 2007 for £20,000. Tay Ltd had spent £2,000 on draining the land in January 2011. The indexation factor from June 2007 to December 2017 was 0.342, from January 2011 to December 2017 was 0.214.

In the year to 31 March 2023, Tay Ltd will dispose of an investment property which will realise a loss. The company wants to know how this loss can be relieved.

223   **What is the base cost of the new warehouse purchased in March 2022, assuming any relevant claim was made?**

    ○   £162,000

    ○   £155,000

    ○   £144,000

    ○   £140,000   (2 marks)

224   **What was the chargeable gain or allowable loss arising on the takeover of Grey Ltd?**

    ○   £8,000 gain

    ○   £24,000 gain

    ○   £16,000 gain

    ○   £(24,000) loss   (2 marks)

225   **What was the chargeable gain (if any) arising on the disposal of the machinery?**

    ○   £0

    ○   £5,500

    ○   £2,500

    ○   £5,000   (2 marks)

BPP
LEARNING
MEDIA

226　What was the chargeable gain arising on the disposal of the plot of land?

- ○　£16,160
- ○　£15,476
- ○　£15,732
- ○　£15,134　　　　　　　　　　　　　　　　　　　　　　　　　　　　(2 marks)

227　**Which TWO of the following statements about the use of the capital loss in the year ended 31 March 2023 are correct?**

(1)　The capital loss can be carried back against chargeable gains made in the year ended 31 March 2022.

(2)　The capital loss can be set against chargeable gains made in the year ended 31 March 2023.

(3)　The capital loss can be set against total profits in the year ended 31 March 2023.

(4)　The capital loss can be carried forward and set against the first available chargeable gains.

- ○　1 and 2
- ○　1 and 3
- ○　2 and 4
- ○　3 and 4　　　　　　　　　　　　　　　　　　　　　　　　　　　　(2 marks)

(Total = 10 marks)

OT case – Hyde plc group

18 mins

The following scenario relates to Questions 228 to 232.

The Hyde plc group has the following structure:

All the group companies prepared accounts to 31 March 2022. However, Greenwich plc intends to change its accounting reference date to 31 December and will prepare accounts to 31 December 2022.

Hyde plc and Greenwich plc are in a group relief group.

In the year ended 31 March 2022, Greenwich plc had the following results:

	£
Trading loss	(68,000)
Capital loss	(4,000)
Interest income	3,000
Qualifying charitable donations	(5,000)

Greenwich plc will surrender the maximum amount possible for the year ended 31 March 2022 to Hyde plc under current period group relief.

In the year ended 31 March 2022, Hyde plc had the following results:

	£
Trading loss	(8,000)
Chargeable gain	48,000
Interest income	12,000
Qualifying charitable donations	(1,500)

Greenwich plc will make a trading loss in the period ended 31 December 2022 and will surrender the maximum amount possible to Hyde plc under current period group relief.

Regent plc and Primrose plc are in a chargeable gains group. In the year to 31 March 2022, Regent plc sold a factory to Primrose plc for £250,000. The market value of the factory at that date was £300,000. Regent plc had acquired the factory for £100,000. The indexation factor between the date of acquisition and December 2017 is 0.200.

228 **Identify, by clicking on the relevant boxes in the table below, which of the following companies are also members of the Hyde plc group for group relief purposes.**

Hampstead plc	Regent plc
Richmond plc	Primrose plc

(2 marks)

229 What is the maximum amount that Greenwich plc could surrender as current period group relief of the year ended 31 March 2022?

    ◯   £68,000

    ◯   £70,000

    ◯   £73,000

    ◯   £77,000   (2 marks)

---

230 What are the maximum available taxable total profits of Hyde plc that could be current period group relieved for the year ended 31 March 2022?

[▼]

Pull down list:

£58,500
£2,500
£52,000
£50,500   (2 marks)

---

231 Which TWO of the following statements about current period group relief claims between Hyde plc and Greenwich plc are correct?

☐   A claim for current period group relief will be ineffective unless Greenwich plc gives a notice of consent.

☐   If Hyde plc pays Greenwich plc an amount up to the amount of the loss surrendered, the payment will be deducted from the current period group relief.

☐   A claim for current period group relief between Greenwich plc and Hyde plc will be available against the whole of the taxable total profits of Hyde plc for the year to 31 March 2023.

☐   The claim for current period group relief would be made on Hyde plc's corporation tax return.   (2 marks)

---

232 What is base cost of the factory acquired by Primrose plc in August 2021?

    ◯   £100,000

    ◯   £120,000

    ◯   £250,000

    ◯   £300,000   (2 marks)

(Total = 10 marks)

233 Problematic Ltd (June 2010) (amended)   18 mins

Problematic Ltd sold the following assets during the year ended 31 March 2022:

(1) On 14 June 2021 16,000 £1 ordinary shares in Easy plc were sold for £54,400. Problematic Ltd had originally purchased 15,000 shares in Easy plc on 26 June 2005 for £12,600. On 28 September 2008 Easy plc made a 1 for 3 rights issue. Problematic Ltd took up its allocation under the rights issue in full, paying £2.20 for each new share issued. Indexation factors are as follows:

June 2005–September 2008 = 0.136
September 2008–December 2017 = 0.273

(2) On 28 January 2022 a freehold factory was sold for £171,000. The indexed cost of the factory on that date was £127,000. Problematic Ltd has made a claim to hold over the gain on the factory against the cost of a replacement leasehold factory under the rollover relief (replacement of business assets) rules. The leasehold factory has a lease period of 20 years, and was purchased on 10 December 2021 for £154,800. The two factory buildings have always been used entirely for business purposes.

Required

(a) Calculate Problematic Ltd's chargeable gains for the year ended 31 March 2022. **(9 marks)**

(b) Advise Problematic Ltd of the carried forward indexed base cost of the leasehold factory.
(1 mark)

(Total = 10 marks)

234 Volatile Ltd (December 2009) (amended)   18 mins

Volatile Ltd commenced trading on 1 July 2020. The company's results for its first five periods of trading are as follows:

	Period ended 31 December 2020	Year ended 31 December 2021	Year ended 31 December 2022	Period ended 30 September 2023	Year ended 30 September 2024
	£	£	£	£	£
Trading profit/(loss)	44,000	(73,800)	86,500	78,700	(186,800)
Property business profit	9,400	6,600	6,500	–	–
Chargeable gain/(loss)	5,100	–	(2,000)	11,700	–
Qualifying charitable donations	(800)	(1,000)	(1,200)	–	–

Required

(a) State the factors that will influence a company's choice of loss relief claims.

Note. You are not expected to consider group relief.   **(2 marks)**

(b) Assuming that Volatile Ltd claims relief for its trading losses as early as possible, calculate the company's taxable total profits for the six-month period ended 31 December 2020, each of the years ended 31 December 2021 and 2022 and the nine-month period ended 30 September 2023. Your answer should also clearly identify the amount of any unrelieved trading losses as at 30 September 2024.   **(8 marks)**

(Total = 10 marks)

235 Maison Ltd (September/December 2019)   27 mins

This scenario relates to one requirement.

You are a trainee Chartered Certified Accountant dealing with the tax affairs of Maison Ltd.

Your assistant has prepared a partly completed draft corporation tax computation for the year ended 31 March 2022. All of your assistant's workings for the figures provided are correct, but there are four uncompleted sections, all related to property, which your assistant does not know how to deal with.

The assistant's corporation tax computation, along with references to the uncompleted sections (with missing figures indicated by a question mark (?)), is shown below:

Maison Ltd – Corporation tax computation for the year ended 31 March 2022

	Uncompleted section	£
Operating profit		892,900
Non-deductible expenditure		22,340
Deduction for lease premium	1	?
Capital allowances	2	?
Trading profit		?
Property business income	3	?
Loan interest receivable		1,460
Chargeable gains	4	?
Taxable total profits		?
Corporation tax		?

Uncompleted section 1 – Deduction for lease premium

Your assistant has identified that on 1 January 2022, Maison Ltd acquired a leasehold office building, paying a premium of £44,000 for the grant of a 12-year lease. The office building was used for business purposes by Maison Ltd throughout the period 1 January to 31 March 2022.

Uncompleted section 2 – Capital allowances

Your assistant has correctly calculated that capital allowances of £12,037 are available on the main pool. However, she is unsure of the amount of capital allowance and structures and buildings allowance which are available in respect of the £140,000 spent by Maison Ltd during November 2021 constructing an extension which is adjacent to the company's existing freehold office building. The extension is used by the company's employees as a staff room and was ready for use on 1 December 2021. The total cost of £140,000 is made up as follows:

Integral to the building	£
Building costs of extension	93,300
Ventilation system	6,700
Heating system	3,900
Not integral to the building	
Furniture and furnishings	33,500
Refrigerator and microwave cooker	2,600
Total cost	140,000

Uncompleted section 3 – Property business income

On 1 July 2021, Maison Ltd purchased a freehold warehouse. The warehouse is currently surplus to requirements, so it was let out from 1 November 2021. However, the warehouse was purchased in a dilapidated state and could not be let until repair work was carried out during August 2021. This fact was represented by a reduced purchase price. Your assistant has listed any income and expenditure that is potentially relevant:

Date received/(paid)		£
1 July 2021	Insurance for the period to 31 March 2022	(1,035)
August 2021	Initial repairs	(17,680)
28 September 2021	Advertising for tenants	(780)
1 November 2021	Security deposit of two months' rent	12,200
1 November 2021	Rent for the quarter ended 31 January 2022	18,300
1 February 2022	Rent for the quarter ended 30 April 2022	18,300

Uncompleted section 4 – Chargeable gains

Maison Ltd disposed of two investment properties during August 2021, both resulting in gains. Your assistant has correctly calculated the gains but is unsure of the amount of indexation allowance available. The assistant's workings are as follows:

	Date	First property £	Second property £
Disposal proceeds	August 2021	237,000	143,000
Cost	April 2009	(101,000)	(117,000)
Enhancement expenditure	May 2018	(26,200)	0
Gain		109,800	26,000

Indexation factors are:

April 2009 to December 2017	0.315

No rollover relief claim is possible in respect of these gains.

Required

Prepare a completed version of Maison Ltd's corporation tax computation for the year ended 31 March 2022 after dealing with the sections uncompleted by your assistant.

Notes

1   Your computation should commence with the operating profit figure of £892,900, and you should indicate by the use of zero (0) any items which are not included in your calculation.

2   In calculating the operating profit figure of £892,900, no deduction has been made for the lease premium (uncompleted section 1) or any capital allowances (uncompleted section 2). It also does not include any income or expenditure in relation to property business income (uncompleted section 3) or any chargeable gains in relation to the disposal of the two investment properties (uncompleted section 4).

(Total = 15 marks)

236 Black Ltd (December 2011) and Gastron Ltd (June 2009) (amended)

18 mins

(a) Black Ltd owns 100% of the ordinary share capital of White Ltd and 80% of the ordinary shares of Grey Ltd. The results of Black Ltd, White Ltd and Grey Ltd for the year ended 31 March 2022 are as follows:

	Black Ltd	White Ltd	Grey Ltd
	£	£	£
Trading profit/(loss)	338,900	(351,300)	50,000
Property business profit	21,100	26,700	4,500
Qualifying charitable donations	(4,400)	(5,600)	0

At 1 April 2021 Grey Ltd had brought forward trading losses of £57,500 arising from the year ended 31 March 2021.

Required

Advise Black Ltd as to the maximum amount of group relief that it can set off in the year ended 31 March 2022 if claims are made both from White Ltd in respect of its losses for the year ended 31 March 2022 and from Grey Ltd in respect of its losses for the year ended 31 March 2021.

Note. You are not expected to calculate either company's corporation tax liability.

(5 marks)

(b) Gastron Ltd is a manufacturing company. In the year to 31 March 2022 Gastron Ltd had taxable total profits of £600,000. The taxable total profits included a chargeable gain of £74,800 on the sale of a 1% shareholding. This figure is after taking account of indexation.

Gastron Ltd owns 100% of the ordinary share capital of Culinary Ltd. On 13 February 2022 Culinary Ltd sold a freehold factory and this resulted in a capital loss of £66,000. For the year ended 31 March 2022 Culinary Ltd made no other disposals.

Required

(i) Explain the group relationship that must exist in order for two or more companies to form a group for chargeable gains purposes. **(2 marks)**

(ii) Explain why it would be beneficial for Gastron Ltd and Culinary Ltd to make a joint election to transfer the whole of the capital gain on Gastron Ltd's disposal of shares to Culinary Ltd. **(1 mark)**

(iii) Explain what two other taxation consequences arise as a result of companies being in a chargeable gains group. **(2 marks)**

(Total = 10 marks)

237 Alimag Ltd (September/December 2017)   18 mins

You should assume that today's date is 15 March 2021.

You are a trainee chartered certified accountant dealing with the tax affairs of Gamila, who is the managing director of, and (currently) 100% shareholder in, Alimag Ltd.

For the year ended 5 April 2022, Alimag Ltd's taxable total profits, before taking account of director's remuneration, are forecast to be £180,000.

Original basis of profit extraction

Gamila originally intended to withdraw £130,000 of the profits as director's remuneration, and you have calculated that this approach would result in the following tax liabilities and national insurance contributions (NICs):

	£
Alimag Ltd	
Corporation tax for the year ended 5 April 2022	6,323
Class 1 employer NICs for the tax year 2021/22	16,720
Gamila	
Income tax for the tax year 2021/22	44,460
Class 1 employee NICs for the tax year 2021/22	6,479
	73,982

Revised basis of profit extraction

After a meeting with Gamila, a more beneficial approach to withdrawing £130,000 of profits from Alimag Ltd has been agreed for the tax year 2021/22

(1)   Gamila will withdraw gross director's remuneration of £30,000.
(2)   Gamila's husband, Magnus, will become a 30% shareholder in Alimag Ltd.
(3)   Alimag Ltd will then pay dividends of £70,000 to Gamila and £30,000 to Magnus.

Neither Gamila nor Magnus will have any other income for the tax year 2021/22.

Required

Calculate the overall saving of taxes and NICs for the tax year 2021/22 if the revised basis of profit extraction is used instead of the original basis of profit extraction.

Notes

1   You are expected to calculate the income tax payable by Gamila and Magnus, the class 1 NIC payable (if any) by Gamila, Magnus and Alimag Ltd, and the corporation tax liability of Alimag Ltd for the year ended 5 April 2022.

2   Alimag Ltd is not entitled to the NIC annual employment allowance.

3   You should assume that the rate of corporation tax remains unchanged.   (10 marks)

_____

(Total = 10 marks)

238 Hopi Ltd (March/June 2018)   18 mins

You should assume that today's date is 25 March 2022.

Kaya is the managing director of, and 100% shareholder in, Hopi Ltd. Hopi Ltd has no other employees.

For the year ended 5 April 2022, Hopi Ltd's tax adjusted trading profit, after taking account of director's remuneration and employer's class 1 national insurance contributions (NICs), is forecast to be £80,000. Hopi Ltd has already paid Kaya gross director's remuneration of £30,000 and dividends of £45,000 for the tax year 2021/22. Kaya does not have any other income. Based on these figures, the tax and NICs for Kaya and Hopi Ltd for the year ended 5 April 2022 will be:

	£
Kaya	
Income tax	12,893
Employee class 1 NICs	2,452
Hopi Ltd	
Employer class 1 NICs	2,920
Corporation tax	15,200

However, on 31 March 2022, Kaya is planning to pay herself a bonus of £25,000, but is unsure whether to take this as additional director's remuneration (the gross remuneration will be £25,000) or as an additional dividend.

Required

Calculate the revised tax and NICs for Kaya and Hopi Ltd for the year ended 5 April 2022 if, on 31 March 2022, Kaya pays herself the bonus of £25,000 (1) as additional director's remuneration or (2) as an additional dividend.

Notes

1   You are expected to calculate the revised income tax liability and NICs for Kaya and the revised corporation tax liability and NICs for Hopi Ltd under each of options (1) and (2).

2   You should assume that the rate of corporation tax remains unchanged   **(10 marks)**

(Total = 10 marks)

239 Kat (September/December 2018)

You should assume that today's date is 15 March 2021.

On 6 April 2021, Kat will purchase a residential freehold property which she will let out. However, Kat is unsure whether to purchase the property personally or via a limited company. The limited company would be incorporated for the sole purpose of purchasing and letting out the property, and Kat would hold all of the shares in the company.

Regardless of whether the property is purchased personally or via a limited company:

(1)   The property will be let throughout the year ended 5 April 2022 at a monthly rent of £2,600 which will be paid when due.

(2)   The purchase of the property will be partly financed with a repayment mortgage. Mortgage interest of £12,000 will be paid during the year ended 5 April 2022.

(3)   The other expenditure on the property for the year ended 5 April 2022 will amount to £7,600, and this will all be allowable.

(4)   Kat will also have employment income of £60,000 for the tax year 2021/22.

If the property is purchased via a limited company, then the company's corporation tax liability for the year ended 5 April 2022 will be £2,204 and Kat will withdraw dividends from the company totalling £6,000 during the tax year 2021/22.

Kat will not have any other income for the tax year 2021/22.

Required

(a)   Determine if there will be an overall saving of tax for the year ended 5 April 2022 if Kat purchases the property via a limited company rather than purchasing it personally.

    Notes

    1   Your answer should include a calculation of Kat's income tax liability if she purchases the property personally and if she purchases it via a limited company.

    2   You should ignore national insurance contributions (NICs).   **(9 marks)**

(b)   Explain the ONE way in which the calculation of a future taxable gain on a property disposal made by the limited company would differ from the calculation of a taxable gain on a disposal made personally by Kat.   **(1 mark)**

(Total = 10 marks)

240 Jogger Ltd (A) (December 2008) (amended)   27 mins

Jogger Ltd is a manufacturing company. The company's summarised statement of profit or loss for the year ended 31 March 2022 is as follows:

	Note	£	£
Operating profit	1		1,052,482
Income from investments			
Bank interest	3	8,460	
Loan interest	4	24,600	
Income from property	5	144,000	
Dividends		45,000	
			222,060
Profit from sale of non-current assets			
Disposal of shares	6		102,340
Profit before taxation			1,376,882

Notes

1   *Operating profit*

Depreciation of £58,840 has been deducted in arriving at the operating profit of £1,052,482.

2   *Plant and machinery*

On 1 April 2021 the tax written down values of plant and machinery were as follows:

	£
Main pool	26,600
Special rate pool	21,167

The following transactions took place during the year ended 31 March 2022:

		Cost/(proceeds)
		£
20 July 2021	Sold a special rate pool motor car	(11,700)
31 July 2021	Purchased motor car CO_2 emissions 40 g/km	11,800
15 August 2021	Purchased new motor car CO_2 emissions 0 g/km	9,000
30 September 2021	Purchased integral features	1,300,000
15 December 2021	Purchased second hand machinery	12,500
14 March 2022	Sold a lorry	(8,600)

The motor car sold on 20 July 2021 for £11,700 originally cost more than this amount. The machinery purchased on 15 December 2021 has a predicted working life of six years and any relevant election has been made. The lorry sold on 14 March 2022 for £8,600 originally cost £16,600.

3   *Bank interest received*

The bank interest was received on 31 March 2022. The bank deposits are held for non-trading purposes.

4   *Loan interest receivable*

The loan was made for non-trading purposes on 1 July 2021. Loan interest of £16,400 was received on 31 December 2021, and interest of £8,200 was accrued at 31 March 2022.

5   *Income from property*

Jogger Ltd lets out an unfurnished freehold office building that is surplus to requirements. The office building was let throughout the year ended 31 March 2022. On 1 April 2021 Jogger Ltd received a premium of £100,000 for the grant of a ten-year lease, and the annual rent of £44,000 which is payable in advance.

6   *Profit on disposal of shares*

The profit on disposal of shares is in respect of a shareholding that was sold in December 2021 for £150,000. The shares were acquired in August 2006 at a cost of £47,660. The relevant indexation factor is 0.396.

Required

(a)   Calculate Jogger Ltd's tax adjusted trading loss for the year ended 31 March 2022.

Notes

1   Your computation should start with the operating profit of £1,052,482.

2   You should assume that the company claims the maximum available capital allowances.

3   Ignore VAT.   **(8 marks)**

(b)   Assuming that Jogger Ltd claims relief for its trading loss against total profits, calculate the company's corporation tax liability for the year ended 31 March 2022.   **(7 marks)**

(Total = 15 marks)

241 Long Ltd group (A) (June 2014) (amended)   27 mins

Long Ltd owns 100% of the ordinary share capital of both Wind Ltd and Road Ltd. Long Ltd and Road Ltd run freight transport businesses, whilst Wind Ltd provides transport related insurance services.

Long Ltd's shareholding in Wind Ltd was acquired on 1 April 2012 and the shareholding in Road Ltd was acquired on 15 January 2021 when that company was incorporated. Long Ltd and Wind Ltd have prepared accounts for the year ended 31 March 2022, whilst Road Ltd has prepared accounts for the period 1 January 2022 (when the company commenced trading) to 31 March 2022. The following information is available:

Long Ltd

(1)   The operating profit for the year ended 31 March 2022 is £817,820. Depreciation of £10,170 has been deducted in arriving at this figure.

(2)   On 1 April 2021, the tax written down value of the plant and machinery main pool was £44,800. On 10 June 2021, Long Ltd purchased a lorry for £28,308 and a motor car for £15,700. The motor car has a CO_2 emission rate of 42 grams per kilometre. The motor car is used by the managing director of Long Ltd, and 40% of the mileage is for private journeys.

(3)   On 29 July 2021, Long Ltd disposed of a 2% shareholding in an unconnected company. The disposal resulted in a capital loss of £21,300.

(4)   During the year ended 31 March 2022, Long Ltd received a dividend of £41,400 from Wind Ltd, and dividends totalling £32,000 from unconnected companies.

Wind Ltd

(1)   The operating profit for the year ended 31 March 2022 is £59,490. Depreciation of £5,000 has been deducted in arriving at this figure.

(2)   On 1 April 2021, the tax written down value of the plant and machinery main pool was £900. There were no additions or disposals during the year ended 31 March 2022.

(3)   On 18 August 2021, Wind Ltd disposed of a 1% shareholding in an unconnected company. The disposal resulted in a chargeable gain of £29,800. This figure is after taking account of indexation.

Road Ltd

(1)   The operating loss for the three-month period ended 31 March 2022 is £26,100. Donations of £2,800 have been deducted in arriving at this figure. The donations consist of political donations of £400, and qualifying charitable donations of £2,400.

(2)   On 3 October 2021, Road Ltd purchased a new motor car for £11,600. The motor car has a CO_2 emission rate of 0 grams per kilometre.

(3)   For the three-month period ended 31 March 2022, loan interest receivable was £4,300. The loan was made for non-trading purposes.

Other information

(1)   Long Ltd, Wind Ltd and Road Ltd do not have any other shareholdings in any other company.

(2)   Road Ltd is not expected to be profitable for the foreseeable future.

Required

(a)   On the assumption that any available reliefs are claimed on the most beneficial basis, calculate the corporation tax liabilities of Long Ltd and Wind Ltd for the year ended 31 March 2022, and of Road Ltd for the three-month period ended 31 March 2022.

(11 marks)

(b)   Explain whether or not Long Ltd is a large company for the purpose of paying corporation tax by instalments for the year ended 31 March 2022.   (4 marks)

(Total = 15 marks)

242 Retro Ltd (June 2015) (amended)

27 mins

Retro Ltd's summarised statement of profit or loss for the year ended 31 March 2022 is as follows:

	Note	£	£
Gross profit			166,760
Operating expenses			
Gifts and donations	1	2,300	
Impairment loss	2	1,600	
Leasing costs	3	4,400	
Other expenses	4	232,400	
			(240,700)
Finance costs			
Interest payable	5		(6,400)
Loss before taxation			(80,340)

Notes

1   *Gifts and donations*

Gifts and donations are as follows:

	£
Gifts to employees (food hampers costing £60 each)	720
Gifts to customers (calendars costing £8 each and displaying Retro Ltd's name)	480
Qualifying charitable donations	1,100
	2,300

2   *Impairment loss*

On 31 March 2022, Retro Ltd wrote off an impairment loss of £1,600 relating to a trade debt. This was in respect of an invoice which had been due for payment on 10 November 2021.

3   *Leasing costs*

The leasing costs of £4,400 are in respect of a motor car lease which commenced on 1 April 2021. The leased motor car has CO_2 emissions of 75 grams per kilometre.

4   *Other expenses*

The figure of £232,400 for other expenses includes a fine of £5,100 for a breach of health and safety regulations. The remaining expenses are all fully allowable.

5   *Interest payable*

The interest payable is in respect of the company's 5% loan notes which were repaid on 31 July 2021. Interest of £9,600 was paid on 31 July 2021, and an accrual of £3,200 had been provided for at 1 April 2021. The loan notes were issued in order to finance the company's trading activities.

BPP
LEARNING
MEDIA

Additional information

Plant and machinery

On 1 April 2021, the tax written down value of the plant and machinery main pool was £39,300.

The following new vehicles were purchased during the year ended 31 March 2022:

	Date of purchase	Cost	CO_2 emission rate
		£	
Motor car [1]	8 June 2021	14,700	44 grams per kilometre
Delivery van	3 August 2021	21,769	122 grams per kilometre
Motor car [2]	19 October 2021	12,400	0 grams per kilometre

New Offices

On 1 October 2021 Retro Ltd spent £850,000 on a new office block, including acquisition fees of £50,000. The offices were moved into immediately. Retro Ltd intends to claim the maximum SBAs on this expenditure.

Previous results

Retro Ltd commenced trading on 1 September 2019. The company's results for its two previous periods of trading are as follows:

	Year ended 31 August 2020	Period ended 31 March 2021
	£	£
Tax adjusted trading profit	56,600	47,900
Bank interest receivable	1,300	0
Qualifying charitable donations paid	(540)	(330)

Future results

Retro Ltd is expected to return to profitability in the year ended 31 March 2023 and to continue to be profitable in subsequent years.

Required

(a) Calculate Retro Ltd's tax adjusted trading loss for the year ended 31 March 2022.

   Note. Your computation should commence with the loss before taxation figure of £80,340, and should also list all of the items referred to in notes (1) to (5), indicating by the use of zero (0) any items which do not require adjustment. **(9 marks)**

(b) Assuming that Retro Ltd claims relief for its trading loss as early as possible, calculate the company's taxable total profits for the year ended 31 August 2020 and for the seven-month period ended 31 March 2021. **(4 marks)**

(c) Identify the amount of unrelieved trading loss which Retro Ltd will have at 31 March 2022, and state how this can be relieved. **(2 marks)**

(Total = 15 marks)

243 Lucky Ltd (September/December 2015) (amended)
27 mins

Lucky Ltd was incorporated on 20 July 2021, and commenced trading on 1 December 2021. The following information is available for the four-month period 1 December 2021 to 31 March 2022:

(1) The operating profit for the four-month period ended 31 March 2022 is £716,903. Advertising expenditure of £4,700 (incurred during September 2021), depreciation of £14,700, and amortisation of £9,000 have been deducted in arriving at this figure.

The amortisation relates to a premium which was paid on 1 December 2021 to acquire a leasehold warehouse on a 12-year lease. The amount of premium assessed on the landlord as income was £46,800. The warehouse was used for business purposes by Lucky Ltd throughout the period ended 31 March 2022.

(2) Lucky Ltd purchased the following assets during the period 20 July 2021 to 31 March 2022:

		£
19 August 2021	Computer	6,300
22 January 2022	Integral features	291,200
31 January 2022	Office equipment	49,566
17 March 2022	Motor car	12,800

The integral features of £291,200 are in respect of expenditure on electrical systems, a ventilation system and lifts which are integral to a freehold office building owned by Lucky Ltd.

The motor car has a CO_2 emission rate of 42 grams per kilometre.

(3) Lucky Ltd made a loan to another company for non-trading purposes on 1 February 2022. Loan interest income of £700 was accrued at 31 March 2022.

Lucky Ltd will make a company car available to its chief executive officer. The car will be purchased, rather than leased, and will be made available to the chief executive officer in December 2022 onwards.

Required

(a) State when an accounting period starts for corporation tax purposes. **(2 marks)**

(b) Calculate Lucky Ltd's corporation tax liability for the four-month period ended 31 March 2022.

Note. Your computation should commence with the operating profit of £716,903, and should also indicate by the use of zero (0) any items referred to in the question for which no adjustment is required. **(9 marks)**

(c) Advise Lucky Ltd as to how long it must retain the records used in preparing its self-assessment corporation tax return for the four-month period ended 31 March 2022, and the potential consequences of not retaining the records for the required period. **(2 marks)**

(d) Advise Lucky Ltd on the effects of the company car on its taxable total profits for the year ended 31 March 2023. **(2 marks)**

(Total = 15 marks)

244 Jump Ltd (March/June 2016)   **27 mins**

Jump Ltd's summarised statement of profit or loss for the three-month period ended 31 March 2022 is as follows:

	Note	£	£
Revenue			264,900
Operating expenses			
Depreciation		8,100	
Employee costs	1	189,700	
Lease of motor car	2	1,200	
Professional fees	3	7,800	
Other expenses	4	202,800	
			(409,600)
Loss before taxation			(144,700)

Notes

1   *Employee costs*

Employee costs are as follows:

	£
Employee training courses	3,400
Employee pension contributions paid	11,600
Cost of annual staff party (for eight employees)	1,500
Balance of expenditure (all allowable)	173,200
	189,700

2   *Lease of motor car*

The lease is in respect of a motor car with CO_2 emissions of 59 grams per kilometre.

3   *Professional fees*

Professional fees are as follows:

	£
Accountancy	2,200
Legal fees in connection with the issue of share capital	3,800
Legal fees in connection with the renewal of a 20-year property lease	1,800
	7,800

4   *Other expenses*

   Other expenses are as follows:

	£
Entertaining UK customers	1,700
Entertaining overseas customers	790
Political donations	800
Balance of expenditure (all allowable)	199,510
	202,800

Additional information

Plant and machinery

On 1 January 2022, the tax written down values of Jump Ltd's plant and machinery were as follows:

	£
Main pool	12,100
Special rate pool	5,700

The following motor cars were sold during the three-month period ended 31 March 2022:

	Date of sale	Proceeds	Original cost
		£	£
Motor car [1]	7 January 2022	9,700	9,300
Motor car [2]	29 March 2022	6,100	13,200

The original cost of motor car [1] was added to the special rate pool when it was purchased, and the original cost of motor car [2] was added to the main pool when it was purchased.

Previous results

Jump Ltd's results for its two previous periods of trading are as follows:

	Year ended 31 May 2021	Period ended 31 December 2021
	£	£
Tax adjusted trading profit	78,600	42,400
Bank interest receivable	1,200	0

Group companies

Jump Ltd owns 80% of the ordinary share capital of Hop Ltd and 60% of the ordinary share capital of Skip Ltd.

Hop Ltd commenced trading on 1 August 2021, and for the eight-month period ended 31 March 2022 has taxable total profits of £63,000.

Skip Ltd has been trading for several years and has taxable total profits of £56,000 for the year ended 31 March 2022.

Required

(a) Calculate Jump Ltd's tax adjusted trading loss for the three-month period ended 31 March 2022.

Notes

1   Your computation should commence with the operating loss figure of £144,700, and should list all of the items referred to in notes (1) to (4), indicating by the use of zero (0) any items which do not require adjustment.

2   You should assume that the company claims the maximum available capital allowances.   (10 marks)

(b) (i)   State the main factor which will influence Jump Ltd's choice of loss relief or group relief claims.   (1 mark)

(ii) Advise Jump Ltd as to the maximum amount of its trading loss which can be relieved against its total profits for the year ended 31 May 2021 and the seven-month period ended 31 December 2021.   (2 marks)

(iii) Advise Jump Ltd as to the maximum amount of its trading loss which can be surrendered as group relief.   (2 marks)

(Total = 15 marks)

245 Online Ltd (March/June 2017)

The following information is available in respect of Online Ltd for the year ended 31 March 2022:

Operating profit

Online Ltd's operating profit for the year ended 31 March 2022 is £896,700. Depreciation of £21,660 and amortisation of leasehold property of £9,000 (see the leasehold property note below) have been deducted in arriving at this figure.

Leasehold property

On 1 April 2021, Online Ltd acquired a leasehold office building, paying a premium of £90,000 for the grant of a ten-year lease. The office building was used for business purposes by Online Ltd throughout the year ended 31 March 2022.

Plant and machinery

On 1 April 2021, the tax written down values of plant and machinery were as follows:

	£
Main pool	56,700
Special rate pool	13,433

The following transactions took place during the year ended 31 March 2022:

		Costs/(proceeds)
		£
14 May 2021	Sold a motor car	(18,100)
18 July 2021	Sold all items included in the special rate pool	(9,300)
27 January 2022	Purchased a motor car	13,700

The motor car sold on 14 May 2021 for £18,100 was originally purchased during the year ended 31 March 2021 for £17,200. This expenditure was added to the main pool.

The motor car purchased on 27 January 2022 for £13,700 has a CO_2 emission rate of 48 grams per kilometre. The motor car is used as a pool car by the company's employees.

Qualifying charitable donations

During the year ended 31 March 2022, Online Ltd made qualifying charitable donations of £6,800. These were not included in arriving at the operating profit above.

Disposal of shareholding in Network plc

On 20 March 2022, Online Ltd sold its entire shareholding of £1 ordinary shares in Network plc for £90,600. Online Ltd had originally purchased 40,000 shares (less than a 1% shareholding) in Network plc on 24 June 2010 for £49,300. On 7 October 2013, Online Ltd sold 22,000 of the shares for £62,200.

Indexation factors are as follows:

June 2010 to October 2013	0.124
June 2010 to December 2017	0.241
October 2013 to December 2017	0.104

Brought forward losses

As at 1 April 2021, Online Ltd had the following brought forward amounts of unused losses:

	£
Capital loss	3,104
Property business loss	12,500

Planned acquisition

Online Ltd currently does not have any 51% group companies. However, Online Ltd is planning to acquire a 60% shareholding in Offline Ltd in the near future. Offline Ltd is profitable and will pay regular dividends to Online Ltd.

Required

(a) Calculate Online Ltd's taxable total profits for the year ended 31 March 2022. **(13 marks)**

(b) Briefly explain how the acquisition of Offline Ltd will affect the calculation and payment of Online Ltd's corporation tax liability in future years. **(2 marks)**

(Total = 15 marks)

246 Last-Orders Ltd (September/December 2017)

27 mins

Last-Orders Ltd ceased trading on 31 January 2022, having traded profitably for the previous ten years. The ordinary share capital of Last-Orders Ltd is owned 80% by Gastro Ltd and 20% by Gourmet Ltd.

Last-Orders Ltd's summarised statement of profit or loss for the ten-month period ended 31 January 2022 is as follows:

	Note	£
Revenue		176,790
Operating expenses		
Depreciation		(9,460)
Employee costs	1	(142,400)
Lease of motor car	2	(1,600)
Other expenses	3	(299,810)
Operating loss		(276,480)
Other income		
Property business income	4	11,500
Profit on disposal of freehold office building	5	47,400
Loss before taxation		(217,580)

Notes

1 *Employee costs*

Employee costs are as follows:

	£
Counselling services provided to employees who were made redundant	5,200
Pension contributions paid on behalf of employees	12,200
Employer class 1 national insurance contributions (NICs)	11,890
Employer class 1A NICs payable on benefits provided for employees	1,160
Employee bonuses declared but unpaid – these will not be paid during 2022	10,400
Balance of expenditure (all allowable)	101,550
	142,400

2 *Lease of motor car*

The lease is in respect of a motor car with CO_2 emissions of 40 grams per kilometre.

3   Other expenses

Other expenses are as follows:

	£
Entertaining UK suppliers	1,920
Entertaining overseas suppliers	440
Qualifying charitable donation	800
Balance of expenditure (all allowable)	296,650
	299,810

4   Property business income

During the ten-month period ended 31 January 2022, Last-Orders Ltd let out a freehold office building. The following income and expenditure was received or incurred during the final 12 months of trading:

Date received/(paid)		£
1 February 2021	Rent for the six months ended 31 July 2021	19,200
1 February 2021	Insurance for the 12 months ended 31 January 2022	(1,800)
1 August 2021	Rent for the six months ended 31 January 2022	19,200
21 November 2021	Repairs following a fire (not covered by insurance)	(7,700)

5   Property business income

The office building was sold on 31 January 2022. The profit has been calculated as disposal proceeds of £126,800 less cost of £79,400. The indexation allowance is £12,900. The office building was never used for business purposes.

Additional information

Plant and machinery – on 1 April 2021, the tax written down value of Last-Orders Ltd's main pool was £24,200. All of the items included in the main pool were sold for £13,600 on 31 January 2022, with none of the items sold for more than their original cost.

Last-Orders Ltd has previously always made up its accounts to 31 March.

Both Gastro Ltd and Gourmet Ltd are profitable and make up their accounts to 31 March.

Required

(a)   Calculate Last-Orders Ltd's tax adjusted trading loss for the ten-month period ended 31 January 2022.

Notes

1   Your computation should commence with the operating loss figure of £276,480, and should also list all of the items referred to in notes (1) to (3), indicating by the use of zero (0) any items which do not require adjustment.

2   You should assume that Last-Orders Ltd claims the maximum possible amount of capital allowances.   **(6 marks)**

(b)   Assuming Last-Orders Ltd claims relief for its trading loss against its taxable total profits for the ten-month period ended 31 January 2022, calculate the company's taxable total profits for this period.

Note. Your answer should show the amount of unused trading loss at 31 January 2022.
                                                                            (5 marks)

(c)   Explain the alternative ways in which Last-Orders Ltd's unused trading loss for the ten-month period ended 31 January 2022 could be relieved.   **(4 marks)**

(Total = 15 marks)

247 Solo Ltd (March/June 2018)

Solo Ltd's results for the previous two periods of trading are:

	Year ended 31 December 2020	Three-month Period ended 31 March 2021
	£	£
Trading profit	35,900	12,300
Property business income	12,100	4,200
Chargeable gains/(capital losses)	(3,300)	(2,100)
Qualifying charitable donations	(1,200)	(1,600)

The following information is available in respect of the year ended 31 March 2022:

Trading loss

The tax-adjusted trading loss based on the draft statement of profit or loss for the year ended 31 March 2022 is £151,300. This figure is before making any adjustments required for:

(1)   A premium which was paid to acquire a leasehold office building on an eight-year lease.
(2)   Capital allowances.

Premium paid to acquire leasehold office building

On 1 April 2021, Solo Ltd acquired a leasehold office building, paying a premium of £20,000 for the grant of an eight-year lease. The office building was used for business purposes by Solo Ltd throughout the year ended 31 March 2022.

Plant and machinery

The tax written down value of the plant and machinery main pool as at 1 April 2021 was £0. During the year ended 31 March 2022, Solo Ltd sold equipment for £4,300. The equipment was originally purchased during the year ended 31 March 2016 for £22,400, with this expenditure qualifying for the 100% annual investment allowance.

Property business income

Solo Ltd lets out a warehouse which is surplus to requirements. The building was empty from 1 April to 31 July 2021, but was let from 1 August 2021 onwards. The following income and expenditure was received or incurred during the year ended 31 March 2022:

Date received/paid

		£
1 April 2021	Insurance for the year ended 31 March 2022	(920)
1 August 2021	Rent for the six months ended 31 January 2022	7,800
1 August 2021	Security deposit equal to two months' rent	2,600
1 March 2022	Rent for the six months ended 31 July 2022	7,800

Disposal of shareholding in Multiple plc

On 12 December 2021, Solo Ltd sold 6,500 £1 ordinary shares in Multiple plc for £31,200. Solo Ltd had originally purchased 20,000 shares (less than a 1% shareholding) in Multiple plc on 18 June 2006 for £27,000, and purchased a further 1,000 shares on 8 December 2021 for £4,600. Indexation factors are:

June 2006 to December 2017	0.401

Required

(a) Calculate Solo Ltd's revised tax-adjusted trading loss for the year ended 31 March 2022.

Note. You should assume that the company claims the maximum available capital allowances. **(3 marks)**

(b) On the basis that Solo Ltd claims relief for its trading loss against its total profits for the year ended 31 March 2022, prepare a corporation tax computation for this year showing taxable total profits. **(8 marks)**

(c) On the basis that Solo Ltd claims relief for the remainder of its trading loss as early as possible, calculate the company's taxable total profits for the year ended 31 December 2020 and the three-month period ended 31 March 2021. **(4 marks)**

(Total = 15 marks)

248 Ash Ltd, Beech Ltd and Cedar Ltd (September/December 2018)

27 mins

You are a trainee chartered certified accountant assisting your manager with the tax affairs of three unconnected limited companies, Ash Ltd, Beech Ltd and Cedar Ltd.

Ash Ltd

Ash Ltd was incorporated in the UK on 1 December 2019 and immediately opened a non-interest bearing bank account. The company commenced trading on 1 February 2020, preparing its first accounts for the 14-month period ended 31 March 2021. Accounts were then prepared for the year ended 31 March 2022.

At the date of incorporation, all three of Ash Ltd's directors (who each own one-third of the company's ordinary share capital) were based in the UK. However, on 1 October 2021, two of the directors moved overseas. The directors have always held Ash Ltd's board meetings in the UK, and will continue to do so despite two of them moving overseas.

Beech Ltd

Beech Ltd's summarised statement of profit or loss for the year ended 31 January 2022 is as follows:

	Note	£
Gross profit		566,175
Operating expenses		
Depreciation		(14,700)
Gifts and donations	1	(4,975)
Impairment loss	2	(3,700)
Leasing costs	3	(12,600)
Other expenses	4	(217,700)
Finance costs		
Interest payable	5	(7,000)
Profit before taxation		305,500

Note 1 – Gifts and donations

Gifts and donations of £4,975 comprise:

	£
Gifts to customers (pens costing £70 each and displaying Beech Ltd's name)	3,500
Gifts to staff (decorative plaques costing £15 each to celebrate Beech Ltd's ten-year anniversary)	375
Qualifying charitable donations	1,100
	4,975

Note 2 – Impairment loss

On 31 January 2022, Beech Ltd wrote off an impairment loss of £3,700 relating to a trade debt. This was in respect of an invoice which had been due for payment on 15 October 2021.

Note 3 – Leasing costs

The leasing costs of £12,600 are in respect of four motor car leases which commenced on 1 February 2021. Each of the four leased motor cars has CO_2 emissions of 60 grams per kilometre.

Note 4 – Other expenses

The other expenses of £217,700 include a fine of £6,400 for a breach of data protection law, and legal fees of £5,700 in connection with the renewal of a 15-year property lease. The remaining expenses are all fully allowable.

Note 5 – Interest payable

The interest payable of £7,000 is in respect of the company's 4% loan notes which were issued on 1 July 2021. Interest of £6,000 was paid on 31 December 2021, with an accrual of £1,000 provided for at 31 January 2022. The loan notes were issued in order to finance the company's trading activities.

Capital allowances

No capital allowances are available for the year ended 31 January 2022.

Cedar Ltd

Cedar Ltd is a 100% subsidiary company of Timber Ltd. The following information is available in respect of the two companies for the year ended 31 March 2022:

(1)   For the year ended 31 March 2022, Cedar Ltd made a trading loss of £19,700.

(2)   On 28 December 2021, Cedar Ltd sold its entire shareholding of 25,000 £1 ordinary shares in Forest plc for £6.00 per share. Cedar Ltd had originally purchased 20,000 shares in Forest plc on 1 July 2010 for £24,800. On 20 July 2010, Forest plc made a 1 for 4 rights issue. Cedar Ltd took up its allocation under the rights issue in full, paying £1.15 for each new share issued. The indexation factor from July 2010 to December 2017 is 0.244.

(3)   For the year ended 31 March 2022, Timber Ltd made:

	£
Trading loss	20,800
Capital loss	8,800

There is no possibility of Cedar Ltd or Timber Ltd offsetting their trading losses against prior year profits. The group has a policy of utilising losses at the earliest opportunity.

Required

(a)   (i)   Identify Ash Ltd's accounting periods throughout the period 1 December 2019 to 31 March 2022. **(2 marks)**

       (ii)   Explain Ash Ltd's residence status throughout the period 1 December 2019 to 31 March 2022. **(2 marks)**

(b)   Calculate Beech Ltd's corporation tax liability for the year ended 31 January 2022.

       Note. Your computation should commence with the profit before taxation figure of £305,500, and should also list all of the items referred to in notes (1) to (5), indicating by the use of zero (0) any items which do not require adjustment. **(6 marks)**

(c)   On the basis that all available claims and elections are made, calculate Cedar Ltd's taxable total profits for the year ended 31 March 2022. **(5 marks)**

(Total = 15 marks)

249 Aoede Ltd, Bianca Ltd and Charon Ltd (March/June 2019)

27 mins

You are a trainee chartered certified accountant dealing with the tax affairs of three unrelated limited companies, Aoede Ltd, Bianca Ltd and Charon Ltd.

Aoede Ltd

Aoede Ltd commenced trading on 1 April 2020. The company's results are:

	Year ended 31 March 2021	Year ended 31 March 2022
	£	£
Trading profit/(loss)	(111,300)	67,800
Property business income/(loss)	(26,400)	23,400
Chargeable gains	5,800	16,200
Qualifying charitable donations	(6,000)	(6,600)

Aoede Ltd owns 100% of the ordinary share capital of Moon Ltd. Moon Ltd commenced trading on 1 April 2021 and for the year ended 31 March 2022 made a trading profit of £19,700.

Bianca Ltd

Bianca Ltd commenced trading on 1 April 2021. The company's tax adjusted trading profit based on the statement of profit or loss for the year ended 31 March 2022 is £256,300. This figure is **before** making any adjustments required for:

(1) Advertising expenditure of £5,800 incurred during January 2020 to promote Bianca Ltd's new business. This expenditure has not been deducted in calculating the profit of £256,300.

(2) Leasing costs of £9,300 which have been deducted in arriving at the profit of £256,300. The leasing costs relate to two motor cars which have been leased since 1 April 2021. The first motor car has CO_2 emissions of 45 grams per kilometre and is leased at an annual cost of £4,200. The second motor car has CO_2 emissions of 65 grams per kilometre and is leased at an annual cost of £5,100.

(3) Capital allowances.

On 1 April 2021, Bianca Ltd purchased four laptop computers at a discounted cost of £1,000 per laptop. The original cost of each laptop was £1,800, but Bianca Ltd was given a discount because they were damaged.

Bianca Ltd also purchased two second-hand motor cars on 1 April 2021. Details are:

	Cost	CO_2 emission rate
	£	
Motor car [1]	12,400	35 grams per kilometre
Motor car [2]	13,900	120 grams per kilometre

Charon Ltd

During the year ended 31 March 2022, Charon Ltd disposed of two investment properties.

The first property was sold for £368,000 during January 2022. This property was purchased for £147,000 during October 1995, and was extended at a cost of £39,000 during June 2018.

The second property was sold for £167,000 during January 2022. This property was purchased for £172,000 during December 2017.

Indexation factors are:

October 1995 to December 2017   0.856

Required

(a) (i)   On the basis that Aoede Ltd claims relief for its losses as early as possible, calculate the taxable total profits of Aoede Ltd for the years ended 31 March 2021 and 31 March 2022, and of Moon Ltd for the year ended 31 March 2022.   **(5 marks)**

     (ii) Explain which aspect of Aoede Ltd's loss relief claim made in part (i) is not beneficial for the company to make.   **(1 mark)**

(b) Calculate Bianca Ltd's revised tax adjusted trading profit for the year ended 31 March 2022.   **(5 marks)**

(c) Calculate Charon Ltd's chargeable gains and capital losses, if any, for the year ended 31 March 2022.   **(4 marks)**

(Total = 15 marks)

PART F VALUE ADDED TAX

Questions 250 to 315 cover value added tax, the subject of Chapters 24 and 25 of the BPP Workbook for Taxation (TX – UK).

OTQ bank – Value added tax 1   **18 mins**

250   Jerome is a value added tax (VAT) registered trader who received an order for goods with a 10% deposit on 18 August. The goods were despatched on 26 August and an invoice was sent on 2 September. The balancing 90% of the payment was received on 10 September.

Match the tax points for the deposit and the balancing payment if Jerome does not use the cash accounting scheme.

18 August	2 September
26 August	10 September

Deposit	

| Balancing payment | | (2 marks)
|---|---|

---

251   Alma runs a financial services business making exempt supplies. Barry runs a children's clothing shop making zero rated supplies. Chris runs an adult clothing shop making standard rated supplies.

Identify, by clicking on the relevant boxes in the table below, who is making taxable supplies and therefore can reclaim input VAT.

ALMA	BARRY	CHRIS

(2 marks)

---

252   Light Ltd is registered for value added tax (VAT). On 1 January 2022 Light Ltd purchased a motor car costing £18,400 (inclusive of VAT) for use by the managing director for business and private purposes. The private use is estimated to be 40%. The managing director is provided with free petrol for business and private mileage which cost Light Ltd £625 (exclusive of VAT). Light Ltd wishes to use the fuel scale charge: the relevant quarterly VAT inclusive scale charge is £377.

What is Light Ltd's VAT repayment in respect of the motor car and the fuel for the quarter ended 31 March 2022?

- ○   £50
- ○   £75
- ○   £62
- ○   £41   (2 marks)

BPP
LEARNING
MEDIA

253 Nora Ltd prepared a value added tax (VAT) return for the quarter ended 31 May 2021 which showed net VAT payable of £2,500.

By which dates should this return have been submitted to HM Revenue & Customs (HMRC) and the payment made to HMRC?

	Return submitted	Payment	
○	30 June 2021	30 June 2021	
○	7 July 2021	7 July 2021	
○	7 July 2021	30 June 2021	
○	30 June 2021	7 July 2021	(2 marks)

254 Mick is a value added tax (VAT) registered trader who prepares quarterly VAT returns to 31 March, 30 June, 30 September and 31 December each year. Mick's accounts are prepared annually to 30 September. Mick made a supply of goods amounting to £6,000 on 22 September 2021 with a due date of payment of 10 October 2021. The customer has defaulted on the payment and Mick has written the debt off in his accounts. He does not use the cash accounting scheme.

Which quarterly VAT return is the earliest in which relief for the impaired debt may be claimed?

- ○ VAT quarter ended 31 December 2021
- ○ VAT quarter ended 31 March 2022
- ○ VAT quarter ended 30 June 2022
- ○ VAT quarter ended 30 September 2022

(2 marks)

(Total = 10 marks)

OTQ bank – Value added tax 2

36 mins

255 Karen is a sole trader and is registered for value added tax (VAT). In October 2021, Karen sold goods for £8,000 exclusive of VAT. The sale was standard rated. Karen's invoice states that there is a discount of 8% on sales if invoices are paid within 21 days. The invoice for the supply was actually paid 25 days after it was issued.

How much VAT should Karen have added to the sale price of £8,000?

£	

(2 marks)

256 Olive is a sole trader who is registered for value added tax (VAT). On 10 October 2021 she purchased a motor car for £12,000 (inclusive of VAT) to use for business and private purposes. The private use is estimated to be 30%. On 1 December 2021, the motor car was damaged in an accident and the repairs amounted to £2,000 (inclusive of VAT).

What is the input tax Olive can recover in relation to the motor car for the quarter ended 31 December 2021?

£	

(2 marks)

257 Price Ltd incurred the following expenditure (inclusive of value added tax) in the quarter to 31 December 2021:

	£
New car for salesman (20% private use)	14,040
New motor van	10,320
Entertaining UK customers	4,200
Entertaining overseas customers	3,600

How much input tax can be recovered by Price Ltd for the quarter to 31 December 2021?

Pull down list:

£5,360
£4,192
£3,020
£2,320

(2 marks)

BPP
LEARNING
MEDIA

258 Ben has been in business for three years. Due to an upturn in trade, he applied to register for value added tax (VAT) with effect from 1 October 2021. Prior to registration, he had incurred the following VAT expenditure:

	£
Legal fees on an invoice dated 13 January 2021	500
Accountancy fees on an invoice dated 5 September 2021	30
Inventory of spare parts acquired in past two years and still held on 30 September 2021	240

What is the total pre-registration input tax that Ben can recover in respect of these items?

£ _____

(2 marks)

259 In the first year of trading to 31 December 2020 Scott's taxable turnover was £5,000 per month.

For the first seven months of 2021 his turnover was as follows:

	£
January 2021	8,400
February 2021	8,600
March 2021	8,800
April 2021	9,600
May 2021	10,000
June 2021	10,200
July 2021	10,300

You have advised Scott that he is compulsorily required to be registered for value added tax (VAT).

From what date will Scott be registered for VAT under compulsory registration?

○ 30 July 2021

○ 1 August 2021

○ 30 June 2021

○ 1 July 2021

(2 marks)

260 During the quarter ended 31 December 2021, Rachel makes purchases of office items for her business of £5,700 and spends £420 entertaining UK customers. Her sales for the period are £35,250. All figures are inclusive of value added tax (VAT) and standard rated.

What is Rachel's total VAT liability for the quarter ended 31 December 2021?

£ _____

(2 marks)

261 Charlie, a United Kingdom (UK) value added tax (VAT) registered trader, made a supply of goods in February 2022 to a customer in France who is VAT registered there.

What rate of VAT will Charlie charge on this sale?

- ○ 0%
- ○ 20%
- ○ 1/6
- ○ 5%

(2 marks)

262 **Which TWO of the following are features of the value added tax (VAT) cash accounting scheme?**

- ○ Date of payment or receipt determines the VAT period in which the transaction is dealt with
- ○ Only need to submit an annual VAT return
- ○ Gives automatic impairment loss relief (bad debt relief)
- ○ Payments on account of VAT are required throughout the quarter

(2 marks)

263 Alice is registered for value added tax (VAT) and calculates her VAT liability based on the flat rate scheme. The relevant flat rate percentage for Alice's business is 10%.

For the year ended 31 March 2022, Alice's sales (exclusive of VAT) were:

	£
Standard rated sales	50,000
Zero rated sales	20,000
Exempt sales	5,000

What amount of VAT is payable by Alice to HM Revenue and Customs (HMRC) in respect of the year ended 31 March 2022?

- ○ £8,500
- ○ £8,000
- ○ £7,500
- ○ £6,000

(2 marks)

264   Match the thresholds for a business to join and to leave the value added tax (VAT) flat
rate scheme.

Tax exclusive annual taxable turnover up to £150,000		Tax inclusive annual taxable turnover up to £150,000
Tax exclusive annual turnover up to £230,000		Tax inclusive annual turnover up to £230,000

Join scheme	

Leave scheme	

(2 marks)

_____

(Total = 20 marks)

OT case – Anne (June 2009) (amended)

18 mins

The following scenario relates to Questions 265 to 269.

Anne runs a retail clothing shop. She is registered for value added tax (VAT) and is in the process of completing her VAT return for the quarter ended 30 November 2021.

The following information is available (all figures are exclusive of VAT):

(1) Cash sales amounted to £42,000, of which £28,000 was in respect of sales of adult clothing (standard rated) and £14,000 was in respect of sales of children's clothing (zero rated).

(2) Sales invoices totalling £12,000 were issued in respect of credit sales. These sales were all standard rated. Anne states on her invoice that there is a 5% discount for payment within one month of the date of the sales invoice. 90% of the customers pay within this period. The sales figure of £12,000 is stated before any deduction for the 5% discount.

(3) Purchase and expense invoices totalling £19,200 were received from VAT registered suppliers. This figure is made up as follows:

	£
Standard rated purchases and expenses	11,200
Zero rated purchases	6,000
Exempt expenses	2,000
	19,200

Anne pays all of her purchase and expense invoices two months after receiving the invoice.

(4) On 30 November 2021 Anne wrote off two impairment losses that were in respect of standard rated credit sales. The first impairment loss was for £300, and was in respect of a sales invoice due for payment on 15 July 2021. The second impairment loss was for £800, and was in respect of a sales invoice due for payment on 10 April 2021.

Anne does not use the cash accounting scheme but she is considering using the scheme.

265 **What is the amount of output tax on cash sales payable by Anne for the quarter ended 30 November 2021?**

£ [   ]

(2 marks)

266 **What is the amount of output tax on credit sales payable by Anne for the quarter ended 30 November 2021, taking into account impairment loss relief?**

○ £2,052

○ £2,400

○ £2,280

○ £2,292

(2 marks)

267 **What is the amount of input tax recoverable by Anne for the quarter ended 30 November 2021?**

£ [   ]

(2 marks)

BPP
LEARNING
MEDIA

268   Which TWO of the following statements about the cash accounting scheme are correct?

☐   Anne will be permitted to join the scheme if her expected taxable turnover for the next 12 months does not exceed £1,350,000.

☐   Anne must pay her 90% of the previous year's net VAT liability during the year by means of nine monthly payments commencing at the end of the fourth month of the year.

☐   Anne will be permitted to join the scheme if she is up to date with her VAT payments but not necessarily up to date with her VAT returns.

☐   If the value of Anne's taxable supplies exceeds £1,600,000 in the 12 months to the end of a VAT period she must leave the scheme immediately.   (2 marks)

269   Identify, by clicking on the relevant boxes in the table below, whether each of the following statements are the advantages of Anne using the cash accounting scheme.

Reduced amount of output VAT payable	ADVANTAGE	NOT ADVANTAGE
Automatic impairment loss relief (bad debt relief)	ADVANTAGE	NOT ADVANTAGE
Only one VAT return each year	ADVANTAGE	NOT ADVANTAGE
Output VAT on 10% of credit sales will be accounted for up to 1 month later than at present	ADVANTAGE	NOT ADVANTAGE

(2 marks)

(Total = 10 marks)

OT case – Auy and Bim (June 2010) (amended)   18 mins

The following scenario relates to Questions 270 to 274.

Auy and Bim have been in partnership since 6 April 2006 and have been registered for value added tax (VAT) since that date.

In the year ended 5 April 2022 the partnership's summarised statement of profit or loss shows sales revenue of £140,762, which is exclusive of output VAT of £25,600, and expenses of £60,200 which are exclusive of recoverable input VAT of £180 for motor expenses and £140 for other expenses.

The partnership has recently started invoicing for its services on new payment terms, and the partners are concerned about output VAT being accounted for at the appropriate time.

The partnership is considering using the flat rate scheme. The relevant flat rate scheme percentage for the partnership's trade is 14%.

270   **Which TWO of the following statements about the tax point are correct?**

     ☐   The basic tax point for services is the date that services commence.

     ☐   If the VAT invoice is issued within 14 days after the basic tax point and payment has not been received before the basic tax point, the invoice date becomes the tax point.

     ☐   The tax point determines the VAT period in which output tax must be accounted for and credit for input tax will be allowed.

     ☐   If the VAT invoice is issued and payment is received before the basic tax point, the actual tax point is the later of those two dates.   **(2 marks)**

271   **What is the total amount of VAT paid by the partnership to HM Revenue & Customs for the year ended 5 April 2022?**

     ○   £25,600

     ○   £25,420

     ○   £25,280

     ○   £25,460   **(2 marks)**

272   **Which TWO of the following statements about the flat rate scheme are correct?**

     ☐   Businesses using the scheme must still issue VAT invoices to their VAT registered customers.

     ☐   Under the scheme, businesses calculate VAT by applying a fixed percentage to their standard rate income only.

     ☐   Businesses using the scheme cannot reclaim any input tax suffered.

     ☐   A 1% reduction off the flat rate percentage can always be made by businesses in the first year that they use the flat rate scheme.   **(2 marks)**

273 **What are the conditions that the partnership must satisfy in order to join and continue to use the VAT flat rate scheme?**

	Join	Continue to use
○	Expected taxable turnover (excluding VAT) for the next 12 months does not exceed £230,000.	Until its total turnover (including VAT) for the previous year exceeds £1,350,000
○	Expected taxable turnover (excluding VAT) for the next 12 months does not exceed £150,000.	Until its total turnover (including VAT) for the previous year exceeds £230,000
○	Expected taxable turnover (excluding VAT) for the next 12 months does not exceed £150,000.	Until its total turnover (including VAT) for the previous year exceeds £1,350,000
○	Expected taxable turnover (excluding VAT) for the next 12 months does not exceed £230,000.	Until its total turnover (including VAT) for the previous year exceeds £230,000

(2 marks)

274 **What is the amount of VAT that would have been paid to HM Revenue & Customs if the partnership had used the flat rate scheme to calculate the amount of VAT payable for the year ended 5 April 2022?**

- ○ £23,291
- ○ £19,707
- ○ £22,971
- ○ £28,152

(2 marks)

(Total = 10 marks)

OT case – Aston (June 2011) (amended)   18 mins

The following scenario relates to Questions 275 to 279.

Aston commenced self-employment on 1 August 2021 providing consultancy services. His sales revenue has been as follows:

		Standard rated	Zero rated
		£	£
2021	August	6,300	–
	September	6,400	–
	October	21,900	4,800
	November	11,700	–
	December	17,100	–
2022	January	14,800	2,200
	February	4,200	–
	March	31,500	3,300
	April	44,600	6,600

Where applicable, the above figures are stated exclusive of value added tax (VAT). Aston only supplies services and all of his supplies are to VAT registered businesses. He does not offer any discount for prompt payment.

Aston wants advice about when he will need to submit his VAT returns and pay the associated VAT due.

The following is a sample of the new sales invoice that Aston is going to issue to his customers:

SALES INVOICE

Aston
111 Long Road
London W1 9MG
Telephone 0207 123 3456

Customer: Faster Motors plc
Address: 22 Short Lane
Manchester M1 8MB

Invoice Date	6 June 2022
Tax Point	6 June 2022

Description of services
Business advice

	£
Total price (excluding VAT)	12,000.00
Total price (including VAT)	14,400.00

You have advised Aston that he also needs to include the rate of VAT for each supply and the amount of VAT payable.

Aston sometimes receives supplies of standard rated services from VAT registered businesses situated elsewhere within the European Union. Aston wants to know how he should account for these services for VAT purposes.

Because of the complexity of the VAT legislation, Aston is concerned that despite his best efforts he will incorrectly treat a standard rated supply as zero rated, thus understating the amount of VAT payable. He wants to know if such an error will result in a penalty, and if so how much the penalty will be.

275 Match the dates on which Aston was liable to be registered for VAT and the date from which Aston's business should be registered for VAT.

| 28 February 2022 | | 28 February 2022 |
| 31 January 2022 | | 1 March 2022 |

| Liable for registration | |
| Date of registration | | (2 marks)

---

276 When must Aston submit his VAT returns and pay the associated VAT?

	Submission	Payment
○	One month after the end of the VAT period	One month after the end of the VAT period
○	One month after the end of the VAT period	One month and seven days after the end of the VAT period
○	One month and seven days after the end of the VAT period	One month and seven days after the end of the VAT period
○	One month and seven days after the end of the VAT period	One month after the end of the VAT period

(2 marks)

---

277 Which TWO pieces of information must Aston show on his new sales invoices in order for them to be valid for VAT purposes in addition to those about which you have already advised him?

☐ Date for payment

☐ Aston's VAT registration number

☐ HMRC reference number

☐ An identifying number (invoice number)   (2 marks)

---

278 Which TWO of the following statements about when and how Aston should account for VAT in respect of the supplies of services he receives from VAT registered businesses situated elsewhere within the European Union are correct?

☐ The transaction is entered on Aston's VAT return as an output and an input.

☐ The tax point is the earlier of the 15th day of the month following that in which the service is completed and the date it is paid for.

☐ Supplies of services from VAT registered businesses situated elsewhere within the European Union are always zero rated for the customer.

☐ The service is treated as being supplied in the UK since this is where Aston is situated.

(2 marks)

---

279   Assuming that Aston incorrectly treats a standard rated supply as zero rated with the result that the amount of VAT payable is understated, what is the maximum amount of penalty that is likely to be charged by HM Revenue & Customs and the minimum penalty that could be charged as a result of a subsequent unprompted disclosure?

	Maximum penalty	Minimum penalty for unprompted disclosure
○	70% of the VAT underpaid	15% of the VAT underpaid
○	70% of the VAT underpaid	0% of the VAT underpaid
○	30% of the VAT underpaid	15% of the VAT underpaid
○	30% of the VAT underpaid	0% of the VAT underpaid

(2 marks)

(Total = 10 marks)

OT case – Starfish Ltd (December 2011) (amended)

18 mins

The following scenario relates to Questions 280 to 284.

Starfish Ltd, a retailing company, ceased trading on 31 March 2022 and deregistered from value added tax (VAT) on that date.

The following information relates to the company's final VAT return for the quarter ended 31 March 2022:

(1)   Cash sales revenue amounted to £41,160, of which £38,520 was in respect of standard rated sales and £2,640 was in respect of zero rated sales.

(2)   Sales invoices totalling £2,000 were issued in respect of credit sales revenue. This figure is exclusive of VAT, and the sales were all standard rated. Starfish Ltd states on its invoices that it offers all of its credit sale customers a 4% discount for payment within 14 days of the date of the sales invoice. 60% of the customers paid within this period.

(3)   In addition to the above sales revenue, Starfish Ltd sold its remaining inventory on 31 March 2022 for £28,800.

(4)   There were no purchases of inventory during the period.

(5)   Standard rated expenses amounted to £69,960, of which £4,320 was in respect of entertaining UK customers.

(6)   Starfish Ltd wrote off an impairment loss on 31 March 2022 in respect of a sales invoice (exclusive of VAT) that was due for payment on 8 August 2021. Output VAT of £384 was originally paid in respect of this sale.

(7)   On 31 March 2022 the company sold all of its machinery for £31,200 and a motor car for £9,600. The motor car was used 30% privately by a director of Starfish Ltd.

Unless otherwise stated, all of the above figures are inclusive of VAT where applicable.

Starfish Ltd did not use the cash accounting scheme for VAT.

280   **What is the amount of output tax on credit sales payable by Starfish Ltd for the quarter ended 31 March 2022?**

   ○   £384

   ○   £480

   ○   £390

   ○   £325   (2 marks)

---

281   **What is the amount of output tax, other than on credit sales, payable by Starfish Ltd for the quarter ended 31 March 2022?**

   ○   £16,420

   ○   £11,620

   ○   £11,220

   ○   £10,000   (2 marks)

---

282 What is the amount of input tax recoverable by Starfish Ltd for the quarter ended
31 March 2022?

    ○   £12,744

    ○   £11,324

    ○   £10,940

    ○   £11,276   (2 marks)

283 From which date would default interest be payable if Starfish Ltd is late in paying the VAT
for the quarter ended 31 March 2022?

    ○   30 April 2022

    ○   7 May 2022

    ○   14 May 2022

    ○   31 March 2022   (2 marks)

284 Which of the following would be the consequences for VAT if Starfish Ltd had instead sold
its entire business as a going concern to a single VAT registered purchaser?

    ○   Output VAT would have been due on the sale of the inventory or the sale of the
non-current assets but would be payable by the purchaser.

    ○   No output VAT would have been due on the sale of the inventory but would have
been due on the sale of the non-current assets.

    ○   No output VAT would have been due on the sale of the non-current assets but would
have been due on the sale of the inventory.

    ○   No output VAT would have been due on the sale of the inventory or the sale of the
non-current assets.   (2 marks)

(Total = 10 marks)

OT case – Greenzone Ltd (June 2013)

18 mins

The following scenario relates to Questions 285 to 289.

Greenzone Ltd owns 60% of Are Ltd, 40% of Be Ltd, 90% of Can Ltd and 70% of Doer Inc. All the companies are UK resident except for Doer Inc which also does not have a fixed establishment in the UK.

The following information is available in respect of Greenzone Ltd's value added tax (VAT) for the quarter ended 31 March 2022:

(1)   Output VAT of £38,210 was charged in respect of sales. This figure includes output VAT of £400 on a deposit received on 29 March 2022, which is in respect of a contract that is due to commence on 20 April 2022.

(2)   In addition to the above, Greenzone Ltd charged output VAT of £4,330 on sales to Can Ltd. Greenzone Ltd does not have group registration.

(3)   The managing director of Greenzone Ltd is provided with free fuel for his company motor car. The total cost of fuel for the motor car for the quarter is £500 and 60% of the total mileage is private mileage.

Greenzone Ltd wishes to use the fuel scale charge. The relevant quarterly scale charge is £334. Both these figures are inclusive of VAT.

(4)   Input VAT of £12,770 was incurred in respect of expenses (excluding the fuel in (3)). This figure includes the following input VAT:

	£
Entertaining UK customers	210
Entertaining overseas customers	139
Repainting the exterior of the company's office building	1,678
Extending the office building in order to create a new reception area	3,300

285   **What is the amount of output VAT charged on the sales in (1) and (2) for the quarter to 31 March 2022?**

○   £42,540

○   £38,210

○   £42,140

○   £37,810   (2 marks)

286   **What is the net amount of VAT payable or recoverable for the provision of the fuel for the managing director's company motor car in (3)?**

○   £23 payable

○   £33 recoverable

○   £56 payable

○   £27 recoverable   (2 marks)

287 What is the amount of input VAT that can be recovered on the expenses in (4)?

£ [   ]

(2 marks)

288 Identify, by clicking on the relevant boxes in the table below, which of the following companies (apart from Can Ltd) could be registered in a VAT group with Greenzone Ltd.

ARE LTD	BE LTD	DOER INC

(2 marks)

289 Which TWO of the following statements about VAT group registration are correct?

☐ Each VAT group must appoint a representative member which accounts for the group's output tax and input tax.

☐ Each VAT group must appoint a representative member which is solely liable for paying the group VAT liability.

☐ All eligible companies must be part of the group registration.

☐ Any supply of goods or services by a member of the group to another member of the group is disregarded for VAT purposes.

(2 marks)

(Total = 10 marks)

OT case – Long Ltd group (B) (June 2014) (amended)

18 mins

The following scenario relates to Questions 290 to 294.

Long Ltd owns 100% of the ordinary share capital of both Wind Ltd and Road Ltd. Long Ltd and Road Ltd run freight transport businesses, whilst Wind Ltd provides transport related insurance services.

Long Ltd, Wind Ltd and Road Ltd are not registered as a group for value added tax (VAT) purposes, but such a registration is being considered, with Long Ltd being the representative member.

The following VAT information is available for the quarter ended 31 March 2022:

Long Ltd

(1)   All of Long Ltd's sales are standard rated for VAT.

(2)   Output VAT of £52,640 was charged in respect of sales. This figure includes output VAT of £1,760 on a deposit received on 28 December 2021. The deposit was in respect of a contract which was completed on 6 January 2022, with a sales invoice being issued on 20 January 2022.

(3)   In addition to the above, Long Ltd also charged output VAT of £1,940 on sales to Wind Ltd and output VAT of £960 on sales to Road Ltd.

(4)   Input VAT of £14,720 was incurred in respect of expenses.

(5)   In addition to the above, Long Ltd has discovered that it has not been claiming for the input VAT of £18 which it has paid each month since 1 January 2016 for the hire of a photocopier.

Wind Ltd

(1)   All of Wind Ltd's sales are exempt from VAT.

(2)   Input VAT of £7,330 was incurred in respect of expenses. This includes input VAT of £1,940 incurred on purchases from Long Ltd.

Road Ltd

(1)   All of Road Ltd's sales are zero rated for VAT.

(2)   Road Ltd registered for VAT on 1 January 2022 and this is the company's first VAT return.

(3)   Input VAT of £3,120 was incurred in respect of expenses. This includes input VAT of £960 incurred on purchases from Long Ltd.

(4)   In addition to the above, Road Ltd incurred input VAT in respect of advertising expenditure as follows:

	£
April 2021	640
November 2021	380
	1,020

290   **What is the amount of output tax payable by Long Ltd for the quarter ended 31 March 2022?**

£ [   ]

(2 marks)

291   What is the amount of input tax recoverable by Long Ltd for the quarter ended 31 March 2022?

      ○   £14,720

      ○   £14,774

      ○   £14,882

      ○   £15,638

                                           (2 marks)

292   What is the amount of input tax recoverable by Wind Ltd for the quarter ended 31 March 2022?

      £ [   ]

                                           (2 marks)

293   What is the amount of input tax recoverable by Road Ltd for the quarter ended 31 March 2022?

      [▼]

      Pull down list:

      £3,120
      £4,140
      £3,500
      £3,760

                                             (2 marks)

294   Which TWO of the following statements about the Long Ltd group and VAT group registration are correct?

      ☐   If Wind Ltd and Road Ltd were both owned by the same individual they would not be able to be included in a group registration.

      ☐   Supplies of goods or services to Road Ltd from outside the group will be treated as a supply to Long Ltd.

      ☐   Each company in the Long Ltd group must join the VAT group if group registration is applied for.

      ☐   The supplies by Long Ltd to Wind Ltd and Road Ltd would be disregarded for VAT purposes.

                                             (2 marks)

                                             (Total = 10 marks)

OT case – Zim (June 2015) (amended)   18 mins

The following scenario relates to Questions 295 to 299.

Zim has been registered for value added tax (VAT) since 1 April 2007. The following information is available for the year ended 31 March 2022:

(1)   Sales invoices totalling £126,000 were issued, of which £115,200 were in respect of standard rated sales and £10,800 were in respect of zero rated sales. Zim's customers are all members of the general public.

(2)   Purchase invoices totalling £49,200 were received, of which £43,200 were in respect of standard rated purchases and £6,000 were in respect of zero rated purchases.

(3)   On 31 March 2022, Zim wrote off two impairment losses which were in respect of standard rated sales. The first impairment loss was for £780, and was in respect of a sales invoice which had been due for payment on 15 August 2021. The second impairment loss was for £660, and was in respect of a sales invoice which had been due for payment on 15 September 2021.

(4)   During the year ended 31 March 2022, Zim spent £2,600 on mobile telephone calls, of which 40% related to private calls.

(5)   During the year ended 31 March 2022, Zim spent £1,560 on entertaining customers, of which £240 was in respect of overseas customers.

All of the above figures are inclusive of VAT where applicable.

Zim does not use either the cash accounting scheme or the flat rate scheme. If he did use the flat rate scheme the relevant percentage for his business is 12%.

295   **What is the net amount of VAT payable on the sales in (1) and the purchases in (2)?**

£ [   ]   (2 marks)

296   **What is the amount of input VAT which can be recovered on the impairment losses in (3)?**

○   £0
○   £110
○   £130
○   £240   (2 marks)

297   **What is the amount of input VAT which can be recovered on the expenditure on the mobile phone calls in (4) and entertaining customers in (5)?**

	Mobile phone	Customers
○	£0	£220
○	£0	£40
○	£260	£220
○	£260	£40

(2 marks)

298 Match the thresholds for Zim to be able to join and to be required to leave the flat rate scheme.

Taxable turnover excluding VAT not more than £150,000 in next 12 months

Total turnover including VAT not more than £230,000 in next 12 months

Taxable turnover including VAT not more than £150,000 in next 12 months

Total turnover excluding VAT more than £230,000 in previous 12 months

Join

Leave

(2 marks)

299 How much VAT would Zim have paid in the year to 31 March 2022 if he had been in the flat rate scheme for the whole of that year?

Pull down list:

£15,120
£13,860
£13,824
£9,216

(2 marks)

(Total = 10 marks)

OT case – Smart Ltd (September/December 2015) (amended)

18 mins

The following scenario relates to Questions 300 to 304.

Smart Ltd commenced trading on 1 September 2021. The company's sales for the first four months of trading were as follows:

2021	£
September	26,000
October	47,000
November	134,000
December	113,000

On 1 November 2021, the company signed a contract valued at £86,000 for completion during November 2021.

All of the above figures are stated exclusive of value added tax (VAT). Smart Ltd only supplies services and all of the company's supplies are standard rated.

Smart Ltd allows its customers 60 days' credit when paying for services, and it is concerned that some customers will default on the payment of their debts. The company pays its purchase invoices as soon as they are received.

Smart Ltd does not use either the VAT cash accounting scheme or the annual accounting scheme.

Smart Ltd is concerned about the penalties that could be charged if it makes a careless error in its VAT return resulting in underpaid VAT.

300 **Match the dates from which Smart Ltd was required to register for VAT and by when it was required to notify HM Revenue & Customs (HMRC) of the registration.**

1 November 2021		30 December 2021
30 November 2021		31 December 2021

Register	
Notification	

(2 marks)

301 **Identify, by clicking on the relevant boxes in the table below, which of the following statements about how and when Smart Ltd will have to submit its quarterly VAT returns and pay any related VAT liability are true or false.**

Smart Ltd can file its VAT returns by entering figures manually on HMRC's website.	TRUE	FALSE
Smart Ltd can choose whether to pay the VAT which is due electronically or by cheque.	TRUE	FALSE
The deadline for paying any VAT which is due is one month after the end of each quarter.	TRUE	FALSE
The deadline for filing the VAT return is one month and seven days after the end of each quarter.	TRUE	FALSE

(2 marks)

302 **Which TWO of the following statements about the tax point for Smart Ltd's supplies of services are correct?**

☐ The basic tax point is the date on which the invoice is issued.

☐ The basic tax point is the date on which services are completed.

☐ If a customer pays for services before the basic tax point, the payment date will be the tax point.

☐ If a customer pays for services after the basic tax point, the payment date will be the tax point.   (2 marks)

303 **Which TWO of the following statements are advantages for Smart Ltd to use the VAT cash accounting scheme?**

(1)   The scheme will provide automatic relief for an impairment loss should a customer default on the payment of a debt.

(2)   Only one VAT return will be required each year so there are fewer occasions to trigger a default surcharge.

(3)   There will be reduced VAT administration as Smart Ltd will not be required to issue invoices to its customers.

(4)   Output VAT will be accounted for 60 days later than at present, because the scheme will result in the tax point becoming the date when payment is received from customers.

○ 1 and 2

○ 2 and 3

○ 1 and 4

○ 2 and 4   (2 marks)

304 **What is the maximum amount of penalty that could be charged by HMRC if Smart Ltd makes a careless error in its VAT return resulting in underpaid VAT and the minimum penalty that could be charged as a result of a subsequent prompted disclosure?**

	Maximum penalty	*Minimum penalty for prompted disclosure*
○	70% of the VAT underpaid	15% of the VAT underpaid
○	70% of the VAT underpaid	0% of the VAT underpaid
○	30% of the VAT underpaid	15% of the VAT underpaid
○	30% of the VAT underpaid	0% of the VAT underpaid (2 marks)

(Total = 10 marks)

OT case – Thidar (March/June 2019)

18 mins

The following scenario relates to Questions 305–309.

You should assume that today's date is 25 April 2022.

Thidar commenced trading as a builder on 1 January 2021. She voluntarily registered for value added tax (VAT) on 1 January 2021.

Sales

Thidar's sales for the first 15 months of trading have been:

Month	Standard rated £	Zero rated £	Month	Standard rated £	Zero rated £
1	3,400	0	9	8,800	6,300
2	0	1,900	10	2,900	7,300
3	5,700	2,100	11	0	0
4	6,800	0	12	0	2,600
5	9,500	1,200	13	2,800	900
6	7,900	2,200	14	3,200	1,700
7	0	3,700	15	22,200	3,600
8	12,100	0			

Pre-registration expenditure

Thidar paid for the following standard rated services prior to registering for VAT on 1 January 2021:

Date	Cost of service £	Description
10 June 2020	1,800	Advertisement for the building business
8 December 2020	300	Advertisement for the building business

Both figures are exclusive of VAT. Thidar paid for the advertisement of £300 by cash, and she does not have any evidence of this transaction (such as a VAT invoice).

VAT return for the quarter ended 30 September 2021

Thidar's VAT return for the quarter ended 30 September 2021 was filed by the submission deadline of 7 November 2021 and the related VAT liability was paid on time.

However, on 15 February 2022, Thidar discovered that the amount of VAT paid was understated by £1,200 as a result of incorrectly treating a standard rated sale as zero rated. Given that the underpayment does not exceed £10,000, Thidar is permitted to correct this error on her VAT return for the quarter ended 31 March 2022, and this is what she will do. Thidar will file this VAT return by the submission deadline of 7 May 2022 and pay the related VAT liability (including the underpaid £1,200) on time.

VAT return for the quarter ended 31 March 2022

Thidar is currently completing her VAT return for the quarter ended 31 March 2022 and is unsure as to how much input VAT is non-deductible in respect of two items:

(1)   During the quarter ended 31 March 2022, Thidar spent £800 on entertaining UK customers.

(2)   During the quarter ended 31 March 2022, Thidar leased a motor car at a cost of £700. The motor car is used by Thidar and 75% of the mileage is for private journeys.

Both figures are exclusive of VAT.

305   In which month did Thidar exceed the VAT threshold for compulsory registration?

      ○   Month 14

      ○   Month 15

      ○   Month 13

      ○   Not yet exceeded

                                                           (2 marks)

306   What amount of pre-registration input VAT was Thidar able to recover in respect of expenditure incurred prior to registering for VAT on 1 January 2021?

      ○   £360

      ○   £60

      ○   £420

      ○   £0

                                                            (2 marks)

307   Within what period must Thidar issue a VAT invoice after making a standard rated supply, and for how long must these VAT invoices then normally be retained by Thidar?

Option	VAT invoices	Retention
1	Within 14 days	Four years
2	Within 30 days	Six years
3	Within 30 days	Four years
4	Within 14 days	Six years

      ○   Option 1

      ○   Option 2

      ○   Option 3

      ○   Option 4

                                                            (2 marks)

308   Why will VAT default (or penalty) interest not be charged on Thidar's underpayment of VAT of £1,200 for the quarter ended 30 September 2021?

      ○   Because Thidar corrected the error within 12 months

      ○   Because the error was not deliberate

      ○   Because separate disclosure of the VAT underpayment was not required

      ○   Because Thidar paid the underpayment of £1,200 by the submission deadline of 7 May 2022

                                                            (2 marks)

309   For the quarter ended 31 March 2022, what is the amount of non-deductible input VAT in respect of entertaining UK customers and the leasing cost of the motor car?

Option	Entertaining UK customers	Leasing cost
1	£0	£105
2	£160	£105
3	£160	£70
4	£0	£70

○   Option 1

○   Option 2

○   Option 3

○   Option 4   (2 marks)

(Total = 10 marks)

310 Jogger Ltd (B) (December 2008) (amended)   18 mins

Jogger Ltd is a manufacturing company and has been registered for value added tax (VAT) since 1 April 2014. From that date until 30 June 2020 the company's VAT returns were all submitted on time. Since 1 July 2020 the company's VAT returns have been submitted as follows:

Quarter ended	VAT paid	Submitted
	£	
30 September 2020	42,700	One month late
31 December 2020	41,200	On time
31 March 2021	38,900	One month late
30 June 2021	28,300	On time
30 September 2021	49,100	On time
31 December 2021	63,800	On time
31 March 2022	89,100	Two months late

Jogger Ltd always pays any VAT that is due at the same time as the related return is submitted.

Required

(a)   State, giving appropriate reasons, the default surcharge consequences arising from Jogger Ltd's submission of its VAT returns for the quarter ended 30 September 2020 to the quarter ended 31 March 2022 inclusive, at the times stated. You may assume that Jogger Ltd is not a small business for the purposes of the default surcharge regime.   **(6 marks)**

(b)   Advise Jogger Ltd why it might be beneficial to use the VAT annual accounting scheme, and state the conditions that it will have to satisfy before being permitted to do so.   **(4 marks)**

(Total = 10 marks)

311 Flick (June 2012) (amended)

18 mins

On 1 January 2022, Flick commenced in partnership with Art running a small cinema.

The partnership voluntarily registered for value added tax (VAT) on 1 January 2022, and immediately began using the flat rate scheme to calculate the amount of VAT payable. The relevant flat rate scheme percentage for the partnership's trade is 12%.

For the quarter ended 31 March 2022 the partnership had standard rated sales of £59,700, and these were all made to members of the general public. For the same period standard rated expenses amounted to £27,300. Both figures are stated inclusive of VAT.

The partnership has two private boxes in its cinema that can be booked on a special basis by privileged customers. Such customers can book the boxes up to two months in advance, at which time they have to pay a 25% deposit. An invoice is then given to the customer on the day of the screening of the film, with payment of the balance of 75% required within seven days. For VAT purposes, the renting out of the cinema boxes is a supply of services.

Required

(a) Explain whether or not it was beneficial for the partnership to have used the VAT flat rate scheme for the quarter ended 31 March 2022.

   Notes

   1   Your answer should be supported by appropriate calculations.

   2   You should ignore the 1% reduction from the flat rate that is available during the first year of VAT registration. **(3 marks)**

(b) Explain whether or not it was financially beneficial for the partnership to have voluntarily registered for VAT from 1 January 2022.

   Note. Your answer should be supported by appropriate calculations. **(3 marks)**

(c) Advise the partnership as to when it should account for output VAT on the renting out of its private boxes to privileged customers. **(4 marks)**

_____

(Total = 10 marks)

312 Richard (December 2013) (amended)

On 6 April 2021, Richard commenced in self-employment, running a restaurant.

Richard's sales since the commencement of trading have been as follows:

April to July 2021	£10,500 per month
August to November 2021	£15,000 per month
December 2021 to March 2022	£21,500 per month

These figures are stated exclusive of value added tax (VAT). Richard's sales are all standard rated.

As a trainee Chartered Certified Accountant you have advised Richard in writing that he should be registered for VAT, but he has refused to register because he thinks his net profit is insufficient to cover the additional cost which would be incurred.

Required

(a)   Explain from what date Richard was required to be compulsorily registered for VAT and the VAT implications of continuing to trade after this date without registering.

  Note. You are not expected to explain the VAT penalties arising from late VAT registration.

  (4 marks)

(b)   Briefly explain from an ethical viewpoint the issues you, as a trainee Chartered Certified Accountant, should consider in order for your firm to deal with Richard's refusal to register for VAT.

  (2 marks)

(c)   State the circumstances in which a trader can issue a simplified (or less detailed) VAT invoice, when such an invoice should be issued, and FIVE pieces of information which such an invoice must show where the supply is entirely standard rated. **(4 marks)**

(Total = 10 marks)

313 Clueless Ltd (December 2012) (amended)   18 mins

Clueless Ltd is a manufacturing company. It is registered for value added tax (VAT), but currently does not use any of the special VAT schemes. The company has annual standard rated sales of £1,200,000 and annual standard rated expenses of £550,000. Both these figures are exclusive of VAT and are likely to remain the same for the foreseeable future. Clueless Ltd is up to date with all of its tax returns, including those for corporation tax, PAYE and VAT. It is also up to date with its corporation tax, PAYE and VAT payments. However, the company often incurs considerable overtime costs due to its employees working late in order to meet tax return filing deadlines.

Clueless Ltd pays its expenses on a cash basis, but allows customers two months' credit when paying for sales. The company does not have any impairment losses.

Clueless Ltd is planning to purchase some new machinery at a cost of £22,000 (exclusive of VAT). The machinery will be purchased from an overseas supplier. Clueless Ltd is not a regular importer and so is unsure of the VAT treatment for this purchase.

Required

(a)   Explain why Clueless Ltd is entitled to use both the VAT cash accounting scheme and the VAT annual accounting scheme, and why it will probably be beneficial for the company to use both schemes.
(6 marks)

(b)   Explain when and how Clueless Ltd will have to account for VAT in respect of the new machinery:

(i)   If they choose not to use postponed accounting

(ii)   if they do choose to use postponed accounting
(4 marks)

(Total = 10 marks)

314 Garfield (March/June 2016)

Garfield has been registered for valued added tax (VAT) since 1 April 2013. Garfield has previously completed his VAT returns himself, but for the quarter ended 31 March 2022 there are some items for which he is unsure of the correct VAT treatment.

Garfield's partly completed VAT computation for the quarter ended 31 March 2022 is shown below. All of the completed sections of the computation are correct, with the omissions marked as outstanding (O/S).

	Note	£
Output VAT		
Sales (all standard rated)		22,500
Discounted sale	1	O/S
Equipment	2	O/S
Fuel scale charge		414
Input VAT		
Purchases (all standard rated)		(11,200)
Motor car (purchased on 1 January 2022)		0
Equipment	2	O/S
Impairment losses	3	O/S
Entertaining – UK customers		O
– Overseas customers	4	O/S
Motor expenses	5	O/S
VAT payable		O/S

Unless otherwise stated, all of the figures in the following notes are stated exclusive of VAT.

Notes

1   *Discounted sale*

    On 10 February 2022, a sales invoice for £4,300 was issued by Garfield in respect of a standard rated supply. To encourage this previously late paying customer to pay promptly, Garfield offered a 10% discount for payment within 14 days of the date of the sales invoice. The customer paid within the 14-day period.

    This invoice has not been taken into account in calculating the output VAT figure of £22,500, and this is the only sale for which Garfield has offered a prompt payment discount.

2   *Equipment*

    During the quarter ended 31 March 2022, Garfield acquired some new equipment at a cost of £12,400 from an overseas supplier.

3   *Impairment losses*

On 31 March 2022, Garfield wrote off three impairment losses. Details are as follows:

Amount	Invoice date	Payment due date
£1,400	30 July 2021	29 August 2021
£2,700	12 September 2021	12 October 2021
£1,900	4 October 2021	3 November 2021

4   *Entertaining*

During the quarter ended 31 March 2022, Garfield spent £960 on entertaining overseas customers. This figure is inclusive of VAT.

5   *Motor expenses*

The motor car purchased on 1 January 2022 is used by Garfield 60% for business mileage. During the quarter ended 31 March 2022, Garfield spent £1,008 on repairs to the motor car and £660 on fuel for both his business and private mileage. Both of these figures are inclusive of VAT.

Additional information

Garfield does not use the cash accounting scheme, the annual accounting scheme or the flat rate scheme, but has read that the use of these schemes can be beneficial for small businesses such as his.

Garfield's VAT exclusive annual turnover is currently £450,000, and this is expected to steadily decrease over the coming years. He pays for most of his purchases and expenses on a cash basis, but allows many of his customers 30 days' credit when paying for sales.

Required

(a)   Calculate the amount of value added tax (VAT) payable by Garfield for the quarter ended 31 March 2022.   **(7 marks)**

(b)   State which VAT schemes Garfield is currently permitted to use, and explain, with supporting reasons, which **ONE** of the available schemes would appear to be the most beneficial for him to use.

Notes

1   Your answer should be confined to the information given in the question.

2   You are not expected to explain how any of the schemes operate.   **(3 marks)**

(Total = 10 marks)

315 Zhi (March/June 2017)

You should assume that today's date is 15 December 2021.

Zhi has been self-employed since 2001, preparing accounts to 31 December. On 1 December 2021, Zhi purchased a new freehold warehouse for £164,000 for use in his business, but this purchase has resulted in Zhi having cash flow problems. He has various tax payments becoming due over the next two months, and would like to reduce or postpone these payments as much as possible.

Income tax and national insurance contributions (NICs)

Zhi's income tax liabilities and class 4 NICs for the tax years 2019/20, 2020/21 and 2021/22 are, or are forecast to be:

	2019/20	2020/21	2021/22
	£	£	£
Income tax liability	25,200	27,600	18,000
Class 4 NICs	4,084	4,204	3,724

Zhi has not made any claims to reduce his payments on account.

Capital gains tax (CGT)

Zhi has a CGT liability of £12,740 becoming due for payment on 31 January 2022. This is in respect of a freehold office building which was sold for £210,000 on 10 December 2020, resulting in a chargeable gain of £76,000. The office building had always been used for business purposes by Zhi.

Zhi is a higher rate taxpayer. No claim has been made for rollover relief.

Value added tax (VAT)

Zhi has forecast that he will have to pay VAT of £20,200 on 7 February 2022 to HM Revenue & Customs (HMRC) in respect of the VAT quarter ended 31 December 2021.

On 12 December 2021, Zhi despatched goods relating to an exceptionally large credit sale of standard rated goods of £45,600 (inclusive of VAT). He has not yet issued a sales invoice for this sale.

Because the customer is unlikely to pay until 28 February 2022, Zhi is considering not issuing a sales invoice until 1 February 2022.

PAYE and NICs

Zhi will have to pay PAYE and NICs of £5,724 electronically on 22 January 2022 to HMRC in respect of his two employees for the tax month running from 6 December 2021 to 5 January 2022.

This includes amounts for bonuses which Zhi was planning to pay to his two employees on 1 January 2022, but could delay payment until 10 January 2022. The bonuses are in respect of the year ended 31 December 2021, and they will be treated as being received on whichever is the date of payment.

The first employee has a gross annual salary of £20,000 and is to be paid a bonus of £1,500. The second employee has a gross annual salary of £55,000 and is to be paid a bonus of £5,000.

Required

(a)   Calculate the amount by which Zhi can claim to reduce his self-assessment income tax and NICs due for payment on 31 January 2022 without incurring interest or penalties.

(2 marks)

(b)   Calculate the amount by which Zhi's CGT liability due for payment on 31 January 2022 will be reduced if he makes a claim for rollover relief based on the warehouse purchased on 1 December 2021 for £164,000.

(3 marks)

(c)   Explain whether Zhi can reduce the amount of VAT payable on 7 February 2022 by not issuing a sales invoice for the credit sale of £45,600 until 1 February 2022, and, if so, by how much the payment will be reduced.

(2 marks)

(d)   Calculate the amount by which Zhi's PAYE and NICs due on 22 January 2022 will be reduced if he delays the payment of employee bonuses until 10 January 2022, and state when the postponed amount will be payable.

Note. Your calculations should be based on annual income tax and NIC thresholds.

(3 marks)

(Total = 10 marks)

Answers

OTQ bank – The UK tax system and its administration 1

1   It is a progressive tax.

    It is a redistributive tax.

    Inheritance tax is a progressive tax as the amount of tax payable as a proportion of the transfers increases as the transfers get bigger (the amount covered by the nil rate band is charged at 0% and the remainder at 20% or 40%). It is also a redistributive tax as it redistributes wealth.

    Inheritance tax is a direct tax and it is not an environmental tax.

2   A Statutory Instrument

    An Act of Parliament

    Statutes (Acts of Parliament) and Statutory Instruments have legal force.

    HMRC publications such as Revenue and Customs Briefs and Extra Statutory Concessions do not have legal force.

3   By the Upper Tribunal

    The Upper Tribunal deals with complex cases which either involve an important issue of tax law or a large financial sum.

4   Notify by 5 October 2022, payment by 31 January 2023

    The chargeable gain arises in the tax year 2021/22 and so Daren must notify HMRC of his chargeability within six months from the end of the tax year. The tax liability must be paid by 31 January following the end of the tax year.

5   £742

    Potential Lost Revenue is the tax payable of £2,120 (40% × £5,300).

    The minimum penalty for a prompted, deliberate, but not concealed error is 35% × PLR which is

    £742.

    The answer £1,484 uses 70% which is the maximum penalty for a deliberate, but not concealed error. The answer £424 uses 20% which is the minimum penalty for an unprompted deliberate, but not concealed error.

    The answer £1,855 uses £5,300 as the Potential Lost Revenue.

6   £1,441

    Due date 1 April 2022, paid 31 July 2022 so four months late. Interest is

    4/12 × 2.6% × £166,250   £1,441

    The answer £360 assumes the due date is 1 July 2021 so that one month's interest is due. The answer £2,161 assumes the due date is 31 January 2021 so that six months' interest is due. The answer £4,323 is one whole year of interest.

7   Year ended 31 December 2024

    The profit threshold for being a large company is £1,500,000/2 = £750,000 since there is one related 51% group company. This threshold is first exceeded in the year ended 31 December 2023 but a company is not required to pay its corporation tax by instalments in the first year that it is large unless its profits exceed £10,000,000, as reduced by related 51% group companies. Mammoth Ltd is also a large company in the year ended 31 December 2024 and so must pay its corporation tax liability by quarterly instalments for that year for the first time.

8

Value added tax	NEITHER TYPE		
Inheritance tax		CAPITAL TAX	
National insurance contributions			REVENUE TAX

9   £406,600

	£
Unconnected company	5,200
Group dividend	0
Non-51% group dividend	1,400
Taxable total profits	400,000
Profits	406,600

10   Paper return 31 October 2022, Online tax return 31 January 2023

OTQ bank – The UK tax system and its administration 2

11

Submission	31 January 2023

Notification	30 April 2024

As the return is filed after the due filing date, the notification must be made by the quarter day following the first anniversary of the actual filing date.

12   £5,159

	£
Income tax £(12,500 – 10,000 payments on account)	2,500
Class 2 NIC	159
Class 4 NIC £(2,500 – 2,000 payments on account)	500
Capital gains tax	2,000
Amount to pay on 31 January 2023	5,159

The answer £5,000 does not include the Class 2 NIC. The answer £4,000 assumes that payments on account are made also for Class 2 NIC and capital gains tax. The answer £4,159 assumes that payments on account are made also for capital gains tax.

13   £27

£10,000 is paid by the due date of 1 January 2023. The balance of £12,400 is one month late so the interest on late paid tax is £12,400 × 2.60% × 1/12 = £27.

14   £50,000 due on 14 May 2022

The amount of each of the first three instalments is 3/10 × £500,000 = £150,000. The final instalment is the remaining liability of £500,000 – (3 × £150,000) = £50,000, and is due on the 14th day of the 4th month of the next accounting period.

15   £100

There is a £100 penalty for late return which is submitted within three months of the due date (here 12 months after the end of the period to which the return relates).

16   Asset 1 only.

Lying about a disposal date so that a gain is declared a year later amounts to tax evasion, which is illegal. Delaying a disposal until the next tax year is a legitimate example of tax planning.

17   10%

The due date for payment was 31 January 2022. The penalty date is 30 days after the due date for the tax. There is a penalty of 5% of the unpaid tax for failing to pay by the penalty date plus a further penalty of 5% of the unpaid tax as the payment is more than five months after the penalty date but not more than 11 months after the penalty date.

18   5 April 2042

> **Examining team's comments.** This was a straightforward administration question, requiring candidates to identify the latest date by which HMRC can raise a discovery assessment where a taxpayer has made a deliberate error in their tax return. Where deliberate error is involved, the time limit for HMRC to raise a discovery assessment is 20 years from the end of the tax year, in this case 5 April 2042.
>
> The majority of candidates selected 5 April 2023, suggesting that they had confused the deadline for a raising a discovery assessment with the deadline for notifying the taxpayer of a compliance check. 5 April 2026 is the basic deadline for issuing a discovery assessment, and 5 April 2028 is the deadline for issuing a discovery assessment where the taxpayer has made a careless error.
>
> Candidates are reminded to devote sufficient attention to tax administration in their revision.

19   Make a determination

If notice has been served on a taxpayer to submit a return but the return is not submitted by the due filing date, an officer of HMRC may make a determination, to the best of their information and belief, of the amounts liable to income tax and CGT and of the tax due, within four years of the end of the relevant tax year.

> **Examining team's comments.** This question tested candidates' knowledge of how HMRC can make a determination of the amount of tax that a taxpayer is liable to. Perhaps not surprisingly, more than 40% of candidates opted for 'start a compliance check enquiry into the return' – possibly because a compliance check was the most well-known of the options. However, the correct answer (a determination) was the second most popular choice. Although this style of question can be answered very quickly, it does not mean that it doesn't warrant any thought. Realising that a compliance check by its very nature involves a submitted return, could have easily ruled this option out.

20   £49

OTQ bank – The UK tax system and its administration 3

21   The returns for the year ended 31 December 2021 and the period ended 31 March 2022 must both be filed by 31 March 2023.

22   1 March 2022

23   £1,700

24   30 April 2023

> **Examining team's comments.** If the taxpayer amends the return after the due filing date, as in the case of Petula, then the time limit for a compliance check is extended to the quarter day following the first anniversary of the date the amendment was filed. Since Petula amended her return on 29 March 2022, this is within the quarter ended 30 April 2022 and so the time limit for the compliance check is 30 April 2023.
>
> 31 January 2023 is the first anniversary of the due filing date.
>
> 20 September 2022 is the first anniversary of the actual filing date.
>
> 29 March 2023 is the first anniversary of the date that the amended return was filed.
>
> Candidates' answers were mixed, with 30 April 2023 being the least popular answer, suggesting that most candidates weren't prepared for a question on this topic.

25   Partnerships must file a separate return and account for each partner's tax through this return

> **Examining team's comments.** The answer which is false is the second option. This is because each partner must include their share of partnership profits on their own personal tax return, not the partnership tax return. The third option was the most commonly chosen. This suggests that candidates' knowledge of tax administration could be improved.

OT case – Domingo and Fargo

> **Workbook references.** Chapter 17 deals with self-assessment for individuals.
>
> **Top tips.** Note the difference between record keeping requirements for taxpayers in business and those not in business.
>
> **Easy marks.** There were easy marks in question 26 for the requirements for filing tax returns.

26   Domingo 31 October 2022, Fargo 31 January 2023

27   Domingo 31 January 2024, Fargo 31 January 2028

Domingo was not in business during 2021/22, so his records must be retained until one year after 31 January following the tax year, which is 31 January 2024.

Fargo was in business during 2021/22, so all of his records (both business and non-business) must be retained until five years after 31 January following the tax year, which is 31 January 2028.

28   £3,000

29   Balancing payment and first payment on account 31 January 2023, second payment on account 31 July 2023

30   Interest £1,800 × 2.60% × 4/12 = £16

The answer £47 is the interest for a whole year.

Penalty £1,800 @ 5% = £90 (balancing payment not more than five months after the penalty date).

OT case – Ernest

Workbook references. Self-assessment for individuals is covered in Chapter 17. Ethics are covered in Chapter 1.

Top tips. If your firm ceases to act for a client, it must notify HMRC that it has ceased to act but not the reasons for doing so.

Easy marks. The definitions of tax evasion and tax avoidance required for question 31 should be well known.

31

Tax evasion is illegal	TRUE	
Both tax evasion and tax avoidance are illegal		FALSE
Tax avoidance is legal but may fail if challenged in the courts by HMRC.	TRUE	
Tax evasion always involves providing HM Revenue & Customs with false information		FALSE

Tax evasion does not necessarily involve providing HM Revenue & Customs (HMRC) with false information. It could include this situation where Ernest is evading tax by not providing HMRC with information to which it is entitled.

32   Ernest should be advised to disclose details of the capital gain to HMRC. If Ernest does not disclose the gain to HMRC, your firm would be obliged to report under the money laundering regulations.

Your firm should also consider ceasing to act for Ernest. If it does cease to act, your firm should notify HMRC that it no longer acts for him although your firm should not provide any reason for this.

33   £12,600

The maximum penalty for an error which is deliberate but not concealed is 70% of potential lost revenue which is £18,000 × 70% = £12,600.

34   £6,300

The minimum penalty for prompted disclosure of an error which is deliberate but not concealed is 35% of potential lost revenue which is £18,000 × 35% = £6,300.

35   £234

The due date for payment was 31 January 2022 so the payment is six months late. The interest payable is therefore £18,000 × 2.60% × 6/12 = £234.

OT case – Thai Curry Ltd

Workbook references. Chapter 23 deals with corporation tax administration. Chapter 17 contains material on the common penalty regime for errors.

Top tips. Remember that some elements of tax administration are the same for both individuals and companies such as penalties for errors. However, you need to watch out for circumstances where they are different such as the penalties for late filing.

Easy marks. Make sure you know due dates for returns and tax payments.

36   31 March 2023

The CT return must be submitted one year after the end of the period of account ie by 31 March 2023.

37   £3,462

As the return is more than three months late the fixed penalty is £200. As the return is more than six months late there is also a tax geared penalty of 10% × unpaid tax, ie £32,624 × 10% = £3,262. The total amount of penalties is therefore £(200 + 3,262) = £3,462.

38   £32,624 on 1 January 2023

As the company is not large since its profits are below the profit threshold of £1,500,000 it must pay its corporation tax by nine months and one day after the accounting period, ie by 1 January 2023.

39   An internal review is a less costly and more effective way to resolve disputes informally than a formal appeal.

HMRC must usually carry out the review within 45 days.

An internal review is a less costly and more effective way to resolve disputes informally than a formal appeal and HMRC must usually carry out the review within 45 days. The internal review will be made by an objective HMRC review officer not previously connected with the case. After the review conclusion is notified, the company has 30 days to appeal to the Tax Tribunal.

40

Complex track	Upper tier

Standard track	First tier

41 John

Workbook references. Self-assessment for individuals is covered in Chapter 17. The UK tax system is the subject of Chapter 1.

Top tips. There are a number of penalties based on Potential Lost Revenue so you need to be able to explain what this is.

Easy marks. There were some easy marks for the date for notification and the date by which the compliance check needed to be started.

Marking scheme

				Marks
(a)	(i)	Date for notification	1	
		Maximum penalty	1	
		Minimum penalty	1	
				3
	(ii)	Compliance check notification date	1	
		Random basis	1	
		Other reasons	1	
				3
(b)	(i)	Saving		1
	(ii)	Charitable support		1
	(iii)	Capital gains reliefs	1	
		Plant and machinery	1	
				2
				10

(a) (i) **Notification of chargeability**

John should have given notice to HM Revenue & Customs (HMRC) of his chargeability to income tax for 2020/21 by 5 October 2021.

The maximum penalty for careless late notification is 30% of the Potential Lost Revenue (PLR) to HMRC which will be John's tax payable on the return for 2020/21.

However, if John tells HMRC of his failure to notify within 12 months and John has no reason to believe HMRC has discovered, or is about to discover, the error (unprompted disclosure) as appears to be the case here, the penalty can be reduced by HMRC to 0%.

(ii) **Compliance check**

If HMRC intends to carry out a compliance check enquiry into John's 2020/21 tax return, it will have to notify him by the first anniversary of the actual filing date.

HMRC has the right to carry out a compliance check enquiry as regards the completeness and accuracy of any return and some returns are selected for a compliance check enquiry at random.

Other returns are selected for a particular reason; for example, if HMRC believes that there has been an underpayment of tax due to the taxpayer's failure to comply with tax legislation.

(b) (i) Saving is encouraged by offering individuals tax incentives such as income tax and capital gains tax exemptions on individual savings accounts and income tax relief on pension contributions.

(ii) Charitable support is encouraged by giving individuals income tax relief on donations made through the gift aid scheme or by payroll deduction.

(iii) Entrepreneurs are encouraged to build their own businesses through various capital gains tax reliefs such as business asset disposal relief.

Investment in plant and machinery is encouraged through capital allowances.

42 Sugar plc

Workbook references. Chapter 19 deals with computing the corporation tax liability. Chapter 23 includes payment of tax by companies.

Top tips. The rules on related 51% group companies are highly examinable and could be tested as an objective test question or in a constructed response question.

Easy marks. The calculation of the corporation tax liability in part (c) was straightforward.

Marking scheme

		Marks
(a)	Definition	1
	Honey plc	½
	Molasses plc	½
	Treacle plc	1
		3
(b)	*Year ended 31 March 2022*	
	Profit limit	½
	Taxable total profits	½
	Dividends	1
	Profits, therefore large	½
	Year ended 31 March 2023	
	Taxable total profits = profits, therefore large	½
		3

(c)   *Year ended 31 March 2022*
      Corporation tax   ½
      Date payable   ½
      Year ended 31 March 2023
      Corporation tax   ½
      Instalments   ½
      Dates payable   2
                                                               ___
                                                                4
                                                               ___
                                                               10
                                                               ___

(a)   Company B is a related 51% group company of another company A, if A is a 51% subsidiary
      of B (B owns more than 50% of A's ordinary shares directly or indirectly) or B is a 51%
      subsidiary of A or both A and B are 51% subsidiaries of another company. Honey plc is not
      a related 51% group company of Sugar plc because Sugar plc only directly owns 45% of
      the ordinary shares of Honey plc. Molasses plc is a related 51% group company of Sugar
      plc because Sugar plc directly owns 75% of the ordinary shares of Molasses plc. Treacle plc
      is a related 51% group company of Sugar plc because Sugar plc indirectly owns 75% × 70%
      = 52.5% of the ordinary shares of Treacle plc.

(b)   *Year ended 31 March 2022*

      Sugar plc has two related 51% group companies (Molasses plc and Treacle plc) at the end
      of the previous accounting period. The profit limit is therefore £1,500,000/3 = £500,000.
      Sugar plc's profits for the year to 31 March 2022 are:

	£
Taxable total profits	470,000
Dividends from non-group companies	50,000
Profits	520,000

      Sugar plc is therefore a large company in the year to 31 March 2022.

      Year ended 31 March 2023

      The profit limit is the same and Sugar plc's taxable total profits of £600,000 are also
      its profits for these purposes. Sugar plc is therefore a large company in the year to
      31 March 2023.

(c)   *Year ended 31 March 2022*

	£
Corporation tax liability	
£470,000 × 19%	89,300

      Since this is the first year that Sugar plc is a large company, its corporation tax liability will
      be due in one amount on 1 January 2023.

      Year ended 31 March 2023

	£
Corporation tax liability	
£600,000 × 19%	114,000

      This is payable in four equal instalments of £28,500. The instalments will be due on
      14 October 2022, 14 January 2023, 14 April 2023 and 14 July 2023.

BPP
LEARNING
MEDIA

OTQ bank – Income tax and NIC liabilities 1

43   90

> **Examining team's comments.** This question examines the third automatic non-UK residency test. For an individual to meet this test, and therefore be treated as automatically not resident in the UK for the tax year 2021/22, they would have to work full-time overseas and spend less than 91 days in the UK. Therefore, because Hana worked full-time in Egypt throughout 2021/22, he will be treated as automatically not resident in the UK for the tax year as long as he spends no more than 90 days in the UK.
>
> The correct answer is therefore 90, however, answer option 15 was most commonly chosen. This would be the correct answer using the sufficient ties tests. However, the sufficient ties tests are only used to determine residence status if none of the automatic non-UK residence tests (and none of the automatic UK residence tests) is met.
>
> This suggests that candidates may not have been familiar enough with the residence tests and the procedure to determine residence.

44   Premium bond prizes

Dividends on shares held in an Individual Savings Account

Interest on an NS&I Investment account and interest on UK government stocks ('gilts') are taxable as savings income.

45   £2,500

	£
£3,000 @ 20%	600
£(5,000 – 3,000) = £2,000 @ 0% (starting rate band)	0
£1,000 @ 0% (savings income nil rate band)	0
£(12,500 – 2,000 – 1,000) = £9,500 @ 20%	1,900
Tax liability	2,500

The answer £2,900 does not apply the starting rate band. The answer £2,700 does not apply the savings income nil rate band. The answer £3,100 applies 20% to all income.

46   £2,448

	£
Taxable income	13,500
Tax	
£13,500 × 20%	2,700
Less transferred personal allowance tax reducer £1,260 × 20%	(252)
Income tax liability	2,448

The answer £186 assumes that Delia can transfer her full personal allowance to Mike. The answer £1,440 deducts £1,260 as a tax reducer. The answer £2,700 is Mike's income tax liability with no transfer.

47 £3,300

			£
Use	£3,600 × 20%		720
Gift	Current market value	£1,000	
	or		
	Original value	£3,600	
	less use:		
	2020/21 £720 × 5/12	(300)	
	2021/22	(720)	
		£2,580	
	The greater amount is taken		2,580
	Total benefits 2021/22		3,300

Note. That the value of the asset when first provided to any employee is used rather than the value when first provided to John.

The answer £2,880 assumes the first year of provision was taxed in full. The answer £1,720 uses the lower value for the gift rather than the higher value. The answer £1,833 uses the value of £2,000 when the asset was provided to John.

48 £58,960

	£
£(37,700 + 10,000) = £47,700 @ 20%	9,540
£(150,000 + 10,000) = £(160,000 − 47,700) = £112,300 @ 40%	44,920
£(170,000 − 160,000) = £10,000 @ 45%	4,500
Tax liability	58,960

The answer £59,460 does not adjust the higher rate limit. The answer £61,460 does not adjust either the basic rate limit or the higher rate limit. The answer £53,432 deducts the personal allowance.

49 £548

	£
Net income	57,000
Less personal pension contributions (gross)	(2,000)
Adjusted net income	55,000
Less threshold	(50,000)
Excess	5,000
÷ £100	50
Child benefit income tax charge: 1% × £1,095 × 50	548

The answer £1,095 assumes there is full recovery of child benefit. The answer £438 is the child benefit times 40%. The answer £767 does not adjust for pension contributions.

50   £22,500

The bonus received on 30 September 2021 is taxable in 2021/22 as the receipts basis applies to employment income.

The gratuity received on 1 December 2021 is taxable as employment income in 2021/22 as it is a reward of the employment even though it was not received from the employer.

51   Travel from employer's office to visit a client

Travel from home to visit a trade fair relevant to the employer's business 100 miles away from permanent place of work

Travel from home to a workplace to which an employee has been seconded for 36 months does not qualify as travel to a temporary workplace as the secondment exceeds 24 months. Travel from home to a permanent place of work is not a qualifying travel expense.

52   £6,000

> **Examining team's comments.** The provision of job-related accommodation does not give rise to a taxable benefit in kind for the employee however, where ancillary services are also provided (ie the household bills and furniture) an assessable benefit in kind does arise. Where the accommodation is job-related, the assessable amount for these benefits is limited to 10% of net remuneration excluding the household costs, giving £6,000 (10% of £60,000) in this example. However, the answer £9,000 was most commonly chosen. This would be the correct answer if the accommodation was not job-related. It is calculated as the cost to the employer of the household bills, plus the use of furniture, calculated at 20% of the cost of the asset, giving £9,000 (£7,000 + (20% × £10,000)). This suggests that candidates may not have been aware of the rule to restrict the assessable amount where the accommodation is job-related.

OTQ bank – Income tax and NIC liabilities 2

53

Marion	£333

Gerald	£167

Marion

	£
Accrued interest deemed received 31.12.21 taxable savings income	
£20,000 × 5% × 4/12	333

Gerald

Interest received 31.12.21	
£20,000 × 5% × 6/12	500
Less relief for accrued interest (amount taxable on Marion)	
£20,000 × 5% × 4/12	(333)
Taxable savings income	167

54 £5,800

CO$_2$ emission (rounded down)	105
Base figure	(55)
	50
Divided by 5	10
Starting percentage	15
Diesel addition	4
Final percentage	29
Benefit £20,000 (list price) × 29%	£5,800

The answer £4,500 uses actual cost (not list price) and there is no diesel addition. The answer £5,220 uses actual cost. The answer £5,000 does not use the diesel addition.

55 £55,000

	£
2021/22 annual allowance	40,000
2020/21 annual allowance £(40,000 − 25,000)	15,000
	55,000

The annual allowance for 2018/19 and 2019/20 are not available as Troy was not a member of a pension scheme in those years.

The answer £40,000 is the current year annual allowance. The answer £135,000 brings forward allowances from all three previous tax years. The answer £35,000 restricts the current year allowance to £10,000.

56 £300

	£
Rental income £150 × 52	7,800
Less rent a room limit	(7,500)
	300

Luke should elect for the 'alternative basis' under rent a room relief, rather the normal basis which would give taxable property business income of £(150 − 20) = £130 × 52 = £6,760.

57 £3,800

The replacement of an equivalent model of sofa is allowable as a deduction. It is restricted by the amount of proceeds realised by selling the first sofa.

£(4,000 − 200)	£3,800

The answer £5,500 allows the full cost of the enhancement of furniture. The answer £5,300 allows the cost of the enhancement of furniture less the proceeds of the first sofa. The answer £4,000 is the cost of the replacement sofa.

58   £2,470

	£
Rent received 3 × £900	2,700
Security deposit	0
Less: insurance premium paid	(150)
motoring expenses 178 × 45p	(80)
Taxable property business income 2021/22	2,470

The answer £1,932 uses the accruals basis for the rent and the insurance premium paid. The answer £2,970 includes the security deposit: this will only become a receipt when Amrul is legally entitled to retain some or all of it at the end of the tenancy. The answer £2,505 uses the rate of 25p per mile for the motoring expenses.

59   £5,400

Depreciation and customer entertaining are not deductible and must be added back. The amount added back is therefore £(3,000 + 2,400) = £5,400.

Staff entertaining is fully deductible (the £150 limit applies to the taxable benefit for the employees).

60   £20,375

	£
Cash sales	41,000
Invoice sales £(4,000 − 1,500)	2,500
Less: cash expenses	(20,200)
motoring expenses 6,500 × 45p	(2,925)
Taxable trading income 2021/22	20,375

61   £3,600

£(12,000 − 6,000) × 60% = £3,600

The answer £2,400 is the private use amount of £(12,000 − 6,000) × 40%. The answer £648 uses the writing down allowance (WDA) and at the rate of 18% which does not apply to high emission cars. The answer £216 uses the WDA at the rate of 6%.

> **Examining team's comments.** This question required candidates to demonstrate their knowledge in respect of capital allowances on cars, where there was a disposal of a car during the year which was also used for private use by Olive.
>
> As the car was disposed of during the year, candidates need to recognise that a balancing allowance arose on its disposal, and that the amount of capital allowance Olive could claim was restricted to the business use element (ie 60%).
>
> Many candidates instead chose the fourth answer, continuing to write down the cost of the car, rather than calculating a balancing allowance. Candidates are reminded that cars which are used partly for private use by a sole trader are put into their own pool and on disposal a balancing charge or allowance may arise.

62   £417,667

	AIA £	Main pool £	Allowance £
p/e 5.4.22			
Plant	430,000		
AIA £1,000,000 × 5/12	(416,667)		416,667
Transfer to pool	13,333	13,333	
WDA @ 18% × 5/12		(1,000)	1,000
TWDV c/f		12,333	
Allowances			417,667

The answer £339,133 time apportions from the date of acquisition rather than the length of the period of account. The answer £419,067 does not time apportion the WDA. The answer £430,000 is the unrestricted annual investment allowance.

OTQ bank – Income tax and NIC liabilities 3

63   £400

	Main pool £	Allowances £
y/e 5.4.22		
TWDV b/f	12,000	
Disposal (limit to cost)	(11,600)	
	400	
WDA – small pool	(400)	400
TWDV c/f	0	

64

Start date	6 April 2021

End date	5 April 2022

2021/22 is the second year of trading. There is no accounting date ending in this year so the actual basis applies.

65   £13,000

First tax year (2019/20): Actual basis 1.2.20 to 5.4.20

Second tax year (2020/21): First 12 months of trading 1.2.20 to 31.1.21

Third tax year (2021/22): Current year basis 1.12.20 to 30.11.21

Periods of overlap 1.2.20 to 5.4.20 and 1.12.20 to 31.1.21

	£
2/10 × £30,000	6,000
2/12 × £42,000	7,000
	13,000

66   £19,000

	£
y/e 31.12.21	18,000
p/e 31.3.22	3,000
Less overlap profits	(2,000)
	19,000

67

2020/21	£3,000

2021/22	£9,600

	£
2020/21 Actual basis 1.1.21 to 5.4.21	
£9,000 × 3/9	3,000
2021/22 First 12 months 1.1.21 to 31.12.21	
£(9,000 − 3,000)	6,000
£14,400 × 3/12	3,600
	9,600

68   31 January 2024

> **Examining team's comments.** This question examines knowledge of the deadline for an individual taxpayer to claim relief for a trading loss which they wish to offset in the tax year prior to the tax year in which the loss arose. The correct answer is the second option (31 January 2024), as a claim must be made within one year of 31 January following the end of the tax year in which the loss arose. Therefore, as the loss arose in the tax year 2021/22, a claim for relief must be made by 31 January 2024.
>
> The second option was the most common answer selected but a significant number of candidates also chose each of the other answer options, suggesting that many candidates were not well prepared for a question on this topic. The second most common answer was the first option (31 January 2023) which is the deadline for submitting a personal tax return online for the tax year 2021/22. Candidates may have selected this date as they are familiar with this deadline in relation to the tax year 2021/22 and assumed the deadline for claiming the loss would be the same.
>
> Administration deadlines, both for individuals and companies, are an important part of the syllabus and future candidates are reminded of the importance of learning, and being able to distinguish between, the different deadlines as part of their studies.

69   £44,150

	£
1.8.20 to 31.8.20 1/12 × £96,000 × 1/2	4,000
1.9.20 to 31.7.21 Salary 11/12 × £9,000	8,250
1.9.20 to 31.7.21 Profit share ((11/12 × £96,000) − 8,250) × 2/5	31,900
	44,150

70

Robin and Stuart each	£48,000

Tania	£5,600

Robin and Stuart

CYB y/e 31.12.21 £96,000 × 1/2 = £48,000

Tania

Actual basis 1.1.22 – 5.4.22 £112,000 × 1/5 × 3/12 = £5,600

71   £136

	£
Class 2 contributions 14 × £3.05	43
Class 4 contributions £(10,600 − 9,568) × 9%	93
Total contributions	136

72   £282

	£
Class 4 contributions £([14,700 − 2,000] − 9,568) × 9%	282

OT case – Ann, Basil and Chloe

> **Workbook references.** Pensions are covered in Chapter 5. The computation of taxable income and the income tax liability are dealt with in Chapter 2.
>
> **Top tips.** Remember that higher rate tax relief for personal pension contributions made by higher rate taxpayers is given by increasing the basic rate limit.
>
> **Easy marks.** There were some easy marks in question 75 for working out a basic tax liability.

73   Individuals can always make gross pension contributions of £3,600 in 2021/22 even if they do not have any relevant earnings in that tax year.

Relevant earnings relate both to contributions to personal pension schemes and to occupational pension schemes.

Unused relevant earnings cannot be carried forward. Relevant earnings include trading income, employment income and income from furnished holiday lettings.

74

Employer contributions do not count towards the annual allowance.		FALSE
The annual allowance can be carried forward for three years to the extent that it is unused in the tax year.	TRUE	
The annual allowance is available even if the individual is not a member of a pension scheme in a tax year and so can be carried forward.		FALSE
If tax-relievable pension contributions exceed the annual allowance, there is a charge to income tax.	TRUE	

75 £15,200

The available annual allowance is £(40,000 + 20,000) = £60,000 and so there is no annual allowance charge for the tax year 2021/22. The basic rate band limit is £(37,700 + 49,000) = £86,700 so all of Ann's taxable income is within the basic rate band.

Tax £76,000 × 20%	£15,200

76 £6,750

The annual allowance must be tapered because Basil's adjusted income before any deduction for the pension contribution is more than £150,000. Basil is still an additional rate taxpayer because his higher rate limit is lifted by the gross pension contribution.

Annual allowance	
£40,000 – [½ × £(250,000 – 240,000)]	£35,000
Excess pension contribution over annual allowance	
£(50,000 – 35,000) @ 45%	£6,750

77 £720

Maximum personal pension contribution is £3,600 since Chloe has no relevant earnings. The pension tax relief is therefore £3,600 × 20% = £720. This relief will have been given at source. The remaining £4,600 contribution is not given tax relief.

OT case – Ae, Bee, Cae, and Eu

> **Workbook references.** Partnerships are covered in Chapter 11. Assessable trading income is dealt with in Chapter 9 and capital allowances are covered in Chapter 8.
>
> **Top tips.** Remember that there is no annual investment allowance nor writing down allowance in the final period of account.
>
> **Easy marks.** There were easy marks in question 80 for working out the trading income assessment.

78 £32,500

	£
2020/21	
Second year, short period of account (first 12 months trading)	
1 July 2019 to 30 April 2020	
£54,000 × ½	27,000
1 May 2020 to 30 June 2020	
£66,000 × ½ × 2/12	5,500
	32,500

79 £21,750

	£
Y/e 30 April 2022 – Cae joined 1 July 2021	
1 July 2021 to 30 April 2022	
£87,000 × 10/12 = 72,500 × 1/3	24,167
First year	
Actual basis 1 July 2021 – 5 April 2022	
£24,167 × 9/10	21,750

80   £61,200

	£
2022/23	
CYB y/e 30.6.22 Trading income	62,775
Less CAs	(1,575)
	61,200

81   £3,108

	£
p/e 30.9.23	
TWDV b/f	5,883
Addition – office furniture	2,400
Disposal at cessation	(5,175)
Balancing allowance (no AIA or WDA in the final period of account)	3,108

82   £57,908

	£
2023/24	
y/e 30.6.23 £(57,600 – 1,292)	56,308
p/e 30.9.23 £(14,400 – 3,000)	11,400
Less overlap profits	(9,800)
	57,908

OT case – Rosie and Sam

Workbook references. Personal pensions are covered in Chapter 5. The income tax treatment of investments is covered in Chapter 2 and the capital gains tax implications of investments are dealt with in Chapter 13.

Top tips. Remember that there is useful information contained in the Tax Tables provided in the examination. For question 83, the annual allowance amounts were vital and could be found in the Tax Tables. For question 86 the annual limit for ISAs is also in the Tax Tables.

Easy marks. There were easy marks in question 85 for identifying the tax consequences of flexible access drawdown.

83   £38,000

In 2021/22 Rosie's adjusted income is greater than £312,000 so her annual allowance is tapered to £4,000.

Rosie was not a member of a pension scheme in 2018/19, so no annual allowance is available to carry forward from that year.

In 2019/20 she had income of £130,000 so her annual allowance does not need to be tapered. She made a gross pension contribution of £26,000 during that year, and her employer made a contribution of £10,000 so she had (40,000 – 26,000 – 10,000) £4,000 annual allowance available to carry forward.

In 2020/21 her income was also below the threshold so the annual allowance does not need to be tapered. She did not make any pension contributions, but her employer made a contribution of £10,000 leaving £30,000 available to carry forward.

Therefore the available annual allowance for 2021/22 is:

	£
2021/22	4,000
2018/19	0
2019/20	4,000
2020/21	30,000
	38,000

The answer £74,000 does not restrict the 2021/22 annual allowance to the minimum amount. The answer £114,000 gives full allowances for the current year plus three years brought forward, after accounting for the contribution in 2019/20 and 2020/21. The answer £78,000 includes the £40,000 annual allowance for 2018/19 that would have been available if Rosie had been a pension scheme member in that year.

84   Charge at **45%** on excess contributions

The annual allowance charge is calculated by taxing the excess contribution as an extra amount of income received by Rosie and so is charged at her highest rate of income tax.

85   Lump sum: Up to 25% of fund can be taken as tax-free lump sum

Rest of pension fund: Taxable as pension income when received

86   £19,000

The ISA amount 2021/22 is £20,000. Sam has already invested £6,000 in the tax year, so can invest a further £(20,000 − 6,000) = £14,000. He can also replace the £5,000 withdrawn in October 2021 so the total amount he can now invest is £(14,000 + 5,000) = £19,000.

87

Premium bonds	Exempt from both income tax and capital gains tax

Government securities	Chargeable to income tax, exempt from capital gains tax

OT case – Fang and Hong

Workbook references. The basis of assessment for sole traders is covered in Chapter 9. Relief for pre-trading expenditure is described in Chapter 7 and capital allowances in Chapter 8. Trading losses are dealt with in Chapter 10.

Top tips. It is important to identify the relevant tax years when dealing with the basis of assessment.

Easy marks. The identification of relief for overlap profits in question 89 should have been easy marks.

88

2019/20	£30,640

2020/21	£45,960

Tax year	Basis of assessment	£
2019/20	Actual – 1 August 2019 to 5 April 2020	
	£45,960 × 8/12	30,640
2020/21	12 months to accounting date in tax year	
	y/e 31 July 2020	45,960

89 Against trading income on cessation

90 Trading expenditure: Treated as incurred on 1 August 2019

    Computer equipment: Addition for capital allowances purposes based on its market value at 1 August 2019

91 £31,000

	£
Trading profit	29,700
Less trading loss brought forward	(2,600)
	27,100
Property business profit	3,900
	31,000
Less trading loss carried back	(31,000)
Net income	0

If your choice was £18,430, you restricted the loss relief to keep the personal allowance in charge which is not permitted.

92 The trading loss is first set against general income of the tax year 2020/21 and only any excess loss is set against chargeable gains of that year.

    The amount of chargeable gains for the tax year 2020/21 is computed ignoring the annual exempt amount for the purposes of this relief.

    Both capital losses of the tax year 2020/21 and brought forward losses are taken into account for the purposes of this relief. Hong cannot specify the amount to be set against chargeable gains, so her annual exempt amount for the tax year 2020/21 may be wasted.

OT case – Chi

> **Workbook references.** Chapter 2 covers the computation of taxable income and the income tax liability. National insurance contributions are the subject of Chapter 12. The cash basis of assessment is dealt with in Chapter 7.
>
> **Top tips.** If the cash basis is used there are no capital allowances on the office equipment but the expenditure is instead deducted in the same way as a revenue expense.
>
> **Easy marks.** The computation of income tax in question 93 should have been easy marks. There were some easy marks in question 97 for identifying cash receipts and payments.

93 £8,632

	£
Trading income/net income	53,000
Less personal allowance	(12,570)
Taxable income	40,430
Tax	
£37,700 @ 20%	7,540
£2,730 (40,430 – 37,700) @ 40%	1,092
	8,632

94   £3,718

		£
£(50,270 – 9,568) = £40,702 @ 9%		3,663
£(53,000 – 50,270) = £2,730 @ 2%		55
Total Class 4 contributions		3,718

95   The trader can deduct capital expenditure on plant and machinery (other than motor cars) as business expenses rather than using capital allowances.

A trader can start to use the cash basis if his receipts for the tax year do not exceed £150,000.

Accounts can be prepared to any date in the tax year as for the normal basis of assessment. Cash basis traders cannot offset losses against other income or gains; they can only carry them forward against profits of the cash basis trade.

96   £5,300

	£
10,000 miles @ 45p	4,500
3,200 miles @ 25p	800
	5,300

Capital allowances are not relevant, since purchases of equipment are deducted as an expense. The running and capital costs of owning a motor car are replaced by the deduction based on approved mileage allowances.

97   Revenue £70,900, other expenses £7,300

Revenue £(72,500 – 1,600)	£70,900

98 Kagan

Workbook references. Income tax computations are the subject of Chapter 2. Pensions are covered in Chapter 4. Basic capital gains and inheritance tax are dealt with in Chapters 13 and 18.

Top tips. It is important to realise that the first two requirements only score 1 mark each and therefore the answers must be very straightforward. There is no need for lengthy and time-consuming calculations.

Easy marks. There were some easy marks in part (b) ii for dealing with the exempt income and personal allowance.

Examining team's comments. This question involved Kagan who had inherited quoted ordinary shares valued at £510,000. Kagan was unsure whether to retain the shares or sell some of them in order to make four alternative investments.

Retain the inherited shares: Kagan would have received dividend income of £15,300 in addition to his employment income of £400,000 (for which the income tax liability was given) for the tax year 2021/22.

Four alternative investments: These consisted of:

(1)   A personal pension contribution of £100,000, with Kagan having sufficient unused annual allowances to cover the pension contribution. He would immediately have withdrawn £25,000 of the pension fund tax-free.

(2)   Investing £50,000 in premium bonds.

(3)   Investing £20,000 in a cash individual savings account (ISA).

(4)   Purchasing a freehold property for £295,000, with the property then let out unfurnished.

After making the four investments, Kagan would have been left with £65,000 of inherited shares, on which he would have received dividend income of £1,950 for the tax year 2021/22.

Part (a) for 1 mark required candidates to calculate Kagan's revised income tax liability for the tax year 2021/22 if he retained the inherited shares. Although fairly well answered, many candidates used valuable time doing full before and after tax computations. Kagan was clearly an additional rate taxpayer, so all that was required was to calculate the additional rate tax due on the dividend income and then add it to the provided figure of tax on the employment income.

Part (b)(i) for 1 mark required an explanation as to why little or no capital gains tax would have been payable if Kagan had sold some of his inherited shares. This was because assets are inherited at the value at the time of the deceased's death. If these assets are sold soon after being inherited, there will generally be a minimal increase in value (this fact was stated in the question), so any gain is likely to be covered by the annual exempt amount. It was pleasing to see that this part was well answered by those candidates who appreciated the tax treatment.

Part (b)(ii) for 6 marks required a calculation of Kagan's revised income tax liability for the tax year 2021/22 if he sold some of his inherited shares and made the four alternative investments. This section was reasonably well answered, but several points should be noted:

- The question stated that a full tax computation was required, so exempt items (pension lump sum, premium bond prizes and the interest from the ISA) should simply have been listed within the main computation and indicated as such by the use of zero (0) – not by an explanation.

- The non-availability of the personal allowance should have been indicated in the same manner. There was no need to justify the non-availability given the level of Kagan's income.

- Although there might only be a ½ mark available for recognising an exemption, it is important to know the various exemptions so that time is not spent producing unnecessary, and more complicated workings – such as applying the savings income nil rate band where the interest from the ISA was included as savings income.

Part (c) for 2 marks required candidates to state for each of the four alternative investments whether the investment would reduce Kagan's potential inheritance tax liability compared to him retaining the inherited shares. Unfortunately, this section was not well answered. Candidates need to remember, that unlike other taxes, there are few exemptions from inheritance tax. Therefore, the replacement of the quoted shares with either premium bonds, an ISA or freehold property would not have changed the value of Kagan's chargeable estate. However, the investment in the pension fund (which is not withdrawn) would have been outside of Kagan's estate, thereby reducing his potential IHT liability.

Marking scheme

				Marks
(a)		Revised income tax liability		1
(b)	(i)	Base cost value inherited		1
	(ii)	Employment income	½	
		Pension lump sum	½	
		Premium bond prizes	½	
		Interest from ISA	½	
		Property income	½	
		Dividend income	½	
		Personal allowance	½	
		Income tax liability	2½	
				6
(c)	(i)	Pension fund outside estate	½	
	(ii)	Other investments	1½	
				2
				10

(a)　　Kagan's revised income tax liability for 2021/22 will be £170,067 (165,000 + ((15,300 − 2,000) at 38.1%)).

(b)　(i)　The base cost of the shares will be their value at the time of the aunt's death (£510,000), so the minimal increase in value is likely to be covered by Kagan's annual exempt amount of £12,300.

　　(ii)　**Kagan – Income tax liability 2021/22**

	£
Employment income	400,000
Pension lump sum	0
Premium bond prizes	0
Interest from ISA	0
Property income	9,600
Dividend income	1,950
	411,550
Personal allowance	0
Taxable income	411,550

Income tax

£	
37,700 at 20%	7,540
100,000 at 20%	20,000
112,300 at 40%	44,920
159,600 (411,550 − 1,950 − 100,000 − 150,000) at 45%	71,820
1,950 at 0%	0
411,550	
Income tax liability	144,280

(c)　(i)　The amount invested in the pension fund (and not withdrawn) will be outside of Kagan's estate, reducing the potential IHT liability.

　　(ii)　The investments in premium bonds, the ISA and the freehold property will not affect Kagan's potential IHT liability because one asset is simply being replaced with another of equivalent value.

99 Michael and Sean

> **Workbook references.** Chapter 10 deals with trading losses.
>
> **Top tips.** Remember that if a taxpayer claims loss relief against general income, the benefit of the personal allowance may be lost.
>
> **Easy marks.** There were some easy marks for identifying the possible loss relief claims.

Michael

The loss of £26,230 for 2020/21 can be claimed against general income for the three preceding years, under early years loss relief, earliest year first, since the loss is incurred in one of the first four years of Michael's trade.

The loss relief claim will therefore be £20,365 in 2017/18 and £(26,230 – 20,365) = £5,865 in 2018/19.

For 2017/18 this will waste Michael's personal allowance, with the balance of the claim of £(20,365 – 12,570) = £7,795 saving income tax at the basic rate of 20%.

For 2018/19 Michael has income of £(57,095 – 12,570 – 37,700) = £6,825 subject to income tax at the higher rate of 40%, so the claim of £5,865 will save tax at the higher rate.

Alternatively, Michael could have carried the trading loss forward against future trading profits, but the trading profit of £9,665 for 2021/22 is covered by the personal allowance, and there is no information regarding future trading profits.

Tutorial note

A claim for loss relief against general income for 2020/21 and/or 2019/20 is not possible since Michael does not have any income for either of these years.

Sean

The unused overlap profits brought forward are added to the loss for the year ended 31 December 2021, so the total loss for 2021/22 is £(23,100 + 3,600) = £26,700.

The whole of the loss can be claimed as a terminal loss since it is for the final 12 months of trading. The claim is against trading income for the year of the loss (2021/22 – nil) and the three preceding years, latest first.

The terminal loss claim will therefore be £3,700 in 2020/21, £18,900 in 2019/20 and £(26,700 – 3,700 – 18,900) = £4,100 in 2018/19.

The property business profits are sufficient to utilise Sean's personal allowance for each year, so the loss relief claims will save income tax at the basic rate of 20%.

Alternatively, Sean could have initially claimed loss relief against his general income for 2021/22 and/or 2020/21, but this would have wasted his personal allowance in those years.

100 Samantha

Marking scheme

			Marks
(a)	Rate of tax	1	
	Timing of relief	1	
	Waste of personal allowance/annual exempt amount	1	
			3
(b)	Trading income	½	
	Trading loss relief carried forward	1	
	Building society interest	½	
	Trading loss relief against general income	1	
	Personal allowance	½	
	Gains	½	
	Capital loss relief carried forward	1	
	Trading loss relief against gains	1	
	Annual exempt amount	1	
			7
			10

(a)   Factors that will influence an individual's choice of loss relief claim are:

   (1)   The rate of income tax or capital gains tax at which relief will be obtained, with preference being given to income charged at the additional rate of 45%, then the higher rate of 40%

   (2)   The timing of the relief obtained, with a claim against general income/capital gains of the current year or preceding year resulting in earlier relief than a carry forward claim against future trading profits

   (3)   The extent to which the income tax personal allowance and the capital gains tax annual exempt amount will be wasted by using a claim against general income/capital gains

(b)   Samantha – Taxable income

	2019/20 £	2020/21 £	2021/22 £	2022/23 £
Trading income	7,290	42,600	0	19,285
Less trading loss relief carried forward	(0)	(0)	(0)	(7,000)
	7,290	42,600	0	12,285
Building society interest	0	6,100	3,800	2,130
	7,290	48,700	3,800	14,415
Less trading loss relief against general income (N)	(0)	(48,700)	(0)	(0)
Net income	7,290	0	3,800	14,415
Less personal allowance	(7,290)	(0)	(3,800)	(12,570)
Taxable income	0	0	0	1,845

Samantha – Taxable gains

	2019/20 £	2020/21 £	2021/22 £	2022/23 £
Gains	21,800	23,300	0	14,800
Less trading loss relief against gains (Note)	(0)	(23,300)	(0)	(0)
	21,800	0	0	14,800
Less annual exempt amount	(12,300)	(0)	(0)	(12,300)
	9,500	0	0	2,500
Less capital loss carried forward	(0)	(0)	(0)	(2,500)
Taxable gains	9,500	0	0	0

Note. Loss relief has been claimed against general income and gains for 2020/21 since this gives relief at the earliest date and at the highest rates of tax. No claim should be made to set the loss against general income in 2021/22 since this is already covered by the personal allowance for that year.

Trading loss memorandum

	£
Loss 2021/22	79,000
Less: used 2020/21 (income)	(48,700)
used 2020/21 (gains)	(23,300)
Available for c/f	7,000
Less used 2022/23	(7,000)
Loss unused	0

ANSWERS

101 Robinette

Workbook references. Chapter 9 deals with basis of assessment, and capital allowances are dealt with in chapter 8. Employment income is covered in chapter 4. Chapter 6 deals with property income.

Top tips. It is important to follow the requirements carefully to see that there was no need to calculate the income tax liability.

Easy marks. Some of the benefits were only worth half marks and were therefore very straight-forward. It was clear that Robinette's income is too high for a personal allowance, which can simply be indicated by a zero.

Examining team's comments. The income tax question involved Robinette.

- She had ceased self-employment on 30 June 2021, preparing accounts for the 14-month period from 1 May 2020 to 30 June 2021. The trading profit figure was given (before taking account of capital allowances).

- From 1 August 2021 to 31 January 2022, Robinette was employed by Bird plc, who provided her with living accommodation and a place in the company's workplace nursery for Robinette's son. Robinette used her private motor car for business purposes.

- Robinette commenced self-employment again, in a new business, on 1 February 2022. She prepared accounts for the five-month period from 1 February to 30 June 2022. The trading profit figure was again given (before taking account of capital allowances).

- In addition, Robinette received property income from letting out her main residence during the period she was employed by Bird plc.

Part (a) for 12 marks required candidates to calculate Robinette's taxable income for the tax year 2021/22. This section was generally very well answered.

However, candidates should always read the question carefully to ensure they understand what needs to be done before starting their answers. Where only taxable income is required, as in this part, candidates should never spend valuable time in also calculating the income tax liability. However, taxable income is after deducting the personal allowance, and this should have been shown by the use of zero (0) (Robinette's level of income meant that the personal allowance was reduced to nil).

Given that the question involved various changes in Robinette's sources of income, candidates needed to be very careful in regard to time-apportionment and basis periods. Common problems included:

- Time-apportioning profits for the period of cessation.

- Not appreciating that WDAs, the AIA and FYAs are not given for the period of cessation.

- Time-apportioning the trading profits on commencement before capital allowances have been deducted.

With this type of question, candidates should think carefully about which workings can be included as one-line calculations within the main computation, and which need their own separate working. For example, the mileage allowance working of 5,200 at 10p (45p – 35p) = £520 should have been included within the main computation.

Part (b) for 3 marks required candidates to (1) state the period during which HM Revenue and Customs (HMRC) would have to notify Robinette if they intended to carry out a compliance check in respect of her self-assessment tax return for the tax year 2021/22, and the likely reason why such a check would be made, and (2) to advise Robinette as to how long she must retain the records used in preparing her self-assessment tax return for the tax year 2021/22. Although there were a number of good answers, in general this section was not so well answered as part (a). Candidates should note:

- The fact that the requirement was for a total of just three marks should have been a good indication that only a few brief points needed to be made, and not a much longer discussion.

- Where a question asks for dates, then these dates need to be precise – including the year relevant to the question.
- Answers should always be related to the information provided. The question made it clear that Robinette's self-assessment tax return was complete and accurate, so the likely reason for HMRC carrying out a compliance check was because her tax return was selected on a random basis.

			Marks
(a)	(i)	Salary	½
		Living accommodation	1
		Running costs	½
		Workplace nursery	½
		Mileage allowance	1
		Personal allowance	½
		(W1) Trading profit old business	3½
		(W2) Trading profit new business	2½
		(W3) Property income	2
			12
(b)	(i)	(1) 12 months from receipt	1
		(2) Random basis	1
			2
	(ii)	5 years from 31 January after tax year	1
			15

(a) **Robinette – Taxable income 2021/22**

	£
Employment income	
Salary (10,600 × 6)	63,600
Living accommodation – Rent paid (690 × 6)	4,140
Running costs	1,440
Workplace nursery	0
Mileage allowance (5,200 at 10p (45p – 35p))	(520)
	68,660
Trading profit – Old business (working 1)	75,350
– New business (working 2)	11,800
	155,810
Property income (working 3)	6,288
	162,098
Personal allowance	(0)
Taxable income	162,098

Tutorial notes:

1   The provision of a workplace nursery is an exempt benefit regardless of the cost to the employer.

2   No personal allowance is available because Robinette's adjusted net income of £162,098 exceeds £125,140.

Working 1 – Trading profit (old business)

	£
14-month period ended 30 June 2021	106,900
Balancing allowance	
(15,300 + 2,600 – 1,750 – 7,300)	(8,850)
	98,050
Relief for overlap profits	(22,700)
	75,350

Working 2 – Trading profit (new business)

		£
Five-month period ended 30 June 2020		55,700
Capital allowances (26,200 x 100% AIA)		(26,200)
		29,500
Assessed in 2021/22	29,500 × 2/5 =	11,800
1 February - 5 April 2022		

Working 3 – Property income

	£
Rent receivable (1,100 × 6)	6,600
Insurance (624 × 6/12)	(312)
Property income	6,288

(b) (i) (1)   If HMRC intend to carry out a compliance check into Robinette's self-assessment tax return for 2021/22, then they will have to notify her by 14 August 2023 (12 months after they received her tax return).

          (2)   If Robinette is confident that her return is complete and accurate, then the likely reason for HMRC carrying out a compliance check is because the return has been selected on a random basis.

    (ii)   Robinette was in business during 2021/22, so all of her records (both business and non-business) must be retained until five years after 31 January following the tax year, which is 31 January 2028.

102 Lucy

Marking scheme

	Marks
Employee	
Income tax payable	1½
Class 1 NIC	1½
Income	1
Self-employed	
Income tax payable	2
Classes 2 and 4 NIC	2
Income	1½
Determination of working pattern with higher disposable income	½
	10

Disposable income if Lucy is employee

Income tax	£
Employment income/net income	36,000
Less personal allowance	(12,570)
Taxable income	23,430
Income tax @ 20%	4,686

Class 1 NIC	£
Salary	36,000
Less employee's threshold	(9,568)
	26,432
Class 1 NIC @ 12%	3,172

Disposable income	£
Salary	36,000
Less: income tax	(4,686)
Class 1 NIC	(3,172)
travel costs	(1,500)
	26,642

Disposable income if Lucy is self-employed

Income tax

	£
Fees received	36,000
Less fixed rate mileage 4,600 @ 45p per mile	(2,070)
Trading income/net income	33,930
Less personal allowance	(12,570)
Taxable income	21,360
Income tax @ 20%	4,272

Classes 2 and 4 NIC

	£	£
Class 2 NIC £3.05 × 52		159
Class 4 NIC		
Trading income	33,930	
Less lower limit	(9,568)	
	24,362	
Class 4 NIC @ 9%		2,193
Total NICs		2,352

Disposable income

	£
Fees received	36,000
Less: income tax	(4,272)
Classes 2 and 4 NICs	(2,352)
travel costs 4,600 @ 40p	(1,840)
	27,536

Lucy will therefore have a higher disposable income by £(27,536 − 26,642) = £894 if she undertakes the self-employed work arrangement.

103 Daniel, Francine and Gregor

Workbook references. Partnerships are the subject of Chapter 11. Employment benefits are covered in Chapter 4. Trading losses are dealt with in Chapter 10.

Top tips. In part (a) it is important to realise that Daniel is treated as commencing a trade and therefore his trading income assessment for 2021/22 is on an actual basis. In part (c), remember that a trading loss can be relieved against total income in the tax year of the loss and the preceding tax year and can also be extended against chargeable gains.

Easy marks. There were some easy marks in part (b) for dealing with the interest paid by Francine on her loan.

Examining team's comments. This question had three separate scenarios, of which the first and third were fairly well answered and the second was less well answered.

The first scenario in part (a) involved three individuals who were in partnership, preparing accounts to 31 October annually. A fourth partner joined mid-way through an accounting period and the requirement was to calculate the new partner's trading income assessment for his first tax year as a partner. Although many candidates demonstrated satisfactory knowledge here, a large number wasted a significant amount of time by also performing calculations for the three existing partners, despite the requirement only concerning the new partner.

The second scenario in part (b) involved an employee who was provided with a beneficial loan part-way through the tax year. The loan was subsequently increased before the end of the tax year. The basic idea behind this question was that candidates had to calculate the benefit using the average method (they were instructed to use this method), with the interest actually paid to the employer being calculated on a strict basis. However, many candidates failed to read the requirement carefully and thus ignored the instruction to use the average basis when calculating the taxable benefit. In addition, many candidates failed to use proper workings and accordingly became confused mid-way through their calculations.

The third scenario in part (c) involved a self-employed taxpayer who had made a trading loss in the tax year. On the assumption that the taxpayer relieved his trading loss as early as possible, the requirement was to calculate the amount of trading loss carried forward to the next tax year. Once again, many candidates' workings were not well laid out. Many candidates prepared tax computations for both years for which figures were provided, before realising that all that was required was a loss memorandum. The set off of the brought forward capital loss against the current year chargeable gain was also often overlooked.

Marking scheme

			Marks
(a)	1 May 2021 to 31 October 2021	1½	
	1 November 2021 to 5 April 2022	1½	
			3
(b)	Average loan	1½	
	Interest paid	1½	
			3
(c)	2020/21 claim against total income	1	
	2021/22 claim against total income	1	
	claim against chargeable gain	1½	
	Loss carried forward	½	4
			10

(a) Daniel – Trading income assessment 2021/22

	£
1 May 2021 to 31 October 2021	
£96,000 × ¼ × 6/12	12,000
1 November 2021 to 5 April 2022	
£180,000 × ¼ × 5/12	18,750
	30,750

Tutorial note

Daniel joined as a partner on 1 May 2021, so the commencement rules apply to him for 2021/22. The basis period is the 11-month period from 1 May 2021 to 5 April 2022.

(b) Francine – Beneficial loan 2021/22

	£	£
$\dfrac{96{,}000 + (96{,}000 + 14{,}000)}{2} \times 2.0\% \times 8/12$		1,373
Interest paid £96,000 at 1.5% × 2/12	240	
£110,000 at 1.5% × 6/12	825	
		(1,065)
Taxable benefit		308

BPP
LEARNING
MEDIA

(c)   Gregor – Trading loss carried forward

			£
Trading loss			68,800
2020/21	– Claim against total income		
	£(14,700 + 4,600 + 1,300)		(20,600)
2021/22	– Claim against total income		(900)
	– Claim against chargeable gain (working)		(14,500)
Loss carried forward to 2022/23			32,800

Working: Claim against chargeable gain

The loss relief claim against the chargeable gain is restricted to £14,500 (chargeable gain of £17,400 less the capital loss brought forward of £2,900).

Tutorial note

Gregor can claim loss relief against his total income and chargeable gains for 2020/21 and 2021/22.

104 George

> **Workbook references.** Employment income is covered in Chapter 3. National insurance contributions are dealt with in Chapter 12.
>
> **Top tips.** Use your tax tables for all the national insurance limits and rates.
>
> **Easy marks.** There were some easy marks in part (a) for working out the income tax liability and in part (c) the comparison of the national insurance contributions gets some easy credit even if you have made errors in the main calculations.
>
> **Examining team's comments.** In part (a), most candidates missed the fact that the taxpayer would not incur any significant expenses in respect of the contract and would not be taking any significant financial risk. Many candidates incorrectly gave the payment of tax under PAYE for the previous year as an indicator.
>
> Part (b) was well answered, but many candidates produced extremely long answers for what should have been a simple set of workings. For example, the capital allowance was simply a 100% annual investment allowance on the purchase of a new asset and did not require a detailed capital allowances computation.
>
> In part (c), as regards the payment aspect, most candidates just referred to PAYE without any further relevant detail. Very few appreciated that the due date under the self-employed basis was simply 31 January following the tax year – payments on account not being required because the previous year's tax liability was collected under PAYE.

Marking scheme

		Marks
(a)	Factors indicative of employment (½ mark each)	2
(b)	Income	½
	Capital allowances	1
	Personal allowance	½
	Income tax	½
	Class 2	½
	Class 4	1
		4

			Marks
(c)	(i)	PAYE	1
		Self-assessment	1
			2
	(ii)	Class 1	1½
		Additional NIC	½
			2
			10

(a)   The contract is for a relatively long period of time.

George is required to do the work personally.

Xpee plc exercises control over George via the weekly meetings and instructions.

George will not incur any significant expenses in respect of the contract.

George will only be working for Xpee plc.

George is not taking any significant financial risk.

Note. Four items only required.

(b)   George – Income tax liability 2021/22

	£
Income	40,000
Capital allowances – annual investment allowance	(3,600)
Trading income	36,400
Less personal allowance	(12,570)
Taxable income	23,830

Income tax

£23,830 × 20%   4,766

George – National insurance contributions 2021/22

Class 2 national insurance contributions will be £159 (52 × £3.05).

Class 4 national insurance contributions will be £2,415 [(36,400 − 9,568) = 26,832 × 9%)].

(c)   (i)   If George is treated as employed in respect of his contract with Xpee plc, then the company will be required to deduct tax under PAYE every time that George is paid during 2021/22.

If treated as self-employed, George's income tax liability for 2021/22 would not be payable until 31 January 2023.

(ii)   If George is treated as employed in respect of his contract with Xpee plc, then his Class 1 national insurance contributions for 2021/22 will be £3,652 (40,000 − 9,568) = 30,432 × 12%).

The additional amount of national insurance contributions which he will suffer for 2021/22 is therefore £1,078 (3,652 − 159 − 2,415).

Tutorial note

For income tax purposes, capital allowances will reduce employment income in the same way that they are deducted in calculating the trading profit. However, there is no deduction for capital allowances when it comes to calculating Class 1 national insurance contributions.

BPP LEARNING MEDIA

105 Joe

Marking scheme

	Marks
Salary – Firstly plc	½
Occupational pension scheme contributions	1½
Bonus	½
Salary – Secondly plc	½
Personal pension contributions	½
Beneficial loan – Average method	1½
– Strict method	1½
Workplace nursery	1
Home entertainment system – Use	1½
– Acquisition	1½
Living accommodation	2
Furniture	1½
Working at home additional costs	1
	15

Joe – Employment income 2021/22

	£
Salary – Firstly plc (6,360 × 9)	57,240
Pension contributions (57,240 × 6%) (N2)	(3,434)
	53,806
Bonus (N1)	0
Salary – Secondly plc (6,565 × 3)	19,695
Beneficial loan (W1)	1,183
Workplace nursery (N3)	0
Home entertainment system – Use (W2)	660
– Acquisition (W2)	3,860
Living accommodation (W3)	6,750
Furniture (W3)	816
Working at home additional costs (N4)	0
Employment income	86,770

Workings

1   *Loan benefit*

The benefit of the beneficial loan using the average method is £1,267 ((120,000 + 70,000)/ 2 = 95,000 at 2.0% × 8/12).

Using the strict method the benefit is £1,183 ((120,000 at 2.0% × 3/12) + (70,000 at 2.0% × 5/12)).

Joe will therefore elect to have the taxable benefit calculated according to the strict method.

2   *Home entertainment system*

The benefit for the use of the home entertainment system is £660 (4,400 × 20% × 9/12).

The benefit for the acquisition of the home entertainment system is the market value of £3,860, as this is greater than £3,740 (4,400 – 660).

3   *Living accommodation and furniture*

The benefit for the living accommodation is the higher of the annual value of £2,600 (10,400 × 3/12) and the rent paid of £6,750 (2,250 × 3).

The benefit for the use of the furniture is £816 (16,320 × 20% × 3/12).

Notes

1   The bonus of £12,000 will have been treated as being received during 2020/21 as Joe became entitled to it during that tax year.

2   The personal pension contributions will increase Joe's basic rate tax limit and are therefore irrelevant as regards the calculation of employment income. Firstly plc's employer contributions are an exempt benefit.

3   The provision of a place in a workplace nursery does not give rise to a taxable benefit.

4   Additional home working costs up to £26 per month does not give rise to a taxable benefit.

106 Sammi

Workbook references. Chapter 4 deals with employment benefits. National insurance contributions are covered in Chapter 12. Computing taxable total profits and computing corporation tax are dealt with in Chapter 19.

Top tips. Use headings to show the examining team which of the two options you are dealing with.

Easy marks. There were easy marks for computing the car benefit and computing the national insurance contributions.

Marking scheme

		Marks
(a)	*Company motor car*	
	Car benefit	2
	Income tax	1
	NIC implications	½
	Additional director's remuneration	
	Income tax	½
	Class 1 NIC	1
		5

(b) *Company motor car*
Class 1A NIC   1

Allowable leasing costs   1

Corporation tax saving   1

Additional director's remuneration
Class 1 NIC   1

Corporation tax saving   1
         5

(c) *Sammi*
Director's remuneration   – Net of tax income   1

   – Overall result   1

Conclusion   1

Smark Ltd
Director's remuneration   1

Conclusion   1
         5
         15

(a) **Sammi – Company motor car**

The list price used in the car benefit calculation is £80,000. The relevant percentage is restricted to a maximum of 37% (15% + 26% (185 – 55 = 130/5) = 41%).

Sammi will therefore be taxed on a car benefit of £29,600 (80,000 × 37%).

Sammi's marginal rate of income tax is 45%, so her additional income tax liability for 2021/22 will be £13,320 (29,600 at 45%).

There are no national insurance contribution implications for Sammi.

Tutorial note

There is no fuel benefit as fuel is not provided for private journeys.

Sammi – Additional director's remuneration

Sammi's additional income tax liability for 2021/22 will be £12,150 (27,000 at 45%).

The additional employee's Class 1 NIC liability will be £540 (27,000 at 2%).

Tutorial note

Sammi's director's remuneration exceeds the upper earnings limit of £50,270, so her additional Class 1 NIC liability is at the rate of 2%.

(b) **Smark Ltd – Company motor car**

The employer's Class 1A NIC liability in respect of the car benefit will be £4,085 (29,600 at 13.8%).

The motor car has a CO_2 emission rate in excess of 50 grams per kilometre, so only £23,486 (27,630 less 15%) of the leasing costs are allowed for corporation tax purposes.

Smark Ltd's corporation tax liability will be reduced by £5,238 (23,486 + 4,085 = 27,571 at 19%).

Smark Ltd – Additional director's remuneration

The employer's Class 1 NIC liability in respect of the additional director's remuneration will be £3,726 (27,000 at 13.8%).

Smark Ltd's corporation tax liability will be reduced by £5,838 (27,000 + 3,726 = 30,726 at 19%).

(c) **More beneficial alternative for Sammi**

Under the director's remuneration alternative, Sammi will receive additional net of tax income of £14,310 (27,000 – 12,150 – 540).

However, she will have to lease the motor car at a cost of £27,630, so the overall result is additional expenditure of £13,320 (27,630 – 14,310).

If Sammi is provided with a company motor car then she will have an additional tax liability of £13,320, so she is in exactly the same financial position.

More beneficial alternative for Smark Ltd

The net of tax cost of paying additional director's remuneration is £24,888 (27,000 + 3,726 – 5,838).

This is more beneficial than the alternative of providing a company motor car since this has a net of tax cost of £26,477 (27,630 + 4,085 – 5,238).

107 Simon

Workbook references. The badges of trade are discussed in Chapter 7 which also deals with the computation of trading profit. Chapter 2 deals with the computation of taxable income and the income tax computation. National insurance contributions are the subject of Chapter 12. Chapter 13 covers computation of chargeable gains for individuals.

Top tips. Think carefully about what costs are allowable as part of trading expenses in part (b) and, alternatively, as part of the cost of the asset in part (c). Not all the expenses are allowable in both cases.

Easy marks. The question gave you the badges of trade in part (a) so it should have been easy marks to comment on them.

		Marks
(a)	Subject matter	½
	Length of ownership	½
	Frequency of transactions	½
	Work done	½
	Circumstances of realisation	½
	Profit motive	½
		3
(b)	Income	½
	Acquisition of house	½
	Legal fees on acquisition	½
	Renovation costs	½
	Legal fees on sale	½
	Loan interest	1
	Personal allowance	½
	Income tax liability	1
	Class 4 NICs	1½
	Class 2 NICs	1½
		8

		Marks
(c)	Sale proceeds	½
	Legal fees on sale	½
	Cost of house	½
	Legal fees on acquisition	½
	Enhancement expenditure	½
	Loan interest – not allowable	½
	Annual exempt amount	½
	Capital gains tax liability	½
		4
		15

(a) **Badges of trade**

Subject matter

Some assets are commonly held as investments for their intrinsic value, for example an individual may buy shares for dividend income produced by them or may buy a painting to enjoy it as a work of art. A subsequent disposal of an investment asset usually produces a capital gain. Where the subject matter of a transaction is not an investment asset, any profit on resale is usually a trading profit.

Length of ownership

If items purchased are sold soon afterwards, this indicates trading transactions.

Frequency of transactions

Transactions which may, in isolation, be of a capital nature will be interpreted as trading transactions where their frequency indicates the carrying on of a trade.

Work done

When work is done to make an asset more marketable, or steps are taken to find purchasers, this is likely to be indicative of trading.

Circumstances of realisation

A forced sale, for example to realise funds for an emergency, is not likely to be treated as trading.

Motive

The absence of a profit motive will not necessarily preclude a tax charge as trading income, but its presence is a strong indication that a person is trading.

(b) **Simon – Income tax and NICs for 2021/22 if trading**

		£	£
Income			260,000
Less:	costs incurred		
	house	127,000	
	legal fees on acquisition	1,800	
	renovation	50,000	
	legal fees on sale	2,600	
	loan interest		
	£150,000 × 6% × 4/12	3,000	
			(184,400)

	£	£
Trading income/Net income		75,600
Less personal allowance		(12,570)
Taxable income		63,030
Income tax		
£37,700 @ 20%		7,540
£25,330 @ 40%		10,132
Income tax liability		17,672
Class 4 NICs		
£(50,270 – 9,568) = £40,702 @ 9%		3,663
£(75,600 – 50,270) = £25,330 @ 2%		507
Total Class 4 NICs		4,170
Class 2 NICs		
£3.05 × 19 weeks (N)		58

Note. Marks were awarded for any reasonable attempt at calculating the number of weeks. ½ mark was deducted if 52 weeks were used.

(c)   Simon – Capital gains tax 2021/22 if **not trading**

	£	£
Sale proceeds		260,000
Less legal fees on sale		(2,600)
Net proceeds of sale		257,400
Less: cost of house	127,000	
legal fees on acquisition	1,800	
renovation	50,000	
loan interest (N)	0	
		(178,800)
Chargeable gain		78,600
Less annual exempt amount		(12,300)
Taxable gain		66,300
Capital gains tax		

	£
£37,700 @ 18%	6,786
£(66,300 – 37,700) = 28,600 @ 28%	8,008
Capital gains tax liability	14,794

Note. The loan interest is a revenue expense and so is not allowable in computing the chargeable gain.

108 Na

Marking scheme

		Marks	
(a)	First tax year trading profits	1	
	Second tax year trading profits	1½	
	Third tax year trading profits	½	
	Overlap profits	2	
			5
(b)	Net profit	½	
	Depreciation	½	
	Motor expenses	1	
	Legal fees	½	
	Property expenses	1	
	Own consumption	1	
	Fine	½	
	Trade subscription	½	
	Private telephone	1	
	Capital allowances	½	
			7
(c)	Trading profit	½	
	Individual savings account interest (exempt)	½	
	Dividends	½	
	Personal allowance	½	
	Income tax liability	1	
			3
			15

(a) **Na – Trading profits 2018/19, 2019/20 and 2020/21**

Year	Basis period	Working	Taxable profits £
2018/19	1.1.19 – 5.4.19	£25,200 × 3/6	12,600
2019/20	1.1.19 – 31.12.19(N)	£25,200 + £21,600 × 6/12	36,000
2020/21	1.7.19 – 30.6.20		21,600

Note. Because the accounting period ending in the second tax year is less than 12 months, the basis period for that year is the first 12 months of trading.

Overlap profits

Overlap period	Working	Overlap profits £
1.1.19 – 5.4.19	£25,200 × 3/6	12,600
1.7.19 – 31.12.19	£21,600 × 6/12	10,800

(b) **Na – Tax adjusted trading profit for year ended 30 June 2021**

		£	£
Net profit			23,000
Add:	depreciation	2,635	
	motor expenses – private use	1,925	
	7,000/8,000 × £2,200		
	professional fees – lease (N)	1,260	
	property expenses – private use	4,300	
	1/3 × £12,900		
	purchases – goods taken for own use (selling price)	450	
	other expenses – fine	480	
	other expenses – trade subscription	0	
			11,050
			34,050
Less:	telephone – business use 20% × £1,200	240	
	capital allowances	810	(1,050)
Tax adjusted trading profit			33,000

Note. Legal expenses relating to the **grant** of a short lease are not allowable.

(c) **Na – Income tax liability for 2021/22**

	Non-savings income £	Dividend income £	Total £
Trading income (part (b))	33,000		
UK dividends		1,200	
Net income (ISA interest is exempt)	33,000	1,200	34,200
Less personal allowance	(12,570)		
Taxable income	20,430	1,200	21,630

	£
Income tax	
Non-savings income	
£20,430 @ 20%	4,086
Dividend income	
£1,200 @ 0%	0
Tax liability	4,086

109 John

Workbook references. Chapter 2 deals with the computation of taxable income and the income tax liability. Pensions are covered in Chapter 5. Employment income is dealt with in Chapters 3 and 4. Property income is the subject of Chapter 6.

Top tips. Make sure you distinguish between occupational pension contributions (which are given tax relief at all rates by being deducted in the computation of employment income) and personal pension contributions (which are given basic rate relief by the taxpayer making a net contribution and higher and additional rate relief by increasing the basic rate and higher rate limits).

Easy marks. The inclusion of salary, deduction of occupational pension contributions and calculation of the tax liability should have been straightforward in part (a).

Marking scheme

		Marks
(a)	Remuneration	½
	Occupational pension contributions	1
	Beneficial loan	
	Outstanding loan at end of tax year	1
	Average loan	1
	Interest paid	½
	Property business profit	½
	Letting agent fees	½
	Personal allowance – not available	½
	Personal pension contributions	
	Unused allowances	1½
	Available allowance 2021/22	1½
	Increase in basic and higher rate limits	1
	Tax liability	
	Basic rate	½
	Higher rate	½
	Additional rate	½
	Finance costs tax reducer	1
		12
(b)	One for each relevant point (maximum of three)	3
		15

(a) **John – Income tax computation 2021/22**

	Non-savings income £
Employment income	
Remuneration	328,318
Less occupational pension contributions	(18,000)
	310,318

	Non-savings income
	£
Beneficial loan (W1)	1,350
Property business income (W2)	12,980
Net income	324,648
Less personal allowance	(0)
Taxable income	324,648

Tutorial note

No personal allowance is available as John's adjusted net income of £(324,648 − 4,000 (W3)) = £320,648 exceeds £125,140.

Tax

	£
£41,700 (W3) @ 20%	8,340
£112,300 (154,000 (W3) − 41,700) @ 40%	44,920
£170,648 (324,648 − 154,000) @ 45%	76,792
	130,052
Less: finance costs tax reducer £7,500 × 20%	(1,500)
Income tax liability	128,552

Workings

1   *Beneficial loan*

John repaid £(12,000 + 12,000) = £24,000 of the loan during 2021/22, so the outstanding balance at 5 April 2022 is £(84,000 − 24,000) = £60,000.

The benefit calculated using the average method (specified in the question) is as follows:

	£
$\dfrac{[84,000 + 60,000]}{2} \times 2.0\%$	1,440
Less interest paid	(90)
Taxable benefit	1,350

2   *Property business income*

	£
Profit before interest	14,855
Less: Letting agent fees	(1,875)
Property business income	12,980

3 *Effect of personal pension contributions on tax limits*

John has adjusted income which is higher than £240,000 in the tax year 2021/22 so his annual allowance is reduced (tapered) for 2021/22 by £1 for every £2 the adjusted income exceeds £240,000. However, the annual allowance is not reduced to less than £4,000.

Unused allowances can be carried forward for three years.

The maximum gross personal pension contribution possible in 2021/22 is as follows:

	£
2021/22 (tapered)	
Adjusted income = £(324,648 + 18,000 + 12,000) = £354,648 which is at least £312,000 so minimum annual allowance applies	4,000
2020/21	
No tapering required as adjusted income below £240,000	40,000
2019/20	
No tapering required as adjusted income below £240,000	40,000
2018/19	
No tapering required as adjusted income below £240,000	40,000
Occupational pension contributions already made £(18,000 + 12,000) × 4	(120,000)
Personal pension contribution allowable	4,000

John's basic and higher rate limits will be increased by this gross personal pension contribution to £(37,700 + 4,000) = £41,700 and £(150,000 + 4,000) = £154,000.

Tutorial note

Adjusted income for an employee is net income plus employee pension contributions to occupational pension schemes under net pay arrangements plus employer contributions to occupational pension schemes and/or personal pension schemes.

(b) **Furnished holiday lettings**

Any three from:

(1) There is no restriction on finance costs.

(2) The cost of furniture purchased for use in the furnished holiday letting will be an allowable expense under the cash basis (or will qualify for capital allowances under the accruals basis) instead of replacement furniture relief.

(3) The profit from the furnished holiday letting will qualify as relevant earnings for pension tax relief purposes.

(4) Capital gains tax business asset disposal relief, relief for replacement of business assets and gift holdover relief for business assets will potentially be available on a disposal of the furnished holiday letting.

110 Ronald

Marking scheme

		Marks
(a)	Trading profit p/e 30 April 2021: assessable trading profit	½
	Trading profit p/e 30 April 2022: capital allowances	1½
	Trading profit p/e 30 April 2022: assessable trading profit	1
	Property business income: premium assessable	1
	Property business income: rent received	1
	Property business income: roof replacement	1
	Property business income: roof repairs	1
	Property business income: insurance paid	1
	Dividends	1
	Figures given	1
	Tax @ 40%	1
		11
(b)	No annual allowances for previous years	1
	Annual allowance 2021/22	1
	Basic rate relief	1
	Higher rate relief	1
		4
		15

(a) Ronald – Income tax computation 2021/22

	Non-savings income £	Savings income £	Dividend income £	Total £
Trading income (W1)	11,592			
Employment income	70,065*			
Property business income (W2)	8,240			
Building society interest		1,260*		
Dividends £(800 + 2,000)			2,800	
Net income	89,897	1,260	2,800	93,957
Less personal allowance	(12,570)*			
Taxable income	77,327	1,260	2,800	81,387

	£
Income tax	
Non-savings income	
£37,700 @ 20%	7,540*
£39,627 (77,327 – 37,700) @ 40%	15,851
Savings income	
£500 @ 0%	0*
£760 (1,260 – 500) @ 40%	304
Dividend income	
£2,000 @ 0%	0*
£800 (2,800 – 2,000) @ 32.5%	260*
Income tax liability	23,955
Tax suffered at source	
PAYE	(11,513)*
Income tax payable	12,442

* Figures provided in question

Tutorial note

The amount of dividends are not given, but as the dividend nil rate band of £2,000 is available and only £800 is being taxed at the higher rate, the total dividends must be £(2,000 + 800) = £2,800.

Workings

1 Trading profit

	£	£
Period ended 30 April 2021		3,840
Period ended 30 April 2022	12,060	
Capital allowances £24,000 × 6% × 30%	(432)	
	11,628	
	× 8/12	7,752
		11,592

2 Property business income

	£	£
Premium received		12,000
Less £12,000 × 2% × (30 – 1)		(6,960)
		5,040
Rents received £768 × 5		3,840
		8,880
SBA on roof replacement (£8,400 × 3% × 4/12)	84	
Roof repairs £(8,600 – 8,200)	400	
Insurance paid	156	
		(640)
Property business profit		8,240

Tutorial notes

1 The rent received in the tax year is taxable under the cash basis rather than the rent receivable for the period.

2 The initial replacement cost of the shop's roof is not deductible, being capital in nature, as the building was not in a usable state when purchased and this fact was reflected in the reduced purchase price. It will, however, qualify for SBAs as it is qualifying expenditure contracted for on or after 29 October 2018. The allowance can be claimed from the date the shop is let out.

3 The whole of the insurance paid in the tax year is deductible under the cash basis.

(b) Ronald was not a member of a pension scheme prior to 2021/22, so the annual allowances for the three previous tax years are not available.

Although net relevant earnings are £(11,592 + 70,065) = £81,657, the maximum amount of tax relievable personal pension contribution is effectively restricted to the annual allowance of £40,000 for 2021/22.

Personal pension contributions are made net of basic rate tax, so Ronald would have paid £32,000 (£40,000 less 20%) to the pension company.

Higher rate tax relief would have been given by increasing Ronald's basic rate tax limit for 2021/22 by £40,000, being the gross amount of the pension contribution.

111 Wai

Workbook references. Employment income is covered in Chapters 3 and 4. The personal allowance is dealt with in Chapter 2.

Top tips. Make sure you are familiar with the tax rates and allowances which will be given to you in the exam. They include a lot of useful information such as mileage allowance, car benefit and the official rate of interest which will help you in answering this question.

Easy marks. There were some easy marks for calculation of basic employment benefits such as car benefit and living accommodation benefit.

Examining team's comments. Part (a) was generally very well answered. Surprisingly, the aspect that caused the biggest problem was the salary, because many candidates did not appreciate that it was necessary to calculate an annual figure. With calculations such as those for the mileage allowance, candidates are advised to study and replicate the layout followed in model answers rather than attempting their own style of short-cut. It is also a very poor approach to simply refer to a question note when answering, such as (5) instead of incidental expenses.

Many candidates found part (b) difficult, and often based their answers on self-assessment tax return information or PAYE form P45. One clue should have been that the question said 'provided to Wai', so clearly a tax return could not be relevant.

Marking scheme

		Marks
(a)	Salary	½
	Bonus	1
	Mileage allowance	
	Reimbursement	½
	Ordinary commuting	½
	Travel to clients	½
	Temporary workplace	½
	Tax-free amount @ 45p	½
	Tax-free amount @ 25p	½
	Car benefit	
	Percentage	½
	Benefit	1

		Marks
Incidental expenses	½	
Mobile telephone	1	
Living accommodation		
Annual value	½	
Additional benefit		
Cost	½	
Improvements	1	
Limit	1	
Benefit	½	
Personal allowance	1	
		12
(b) Form P60 contents	1½	
Date	½	
Form P11D contents	½	
Date	½	
		3
		15

(a) **Wai – Taxable income 2021/22**

	£
Employment income	
Salary (10,200 × 12)	122,400
Bonus	8,100
Mileage allowance (W1)	2,763
Car benefit (W2)	1,285
Incidental expenses (overseas, up to £10 per night – exempt)	0
Mobile telephone (400 × 20%)	80
Living accommodation – Annual value	4,828
– Additional benefit (W3)	1,824
	141,280
Less personal allowance	(0)
Taxable income	141,280

Tutorial notes

1   The bonus of £4,600 will have been treated as being received during 2020/21 as Wai became entitled to it during that tax year. Similarly, the bonus of £2,900 will be treated as received during 2022/23.

2   The exemption for mobile telephones does not apply to the second telephone.

3   No personal allowance is available as Wai's adjusted net income of £141,280 exceeds £125,140.

Workings

1   *Mileage allowance*

	Miles	£
Reimbursement (13,860 at 55p)		7,623
Business mileage		
Ordinary commuting	0	
Travel to clients' premises	8,580	
Temporary workplace	2,860	
	11,440	
Tax-free amount		
10,000 miles at 45p		(4,500)
1,440 miles at 25p		(360)
Taxable benefit		2,763

Tutorial note

Travel to the temporary workplace qualifies as business mileage because the 24-month limit was not exceeded.

2   *Car benefit*

The relevant percentage for the car benefit is 22% because the motor car has CO2 emissions from 90 to 94 grams per kilometre. The diesel addition does not apply because the car meets the RDE2 standard.

The motor car was available during the period 1 September 2021 to 5 April 2022, so the benefit for 2021/22 is £1,285 (10,013 × 22% × 7/12).

3   *Living accommodation additional benefit*

The benefit is based on the cost of the property plus subsequent improvements incurred before the start of the tax year.

	£
Cost	142,000
Improvements (prior to 6 April 2021 only)	24,200
	166,200
Limit	(75,000)
	91,200

The additional benefit is therefore £1,824 (91,200 at 2.0%).

(b)   **Form P60**

Form P60 will show Wai's taxable earnings, income tax deducted, final tax code, national insurance contributions (NIC), and Qaz plc's name and address.

This form should have been provided to Wai by 31 May 2022.

Form P11D

Form P11D will detail the expenses and benefits provided to Wai.

This form should have been provided to Wai by 6 July 2022.

112 Samson and Delilah

> **Workbook references.** The income tax computation is covered in Chapter 2. Chapters 3 and 4 deal with employment income and taxable and exempt benefits. Partnerships are the subject of Chapter 11.
>
> **Top tips.** Trivial benefits (not exceeding £50) are exempt benefits.
>
> **Easy marks.** There were some easy marks for dealing with the car benefit and computing income tax.
>
> **Examining team's comments.** Part (a) of the question was a typical income tax liability calculation (for both the husband and wife), and it was generally very well answered. Part (b) of the question involved income tax planning, requiring a calculation of the husband's income tax saving for the tax year if the building society deposit account had been in his wife's sole name instead of in joint names for the entire year. Given that the husband's personal allowance restriction would be reduced, the answer was simply the amount of interest (after deducting the savings income nil rate band of £500) at 60%. However, half page answers were quite common. Once again, working at the margin (where appropriate) could have saved an enormous amount of time.

Marking scheme

		Marks
(a)	*Samson*	
	Salary	½
	Building society interest	½
	Personal allowance	1
	Income tax	2
	Delilah	
	Salary	½
	Payroll giving	1
	Car benefit	1
	Chauffeur	½
	Hamper	½
	Business travel	½
	Trading profit	1
	Building society interest	½
	Deductible interest	1
	Personal allowance not available	½
	Income tax	2
		13
(b)	Transfer part of account from Samson to Delilah	2
		15

(a)   **Samson – Income tax computation 2021/22**

	Non-savings income £	Savings income £	Total £
Employment income – Salary	112,000		
Building society interest £9,600/2		4,800	
Net income	112,000	4,800	116,800
Less personal allowance (W)	(4,170)		
Taxable income	107,830	4,800	112,630

Income tax

	£
£37,700 × 20%	7,540
£70,130 (107,830 − 37,700) × 40%	28,052
£500 × 0% (savings rate nil rate band)	0
£4,300 (4,800 − 500) × 40%	1,720
Income tax liability	37,312

Working

Samson's adjusted net income exceeds £100,000, so his personal allowance of £12,570 is reduced to £4,170 (12,570 − 8,400 ((116,800 − 100,000)/2)).

Delilah – Income tax computation 2021/22

	Non-savings income £	Savings income £	Total £
Employment income (W1)	213,248		
Trading profit £85,600 (93,600 − 8,000) × 40%	34,240		
Building society interest £9,600/2		4,800	
Total income	247,488	4,800	252,288
Less interest paid	(6,200)		
Net income/taxable income	241,288	4,800	246,088

Workings

1   *Employment income*

	£
Salary	184,000
Less charitable payroll deductions £250 × 12	(3,000)
	181,000
Car benefit (W2)	22,848
Chauffeur	9,400
Hamper	0
Reimbursement of travel to visit client	0
Employment income	213,248

2   *Car benefit*

The relevant percentage for the car benefit is 34% (15% + (150 − 55)/5).

The motor car was available throughout 2021/22 so the benefit is £22,848 (67,200 × 34%).

Income tax	£
£43,780 (W) × 20%	8,756
£112,300 (156,080 − 43,780) × 40%	44,920
£90,008 (246,088 − 156,080) × 45%	40,504
Income tax liability	94,180

Working

Delilah's basic and higher rate tax limits are increased by £4,864 × $\frac{100}{80}$ = £6,080 to £43,780 (37,700 + 6,080) and £156,080 (150,000 + 6,080) in respect of the charitable gift aid donations.

Tutorial notes

1   The car benefit does not cover the cost of a chauffeur, so this is an additional benefit.

2   The hamper is a trivial benefit as it does not exceed £50.

3   There is an automatic exemption for reimbursement of business expenses such as the train travel by Delilah (which would be a taxable benefit under general principles) provided that the expense would have been a deductible expense for the employee.

4   The loan interest paid of £6,200 is deductible because the loan was used by Delilah for a qualifying purpose.

5   No personal allowance is available as Delilah's adjusted net income of £240,008 (246,088 − 6,080) exceeds £125,140.

6   No savings income nil rate band is available as Delilah is an additional rate taxpayer.

(b)   If the building society deposit account had been in Delilah's sole name instead of in joint names for the entire year, this would have saved Samson income tax of £2,680 (£500 × 20% + £4,300 × 60%).

Tutorial note

Samson's effective marginal rate on the savings income covered by the savings income nil rate band (£500) is 20%. This is 40% of half of the £500 (ie 20% of the whole of the £500) of the savings income which was used to restrict the personal allowance. Samson's effective marginal rate of income tax on the savings income not covered by the savings income nil rate band (ie £4,800 − 500 = £4,300) is 60%. This is 40% (the higher rate) plus 40% of half (ie 20% of the whole) of the remaining £4,300 of savings income which was used to restrict the personal allowance.

113 Patience

> **Workbook references.** Employment income is covered in Chapters 3 and 4 and national insurance contributions in Chapter 12. Assessable trading income is covered in Chapter 9 and capital allowances in Chapter 8. Property business income is the subject of Chapter 6. The computation of taxable income and the income tax liability will be found in Chapter 2. Pensions are the subject of Chapter 5.
>
> **Top tips.** There are no writing down allowances or annual investment allowance in the final year of trading. Remember that gains on the disposal of residential property are taxed at 18% and 28% if they are not covered by the annual exempt amount and private residence relief.
>
> **Easy marks.** Recognising the exempt benefits and mentioning them in your answer is important to get some easy marks.
>
> **Examining team's comments.** Two aspects to this question caused particular difficulty. Firstly, many candidates treated the pension income (state pension, employer's occupational pension scheme and a private pension) as exempt income. Secondly, the format in which information was given for two properties caused a certain amount of confusion, with the information relevant for income tax and the capital gains tax details being shown within the one table; candidates being required to separate out the relevant information for income tax and capital gains tax purposes. Here figures were often duplicated with, for example, revenue expenditure being (correctly) deducted as an expense in calculating the property business profit, but then also (incorrectly) deducted in calculating chargeable gains.

		Marks
Salary		1
Pension contribution	Patience	½
Pension contribution	Employer	½
School place		1
Long-service award		½
Beneficial loan		½
Trading income	y/e 31.7.21	½
	p/e 31.12.21	½
	Overlap relief	1
Capital allowances	TWDV brought forward	½
	Laptop	½
	Disposal proceeds	1
	Balancing allowance	½
Property business profit	Rent received	½
	Expenditure	½
Pension income		1
Personal allowance		½
Increase basic rate limit		1
Income tax liability		1
Capital gains	Property one	½
	Property two	½
	Annual exempt amount	½
	CGT payable	½
		<u>15</u>

Patience – Income tax computation 2020/21

		£
Employment income		
Salary £3,750 × 9		33,750
Pension contributions	Patience £33,750 × 6%	(2,025)
	Employer	<u>0</u>
		31,725
School place		540
Long-service award		0
Beneficial loan		0
Trading income (W1)		16,100
Pension income £(1,450 + 7,000 + 3,650)		12,100
Property business income (W3)		<u>3,500</u>
Net income		63,965
Less personal allowance		<u>(12,570)</u>
Taxable income		<u>51,395</u>
Income tax		
£42,200 (W4) × 20%		8,440
£9,195 (51,395 − 42,200) × 40%		<u>3,678</u>
Income tax liability		<u>12,118</u>

Tutorial notes

1   An employer contribution to a pension scheme is not a taxable benefit.

2   The taxable benefit on the provision of the school place is the additional marginal cost to the employer, not the normal fee payable.

3   A non-cash long-service award is not a taxable benefit if it is for a period of service of at least 20 years, and the cost of the award does not exceed £50 per year of service.

4   There is no taxable benefit if beneficial loans do not exceed £10,000 during the tax year.

Workings

1   *Trading income*

	£	£
Year ended 31 July 2021		14,800
Period ended 31 December 2021	6,900	
Balancing allowance (W2)	(1,900)	
		5,000
		19,800
Relief for overlap profits		(3,700)
		16,100

2   *Capital allowances*

	Main pool £	Allowances £
WDV brought forward	2,200	
Addition – Laptop computer	1,700	
Proceeds £(1,200 + 800)	(2,000)	
Balancing allowance	(1,900)	1,900

3   *Property business income*

	£
Rent received £(3,600 + 7,200)	10,800
Expenditure paid £(4,700 + 2,600)	(7,300)
Property business income	3,500

4   *Basic rate limit*

Patience's basic rate tax limit is increased by £4,500 to £42,200 (37,700 + 4,500 (3,600 × 100/80)) in respect of the personal pension contributions.

Patience – Capital gains tax computation 2021/22

		£	£
Property one	Disposal proceeds	122,000	
	Less cost	(81,000)	
			41,000
Property two	Disposal proceeds	98,000	
	Less cost	(103,700)	
			(5,700)

Patience – Capital gains tax computation 2021/22

	£	£
Net chargeable gains		35,300
Less annual exempt amount		(12,300)
Taxable gains		23,000
Capital gains tax		
£23,000 × 28%		6,440

114 Petula

Workbook references. Employment income is dealt with in Chapters 3 and 4. The income tax computation is covered in Chapter 2. Pensions are the subject of Chapter 5.

Top tips. Part (b) is quite challenging and you need to adopt a logical approach by first working out the annual allowances that have been used and then working out the remaining allowances to be carried forward. Make sure you use the earliest available tax year brought forward allowance first. This maximises the amount that can be carried forward.

Easy marks. There were easy marks in part (a) for dealing with employment income benefits and expenses.

Examining team's comments. Part (a) was very well answered, and there were many perfect answers. However, the following points should be noted when answering this style of question:

(a)   If a question requires just a calculation of taxable income, then that is where candidates should stop. Calculating the income tax liability wastes valuable time.

(b)   As stated in the requirements, candidates should always clearly indicate (by the use of a zero) any items which are not taxable or deductible – such as the employer pension scheme contribution and the disallowable subscription.

(c)   Candidates should think carefully about which workings can be included as one-line calculations within the main taxable income computation, and which need their own separate working. The only aspects which warranted separate workings here were the mileage allowance and property income. These workings should always have a heading or be obviously identifiable. Just referencing adjustments to the bullet list numbers used in the question is not good exam technique.

(d)   The use of abbreviated numbers, such as 15.6k instead of 15,600 for the reimbursed mileage, should be avoided.

(e)   With a computation containing both additions and deductions, candidates should be very careful to indicate which is which. A single column approach with deductions shown in brackets avoids any confusion.

(f)   Where a result is obvious, such as no personal allowance being available (because the adjusted net income of £322,420 exceeded £125,140), all that is needed is a zero entry. There is no need for an explanation or a calculation of the reduction to nil.

(g)   Candidates need to appreciate that each source of income is self-contained. It is not correct to show all the receipts from each source first (such as rent receivable), and then all the various expenses lumped together (such as property income deductions). With a separate working for property income, just the one figure for property income should then be included in the main taxable income computation.

Although most candidates scored some marks for part (b), few achieved full marks. The three marks available for this section should have been a good indication as to the complexity of the requirement.

Marks

(a) Salary ½
 Bonuses 1
 Mileage allowance: reimbursed ½
  first 10,000 miles ½
  remaining miles ½
 Pension contributions ½
 Professional subscription ½
 Golf club membership ½
 Property income: rent received ½
  washing machine 1
  dishwasher 1
  other expenses ½
  furnished room 1
 Savings income 2
 Interest paid 1
 Personal allowance ½
 12

(b) 2021/22 annual allowance used in 2021/22 1
 2018/19 annual allowance used in 2021/22 ½
 2019/20 annual allowance carried forward to 2022/23 ½
 2020/21 annual allowance carried forward to 2022/23 1 3
 15

(a) **Petula – Taxable income 2021/22**

	£
Employment income	
Salary	260,000
Bonuses (18,600 + 22,400)	41,000
Mileage allowance (W1)	8,350
Pension contributions	0
	309,350
Less Professional subscription	(630)
Less Golf club membership	0
	308,720
Property income (W2)	11,340
Savings income (250,000 at 3% × 4/12)	2,500
Less Interest paid	(140)
	322,420
Less Personal allowance	(0)
Taxable income	322,420

Tutorial notes

1   The bonus of £21,200 will have been treated as being received 2020/21 because Petula became entitled to it during that tax year.

2   Under the accrued income scheme, Petula must include the accrued interest from the gilts as savings income for 2021/22, even though she has not received any actual interest.

3   No personal allowance is available because Petula's adjusted net income of £322,420 exceeds £125,140.

Workings

1   *Mileage allowance*

	£
Reimbursement (26,000 at 60p)	15,600
Tax free amount	
10,000 miles at 45p	(4,500)
11,000 miles at 25p	(2,750)
Taxable benefit	8,350

2   *Property income*

	£
Rent received	12,000
Replacement furniture relief	
Washing machine	(420)
Dishwasher	0
Other expenses paid	(1,640)
	9,940
Furnished room (8,900 – 7,500)	1,400
Property income	11,340

Tutorial notes

1   No relief is given for that part of the cost of the washer-dryer which represents an improvement over the original washing machine. Relief is therefore restricted to the cost of a similar washing machine.

2   No relief is available for the cost of the dishwasher because this is an initial cost rather than the cost of a replacement.

3   Claiming rent-a-room relief in respect of the furnished room is more beneficial than the normal basis of assessment (8,900 – 2,890 = £6,010).

(b)   *Annual allowances carried forward to 2022/23*

First work out the annual allowance used in 2021/22, remembering to use the current tax year allowance first and then the previous three tax years, earlier years first:

	£
Used in 2021/22	
Annual allowance 2021/22 (N1)	4,000
Brought forward from 2018/19	
£(40,000 – 25,000)	15,000

	£
Brought forward from 2019/20	
£(40,000 − 25,000)	β 6,000
Annual allowance used in 2021/22	25,000

Then work out the remaining annual allowances carried forward to 2022/23:

	£
Carried forward from 2019/20	
£(40,000 − 25,000 − 6,000)	9,000
Carried forward from 2020/21 (N2)	
£(40,000 − 25,000)	15,000
Annual allowance carried forward to 2022/23	24,000

Notes

1   Petula's adjusted income for 2021/22 exceeds £312,000 so she is only entitled to the minimum annual allowance for this tax year.

2   Tapering of the annual allowance does not apply in 2018/19, 2019/20 and 2020/21 as Petula's adjusted income did not exceed £240,000 in those years.

115 Dill

Workbook references. Residence, exempt income and the restriction of the personal allowance are covered in Chapter 2. Employment income is the subject of Chapters 3 and 4. Pensions are dealt with in Chapter 5. Trading losses are covered in Chapter 10.

Top tips. In part (a), keep your points brief and relevant to the facts given in the question.

Easy marks. In part (b) there were some easy marks for calculating taxable benefits and identifying exempt benefits.

Examining team's comments. Part (a) for 3 marks required candidates to explain why Dill was treated as not resident in the UK for the tax year 2020/21. Although reasonably well answered, very few candidates managed to pick up all the available marks for this section. For example, most candidates simply stated that Dill had been in the UK for 60 days, rather than indicating that this fell in the 46 to 90 day band from the tax tables. A number of candidates wasted time by explaining the automatically resident and not resident tests, when it was obvious that these were not relevant. Then when discussing UK ties, some candidates focused on those ties which were not met, rather than those which were. The three marks available should have been a clear indication that a long, detailed, explanation was not required.

Part (b) for 12 marks required candidates to calculate Dill's taxable income for the tax year 2021/22. This section was generally answered very well, with many candidates achieving high marks. Common problems included:

- Not appreciating that the benefit of a workplace nursery is an exempt benefit.

- Treating subscriptions as benefits rather than as deductions.

- Omitting the personal allowance. Even when shown, it was obvious (given the level of Dill's income) that the personal allowance was not available, so all that was needed was a zero entry. There was no need for an explanation or a calculation of the reduction to nil.

- If a question requires just a calculation of taxable income, then that is where candidates should stop. Calculating the income tax liability just wastes valuable time.

- As stated in the requirements, candidates should always clearly indicate (by the use of a zero) any items which are not taxable or deductible – such as exempt benefits, non-deductible expenses and exempt income.

- Where a computation contains additions and deductions, candidates should be very careful to indicate which is which. A single column approach with deductions shown in brackets avoids any confusion.

- Candidates should think carefully about which workings can be included as one-line calculations within the main taxable income computation, and which need their own separate working. The only aspects which warranted a separate working here was the mileage allowance.

- The use of abbreviated numbers such as 45.5k instead of 45,500 for the bonuses should be avoided.

Marking scheme

		Marks	
(a)	Sufficient ties test relevant	½	
	Number of sufficient ties needed	½	
	Identification of UK ties	1½	
	Conclusion	½	
			3
(b)	Salary	½	
	Bonuses	1	
	Gym	½	
	Home entertainment system	1	
	Workplace nursery	½	
	Beneficial loan	1½	
	Health club membership	½	
	Mileage allowance	1½	
	Professional subscription	½	
	Golf club membership	½	
	Occupational pension contribution	1	
	Premium bond prize	½	
	Interest from savings certificate	½	
	Loss	1½	
	Personal allowance	½	
			12
			15

(a) **Dill – Residence status in the tax year 2020/21**

The sufficient ties test is relevant since Dill does not meet either of the automatic tests.

As Dill spends between 46 and 90 days in the UK in the tax year 2020/21 and was previously UK resident in at least one of the previous three tax years, she will be UK resident in that tax year if she has three or more UK ties.

Dill has two UK ties:

- Available UK accommodation in which she spent at least one night during the tax year; and

- More than 90 days spent in the UK in either or both of the previous two tax years.

On this basis, Dill is not UK resident in the tax 2020/21 as she has less than three UK ties.

BPP
LEARNING
MEDIA

Tutorial notes

1   Dill is not automatically non-UK resident in the tax year 2020/21 since she spends at least 16 days in the UK in that tax year and was resident in the UK for one or more of the three previous tax years, and does not work full-time overseas.

2   Dill is not automatically UK resident in the tax year 2020/21 since she does not spend at least 183 days in the UK in that tax year, has an overseas home as well as a UK home, and does not work full-time in the UK.

3   Dill might have a third UK tie which is that she was present in the UK at midnight for the same or more days in that tax year than in any other country. However, there is insufficient information to conclude on this point.

(b)   **Dill – Taxable income 2021/22**

		£
Employment income		
Salary		430,000
Bonuses £(16,200 + 29,100)		45,300
Company gym		0
Home entertainment system £5,900 × 20%		1,180
Workplace nursery		0
Beneficial loan £96,000 × 2.0% × 10/12		1,600
Health club membership		990
Less:	Mileage allowance (W)	(1,625)
	Professional subscription	(560)
	Golf club membership	(0)
	Occupational pension scheme contribution	(4,000)
		472,885
Premium bond prize		0
Interest from savings certificates		0
Total income		472,885
Less loss relief against total income		(58,000)
Net income		414,885
Less personal allowance		(0)
Taxable income		414,885

Working

	£
10,000 miles @ 45p	4,500
4,500 miles @ 25p	1,125
	5,625
Less mileage allowance paid 16,000 @ 25p	(4,000)
Allowable deduction	1,625

Tutorial notes

1   The bonuses are treated as received on the earlier of the time when payment is made and the time when Dill became entitled to the bonuses. These are 1 November 2021 for the first bonus and 1 March 2022 for the second bonus. Therefore both bonuses are taxable in the tax year 2021/22.

2   The use of the company gym is an exempt benefit as provision of sporting or recreational facilities available to employees generally and not to the general public.

3   The golf club membership is not deductible as it is not incurred wholly, necessarily and exclusively for the purposes of Dill's employment.

4   The maximum occupational pension scheme contribution that Dill can make without triggering an annual allowance charge is £4,000 since she has adjusted income of at least £312,000.

5   The loss relief cap is the greater of £50,000 and 25% of Dill's adjusted total income of £472,885 which is £118,221. Therefore, Dill can relieve the whole of her trading loss of £58,000.

116 Danh

Workbook references. Residence, computing taxable income and the income tax liability are covered in Chapter 2. Property business income is dealt with in Chapter 6. Computing trading income is covered in Chapter 7, capital allowances in Chapter 8 and the basis of assessment in Chapter 9. Trading losses are covered in Chapter 10 and partnerships in Chapter 11.

Top tips. In part (a) you need to deal with Danh's residence position for both the tax years 2019/20 and 2020/21. Don't waste time dealing with ties that Danh does not satisfy, just state the ones which are relevant.

Easy marks. There are easy marks in part (b) for dealing with adjustment of profit. Watch out for the computation of the capital allowance on the car as you need to think about what rate of capital allowance will be given, private use and the length of the period of account.

Examining team's comments. Part (a) for 3 marks required candidates to explain whether Danh was treated as resident or not resident in the UK for each of the tax years 2019/20 and 2020/21. This section was reasonably well answered, although a number of candidates did not appreciate that there would be one additional UK tie for the tax year 2020/21. This is often the case where a question covers two tax years since for the second year a taxpayer will have the additional UK tie of being in the UK for more than 90 days during the previous tax year.

Where a question makes it clear that that the tests of automatic residence and automatic non-residence are not relevant, then there is nothing to be gained from explaining why this is the case. It should have been quite obvious from reading the question that only residence based on UK ties needed to be considered. The three marks available for this section was a good indication as to the length of answer required.

Part (b) for 12 marks required candidates to calculate Danh's income tax liability for the tax year 2021/22. This section was very well answered, and there were many perfect responses. However, the following points should be noted when answering this style of question:

• Candidates should think carefully about which workings can be included as one-line calculations within the main computation and which need their own separate working. For example, the partnership loss calculation of £12,600 × 7/12 × 20% = 1,470 was easily included within the main computation which would have saved candidates time. The only aspects which warranted separate workings here were the trading profit and property income.

• As mentioned above, the calculation for the partnership loss was fairly straightforward. There was no need to work out the loss allocations for the other partners and such workings simply used valuable time.

• Practice as many computations as possible. If this is done, basic mistakes such as applying the motor car benefit rules rather than claiming capital allowances should be avoided.

- As stated in the requirements, candidates should always clearly indicate (by the use of a zero) any items which do not require adjustment – the accountancy fees were deductible when calculating the trading profit, but this needed to be indicated.

- With computations containing both additions and deductions, candidates should be very careful to indicate which is which. A single column approach with deductions shown in brackets should avoid any confusion.

- Candidates need to appreciate that each source of income is self-contained. It is not technically correct to show all the receipts from each source first (such as rent receivable), and then the various deductions shown later in the main computation (such as property income deductions). With a separate working for property income, just the one figure for property income should then be included in the main taxable income computation.

Marking scheme

			Marks
(a)	2019/20	2	
	2020/21	1	
			3
(b)	Trading profit		
	Depreciation	½	
	Motor expenses	1	
	Accountancy	½	
	Legal fees	½	
	Use of office	1	
	Capital allowances	2	
	Property business income		
	Rent received	½	
	Other expenses	½	
	Qualifying interest	1	
	Partnership loss	2	
	Personal allowance	½	
	Income tax @ 20%	½	
	Income tax @ 40%	½	
	Tax reducer	1	
			12
			15

(a) **Danh – Residence status in the tax years 2019/20 and 2020/21**

2019/20

Danh was not resident in the UK. Danh would be UK resident if he had three or more UK ties because he was in the UK between 91 and 120 days and was not UK resident in any of the previous three tax years. Danh had two ties which were available UK accommodation in which he spent at least one night during the tax year and substantive UK work.

2020/21

Danh was resident in the UK. Again, Danh would be UK resident if he had three or more UK ties. Danh had an additional tie which was that he spent more than 90 days in the UK in the previous tax year.

(b) Danh – Income tax liability 2021/22

	£
Trading income (W1)	73,176
Property business income £14,400 - £3,980	10,420
Total income	83,596
Less Qualifying interest	(875)
Partnership loss £12,600 × 7/12 × 20%	(1,470)
Net income	81,251
Less personal allowance	(12,570)
Taxable income	68,681

Tax	
£37,700 @ 20%	7,540
£(68,681 – 37,700) = £30,981 @ 40%	12,392
Less Property finance costs tax reducer £10,000 × 20%	(2,000)
Income tax liability	17,932

Workings

1   *Trading profit for the eight-month period ended 5 April 2022*

		£
Net profit		70,200
Add Depreciation		2,300
Motor expenses private use £3,300 × 4,000/12,000		1,100
Accountancy		0
Legal fees in connection with grant of short new lease		1,460
Less Use of office £4,200 × 1/6		(700)
Capital allowances £(14,800 × 18% × 8/12 × 8,000/12,000)		(1,184)
Trading profit		73,176

117 Martin

Marks

(a)   Employment income
           Salary   ½
           Bonuses   1
           Car benefit 1st car   1
           Car benefit 2nd car   1
           Beneficial loan   ½
           Home entertainment system   1
           Charitable payroll deductions   ½
           Professional subscription   ½
           Health club membership   ½
       Trading profit
           January to September   1
           October to December   1
       Property income   1
       Dividend income   ½
       Savings certificate income   ½
       Personal allowance   ½
                                                                                      ─
                                                                                      11

(b)   (i)   Deadline for amending tax return   1
              Interest   1
                                                                                      ─
                                                                                      2

       (ii)   Compliance check notice   1
              Reasons for check   1
                                                                                      ─
                                                                                      2
                                                                                      ─
                                                                                      15

(a)   Martin – Taxable income 2021/22

	£
Employment income	
Salary	144,000
Bonuses (21,400 + 13,700)	35,100
Car benefit 18,450 × 16% × 9/12	2,214
Car benefit 24,905 × 19% × 3/12	1,183
Beneficial loan	0
Home entertainment system (7,400 × 20%)	1,480
Charitable payroll deductions	(1,000)
Professional subscription	(560)
Health club membership	0
	182,417
Trading profit (working)	20,930
Property income (9,200 – 7,500)	1,700
Dividend income	440
Interest from savings certificate	0
Net income	205,487
Less Personal allowance	0
Taxable income	205,487

Tutorial notes

1   The bonus of £18,200 will have been treated as being received during 2020/21 because Martin became entitled to it during that tax year.

2   There is no taxable benefit in respect of the beneficial loan because it did not exceed £10,000 at any time during 2021/22.

3   No personal allowance is available because Martin's adjusted net income of £205,487 exceeds £125,140.

Working – Trading profit

	£
1 January to 30 September 2021 54,600 × 9/12 × 40%	16,380
1 October to 31 December 2021 54,600 × 3/12 × 1/3	4,550
	20,930

(b)   (i)   Martin's deadline for amending his self-assessment tax return for the tax year 2021/22 will be 31 January 2024 (12 months from the latest (electronic) filing date for the return of 31 January 2023).

Should additional tax become payable, then interest will be charged from 31 January 2023 to the day before the additional tax is paid.

(ii)   If HMRC intend to carry out a compliance check into Martin's self-assessment tax return for 2021/22, then they will have to notify him by 26 December 2023 (12 months after they receive his tax return).

HMRC will carry out a compliance check because of a suspicion that income has been undeclared or deductions have been incorrectly claimed.

118 Tonie

Workbook references. The income tax computation, including residence and the accrued income scheme, is covered in Chapter 2. Employment income is dealt with in Chapters 3 and 4. Property income is the subject of Chapter 6.

Top tips. In part (a) you only need to discuss the relevant UK ties which Tonie satisfied, not all of them. Be guided by the fact that there were only two marks for this part.

Easy marks. There were some easy ½ marks for showing that the premium bond prize and the interest from savings certificates were exempt income – but would you have got them by using a zero in your computation?

Examining team's comments. Part (a) was reasonably well answered, although candidates sometimes did not focus their answers on the information given. For example, there was no point mentioning the UK ties which were not met by Tonie. The section was for just two marks, so this should have been a good indication that only a few brief sentences were required and not a half page discussion on everything a candidate knew about the residence rules.

Part (b) was well answered. However, candidates should avoid repetition by, for example, stating that Tonie (1) attended weekly meetings at Droid plc's offices, and (2) received instructions – these were both indications of control. When asked for a list it is easiest to answer using a list format.

With the exception of the accrued gilt income, part (c) was generally very well answered.

•   Candidates should note that most of the workings for this style of question can be included within the main computation. For example, the mileage allowance deduction was easily included within the main computation. The only aspect which warranted a separate working here was property income.

- With computations containing both additions and deductions, candidates should be very careful to indicate which is which. A single column approach with deductions included as such on the spreadsheet avoids any confusion.

- Candidates should note that taxable income is after the personal allowance has been deducted.

- Reading and understanding a question's requirements will avoid spending time calculating an income tax liability when it is not needed. The requirement was just to calculate Tonie's taxable income.

Marking scheme

			Marks
(a)	Three ties needed	½	
	Two ties identified	1½	
			2
(b)	½ mark for each factor	Max	2
(c)	Employment income		
	Salary	½	
	Mileage allowance	1	
	Leasing costs	1	
	Property income		
	Rent received	½	
	Mortgage interest - no relief	1	
	Washing machine	1	
	Dishwasher	1	
	Other expenses	½	
	Furnished room	1	
	Accrued interest scheme income	2	
	Premium bond prize	½	
	Savings certificate interest	½	
	Personal allowance	½	
			11
			15

(a) Tonie was previously resident and was in the UK between 46 and 90 days. She therefore needed three UK ties or more to be treated as UK resident.

Tonie only had two UK ties, which were being in the UK for more than 90 days during the previous tax year, and spending more time in the UK than in any other country during 2020/21.

(b) The contract was for a relatively long period of time.
Tonie did not take any financial risk. Tonie only worked for Droid plc.
Tonie was required to do the work personally.
Droid plc exercised control over Tonie via the weekly meetings and instructions.

(c)   Tonie – Taxable income 2021/22

	£
Employment income	
Salary (6,200 × 12)	74,400
Mileage allowance (2,300 at 15p (60p – 45p))	345
Less leasing costs (180 × 12)	(2,160)
Property income (working)	7,570
Savings income (100,000 at 3% × 5/12)	1,250
Premium bond prize	0
Interest from savings certificate	0
	81,405
Less personal allowance	(12,570)
Taxable income	68,835

Tutorial note

Under the accrued income scheme, Tonie must include the accrued interest from the gilts as savings income for 2021/22, even though she has not received any actual interest.

Working – Property income

	£
Rent received	10,080
Less mortgage interest - relief as tax reducer	(0)
Less replacement furniture relief	
Washing machine	(380)
Dishwasher	(0)
Less other expenses	(3,210)
	6,490
Furnished room (8,580 – 7,500)	1,080
Property income	7,570

Tutorial notes

1   No relief is given for that part of the cost of the washer-dryer which represents an improvement over the original washing machine. Relief is therefore restricted to the cost of a similar washing machine.

2   No relief is available for the cost of the dishwasher because this is an initial cost rather than the cost of a replacement.

3   Claiming rent-a-room relief in respect of the furnished room is more beneficial than the normal basis of assessment (8,580 – 870 = £7,710).

OTQ bank – Chargeable gains for individuals 1

119 Gift of a motor boat valued at £10,000 (cost £5,000) to his aunt.

The gift of the motor boat is exempt because this is a wasting chattel and is not plant and machinery eligible for capital allowances.

The gift of the unquoted shares is not a gift of tangible moveable property and so the chattels rules do not apply to it.

The gift of the antique jewellery is a gift of a non-wasting chattel but it would only be exempt if the proceeds (market value) were £6,000 or less. The gain cannot exceed 5/3 × (proceeds − £6,000).

The gift of the sculpture is a gift of a non-wasting chattel but results in a loss. The loss will be restricted by deeming the market value to be £6,000.

> **Examining team's comments.** This question examines exempt gifts for capital gains tax purposes. The correct answer is gift of a motor boat valued at £10,000 (cost £5,000) to his aunt. This is an exempt gift because it is a wasting chattel (ie a tangible, movable asset with an expected life not exceeding 50 years). Wasting chattels (other than those eligible for capital allowances) are always treated as exempt disposals. The value and original cost are irrelevant.
>
> Answer option gift of unquoted shares in a United Kingdom company valued at £2,500 (cost £1,800) to his brother was the most commonly chosen, suggesting that candidates may not have known the special rules regarding chattels well enough.

120 £2,712

	£
Chargeable gain	26,300
Less annual exempt amount	(12,300)
Taxable gains	14,000

Tax

	£
£(37,700 − 25,620) = 12,080 × 18% (residential property)	2,174
£(14,000 − 12,080) = 1,920 × 28% (residential property)	538
Total capital gains tax	2,712

The answer £3,920 uses 28% throughout. The answer £6,156 does not deduct the annual exempt amount. The answer £1,592 uses the rates of 10% and 20%.

121 £12,143

The amount of the cost attributable to the part sold is:

$$\frac{£36,000}{£36,000 + £90,000} \times £80,000 = £22,857$$

	£
Proceeds £(36,000 − 1,000)	35,000
Less cost (see above)	(22,857)
Gain	12,143

The answer £12,600 uses the net proceeds in the part disposal fraction. The answer £13,143 ignores the cost of disposal. The answer £11,000 uses 3/10 as the part disposal fraction.

122 £11,400

	2019/20	2020/21	2021/22
	£	£	£
Gains	2,000	4,000	14,900
CY losses	(14,000)	(2,000)	(2,000)
	(12,000)	2,000	12,900
AEA	(0)	(2,000)	(12,300)
	0	0	600
B/f losses			(600)
Losses c/f	12,000	12,000	11,400

Current year losses must be set against current year gains. Brought forward losses are set off after the annual exempt amount.

123 £1,667

	£
Proceeds	7,000
Less cost	(1,500)
Gain	5,500

The maximum gain is $5/3 \times £(7,000 - 6,000) = £1,667$.

The chargeable gain is the lower of £5,500 and £1,667, so it is £1,667.

The answer £1,000 is the excess over £6,000. The answer £0 assumes the chattel is an exempt asset.

OTQ bank – Chargeable gains for individuals 2

124 £2,500

	£
Deemed proceeds	6,000
Less cost	(8,500)
Loss	(2,500)

125 14 years

	Exempt years	Chargeable years	Total years
Actual occupation	3		3
Deemed occupation – any time employed overseas	5		5
Actual occupation	2		2
Deemed occupation – up to 3 years any reason	3		3
Unoccupied		1	
Occupied (including last 9 months of ownership)	1	—	1
Totals	14	1	15

126 12 August 2031

When a depreciating asset is purchased to replace a non-depreciating asset the gain on the sale is deferred until the earliest of:

The sale of the depreciating asset – 14 October 2031

Ceasing to use the depreciating asset in a business – not applicable here

The ten-year anniversary of the purchase of the depreciating asset – 12 August 2031

127 £1,160

Gains subject to business asset disposal relief are taxed at 10%. Other gains will be reduced by the annual exempt amount and then taxed, in this case at 20%, because Louise has taxable income in excess of the basic rate limit of £37,700. The capital gains tax (CGT) payable is therefore:

Tax	£
£8,000 × 10%	800
£(14,100 – 12,300) = 1,800 × 20%	360
Total CGT	1,160

128 £13,650

	Number	Cost
		£
Purchase October 2004	1,000	1,500
Bonus issue November 2006		
1 for 2 bonus issue	500	0
	1,500	1,500
Rights issue July 2011		
3 for 1 rights issue @ £2.70	4,500	12,150
	6,000	13,650
Disposal February 2022	(6,000)	(13,650)

129 £77,500

	£
Cost	73,000
Enhancement expenditure	41,700
Less insurance proceeds	(37,200)
Cost of restored property	77,500

130 £16,200

	£
Proceeds	28,800
Less cost £21,000 × 9/15	(12,600)
Chargeable gain	16,200

A copyright is a wasting asset and so the cost is written down over its life on a straight-line basis.

131 £4,000

	£
Gain	24,400
Less current year loss	(10,000)
Net current year gain	14,400
Less annual exempt amount	(12,300)
	2,100
Less loss brought forward	(2,100)
Taxable gain	0
Loss carried forward £(6,100 – 2,100)	4,000

132 £143,000

The proceeds not reinvested in the new asset are £(184,000 − 143,000) = £41,000. Since this is greater than the gain of £38,600, no rollover relief is available. The cost of the replacement warehouse is therefore £143,000.

133

Earliest date	1 August 2020

Latest date	31 July 2024

OT case – Nim

Workbook references. Transfers between spouses, exempt assets, the annual exempt amount and losses are covered in Chapter 13. The rules on chattels will be found in Chapter 14. The valuation of gifts of quoted shares is dealt with in Chapter 16.

Top tips. Questions may be set about spouses or civil partners. Transfers between these are on a no gain / no loss basis.

Easy marks. The valuation of the quoted shares in question 134 should have been easy.

134 £37,500

The shares in Kapook plc are valued at 3.70 + ½ × (3.80 − 3.70) = £3.75 so the deemed disposal proceeds are 10,000 × £3.75 = £37,500.

Make sure you learn this rule!

135 £26,333

The disposal is first matched against the purchase on 24 July 2021 (this is within the following 30 days) and then against the shares in the share pool. The cost of the shares disposed of is, therefore, £26,333 (5,800 + 20,533).

Share pool	No. of shares	Cost
	£	£
Purchase 19 February 2004	8,000	16,200
Purchase 6 June 2009 1 for 2 @ £3.65 per share	4,000	14,600
	12,000	30,800
Disposal 20 July 2021 £30,800 × 8,000/12,000	(8,000)	(20,533)
Balance c/f	4,000	10,267

The answer £28,500 treats the rights issue as separate holding and disposes of it in priority to the 2004 shares. The answer £25,667 is a disposal of 10,000 shares from the pool only. The answer £20,533 is the pool disposal only.

136 Nim will have deemed proceeds on the transfer of the Jooba Ltd shares to his wife so that neither a gain nor a loss will arise.

Nim's wife will take the Jooba Ltd shares with a cost equal to the deemed proceeds ie the original cost to Nim. The spouse exemption applies for inheritance tax, not capital gains tax.

Nim's wife will not be able to transfer her annual exempt amount to Nim.

137   £3,500

	£
Net proceeds	8,700
Less cost	(5,200)
Gain	3,500

The maximum gain is 5/3 × £([8,700 + 300] − 6,000) = £5,000. The chargeable gain is the lower of £3,500 and £5,000, so it is £3,500.

138   £7,100

The set off of the brought forward capital losses is equal to the gain left in charge after the deduction of the annual exempt amount, £8,700 (21,000 − 12,300). Capital losses carried forward are therefore £(15,800 − 8,700) = £7,100.

OT case – Aloi, Bon and Dinah

Workbook references. Business asset disposal relief is dealt with in Chapter 15. Shares are covered in Chapter 16. Transfers on death, computing chargeable gains and the calculation of capital gains tax will be found in Chapter 13.

Top tips. Par value means the face value of the shares. Aloi therefore had a cost of £50,000 for her first 50,000 £1 shares in Alphabet Ltd.

Easy marks. The dates in question 141 should have been well known.

139   Bon was not an officer or employee of Alphabet Ltd for the requisite time before disposal.

Alphabet Ltd was not Dinah's personal company for the requisite time before disposal.

Bon only became a director on 1 February 2020, so this qualifying condition was not met for two years prior to the date of disposal. Her shareholding of 25% (25,000/100,000 × 100) means that Alphabet Ltd is her personal company and she also satisfies the minimum two years for this condition to be met prior to the date of disposal.

Dinah was an employee for at least two years prior to the disposal but her shareholding of 3% (3,000/100,000 × 100) is less than the minimum required holding of 5% for Alphabet Ltd to be her personal company.

140   £29,140

	£
Gain qualifying for business asset disposal relief	
Ordinary shares in Alphabet Ltd	
Proceeds of sale (60,000 × £6)	360,000
Less cost £(50,000 + 18,600)	(68,600)
Gain	291,400
CGT @ 10% on £291,400	29,140

141   Notification 5 October 2022, payment 31 January 2023

142   £34,320

	£
Deemed proceeds of sale (10,000 × £7.12 (W1))	71,200
Less cost (W2)	(36,880)
Gain	34,320

Workings

1   The shares in XYZ plc are valued at $7.10 + \frac{1}{2} \times (7.14 - 7.10) = £7.12$.

2   Following the takeover, Bon received 25,000 shares in XYZ plc. The cost of the original shareholding is passed on to the new shareholding so the cost attributable to the 10,000 shares sold is £36,880 ($92,200 \times 10,000/25,000$).

143   £0

There is no CGT liability on the sale of the XYZ plc shares as the gain of £5,000 (6,600 – (4,800 × 1,000/3,000)) is less than the annual exempt amount.

The transfer of the XYZ plc shares on Dinah's death is an exempt disposal.

OT case – Ginger, Innocent and Nigel

Workbook references. Chapter 13 covers the basics of computing chargeable gains. Chapter 15 deals with business reliefs.

Top tips. In questions 147 and 148 think why the disposals by Innocent and Nigel would give rise to different capital gains tax liabilities. Are there different rates of capital gains tax? When do those rates apply?

Easy marks. There were easy marks in question 145 for working out the number of shares that could be sold without incurring a charge to CGT.

144   £1.60

The disposal is at an undervalue, so only the gift element of the gain can be deferred under gift holdover relief. The consideration paid for each share will be immediately chargeable to capital gains tax to the extent that it exceeds the allowable cost. The chargeable amount is therefore £(4.00 – 2.40) = £1.60 per share.

145   8,506

Ginger's annual exempt amount for 2021/22 is £12,300 and she has a loss of £(800) brought forward from 2020/21. She can therefore sell (13,100/1.54) = <u>8,506 shares</u> to her daughter without this resulting in any capital gains tax liability for 2021/22.

146   There is a lifetime limit of £1,000,000 for business asset disposal relief.

Business asset disposal relief is only available on shareholdings if they are held in a trading company.

The individual can be an officer (eg a director) or an employee of the company in which the shares are held. The conditions for business asset disposal relief must be satisfied for two years before the disposal.

147   £6,300

Innocent makes disposal

	£
Disposal proceeds	65,000
Less cost	(2,000)
Gain	63,000
CGT on £63,000 @ 10%	6,300

148   £6,840

Nigel makes disposal

	£
Disposal proceeds	65,000
Less cost (£46,200 × 2,000/3,000)	(30,800)
Gain	34,200
CGT on £34,200 @ 20%	6,840

OT case – Jerome

> **Workbook references.** Computing chargeable gains is dealt with in Chapter 13. Chattels are covered in Chapter 14. Business reliefs are the subject of Chapter 15.
>
> **Top tips.** If you are dealing with the disposal of a chattel, do not assume that the 5/3 rule always applies. Test it against the actual gain.
>
> **Easy marks.** There were some easy marks for identifying the base cost of the house for Jerome's wife in question 149 and for the administrative aspects of the election to hold over the gain on the Reward Ltd shares in question 151.

149   £112,800

The disposal of the house does not give rise to a gain or a loss because it is a transfer between spouses. The base cost of the house for Jerome's wife is therefore Jerome's base cost which was the value of the house at the uncle's death.

150   £50,600

	£
Deemed proceeds	98,400
Less cost	(39,000)
Gain before gift holdover relief	59,400

Gift holdover relief is restricted to £50,600 (£59,400 × 460,000/540,000), being the proportion of chargeable business assets to chargeable assets.

151

Latest date for election	5 April 2026

Person(s) making election	Jerome and his son

152   £10,100

	£
Proceeds	12,200
Less cost	(2,100)
Chargeable gain	10,100

The maximum gain is 5/3 × £(12,200 − 6,000) = £10,333. The chargeable gain is the lower of £10,333 and £10,100, so it is £10,100.

If your choice was £3,900 make sure you don't confuse the rules on gains and the rules on losses – the deemed proceeds are only £6,000 for computing the restricted loss.

153   £51,940

	£
Proceeds	78,400
Less cost (W)	(26,460)
Chargeable gain	51,940
Working	

The amount of the cost attributable to the part sold is:

$$\frac{£78,400}{£78,400 + £33,600} \times £37,800 = £26,460$$

OT case – Hali and Goma

> **Workbook references.** Capital gains tax (CGT) computation is covered in Chapter 13 and business reliefs in Chapter 15.
>
> **Top tips.** In question 154, remember that current year losses are set against gains before the annual exempt amount (AEA), but brought forward losses are set against gains remaining after the AEA.
>
> **Easy marks.** There were easy marks in question 158 for knowledge of exempt assets for CGT.

154   Option 4

Hali

	£
Gains	16,300
Less AEA	(12,300)
	4,000
Less losses b/f	(4,000)
	0
Losses c/f £(39,300 – 4,000)	35,300

Goma

	£
Gains	6,900
Less current year losses	(9,100)
Losses c/f	(2,200)

For Hali, the answer £23,000 uses the carried forward loss against the gains first, before the annual exempt amount. For Goma, the answer £9,100 uses the annual exempt amount first so that there are no gains left to relieve.

155   Option 1

The transfer of the shares between Goma and Hali was on a no gain/ no loss basis so Hali's cost is Goma's cost of £1 per share (par value). His cost of 5,000 shares is therefore 5,000 × £1 = £5,000.

The answer £14,500 is the value of 5,000 shares at the time of the transfer between Goma and Hali.

The value per share is £4.95.

The answer £5.30 could be the market value per share. This is used where there is a sale which is not at arm's length but not just because Hali wanted a quick sale.

156   Lima Ltd must be a trading company

The answer Hali and Goma must be directors of Lima Ltd is incorrect because the condition is that that they are either officers (could include company secretary, not just directors) or employees of the company.

The answer Hali and Goma must have shareholdings of at least 10% each in Lima Ltd is incorrect because the condition is at least 5%.

The answer The qualifying conditions must be met for a period of three years prior to the date of disposal is incorrect because the qualifying period is two years.

157   £45,600

	£
Proceeds (compensation received)	62,000
Less cost	(44,000)
Gain	18,000

All proceeds reinvested so whole gain can be rolled over into the cost of the replacement asset.

The base cost of the replacement antique table is £(63,600 – 18,000) = £45,600.

The answer £62,000 is the compensation received. The answer £63,200 is the cost of the replacement antique table (ie no roll-over). The answer £44,000 is the cost of the original table.

158   Three

Qualifying corporate bonds sold for £38,300

A motor car (suitable for private use) sold for £11,600

Quoted shares held within an individual savings account (ISA) sold for £24,700

The antique vase sold for £6,200 is a chargeable asset but the restriction applies of the gain to 5/3 × proceeds.

The copyright (with an unexpired life of eight years when purchased) sold for £5,400 is a chargeable asset but the cost will be written down on a straight line basis so that only the remaining eight years of cost will be available.

159 Jorge

Workbook references. Chapter 13 deals with the basic computation of chargeable gains, including the annual exempt amount. Chapter 14 covers wasting assets, chattels, and the private residence exemption.

Top tips. Remember that deemed periods of occupation for private residence relief must usually be preceded by a period of actual occupation and followed by a period of actual occupation.

Easy marks. The painting and the motor car were easy half marks. Don't forget to deduct the annual exempt amount for another easy half mark.

Marking scheme

	Marks
House	
Proceeds	½
Cost	½
Enhancement expenditure	½
Period of exemption	3
Private residence exemption	1
Copyright	
Proceeds	½
Cost	1½
Painting	½
Motor car	½
Annual exempt amount	½
Capital loss bf	1
	10

Jorge – Taxable gains computation 2021/22

	£
House (W1)	31,000
Copyright (W4)	24,300
Painting – exempt as proceeds and cost £6,000 or less	0
Motor car – exempt asset so loss not allowable	0
Chargeable gains	55,300
Less annual exempt amount	(12,300)
Less capital loss bf	(25,000)
Taxable gains	18,000

Workings

1   *House*

	£
Proceeds	308,000
Less cost	(93,000)
Less enhancement expenditure (defending title to property)	(5,000)
Gain	210,000
Less private residence exemption (W2)	(179,000)
Gain after exemptions	31,000

2   *Private residence exemption*

	Exempt months	Chargeable months	Total months
Actual occupation	34		34
Deemed occupation – up to 3 years any reason	18		18
Deemed occupation – any time employed overseas	24		24
Actual occupation	11		11
Deemed occupation – up to 4 years working elsewhere in UK	30		30
Deemed occupation – up to 3 years any reason balance (36 − 18) = 18, (22 − 18) = 4 chargeable	18	4	22
Deemed occupation – up to 4 years working elsewhere in UK balance (48 − 30) = 18, (26 − 18) = 8 chargeable	18	8	26
Actual occupation	17		17
Working overseas – not followed by actual occupation		12	12
Unoccupied – travelling		7	7
Last 9 months – always treated as period of occupation	9		9
Totals	179	31	210

Private residence exemption £210,000 × 179/210   £179,000

Tutorial note

In calculating the private residence exemption, any periods of absence while working overseas, a maximum of four years' absence while working elsewhere in the UK, and a maximum of three years' absence for any reason are treated as deemed occupation, usually provided that they are preceded and followed by a period of actual occupation. The second period working overseas is therefore not a period of deemed occupation as it was not followed by a period of actual occupation.

No letting relief is available since Jorge let out the whole property while he was away, rather than sharing occupation.

Alternative approach

An alternative approach to calculate the chargeable months as follows:

Total period of ownership	210
Less actual occupation (34 + 11 + 17)	(62)
Deemed occupation – any reason up to 3 years	(36)
– employed overseas without limit	(24)
– working in UK up to 4 years	(48)
Last 9 months – always treated as period of occupation	(9)
Chargeable months	31

3   *Copyright*

	£
Proceeds	80,300
Less cost £70,000 × 8/10 (N)	(56,000)
Gain	24,300

Tutorial note

The copyright is a wasting asset. The cost of £70,000 must therefore be depreciated based on an unexpired life of ten years at the date of acquisition and an unexpired life of eight years at the date of disposal.

160 Winston

Workbook references. Chapter 13 covers transfers on death, computing chargeable gains, transfers between spouses, part disposals and CGT liability. Chapter 15 includes business asset disposal relief.

Top tips. Losses on assets not qualifying for business asset disposal relief and the annual exempt amount should be deducted to produce the lowest CGT liability. This means that they should be deducted from gains taxed at 20% in priority to gains taxed at 10%.

Easy marks. The calculation of capital gains tax in part (a)(i) was straightforward.

Marking scheme

			Marks	
(a)	(i)	Annual exempt amount	1	
		Unused basic rate band	½	
		Capital gains tax	1½	
				3
	(ii)	Freehold shop	½	
		Painting	½	
		Capital loss	1	
		Annual exempt amount	½	
		Capital gains tax	1½	
				4
(b)		Net proceeds	1	
		Cost – probate value taken over on transfer from spouse	1	
		Apportionment of cost	1	
				3
				10

(a) (i) Winston – CGT liability 2021/22

	£
Chargeable gain on painting	47,560
Less annual exempt amount	(12,300)
Taxable gain	35,260

CGT liability:	£(37,700 – 25,100) = 12,600 @ 10%	1,260
	£(35,260 – 12,600) = 22,660 @ 20%	4,532
		5,792

(ii) Winston – Revised CGT liability 2021/22

	£
Gain qualifying for business asset disposal relief	
Gain on freehold shop £(140,000 – 80,000)	60,000
Gain not qualifying for business asset disposal relief	
Painting	47,560
Less allowable loss on warehouse £(102,000 – 88,000)	(14,000)
Net gain	33,560
Less annual exempt amount	(12,300)
Taxable gain	21,260

		£
CGT liability:	£60,000 @ 10%	6,000
	£21,260 @ 20%	4,252
		10,252

Tutorial notes

1   The capital loss on the sale of the freehold warehouse and the annual exempt amount are set against the chargeable gain from the sale of the painting as this saves CGT at the higher rate of 20%. Although the warehouse is being sold with the business, it was never actually used in the business, and so this aspect of the sale does not qualify for business asset disposal relief. If it had been used in the business, the loss of £14,000 would have been deducted from the gain on the shop to give a net gain on sale of the business of £46,000. CGT would then be charged on £46,000 at 10%.

2   The unused basic rate tax band of £12,600 is effectively used by the gain qualifying for business asset disposal relief of £60,000 even though this has no effect on the 10% tax rate.

(b) Renaldo – Chargeable gain 3 December 2021

	£
Gross proceeds	92,000
Less auctioneers' commission (cost of disposal) £92,000 × 5%	(4,600)
Net proceeds	87,400
Less cost £28,600 × $\dfrac{92,000}{92,000 + 38,000}$	(20,240)
Chargeable gain	67,160

Tutorial notes

1   The cost of the land is £28,600 which is the value when Renaldo's father in law died. Renaldo would have taken over this cost when his wife transferred the land to him.

2   The gross proceeds of sale are used in the part-disposal fraction.

161 Mick

Marking scheme

		Marks
(a)	*Warehouse*	
	Disposal proceeds	½
	Cost	½
	Extension	½
	Floor	½
	Shares in Rolling Ltd	
	Disposal proceeds	½
	Purchase	½
	Bonus issue	½
	Disposal cost	½
		4
(b)	*Warehouse*	
	Replacement of business assets relief	1
	Acquisition date of new warehouse	1
	Cost of new warehouse	1
	Shares in Rolling Ltd	
	Business asset disposal relief	1
	Rolling Ltd share capital	1
	Previous claims	1
		6
		10

(a) **Mick – Chargeable gains 2021/22**

Freehold warehouse

	£	£
Disposal proceeds		522,000
Less: cost	258,000	
enhancement expenditure: extension	99,000	
enhancement expenditure: floor	0	
		(357,000)
Chargeable gain		165,000

Tutorial note

The cost of replacing the warehouse's floor is revenue expenditure as the floor is a subsidiary part of the property.

Shares in Rolling Ltd

	£
Disposal proceeds	3,675,000
Less cost (W)	(537,600)
Chargeable gain	3,137,400

Working: Share pool

	Number	Cost £
Purchase June 2007	500,000	960,000
Bonus issue December 2012		
500,000 × 3/2	750,000	0
Disposal September 2021	1,250,000	960,000
960,000 × 700,000/1,250,000	(700,000)	(537,600)
Balance carried forward	550,000	422,400

(b)   **Freehold warehouse**

Replacement of business assets relief (rollover relief) may be available in respect of the chargeable gain arising on the disposal of the freehold warehouse.

The acquisition date of the replacement warehouse is required, since relief will only be available if this is after 19 May 2020 (one year before the date of disposal).

The cost of the replacement warehouse is required, since relief will be restricted if the sale proceeds of £522,000 have not been fully reinvested.

Shares in Rolling Ltd

Business asset disposal relief may be available in respect of the chargeable gain arising on the disposal of the shares in Rolling Ltd.

Details of Rolling Ltd's share capital are required, since relief will only be available if Mick had the minimum required holding of 5%.

Details of any previous business asset disposal relief claims made by Mick are required, since there is a lifetime limit of £1 million of gains.

162 Ruby

Workbook references. The computation of chargeable gains and capital gains tax is covered in Chapter 13. Business reliefs are the subject of Chapter 15 and shares are dealt with in Chapter 16.

Top tips. The annual exempt amount should be set against gains which do not qualify for investors' relief in priority to those which do qualify for the relief.

Easy marks. There were easy marks in part (a) for a basic computation of capital gains tax.

Examining team's comments. Part (a) of the question was well answered.

In part (b), the main problem was that candidates did not appreciate that both disposals would impact on the capital gains tax payable in respect of the disposal of the investment property. The disposal of the shares in the unquoted trading company (qualifying for investors' relief) would utilise the remaining basic rate tax band, meaning that the 28% rate was now applicable. The capital loss arising on the disposal of the shares in the quoted trading company would be offset against the chargeable gain on the investment property. Another common problem was the 50p nominal value of the shares in the quoted trading company. This did not impact on the calculation of the capital loss, although many candidates incorrectly divided their cost figure by two.

		Marks
(a)	Annual exempt amount	½
	CGT at 18%	1
	CGT at 28%	½
		2
(b)	*Pola Ltd*	
	Disposal proceeds	½
	Cost	½
	Investment property	½
	Annual exempt amount (best use)	1
	CGT at 10%	1
	CGT at 28%	1
	Aplo plc	
	Disposal proceeds	½
	Cost	1½
	Investment property	½
	Annual exempt amount	½
	CGT at 18%	½
		8
		10

(a) Ruby's CGT liability

	£
Chargeable gain on investment property	47,000
Less annual exempt amount	(12,300)
	34,700
Capital gains tax	
£14,185 (37,700 – 23,515) @ 18% (residential property)	2,553
£20,515 (34,700 – 14,185) @ 28% (residential property)	5,744
	8,297

(b) Choice of disposal

Shareholding in Pola Ltd

	Investors' relief £	No reliefs £
Pola Ltd shares £(61,000 – 23,700)	37,300	
Investment property (part (a))		47,000
Less annual exempt amount (best use)		(12,300)
	37,300	34,700
Capital gains tax		
£37,300 @ 10%	3,730	
£34,700 @ 28%		9,716
Total CGT £(3,730 + 9,716)		13,446

Tutorial note

The shares in Pola Ltd qualify for investors' relief because they are shares in an unlisted trading company of which Ruby is neither an officer nor an employee, were subscribed for by Ruby on or after 17 March 2016 and held by her for at least 3 years before the disposal.

Shareholding in Aplo plc

	£
Aplo plc shares	
£59,000 – (40,000 × £2.15(W))	(27,000)
Investment property (part (a))	47,000
Less annual exempt amount	(12,300)
Taxable gain	7,700
Capital gains tax	
£7,700 @ 18%	1,386

Working: The Aplo plc shares are valued at £2.12 + ½ × (£2.18 − £2.12) = £2.15.

OTQ bank – Inheritance tax 1

163   £150,000

	£
Before the gift: 70% shareholding	350,000
After the gift: 50% shareholding	(200,000)
Transfer of value	150,000

164   £461,250

	£
Sunita's unused nil rate band £325,000 × 65%	211,250
Joel's nil rate band	325,000
	536,250
Less used against Joel's PET now chargeable	(75,000)
Available nil rate band to set against Joel's death estate	461,250

Sunita's nil rate band is increased pro-rata to that available at the time of Joel's death.

The answer £325,000 does not involve a spouse transfer and does not take account of the PET. The answer £452,800 transfers 65% of £312,000. The answer £536,250 does not deduct the PET.

165   £29,750

	£
Gift	190,000
Less AE × 2 (current year + b/f)	(6,000)
	184,000
Less nil rate band available £(325,000 – 260,000)	(65,000)
	119,000
IHT @ $^{20}/_{80}$	29,750

The answer £28,250 deducts annual exemptions from the earlier transfer. The answer £31,250 does not deduct annual exemptions from the current transfer. The answer £23,800 does not gross up ie uses a rate of 20%.

166   £0

The gift to the granddaughter is covered by the marriage exemption of £2,500 by a remoter ancestor.

The sale of the vase is not a transfer of value because there is no gratuitous intent as Donald and Alan believed that the vase was worth what Alan paid for it.

167   £136,000

	£
PET on 10.7.18 PET now chargeable	600,000
Less nil rate band available £(325,000 – 150,000)	(175,000)
	425,000
IHT @ 40%	170,000
Less taper relief (3 to 4 years) @ 20%	(34,000)
Death tax payable on lifetime transfer	136,000

The chargeable lifetime transfer on 15 September 2012 is cumulated with the later PET since it was made in the seven years before that transfer.

The answer £170,000 does not deduct taper relief. The answer £88,000 treats the earlier gift as exempt so the full nil rate band is available. The answer £134,080 deducts annual exemptions from the current transfer.

BPP LEARNING MEDIA

OTQ bank – Inheritance tax 2

168   £350

The gifts to the grandson are exempt as normal expenditure out of income because they are part of the normal expenditure of the donor, made out of income and left the donor with sufficient income to maintain her usual standard of living.

The small gifts exemption only applies to gifts up to £250 per donee per tax year. If gifts total more than £250 the whole amount is chargeable. Since the gifts to the grandnephew totalled £(100 + 250) = £350 in the year, this exemption does not apply.

169   £66,000

	£
Before the gift: 100% shareholding 1,000 × £150	150,000
After the gift: 70% shareholding 700 × £120	(84,000)
Transfer of value	66,000

170   £24,000

	£
Main residence (net of mortgage) £(300,000 – 195,000)	105,000
Investments and cash	385,000
Chargeable death estate	490,000
Less: residence property nil rate band	
(lower of £105,000 and £175,000)	(105,000)
available nil rate band (no lifetime transfers)	(325,000)
	60,000
IHT @ 40%	24,000

The residence nil rate band applies because the main residence is left to direct descendants. Note that the residence nil rate band is the lower of the net value of the main residence and the maximum amount of £175,000 (2021/22).

171   £351,000

	£
Cash to nephews £200 × 5	1,000
ISA investments	350,000
Chargeable estate	351,000

The small gifts exemption only applies to lifetime transfers. The ISA exemption only applies for income tax and capital gains tax. The residue to the wife is covered by the spouse exemption.

172   Sandeep is liable to make the payment by 31 May 2022

> **Examining team's comments.** This question tested candidates' knowledge of the payment of IHT on a chargeable lifetime transfer (CLT) to a trust.
>
> The donor, Sandeep, is primarily liable for the tax due on a CLT and the due date is the later of the following:
>
> - Six months after the end of the month of transfer
> - 30 April after the end of the tax year of transfer
>
> The later of these dates is therefore 31 May 2022 and so the correct answer was the third option. Many candidates were able to select the correct date, but were less successful in determining who was primarily liable for payment.
>
> Tax administration and the payment of tax are important aspects of the syllabus and candidates are reminded to devote sufficient attention to these topics when preparing for the TX–UK exam.

173   £234,000

	£
Estate	890,000
Less: IHT	(276,000)
legacy to wife	(260,000)
legacy to brother	(120,000)
Residue to grandchildren	234,000

174

Changing the terms of her will so that the residue of her estate goes to her grandchildren rather than her children		WILL NOT ACHIEVE
Making lifetime gifts to trusts up to the value of the nil rate band every seven years	WILL ACHIEVE	
Changing the terms of her will so that the residue of her estate goes to her husband rather than her children	WILL ACHIEVE	
Making lifetime gifts to her grandchildren early in life	WILL ACHIEVE	

There will be the same amount of inheritance tax on the residue of the estate if it is left to Heng's children or grandchildren. However, if the estate is left to her husband the spouse exemption will apply. Heng could reduce the potential inheritance tax liability on her estate when she dies by making lifetime gifts to trusts up to the value of the nil rate band every seven years as these will reduce her assets and will not be cumulated if she survives seven years. She could also make lifetime gifts to her grandchildren early in life as these would be potentially exempt transfers and she is more likely to survive seven years the earlier in life she makes the gifts.

175

Due date	30 June 2022

Persons responsible	The trustees

Examining team's comments. This question tested knowledge of when IHT will be payable and by whom. The correct answer was the trustees on 30 June 2022, which is six months following the month of death. More candidates selected this option than any of the others, but 'The personal representatives of Chan's estate on 30 June 2022' and 'The trustees on 8 June 2022' were both popular choices. This is fairly basic knowledge, and it is the type of question which should represent a very easy (and quick) two marks.

176   £220,000

Nadia is entitled to her husband's residence nil rate band (as it was unused at the date of his death). It is assumed to be £175,000. The maximum residence nil rate band is therefore £(175,000 + 175,000) = £350,000.

The residence nil rate band is the lower of the maximum residence nil rate band of £350,000 and the net value of the main residence of £(360,000 − 140,000) = £220,000 ie £220,000.

BPP
LEARNING
MEDIA

177   The inheritance tax liability on Rachel's estate will [decrease] by [£70,000] if she leaves her main residence to her son rather than her brother.

This is because the residence nil rate band will apply since Rachel will be leaving her main residence to a direct descendent. The available residence nil rate band is the lower of £175,000 and £300,000 ie £175,000. This gives a decrease in the inheritance tax liability of £175,000 × 40% = £70,000.

OT case – Ning

> **Workbook references.** Inheritance tax is covered in Chapter 18.
>
> **Top tips.** If the nil rate band has increased since the death of the first spouse, the available nil rate band to be transferred on the death of the surviving spouse is calculated with reference to the increased nil rate band.
>
> **Easy marks.** Question 179 was quite straightforward as long as you did not confuse the exemptions for income tax and capital gains tax on certain investments with the inheritance tax position.

178   £956,000

	£
Property one	674,000
Less repayment mortgage	(160,000)
	514,000
Property two	442,000
	956,000

179   £324,000

	£
Motor cars	172,000
Investments £(47,000 + 36,000 + 69,000)	152,000
	324,000

There are no exempt assets for inheritance tax.

180   £27,900

	£
Bank loan	22,400
Nephew's legal fees	0
Funeral expenses	5,500
	27,900

The promise to pay the nephew's legal fees is not deductible as it is purely gratuitous (not made for valuable consideration).

181   £105,000

The potentially exempt transfer on 14 August 2010 is exempt from inheritance tax as it was made more than seven years before 20 March 2022.

The potentially exempt transfer on 7 November 2020 will utilise £220,000 of the nil rate band, so only £(325,000 − 220,000) = £105,000 is available against the death estate. The residence nil rate band is not available as it cannot be used against lifetime gifts.

182   Amount £227,500, Claim by 31 March 2024

Ning's personal representatives could claim her deceased husband's unused nil rate band of £325,000 × 70% = £227,500. The time limit for the claim is two years from the end of the month of Ning's death ie by 31 March 2024.

OT case – Jimmy

183   £8,500

	£
Marriage exemption	2,500
Annual exemption 2020/21	3,000
Annual exemption 2019/20 b/f	3,000
	8,500

The answer £3,000 is just the current year annual exemption. The answer £6,000 is the annual exemptions for the current year and the previous year. The answer £11,000 uses £5,000 as the marriage exemption.

184   £55,000

	£
Before the gift: 5,100 shares × £30	153,000
After the gift: 4,900 shares × £20	(98,000)
Diminution in value	55,000

The answer £4,000 is 200 shares at £20 each. The answer £6,000 is 200 shares at £30 each. The answer £1,000 is the actual value of the shares gifted which is 200 shares at £5 each.

185   £118,750

	£
Net transfer of value (Jimmy pays IHT)	800,000

IHT	£325,000	× 0% =	Nil
	£475,000	× 20/80 =	118,750
	£800,000		118,750

The annual exemptions have been used by the PET in August 2020.

186

Due date	31 August 2022

By whom paid	Trustees of trust

187   £312,000

	£
Death estate	980,000
Less spouse exemption	(200,000)
Chargeable death estate	780,000

£780,000 × 40%	312,000

The nil rate band has been used up by the lifetime transfers (stated in question) so the chargeable death estate is all taxed at 40%.

OT case – Zoe and Luke

188   The payments could be exempt without any cash limit under the normal expenditure out of income exemption.

The payments must have left Luke with sufficient income to maintain his usual standard of living to qualify for the normal expenditure out of income exemption.

Payments can qualify for the normal expenditure out of income exemption even if they are not paid directly to the individual who benefits from them. The payments did not have been reported each tax year to HM Revenue & Customs in Luke's income tax return to qualify for the normal expenditure out of income exemption (they will be reported in the inheritance tax account submitted on Luke's death).

189   £710,000

	£
Net chargeable transfer (AEs already used)	633,000

IHT	
£325,000 × 0%	0
£308,000 × 20/80	77,000
£633,000	77,000

Gross chargeable transfer £(633,000 + 77,000)	710,000

The answer £702,500 deducts two annual exemptions. The answer £694,600 treats the transfer as a gross chargeable transfer so uses the rate of 20%. The answer £756,200 uses the death rate of 40%.

190   £24,000

	£
Gross chargeable transfer	200,000

IHT on death (nil rate band already used)	
£200,000 × 40%	80,000
Less taper relief (3 to 4 years) £80,000 × 20%	(16,000)
	64,000
Less lifetime tax £200,000 × 20%	(40,000)
Additional IHT payable	24,000

The answer £40,000 does not deduct taper relief. The answer £80,000 is the death tax without deducting taper relief or lifetime tax. The answer £64,000 does not deduct lifetime tax.

191   £259,000

	£
Gift	270,000
Less: marriage exemption	(5,000)
annual exemption current year	(3,000)
annual exemption b/f	(3,000)
Potentially exempt transfer	259,000

192   £75,000

	£
Unused nil rate band at wife's death £(312,000 − 240,000)	72,000
Amount to transfer £325,000 × 72,000/312,000	75,000

The answer £72,000 does not adjust for the change in the nil rate band between the death of Luke's wife and Luke. The answer £312,000 is the nil rate band at the date of Luke's wife's death. The answer £325,000 is the nil rate band at Luke's death.

OT case – Marcus

Workbook references. Inheritance tax is dealt with in Chapter 18.

Top tips. In question 197, do not mix up the rules for transfers between spouses for capital gains tax (no gain/no loss transfer) and inheritance tax (exempt transfer).

Easy marks. There were some easy marks for a basic inheritance tax computation in question 193 provided that you remembered that the nil rate band at the date of the transfer should be used.

193   £600

			£
IHT	£325,000	× 0% =	Nil
	£3,000	× 20% =	600
	£328,000		600

194   £98,250

			£
IHT	£0	(325,000 − 328,000) × 0% =	Nil
	£491,250	× 20% =	98,250
	£491,250		98,250

Although Marcus pays the inheritance tax due, since the gross chargeable transfer is given, in order to work out the tax he pays, this is 20% of the excess over the available nil rate band.

The answer £122,812 grosses up (ie uses 20/80). The answer £33,250 uses the full nil rate band. The answer £41,562 uses the full nil rate band and grosses up.

195   £78,600

			£
IHT	£0	× 0% =	Nil
	£491,250	× 40% =	196,500
	£491,250		196,500

	£
Taper relief (4 to 5 years) £196,500 @ 40%	78,600

The answer £117,900 is the tax payable after taper relief. The answer £26,600 does not take account of the brought forward transfer. The answer £39,900 is does not take account of the brought forward transfer and is the tax payable after taper relief.

196   £570,000

	£
Before: 100,000 × £12	1,200,000
After: 70,000 × £9	(630,000)
Potentially exempt transfer of value	570,000

The answer £360,000 is 30,000 shares at £12 each. The answer £270,000 is 30,000 shares at £9 each. The answer £150,000 is 30,000 shares at £5 each.

197   If Barbara remarries, any unused nil rate band on her death can be transferred to her spouse if they survive her.

The transfer of Marcus's estate to Barbara on his death is an exempt transfer.

Married couples (and registered civil partnerships) are not chargeable persons for inheritance tax (IHT) purposes, because each spouse (or civil partner) is taxed separately.

The gift of the land on 29 June 2019 by Marcus to Barbara is an exempt transfer.

OT case – Lebna and Lulu

> **Workbook references.** Inheritance tax (IHT) is the subject of Chapter 18.
>
> **Top tips.** In question 200, remember that IHT is charged on the diminution of the donor's estate, not on the value of the property transferred.
>
> **Easy marks.** In question 201, the taper relief percentage will be found in the Tax Rates and Allowances in the exam and you should have known the payment date for IHT as a result of death.

198   £205,000

	£
Nil rate band at Lulu's death	325,000
Less Potentially exempt transfer (PET) now chargeable (within seven years of death)	(80,000)
Legacy to brother	(40,000)
Lulu's nil rate band for transfer to Lebna	£205,000

Since the nil rate band at the date of both Lulu's and Lebna's death is the same (£325,000) there is no need to adjust the amount available to transfer.

The chargeable lifetime transfer (CLT) is more than seven years before Lulu's death and is therefore not cumulated on death. It would be cumulated to work out any inheritance tax on the PET (although in this case the cumulative amount would be within the nil rate band at Lulu's death and so no tax would be payable on the PET).

The answer £155,000 cumulates the CLT. The answer £35,000 deducts the PET twice, the legacy twice and the CLT once. The answer £285,000 only deducts the legacy.

199   £188,000

	£	£
Lebnar's available residence nil rate band (RNRB) is lower of:		
Value of house	340,000	
Less mortgage	(152,000)	
		188,000
Maximum RNRB at date of death = £175,000	175,000	
Lulu's RNRB	175,000	
Maximum RNRB		350,000
Available RNRB		188,000

The whole of Lulu's RNRB is available for transfer because she died before 6 April 2017 (so even if she had had a main residence at her death it could not have been used since this was the date of introduction of the RNRB). It is not necessary that Lulu had a main residence at her death, the condition is that Lebnar has a main residence at his death which he leaves to a direct descendent (his son).

The answer £175,000 is just Lebnar's RNRB. The answer £350,000 is the maximum RNRB. The answer £340,000 is the gross value of Lebnar's main residence.

200 £536,000

	£
Before transfer: 100,000 @ £7.10	710,000
Less After transfer: 40,000 @ £4.20	(168,000)
Transfer of value (diminution in value)	542,000
Less Current year and previous year annual exemptions £3,000 × 2	(6,000)
Potentially exempt transfer	£536,000

The answer £542,000 does not deduct the annual exemptions (make sure you read the question carefully if you chose this answer!). The answer £372,000 is the value of the gifted holding (60,000 @ £6.30) less annual exemptions. The answer £378,000 is just the value of the gifted holding.

201 Option 1

The period between the date of the PET (22 February 2017) and the date of Lebnar's death (1 March 2022) is between five and six years so the taper relief reduction is 60% (in the Tax Rates and Allowance available in the exam).

The answer 40% is the amount of the transfer on which tax will be charged at the death rate.

The due date for payable of death tax on a PET is the end of six months following the month of death which is 30 September 2022.

The answer 1 September 2022 is exactly six months from the date of Lebnar's death.

202 £225

Only the gift of £225 is exempt under the small gifts exemption.

The limit of £250 applies per donee per tax year so the gifts of £(85 + 190) = £275 and £490 both exceed the limit.

The answer £500 exempts the gifts of £85, £225 and £190. The answer £990 exempts all the gifts. The answer £275 exempts the gifts of £85 and £190.

203 Pere and Phil

Workbook references. Inheritance tax is dealt with in Chapter 18. Chargeable gains and the computation of capital gains tax are in Chapter 13. The points on distinguishing between revenue and capital expenditure are covered in Chapter 7.

Top tips. You don't need to know names of tax cases in the Taxation (TX – UK) exam, but you are expected to know, and be able to apply, the principles decided, as in part (b) here.

Easy marks. There were some easy marks in part (a) for using the exemptions.

Marking scheme

		Marks
(a)	Lifetime gift	
	Marriage exemption	1
	Annual exemption – current year	½
	Annual exemption – brought forward	½
	Potentially exempt transfer	½
	IHT @ 0%	½
	IHT @ 40%	½
	Taper relief	1
	Death estate	
	Spouse exemption	1
	IHT @ 40%	½
		6

(b)

	Marks
Disposal proceeds	½
Cost	1
Enhancement	1
Annual exempt amount	½
Capital gains tax @ 18%	½
Capital gains tax @ 28%	½
	4
	10

(a) **Pere – Inheritance tax (IHT) arising on death**

Lifetime transfer 23 August 2015

	£
Gift	420,000
Less: marriage exemption	(5,000)
annual exemption current year	(3,000)
annual exemption b/f	(3,000)
Potentially exempt transfer	409,000
IHT	
£325,000 @ 0%	0
£84,000 @ 40%	33,600
£409,000	
Less taper relief (6 to 7 years @ 80%)	(26,880)
IHT payable	6,720

Tutorial note

The potentially exempt transfer becomes chargeable as a result of Pere dying within seven years of making it.

Death estate

	£
Value of estate	880,000
Less spouse exemption £880,000/2	(440,000)
Chargeable estate	440,000
IHT on £440,000 @ 40%	176,000

(b) **Phil – Capital gains tax computation 2021/22**

	£
Net disposal proceeds	496,700
Less: cost	(420,000)
enhancement expenditure	(5,200)
Gain	71,500
Less annual exempt amount	(12,300)
Taxable gain	59,200

	£
CGT on £23,550 (37,700 – 14,150) @ 18%	4,239
CGT on £35,650 (59,200 – 23,550) @ 28%	9,982
	14,221

Tutorial notes

1   The cost of replacing the property's chimney is revenue expenditure because the chimney is a part of the house and so this is a repair to the house. The cost of the new boundary wall is capital expenditure because the wall is a separate structure which is not part of the house.

2   Because the house is residential property, the gain is taxed at 18% and 28% rather than 10% and 20%.

204 Afiya

Workbook references. Inheritance tax is covered in Chapter 18.

Top tips. A potentially exempt transfer is treated as if it were an exempt transfer during the lifetime of the donor so it does not affect the computation of lifetime tax on subsequent chargeable lifetime transfers.

Easy marks. The calculation of the residue in part (b) was an easy mark.

Marking scheme

			Marks
(a)	*Lifetime transfers*		
	Cassava Ltd shares	Value of shares before transfer	1
		Value of shares after transfer	1
		Annual exemption current year	½
		Annual exemption brought forward	½
	Cash	Nil rate band	½
		Balance @ 20/80	½
	Additional liabilities arising on death		
	Cassava Ltd shares	Potentially exempt transfer now chargeable	1
	Cash	Gross chargeable transfer	½
		Nil rate band	½
		Balance @ 40%	½
		Lifetime tax already paid	½
	Death tax		
	Value of estate		½
	Spouse exemption		½
	Residence nil rate band		½
	Charge @ 40%		½
			9
(b)	Residue of estate		1
			10

(a)   Afiya – Inheritance tax on death

   Lifetime transfers

   14 September 2020

	£
Value of shares held before transfer 8,000 × £8	64,000
Less value of shares held after transfer 1,500 × £3	(4,500)
Transfer of value	59,500
Less: annual exemption current year	(3,000)
annual exemption b/f	(3,000)
Potentially exempt transfer	53,500

   27 January 2021

	£
Net chargeable transfer	400,000

IHT	
325,000 × 0%	0
75,000 × 20/80 (donor pays tax)	18,750
400,000	18,750
Gross chargeable transfer £(400,000 + 18,750)	418,750

   Additional tax on lifetime transfer on death of donor

   14 September 2020

   Potentially exempt transfer of £53,500 becomes chargeable as donor dies within 7 years.

   Within nil rate band at death, no tax to pay.

   27 January 2021

   Nil rate band available £(325,000 – 53,500) = £271,500.

	£
Gross chargeable transfer	418,750

IHT	
271,500 × 0%	0
147,250 × 40%	58,900
418,750	58,900
No taper relief (death within three years of transfer)	
Less lifetime tax paid	(18,750)
Additional tax payable on death	40,150

   Death estate

	£
Assets at death	623,000
Less funeral expenses	(3,000)
Value of estate for IHT purposes	620,000
Less exempt legacy to spouse	(150,000)
Chargeable estate	470,000
Less residence nil rate band (lower of £90,000 and £175,000)	(90,000)
Taxable estate	380,000
IHT liability £380,000 × 40%	152,000

   The nil rate band was used by lifetime transfers.

(b)   Afiya's children will inherit the residue of £(620,000 – 150,000 – 40,000 – 152,000)
   = £278,000.

205 Kendra

Marking scheme

			Marks
(a)	Property	½	
	Building society deposits	½	
	ISAs	½	
	NS&I certificates	½	
	Proceeds of life assurance policy	1	
	Income tax	½	
	Loan	½	
	Inheritance tax	1	
			5
(b)	No IHT benefit	1½	
	No CGT benefit	1½	
			3
(c)	Skip a generation	1	
	Avoids double charge to IHT	1	
			2
			10

(a)   Kendra – Inheritance tax on death

	£
Property	970,000
Building society deposits	387,000
Individual Savings Accounts	39,000
NS&I certificates	17,000
Proceeds of life policy	225,000
Gross estate	1,638,000
Less: income tax	(12,800)
loan	(1,200)
Net estate	1,624,000

	£
Inheritance tax	
£325,000 @ 0%	0
£1,299,000 @ 40%	519,600
Inheritance tax liability	519,600

(b)   As the property is not expected to increase in value in the near future, there is no inheritance tax benefit in making a lifetime gift. Kendra would need to live for three more years for taper relief to be available.

Also, a lifetime gift would result in a capital gains tax liability of £48,720 (£174,000 at 28%) for 2021/22, whereas a transfer on death would be an exempt disposal.

(c)   It can be beneficial to skip a generation so that gifts are made to grandchildren rather than children, particularly if the children already have significant assets.

This avoids a further charge to inheritance tax when the children die. Gifts will then only be taxed once before being inherited by the grandchildren, rather than twice.

BPP
LEARNING
MEDIA

206 James

> **Workbook references.** Chapter 18 deals with inheritance tax.
>
> **Top tips.** When working out the inheritance death tax on the lifetime transfer, remember to look back seven years from the date of the lifetime transfer (not the date of death) to see whether there are any previous transfers to cumulate.
>
> **Easy marks.** The nil rate band is used up on the first gift so the calculation of the inheritance tax on the CLT and death estate are easy.

Marking scheme

		Marks	
(a)	Potentially exempt transfer (after annual exemptions)	1	
	Nil rate band available	1½	
	Inheritance tax	½	
	Daughter to pay	½	
	Chargeable lifetime transfer	½	
	Inheritance tax	½	
	Trustees to pay	½	
	Death estate – IHT liability	½	
	James's personal representatives to pay	½	
			6
(b)	Avoidance of double taxation		2
(c)	Taper relief	½	
	Lifetime transfer values fixed	½	
	IHT saving	1	
			2
			10

(a)   **James – Inheritance tax arising on death**
Lifetime transfers within seven years of death
14 May 2020

			£
Gift			420,000
Less: annual exemption	current year		(3,000)
annual exemption	b/f		(3,000)
Potentially exempt transfer			414,000
Inheritance tax liability	£296,000 (W) @ 0%		0
	£118,000 @ 40%		47,200
			47,200

James's daughter will be responsible for paying the inheritance tax of £47,200.

2 August 2020

	£
Chargeable lifetime transfer	260,000

	£
Inheritance tax liability £260,000 @ 40%	104,000

The trustees will be responsible for paying the inheritance tax of £104,000.

Death estate

	£
Chargeable estate	870,000

	£
Inheritance tax liability £870,000 @ 40%	348,000

The personal representatives of James's estate will be responsible for paying the inheritance tax of £348,000.

Working: Available nil rate band

		£	£
Nil rate band at date of death			325,000
Gift 9 October 2014		35,000	
Less: annual exemption — current year		(3,000)	
annual exemption — b/f		(3,000)	(29,000)
Nil rate band available			296,000

(b) Skipping a generation avoids a further charge to inheritance tax when the children die. Gifts will then only be taxed once before being inherited by the grandchildren, rather than twice.

(c) Even if the donor does not survive for seven years, taper relief will reduce the amount of IHT payable after three years.

The value of potentially exempt transfers and chargeable lifetime transfers are fixed at the time they are made.

James therefore saved inheritance tax of £20,000 (£(310,000 − 260,000) @ 40%) by making the lifetime gift of property.

207 Dembe

Workbook references. The income tax computation is covered in Chapter 2 and pensions in Chapter 5. Chargeable gains computation is dealt with in Chapter 13. Inheritance tax is the subject of Chapter 18.

Top tips. In part (c) think about the nil rate bands available for each spouse. What happens if the first spouse dies without using up their nil rate bands?

Easy marks. There were some easy marks for basic computation of capital gains tax in part (b) but you should make sure that you clearly show which individual is making the disposal in each case.

Examining team's comments. Although there were some good answers to part (a), many candidates used up valuable time by producing full tax computations. The question stated that these were not required, indicating that workings were to be done at the margin.

Many candidates did not appreciate that the personal pension contribution would have no impact on NICs. This fact should have just been stated, without any need to perform calculations. Many candidates did not realise that the personal pension contribution would bring Dembe's adjusted net income down from in excess of £125,140, to less than £100,000. Therefore, the personal allowance would have been fully reinstated. This shows the importance of carefully considering the impact of all the information provided.

Part (b) was generally well answered provided the basic tax planning involved was understood. Transferring the property to Kato prior to its disposal meant a lower rate of capital gains tax (CGT) on part of the gain, plus Kato's annual exempt amount was available (Dembe's was not).

Somewhat surprisingly, quite a few candidates used the incorrect rates of CGT, despite the fact that these rates are provided in the tax rates and allowances. The £2,000 in additional legal fees were often not taken into account in the comparison.

Part (c) was not particularly well answered, with many candidates not appreciating how straightforward the answer actually was.

The couple's estate, with a value of £950,000, would have been fully covered by the available nil rate bands totalling £1,000,000 (two nil rate bands of £325,000, and two residence nil rate bands of £175,000). The IHT liability was therefore nil.

Even if IHT were payable (for example, if the value of the estate increased faster than the available nil rate bands), then there would be no advantage to leaving assets to children on the first death. This is because unused nil rate bands can be transferred to the surviving spouse. This very basic IHT planning was often overlooked.

Marks

(a) Extension of basic rate band 2
Reinstatement of personal allowance 1½
National insurance contributions ½

4

(b) Disposal by Dembe ½
Disposal by Kato
Taxable at basic rate 1
Taxable at higher rate 1
Overall saving ½

3

(c) Spouse exemption ½
Residence nil rate bands ½
Nil rate bands ½
Chargeable at death rate ½
Transfer of unused nil rate band 1

3

10

(a)

	£
Extension of basic rate tax band	
40,000 (32,000 × 100/80) at 20% (40% – 20%)	8,000
Reinstatement of personal allowance	
12,570 at 40%	5,028
Reduction in income tax liability	13,028
National insurance contributions (NICs)	0
Total tax reduction	13,028

Tutorial notes

1   Before making the personal pension contribution, Dembe's adjusted net income of £130,000 exceeds £125,140, so no personal allowance is available. The personal pension contribution will reduce Dembe's adjusted net income to less than £100,000 (130,000 – 40,000 = 90,000), so the personal allowance will be fully reinstated.

2   Pension contributions have no impact on NICs.

(b)

	£	£
Disposal made by Dembe		
67,000 at 28%		18,760
Disposal made by Kato		
16,350 (37,700 – 21,350) at 18%	2,943	
36,350 (65,000 – 12,300 – 16,350) at 28%	10,178	
		(13,121)
Capital gains tax (CGT) saving		5,639
Additional legal fees		(2,000)
Overall saving		3,639

(c)   On first death, there will be no inheritance tax (IHT) liability because of the spouse exemption.

There will also be no IHT liability on second death because the couple's residence nil rate bands and nil rate bands will exceed the value of the combined chargeable estate:

	£
Combined chargeable estate	950,000
Residence nil rate bands (175,000 × 2)	(350,000)
Nil rate bands (325,000 × 2)	(650,000)
Chargeable at 40%	0

Even if IHT were payable (for example, if the value of the estate increases faster than the available nil rate bands), then there is no advantage to leaving assets to children on the first death. This is because unused nil rate bands can be transferred to the surviving spouse.

BPP
LEARNING
MEDIA

OTQ bank – Corporation tax liabilities

208

Legal expenses relating to the acquisition of a new 40-year lease on its factory		NOT ALLOWABLE
Cost of arranging a new bank loan to purchase machinery for trade	ALLOWABLE	
Write off of an irrecoverable loan to a former employee		NOT ALLOWABLE
Donation to local charity with mention of Jet Ltd's support in programme for fundraising concert (not a qualifying charitable donation)	ALLOWABLE	

Legal expenses in respect of leases are only allowable if they relate to the **renewal** of a short lease. The cost of arranging a bank loan for trade purposes is allowable. A debt written off in respect of a former employee is accounted for under the non-trade loan relationship rules as it does not relate to the trade of the company. A small donation to a local charity with publicity would normally be allowable as being for the purposes of the trade.

209   12 months to 30 November 2021, 4 months to 31 March 2022

If the company has a long period of account it is divided into one period of 12 months and one of the remainder.

210   £40,500

£1,800,000 × 3% × 9/12 = £40,500

The qualifying cost for SBAs excludes acquisition fees. The SBA must be time-apportioned in the year of acquisition from the date the building is brought into use.

211   £3,198

	Main pool	Special rate pool	Allowances
	£	£	£
Additions	30,400	15,400	
WDA 6% × 6/12		(462)	462
18% × 6/12	(2,736)		2,736
TWDV c/f / Allowances	27,664	14,938	3,198

Do not forget to pro-rate writing down allowances in a short accounting period. No adjustment is made for private use by a director for a company.

The answer £4,122 uses 18% for both WDAs. The answer £6,396 is the full year's WDAs. The answer £3,106 adjusts for private use – this is a common mistake. Remember that there is never any private use by a company!

212   £0

	£
Proceeds	70,000
Less cost 15,000 × £3.50	(52,500)
Unindexed gain	17,500
Less indexation allowance	
0.578 × £52,500 = £30,345 restricted to	(17,500)
Indexed gain	0

The answer £12,845 allows the indexation allowance to create a loss. The answer £105,000 loss uses the cost of all 50,000 of the shares. The answer £17,500 is the unindexed gain.

> **Examining team's comments.** This was a straightforward chargeable gain computation on the disposal of shares. The correct answer is £0. However, the vast majority of candidates chose £12,845, suggesting they simply forgot that indexation cannot create a loss.

213 £33,300

Crane plc can make a carry forward loss relief claim against total profits but can leave sufficient profits to cover the qualifying charitable donation, thus maximising the unrelieved loss carried forward to the next accounting period. The most beneficial claim is therefore £(30,000 + 6,000 − 2,700) = £33,300. The remaining £(40,000 − 33,300) = £6,700 will be carried forward to the accounting period ending 31 December 2023.

214 £83,750

	£
Loss	160,000
Less loss relief y/e 31.12.22	(5,000)
Less loss relief p/e 31.12.21 (40,000 + 15,500)	(55,500)
Less loss relief y/e 31.3.21 3/12 × (45,000 + 18,000)	(15,750)
Loss c/f	83,750

215 £38,000

> **Examining team's comments.** This calculative question tested candidates' knowledge of group relief. The question asked candidates to calculate the maximum amount of group relief which Boon Ltd could claim from Bab Ltd. The correct answer was £38,000. Boon Ltd can claim group relief against its taxable total profits, in this case £40,000 (£36,000 + £4,000). Bab Ltd does not need to use its trading loss against its own profits first, so it can surrender the full amount of £38,000 to Boon Ltd.
>
> Most candidates answered £31,000, indicating that they may have thought that Bab Ltd had to use the loss against its chargeable gains first. Many candidates answered £36,000, perhaps because they thought that group relief can only be set against trading income.
>
> Group relief is an important aspect of the syllabus in respect of corporation tax, and candidates should ensure they are familiar with the rules and can apply them to a given scenario.

216

Daffodil plc	
Flora Ltd	

Group relief can be made to UK companies only, so not to Geranium Inc, and where there is a ≥75% direct and indirect holding by the controlling company. Daffodil plc only has a (80% × 90%) = 72% interest in Hellebore Ltd.

217

Pine plc	Willow Ltd
Juniper Ltd	

Losses can only be transferred to UK companies where there is a ≥75% direct interest at each level and >50% indirect holding by the top company. Pine plc has a (75% × 75%) = 56.25% interest in Maple Ltd.

OT case – Luna Ltd

218

Indexation allowance can reduce a gain to nil but not create a loss	TRUE	
Indexation allowance can increase an unindexed loss		FALSE

Indexation allowance cannot increase or create a loss although it can reduce a gain to nil.

219   £6,186

	£
Proceeds	53,400
Less cost	(36,800)
	16,600
Less indexation allowance to December 2017 0.283 × £36,800	(10,414)
Gain	6,186

220   £14,928

	No. of shares	Indexed cost £
Acquisition	16,000	32,000
Indexed rise to December 2017		
0.244 × £32,000		7,808
		39,808
Disposal	(10,000)	(24,880)
	6,000	14,928

The answer £12,000 is the unindexed pool of cost immediately after the sale. The answer £39,808 is the indexed cost of the pool immediately before the disposal. The answer £24,880 is the amount of indexed cost used on the disposal.

221   £13,125

	No. of shares	Cost £
Acquisition	5,000	7,500
Bonus 1 for 1	5,000	0
	10,000	7,500
Rights 1 for 4 @ £2.25	2,500	5,625
	12,500	13,125

222   £19,500

$$£33,000 \times \frac{(£6.50 \times 10,000)}{(£6.50 \times 10,000) + (£4.50 \times 10,000)} \qquad £19,500$$

OT case – Tay Ltd

Workbook references. Chargeable gains for companies is the subject of Chapter 20.

Top tips. The application of the rules on the destruction of assets in question 213 is similar to rollover relief for replacement of business assets.

Easy marks. The chattels rules in question 225 should have been well known.

223 £155,000

	£
Proceeds	180,000
Less indexed cost	(155,000)
Gain	25,000
Gain immediately chargeable £(180,000 – 162,000)	(18,000)
Deduction from base cost of new warehouse	7,000

The base cost of the new warehouse is £(162,000 – 7,000) = £155,000.

The answer £162,000 does not give any relief. The answer £144,000 deducts the gain immediately chargeable. The answer £140,000 uses the unindexed cost to work out the gain.

224 £8,000

	Market value	Indexed cost	Gain
	£	£	£
20,000 £1 ordinary shares @ £4 each	80,000	64,000	
£40,000 (20,000 × £2) cash	40,000	32,000	8,000
	120,000	96,000	

The answer £24,000 gain is the total gain if the acquisition of the shares was treated as a disposal. The answer £16,000 gain is the gain on the shares if the acquisition of the shares was treated as a disposal. The answer £(24,000) loss is the loss on cash if the nominal value of the shares of £1 is used for the apportionment.

225 £5,000

Although the general rule is that wasting chattels are exempt, there is an exception for assets used for the purpose of a trade in respect of which capital allowances have been or could have been claimed. The usual chattel rules therefore apply as follows:

	£
Proceeds	9,000
Less indexed cost	(3,500)
Gain	5,500

The maximum gain is 5/3 × £(9,000 – 6,000) = £5,000.

The chargeable gain is the lower of £5,500 and £5,000, so it is £5,000.

226 £15,732

	£
Proceeds	45,000
Less: cost	(20,000)
enhancement (drainage)	(2,000)
Unindexed gain	23,000
Less: indexation on cost £20,000 × 0.342	(6,840)
indexation on enhancement £2,000 × 0.214	(428)
Chargeable gain	15,732

The answer £16,160 does not index the enhancement. The answer £15,476 uses the indexation factor on cost for both cost and enhancement. The answer £15,134 indexes the unindexed gain using the indexation factor on cost.

227 2 and 4

The capital loss can be set against chargeable gains made in the year ended 31 March 2023 and the capital loss can be carried forward and set against the first available chargeable gains.

Capital losses cannot be carried back and cannot be set against profits other than chargeable gains.

OT case – Hyde plc group

> **Workbook references.** Groups are the subject of Chapter 22.
>
> **Top tips.** Make sure you know the difference between the rules for relationships between companies for group relief and those applying to chargeable gains groups.
>
> **Easy marks.** The identification of the base cost of the factory in question 232 should have been easy marks if you remembered that transfers between chargeable gains group companies are on a no gain, no loss basis.

228

Hampstead plc	Regent plc
	Primrose plc

A company is in a group relief group where there is a ≥75% direct and indirect holding by the controlling company (Hyde plc). Hyde plc has a (95% × 80%) = 76% interest in Primrose Ltd but only has a (85% × 85%) = 72.25% interest in Richmond Ltd.

229 £70,000

	£
Trading loss	68,000
Excess qualifying charitable donations £(5,000 – 3,000)	2,000
Maximum current period group relief	70,000

230   £50,500

	£
Chargeable gain	48,000
Interest income	12,000
Trading loss	(8,000)
Qualifying charitable donations	(1,500)
Available taxable total profits	50,500

Hyde plc is assumed to use its own current year losses in working out the taxable total profits against which it may claim current group relief, even if it does not in fact claim relief for current losses against total profits. Group relief is set against taxable total profits after all other reliefs for the current period such as qualifying charitable donations.

231   A claim for current period group relief will be ineffective unless Greenwich plc gives a notice of consent.

The claim for current period group relief would be made on Hyde plc's corporation tax return.

Any payment by Hyde plc for current period group relief, up to the amount of the loss surrendered, is ignored for all corporation tax purposes. A claim for current period group relief between Greenwich plc and Hyde plc will be available against 9/12ths of the taxable total profits of Hyde plc for the year to 31 March 2023, since surrendered losses must be set against taxable total profits of a corresponding accounting period (1 April 2022 to 31 December 2022).

232   £120,000

	£
Cost	100,000
Indexation allowance to date of transfer £100,000 × 0.200	20,000
Base cost for Primrose plc	120,000

The transfer of assets within a chargeable gains group is on a no gain / no loss basis including indexation to the date of the transfer.

233 Problematic Ltd

> **Workbook references.** Chargeable gains for companies are covered in Chapter 20.
>
> **Top tips.** Make sure you use the three column proforma for the FA 1985 pool.
>
> **Easy marks.** The base cost required in part (b) is easy provided you remember that the leasehold factory is a depreciating asset, and so do not reduce the base cost by rollover relief.

Marking scheme

		Marks
(a)	**Easy plc**	
	FA 1985 pool – Purchase	½
	– Rights issue	1
	– Indexation	2
	– Disposal	1
	Chargeable gain	1½

Freehold factory

Disposal proceeds	½
Indexed cost	½
Rollover relief	2
	9

(b) **Leasehold factory** 1

10

(a) **Easy plc shares**

FA85 pool

	No. of shares	Cost	Indexed cost
		£	£
Purchase 26.6.05	15,000	12,600	12,600
Index to September 2008			
0.136 × £12,600			1,714
Rights issue 1 for 3 @ £2.20	5,000	11,000	11,000
c/f	20,000	23,600	25,314
Index to December 2017			
0.273 × £25,314			6,911
			32,225
Sale	(16,000)	(18,880)	(25,780)
C/f	4,000	4,720	6,445

Gain	£
Proceeds	54,400
Less cost	(18,880)
	35,520
Less indexation £(25,780 – 18,880)	(6,900)
Chargeable gain	28,620

Freehold factory

	£
Proceeds	171,000
Less indexed cost	(127,000)
	44,000
Less gain deferred on purchase of leasehold factory £(44,000 – 16,200)	(27,800)
Chargeable gain (amount not reinvested £(171,000 – 154,800))	16,200

(b)   The leasehold factory is a depreciating asset, so there is no adjustment to the base cost of £154,800.

Tutorial note

When a replacement asset is a depreciating asset then the gain is not rolled over by reducing the cost of the replacement asset. Instead, the gain is deferred until it crystallises on the earliest of:

- The disposal of the replacement asset

- The date the replacement asset is no longer used in the business

- Ten years after the acquisition of the replacement asset which in this case is 10 December 2031

234 Volatile Ltd

Workbook references. Corporation tax losses are covered in Chapter 21.

Top tips. Don't forget to set up a loss memorandum for each loss so that you can see how the loss is utilised.

Easy marks. You should have been able to state at least one of the principles of claiming loss relief in part (a).

Marking scheme

			Marks
(a)	Timing of relief	1	
	Loss of QCDs	1	
			2
(b)	Trading income	½	
	Property business income	½	
	Chargeable gains	1½	
	Loss relief – y/e 31 December 2020	2	
	Loss relief – y/e 30 September 2024	2½	
	Qualifying charitable donations	½	
	Unrelieved losses	½	
			8
			10

(a)   **Choice of loss relief**

The two factors that will influence a company's choice of loss relief claims are:

(1)   Timing of relief: both in terms of tax rate and cash flow (saving tax sooner is beneficial for cash flow)

(2)   The extent to which relief for qualifying charitable donations might be lost so it may be beneficial to restrict carry forward loss relief claims to keep an amount of total profits in charge after loss relief to match donations.

(b)   **Volatile Ltd**

	P/e 31.12.20	Y/e 31.12.21	Y/e 31.12.22	P/e 30.9.23
	£	£	£	£
Trading income	44,000	0	86,500	78,700
Property business income	9,400	6,600	6,500	0
Chargeable gains (11,700 − 2,000)	5,100	0	0	9,700
Total profits	58,500	6,600	93,000	88,400
Less current period loss relief	(0)	(6,600)	(0)	(0)
Less carry back loss relief	(58,500)		(23,250)	(88,400)
Less carry forward loss relief	(0)	(0)	(8,700)	(0)
Less qualifying charitable donations	(0)	(0)	(1,200)	(0)
Taxable total profits	0	0	59,850	0

Loss memorandum

	£
Loss in y/e 31.12.21	73,800
Less used y/e 31.12.21	(6,600)
Less used p/e 31.12.20	(58,500)
Less used y/e 31.12.22	(8,700)
Loss remaining unrelieved	0

	£
Loss in y/e 30.9.24	186,800
Less used p/e 30.9.23	(88,400)
Less: used y/e 31.12.22	
3 months to 31.12.22	
£93,000 × 3/12	(23,250)
Loss remaining unrelieved at 30.9.24	75,150

The loss of y/e 30.9.24 can be carried back against total profits of the previous 12 months ie against the 9-month period ending 30.9.23 and 3 months of the y/e 31.12.22.

235 Maison Ltd

Marking scheme

		Marks
(W1)	Deduction for lease premium	
	Premium paid	½
	Deduction	1
	Per annum and time apportioned	1

		Marks
(W2)	Capital allowances	
	Main pool	½
	AIA on integral features	1
	130% FYA on P&M	1
	SBA on building costs	1
(W3)	Property income	
	Rent receivable	1
	Security deposit	½
	Insurance	1
	Initial repairs	1
	Advertising	½
(W4)	Chargeable gains	
	First property	
	Gain	½
	Indexation allowance	1
	Enhancement expenditure	½
	Second property	
	Gain	½
	Indexation allowance	1
Corporation Tax		½
Figures provided in question		1
		15
		15

Maison Ltd – Corporation tax computation for the year ended 31 March 2022

	£
Operating profit	892,900*
Non-deductible expenditure	22,340*
Deduction for lease premium (working 1)	(715)
Capital allowances (working 2)	(70,500)
Trading profit	844,025
Property business income (working 3)	28,685
Loan interest receivable	1,460*
Chargeable gains (working 4)	77,985
Taxable total profits	952,155
Corporation tax (952,155 at 19%)	180,909

*Figures provided in question

Working 1 – Deduction for lease premium

	£
Premium paid	44,000
Less: 44,000 × 2% × (12 – 1)	(9,680)
Amount assessed on the landlord as income	34,320
Deduction (34,320/12 years × 3/12)	715

Working 2 – Capital allowances

	£	£
Main pool		12,037
Capital allowances		
Building costs	0	
Ventilation system - AIA preferable to 50% FYA	6,700	
Heating system - AIA preferable to 50% FYA	3,900	
Furniture and furnishings - 130% FYA (£33,500 × 130%)	43,550	
Refrigerator and microwave cooker- 130% FYA (£2,600 × 130%)	3,380	
		57,530
Structures and buildings allowance (£93,300 × 3% × 4/12)		933
Total allowances		70,500

Working 3 – Property business income

	£
Rent receivable (18,300 + (18,300 × 2/3))	30,500
Security deposit	0
Insurance	(1,035)
Initial repairs	0
Advertising	(780)
Property business income	28,685

Tutorial notes:

1 A security deposit, less the cost of making good any damage, is returned to the tenant on the cessation of a letting. It is therefore initially not treated as income.

2 The cost of insurance for the period 1 July to 1 November 2021 is deductible as pre-trading expenditure.

3 The cost of the initial repairs to the warehouse are disallowable capital expenditure as the warehouse could not be let out in its original state and this was reflected in the purchase price paid.

Working 4 – Chargeable gains

	£
First property	
Gain	109,800
Indexation allowance	
Cost (101,000 × 0.315)	(31,815)
Enhancement expenditure	0
Chargeable gain	77,985

BPP
LEARNING
MEDIA

	£
Second property	
Gain	26,000
Indexation allowance	
Cost (117,000 × 0.315) – Restricted	(26,000)
Chargeable gain	0

Tutorial notes:

1   There is no indexation allowance for the first property's enhancement expenditure of £26,200 because this was incurred after December 2017.

2   For the second property, the indexation allowance cannot create a capital loss.

236 Black Ltd and Gastron Ltd

Workbook references. Groups are covered in Chapter 22.

Top tips. It is very important that you read the questions carefully and comply with any detailed instructions. For example, in part (a) you were given a note about what you were not expected to do.

Easy marks. You should have been able to outline the group structure in part (b)(i).

Marking scheme

				Marks
(a)		*Maximum potential claim by Black Ltd in relation to White Ltd*		
		Maximum claim	1	
		Maximum surrender by White Ltd		
		Current period trading loss – maximum claim	½	
		Qualifying charitable donations	1	
		Maximum group relief claim Black Ltd and White Ltd	½	
		Maximum potential claim by Black Ltd in relation to Grey Ltd		
		Maximum claim	½	
		Maximum surrender by Grey Ltd		
		Carried forward trading loss – maximum claim	1	
		Maximum group relief claim Black Ltd and Grey Ltd	½	
				5
(b)	(i)	75% shareholding	1	
		50% effective interest	1	
				2
	(ii)	Set-off of capital loss		1
	(iii)	No gain no loss transfers	1	
		Rollover relief	1	
				2
				10

(a) **Black Ltd – Group relief claims for year ended 31 March 2022**

Maximum potential claim by Black Ltd from White Ltd

Group relief is against taxable total profits after all other reliefs for the current period (for example qualifying charitable donations).

The maximum potential current period group relief claim by Black Ltd in relation to White Ltd is therefore £(338,900 + 21,100 − 4,400) = £355,600.

Maximum potential surrender by White Ltd to Black Ltd

White Ltd may surrender its current period trading losses of £351,300.

White Ltd may also surrender excess qualifying charitable donations (ie to the extent that they exceed total profits before taking account of any losses). Since the qualifying charitable donations of £5,600 do not exceed the total profits of £26,700, there is no excess.

The maximum potential surrender by White Ltd is therefore £351,300.

Maximum group relief claim by Black Ltd from White Ltd

The maximum current period group relief claim is the lower of the claim that can be made by Black Ltd and the surrender that can be made by White Ltd ie £351,300.

Maximum potential claim by Black Ltd from Grey Ltd

Current period group relief is taken before carry forward group relief. The maximum potential claim by Black Ltd in relation to Grey Ltd is therefore £(355,600 − 351,300) = £4,300.

Maximum potential surrender by Grey Ltd

Grey Ltd may surrender its carried forward trading losses after deducting the amount it can set against its own current period total profits ie £(57,500 − 50,000 − 4,500) = £3,000.

Maximum group relief claim by Black Ltd from Grey Ltd

The maximum carry forward group relief claim is the lower of the claim that can be made by Black Ltd and the surrender that can be made by Grey Ltd ie £3,000.

(b) (i) Companies form a chargeable gains group if at each level in the group structure there is a 75% shareholding.

However, the parent company must also have an effective interest of over 50% in each group company.

(ii) The election will enable the capital loss of £66,000 to be set against the capital gain of £74,800 and so save tax in the current year. Otherwise the loss would have to be carried forward by Culinary Ltd and set against future gains.

Tutorial note

Alternatively, an election could have been made to transfer the loss of Culinary Ltd to Gastron Ltd to set against the gain. The overall corporation tax effect for the chargeable gains group would have been the same.

(iii) Companies in a chargeable gains group make intra-group transfers of chargeable assets without a chargeable gain or an allowable loss arising.

If a member of a chargeable gains group disposes of an asset eligible for chargeable gains rollover relief it may treat all of the group companies as a single unit for the purpose of claiming such relief.

237 Alimag Ltd

Marking scheme

	Marks
Gamila income tax liability	
Director's remuneration	½
Dividend income	½
Personal allowance	½
Income tax (½ mark for each amount)	2
Magnus income tax liability	
Dividend income	½
Personal allowance	½
Income tax (½ mark for each amount)	1
Gamila and Alimag Class 1 national insurance contributions	1
Magnus Class 1 national insurance contributions	½

		Marks
Alimag Ltd corporation tax liability		
Trading profit		½
Director's remuneration		½
Employer's Class 1 NIC		½
Corporation tax		½
Overall tax and NICs savings		1
		10

Gamila – Income tax liability 2021/22

	Non-savings income £	Dividend income £
Director's remuneration	30,000	
Dividend income		70,000
Net income	30,000	70,000
Less Personal allowance	(12,570)	
Taxable income	17,430	70,000

Tax

	£
£17,430 @ 20%	3,486
£2,000 @ 0% (dividend nil rate band)	0
£(37,700 – 17,430 – 2,000) = 18,270 @ 7.5%	1,370
£(70,000 – 2,000 – 18,270) = 49,730 @ 32.5%	16,162
Income tax liability	21,018

Magnus – Income tax liability 2021/22

	Dividend income £
Dividend income/net income	30,000
Less Personal allowance	(12,570)
Taxable income	17,430

Tax

	£
£2,000 @ 0%	0
£(17,430 – 2,000) = 15,430 @ 7.5%	1,157
Income tax liability	1,157

Gamila and Alimag Ltd – National insurance contributions 2021/22

	£
Employee Class 1 £(30,000 – 9,568) = 20,432 @ 12%	2,452
Employer Class 1 £(30,000 – 8,840) = 21,160 @ 13.8%	2,920

Marcus – National insurance contributions 2021/22

There will be no employee or employer Class 1 contributions for Marcus as he does not have any earnings.

Alimag Ltd – Corporation tax liability for year ended 5 April 2022

	£
Trading profit	180,000
Less Director's remuneration	(30,000)
Employer's Class 1 NIC	(2,920)
Taxable total profits	147,080
Tax	
£147,080 @ 19%	27,945

Overall tax saving if revised basis of profit extraction used

	£
Original basis	73,982
Revised basis (21,018 + 1,157 + 2,452 + 2,920 + 27,945)	(55,492)
Overall savings	18,490

238 Hopi Ltd

Workbook references. The income tax computation is covered in Chapter 2. National insurance contributions are the subject of Chapter 12. Corporation tax liability is dealt with in Chapter 19.

Top tips. When computing Kaya's income tax liability if she receives additional dividend income, simply calculate the additional tax on the dividend income rather than rework the whole income tax computation.

Easy marks. There were easy marks for stating that, if Kaya receives additional dividend income, there will be no change to the national insurance contributions for Kaya and Hopi Ltd and no change to Hopi Ltd's corporation tax liability.

Examining team's comments. The requirement for 10 marks was to calculate the revised tax and national insurance contributions (NICs) for Kaya and Hopi Ltd for the year ended 5 April [2021] if, on 31 March [2021], Kaya paid herself a bonus of £25,000 (1) as additional director's remuneration or (2) as an additional dividend. Those candidates who understood basic tax rules had no difficulty answering this question.

As warned in previous reports, where tax figures are given for the original scenario, candidates should never attempt to recalculate these figures for themselves. All this does is lose valuable time with candidates producing three sets of workings rather than the expected two. Candidates should always read the requirements very carefully. These types of questions often require a summary or a conclusion, but neither was necessary for this question – again those candidates who provided one lost a bit more time.

Where computations are required for two different scenarios, candidates should clearly indicate which scenario is being answered. It is much better to deal with one scenario first, then the second, rather than have a mix of computations dealing with one tax at a time, such as all the income tax and class 1 NIC computations for Kaya, then the corporation tax and class 1 NIC calculations for Hopi Ltd. Although full marks are awarded for correct answers however the information is presented, dealing with one scenario at a time can help candidates to ensure they have covered all aspects in their answers.

Some of the calculations in this question required full computations (such as Kaya's income tax liability under the additional director's remuneration alternative), whereas others (such as Kaya's income tax liability under the additional dividend alternative) could be calculated by working at the margin. Appreciating where full computations can be avoided saves time as well as reducing the complexity of the workings. Also, under the additional dividend alternative, many candidates did not appreciate that the class 1 NICs and Hopi Ltd's corporation tax liability would not change from the original figures provided.

In summary, although many candidates correctly calculated most, if not all, of the revised tax and NICs, they often took a much longer route in reaching their answer than was necessary. Working through past examination questions will help candidates familiarise themselves with the best approach to be taken when answering these types of questions. Also, it is important that candidates appreciate the interactions which can arise in these questions, and an article has been published covering many of the scenarios which could be examined.

Marking scheme

	Marks
Revised liabilities if Kaya receives additional director's remuneration	
Kaya income tax liability	
Director's remuneration	½
Dividend income	½
Personal allowance	½
Income tax (½ mark for each amount)	2
Kaya Class 1 national insurance contributions	1½
Hopi Ltd Class 1 national insurance contributions	1
Hopi Ltd corporation tax	1
Revised liabilities if Kaya receives additional dividend income	
Kaya income tax liability	1½
Kaya and Hopi Ltd Class 1 national insurance contributions	1
Hopi Ltd corporation tax	½
	10

BPP
LEARNING
MEDIA

Revised liabilities if Kaya receives additional director's remuneration

Kaya – Income tax liability 2021/22

	Non-savings income	Dividend income
	£	£
Director's remuneration £(30,000 + 25,000)	55,000	
Dividend income		45,000
Net income	55,000	45,000
Less Personal allowance	(12,570)	
Taxable income	42,430	45,000

Tax

	£
£37,700 @ 20%	7,540
£(42,430 − 37,700) = £4,730 @ 40%	1,892
£2,000 @ 0% (dividend nil rate band)	0
£(45,000 − 2,000) = £43,000 @ 32.5%	13,975
Revised income tax liability	23,407

Kaya and Hopi Ltd – National insurance contributions 2021/22

	£
£(50,270 − 9,568) = 40,702 @ 12%	4,884
£(55,000 − 50,270) = 4,730 @ 2%	95
Revised employee Class 1 NICs	4,979

	£
Revised employer Class 1 NICs £(55,000 − 8,840) = £46,160 @ 13.8%	6,370

Hopi Ltd – Corporation tax liability for year ended 5 April 2022

	£
Trading profit before additional director's remuneration	80,000
Less Additional director's remuneration	(25,000)
Additional employer's Class 1 NIC £(6,370 − 2,920)	(3,450)
Taxable total profits	51,550

Tax

	£
£51,550 @ 19%	9,794

Revised liabilities if Kaya receives additional dividend income

Kaya – Income tax liability 2021/22

	£
Original income tax	12,893
Add: tax on additional dividend income £25,000 @ 32.5%	8,125
	21,018

Kaya and Hopi Ltd – National insurance contributions 2021/22

There are no NICs payable on dividends so the Class 1 NICs for Kaya and Hopi Ltd will remain unchanged.

Hopi Ltd – Corporation tax liability for year ended 5 April 2022

Hopi Ltd's corporation tax liability will remain unchanged.

239 Kat

Workbook references. The income tax computation is the subject of Chapter 2. Property income is dealt with in Chapter 6. Corporation tax computation is covered in Chapter 19. The computation of chargeable gains for individuals is covered in Chapter 13 and for companies in Chapter 20.

Top tips. When you are given a figure for a tax liability in the question don't waste time proving that the figure is correct – just use it!

Easy marks. There were some easy marks for basic income tax and corporation tax computations but you needed to keep them separate and then compare them at the end of your answer.

Examining team's comments. In part (a), those candidates who made sure that they understood the scenario and worked carefully through each calculation had no difficulty answering this section.

As warned in previous reports, where a tax figure is given for one of the scenarios (in this case, the corporation tax figure), candidates should never attempt to recalculate the figure for themselves. All this does is use up valuable time. As regards the conclusion, this should have just been a calculation of the tax difference between the two scenarios. There was no need for a detailed explanation.

Where computations are required for two different scenarios, candidates should clearly indicate which scenario is being answered. This is particularly important where some of the same information is used in both scenarios. In this case employment income and the personal allowance were common across both scenarios. Some candidates attempted to answer this question with just the one computation; impossible given that property income formed part of the first computation, with dividend income included in the second.

It should have been quite clear from the information provided that full computations were necessary for both scenarios. Those candidates who calculated the tax liability for a personal purchase and then attempted to adjust the figures for a corporate purchase invariably ended up with a very confused answer.

The personal purchase required candidates to apply the recently introduced restriction whereby relief for property income finance costs is restricted to the basic rate. Candidates should be particularly aware of such recent tax changes and this is why an annual Finance Act update article is published.

Working through past examination questions will help candidates familiarise themselves with the best approach to be taken when answering questions which examine more than one tax. Also, it is important that candidates appreciate the interactions that can arise in such questions, and an article has been published covering many of the scenarios which could be examined. Although there were many good answers to part (b), some candidates discussed the finance costs restriction when this has nothing to do with taxable gains. All that was required was a brief mention (not a detailed answer) of the annual exempt amount.

BPP
LEARNING
MEDIA

		Marks
(a)	**Property purchased personally**	
	Employment income	½
	Property income	
	Rent received	1
	Other expenses	½
	Personal allowance	½
	Income tax at basic rate	½
	Income tax at higher rate	½
	Finance costs tax reducer	1
	Property purchased via limited company	
	Employment income	½
	Dividend income	½
	Personal allowance	½
	Income tax on non-savings income at basic rate	½
	Income tax on non-savings income at higher rate	½
	Dividend nil rate band	½
	Income tax on dividend income at higher rate	½
	Conclusion	1
		9
(b)	Annual exempt amount	1
		10

(a) **Property purchased personally**

	Non-savings income
	£
Employment income	60,000
Property income (W)	23,600
Net income	83,600
Less Personal allowance	(12,570)
Taxable income	71,030

	Non-savings income
Income tax	
£	
37,700 at 20%	7,540
<u>33,330</u> at 40%	13,332
<u>71,030</u>	
	20,872
Interest relief (12,000 at 20%)	(2,400)
Income tax liability	18,472

Working – Property income

	£
Rent receivable (2,600 × 12)	31,200
Other expenses	(7,600)
Property income	23,600

Property purchased via a limited company

	Non-savings income	Dividend income
	£	£
Employment income	60,000	
Dividends		6,000
Net income	60,000	6,000
Less Personal Allowance	(12,570)	
Taxable income	47,430	6,000

Income tax

Non-savings income

£37,700 at 20%	7,540
£9,730 at 40%	3,892
£47,430	

Dividend income

£2,000 at 0%	0
£4,000 at 32.5%	1,300
£6,000	
Income tax liability	12,732

Conclusion

If Kat purchases the property via a limited company, then the overall tax saving will be £3,536 compared to purchasing the property personally:

	£
Property purchased personally	18,472
Property purchased via a limited company (2,204 + 12,732)	(14,936)
Tax saving	3,536

Tutorial note

The comparison ignores the fact that not all of the profits are withdrawn under the company purchase option. However, profits might typically be retained within a company to repay the mortgage borrowing or to fund a future property purchase.

(b)   The annual exempt amount of £12,300 will not be available if the gain occurs within a limited company.

240 Jogger Ltd (A)

Workbook references. Computing taxable total profits, including capital allowances, and the corporation tax liability are dealt with in Chapter 19. Losses are covered in Chapter 21.

Top tips. Make sure you use the capital allowances proforma in part (a).

Easy marks. There were easy marks in part (b) for the corporation tax computation.

Marking scheme

		Marks
(a)	Operating loss	½
	Depreciation	½
	P&M – AIA set against integral features in priority to SLA	1
	– FYA @ 50%	1
	– FYA @ 100%	1
	– Main pool	1½
	– Special rate pool	1
	– Short life asset	1½
		8
(b)	Bank interest	½
	Loan interest	1
	Property business profit	2
	Chargeable gain	2
	Loss relief	1
	Corporation tax	½
		7
		15

(a) Jogger Ltd – Trading loss y/e 31 March 2022

	£
Operating profit	1,052,482
Add depreciation	58,840
	1,111,322
Less capital allowances (W)	(1,167,182)
Adjusted trading loss	(55,860)

Working: Plant and machinery

	AIA/FYA £	Main pool £	Special rate pool £	SLA £	Allowances £
TWDV b/f		26,600	21,167		
30.9.21 Integral features	1,300,000				
AIA	1,000,000				1,000,000
	300,000				
50% FYA	(150,000)				150,000
15.12.21 second hand machinery				12,500	
15.8.21 Car	9,000				
100% FYA	(9,000)				9,000
31.7.21 Car		11,800			
Disposal					
20.7.21 Car			(11,700)		
			9,467		
14.3.22 Lorry		(8,600)			
		29,800			
WDA @ 18%		(5,364)		(2,250)	7,614
WDA @ 6%			(568)		568
Transfer balance of 50% FYA addition	(150,000)		150,000		
TWDV c/f		24,436	158,899	10,250	
Allowances					1,167,182

(b)   **Jogger Ltd – Corporation tax liability y/e 31 March 2022**

		£
Interest income (W1)		33,060
Property income (W2)		126,000
Chargeable gain (W3)		83,467
Total profits		242,527
Less loss relief		(55,860)
Taxable total profits		186,667
£186,667 × 19%		35,467

Workings

1   *Interest income*

	£
Bank interest receivable	8,460
Loan interest – received 31.12.21	16,400
– accrued 31.3.22	8,200
	33,060

2   *Property income*

	£
Premium received	100,000
Less 2% × (10 − 1) × £100,000	(18,000)
Taxable as property income	82,000
Add rental income accrued	44,000
	126,000

3   *Chargeable gain*

	£
Disposal proceeds	150,000
Less cost	(47,660)
	102,340
Less indexation allowance £47,660 × 0.396	(18,873)
Gain	83,467

241 Long Ltd group (A)

Workbook references. The computation of taxable total profits and the corporation tax liability are covered in Chapter 19. Groups of companies are covered in Chapter 22.

Top tips. A capital loss transferred between group companies can only be set against a capital gain, whereas a trading loss transferred between group companies is deducted in computing taxable total profits.

Easy marks. There were some easy marks for computing the corporation tax.

Marking scheme

		Marks
(a)	Long Ltd	
	Depreciation	½
	Capital allowances	
	TWDV b/f	½
	Lorry	½
	FYA	½
	Motor car	½
	WDA	½
	Group relief	1½
	Wind Ltd	
	Amortisation	½
	Capital allowances	1
	Chargeable gain after loss relief	1½
	Corporation tax	½
	Road Ltd	
	Trading loss	½
	Donations	½
	Capital allowances	½
	Corporation tax computation	
	Interest income	½
	Qualifying charitable donations	½
	Corporation tax	½
		11

		Marks
(b)	Definition of large company	1
	Application to Long Ltd group	1
	Profit threshold adjusted	½
	Taxable total profits	½
	Dividends from non-group companies	1
		4
		15

(a) **Long Ltd – Corporation tax computation for the year ended 31 March 2022**

	£
Operating profit	817,820
Add depreciation	10,170
	827,990
Less capital allowances (W)	(47,690)
Trading profit	780,300
Less group relief from Road Ltd	(34,900)
Taxable total profits	745,400
Corporation tax	
£745,400 × 19%	141,626

Tutorial note

Group relief is not restricted as the amount claimed is clearly less than 3/12ths of Long Ltd's taxable total profits.

Working: Capital allowances

	FYA £	Main pool £	Allowances £
TWDV b/f		44,800	
Lorry (28,308 × 130%)	36,800		
FYA @ 130%	(36,800)		36,800
Motor car		15,700	
		60,500	
WDA @ 18%		(10,890)	10,890
TWDV c/f		49,610	
Allowances			47,690

Wind Ltd – Corporation tax computation for the year ended 31 March 2022

	£
Operating profit	59,490
Add depreciation	5,000
	64,490
Less capital allowances: small pool w/off	(900)
Trading profit	63,590
Chargeable gain £(29,800 – 21,300)	8,500
Taxable total profits	72,090
Corporation tax	
£72,090 × 19%	13,697

Tutorial notes

1   The balance on the main pool is less than £1,000, so a writing down allowance equal to the unrelieved expenditure can be claimed.

2   A joint election can be made to transfer Long Ltd's capital loss since this will give loss relief earlier than if the loss is carried forward against future gains made by Long Ltd.

Road Ltd – Trading loss for the three-month period ended 31 March 2022

	£
Operating loss	(26,100)
Add donations	2,800
	(23,300)
Less capital allowances: FYA £11,600 × 100%	(11,600)
Trading loss (surrendered as group relief)	(34,900)

Tutorial notes

1   Political donations are not allowable. The qualifying charitable donations are not allowable in the calculation of the trading loss but will be deducted from total profits (see below).

2   The motor car purchased on 3 October 2021 is pre-trading expenditure and is treated as incurred on 1 January 2022. The motor car has zero CO_2 emissions per kilometre and therefore qualifies for the 100% first year allowance.

3   Road Ltd's loss can be surrendered under group relief to either Long Ltd or Wind Ltd but if surrendered to Wind Ltd group relief would be restricted as 3/12ths of Wind Ltd's taxable total profits is less than Road Ltd's loss.

Road Ltd – Corporation tax computation for the three-month period ended 31 March 2022

	£
Interest income/Total profits	4,300
Less qualifying charitable donations	(2,400)
Taxable total profits	1,900
Corporation tax	
£1,900 × 19%	361

BPP
LEARNING
MEDIA

Tutorial notes

1   The qualifying charitable donations cannot be surrendered as group relief as they are fully relieved against Road Ltd's interest income: only **excess** qualifying charitable donations can be group relieved.

2   A current year claim in Road Ltd would have wasted the qualifying charitable donations, therefore group relief is the most beneficial use of Road Ltd's loss.

(b)   A large company is one whose profits exceed the profit threshold. Profits are the taxable total profits of the company plus the dividends received from other companies, other than those from 51% subsidiaries (group dividends). The threshold must also be divided by the number of related 51% group companies.

For Long Ltd for the year ended 31 March 2022, it is necessary to look at the situation at 31 March 2021 in respect of related 51% group companies. Wind Ltd was a related 51% group company at that date but Road Ltd was not since it only started trading on 1 January 2022.

The profit threshold is therefore £1,500,000/2 = £750,000.

Long Ltd's profits for the year ended 31 March 2022 are:

	£
Taxable total profits	745,400
Add dividends from non-group companies	32,000
Profits	777,400

Long Ltd is therefore a large company in the year ended 31 March 2022. Long Ltd would have to pay instalments for the year ended 31 March 2022 if it had also been large in the year ended 31 March 2021.

242 Retro Ltd

> **Workbook references.** The computation of taxable total profits is covered in Chapter 19. Losses are dealt with in Chapter 21.
>
> **Top tips.** For part (a) you might want to start this question by computing the capital allowances. You can then just slot this into the adjustment of profit proforma at the appropriate place.
>
> **Easy marks.** There were some easy marks for standard adjustments to profit in part (a).
>
> **Examining team's comments.** Most candidates had little difficulty with part (a). One poor practice was the use of notes and explanations. It was a simple matter, as per the model answer, to just list all the items of expenditure (and show whether or not an adjustment was required), so the use of notes (such as for the gifts and donations) was completely unnecessary and against the guidance given in the note to the requirement. Since the requirement was for a calculation, explanations are not required, and result in wasted time. As regards the capital allowances, many candidates did not appreciate that the delivery van qualified for the 100% annual investment allowance – instead including it in the special rate pool.
>
> There were many perfect answers to part (b), although disappointingly a few candidates tried to time-apportion profits using the opening year rules.
>
> Part (c) caused few problems.

Marks

(a)   *Adjustment to profit*

      Gifts to employees   ½

      Gifts to customers   ½

      Qualifying charitable donations   ½

      Impairment loss   ½

      Lease of motor car   1

      Health and safety fine   ½

      Interest payable   ½

      Capital allowances

            WDV b/f   ½

            Delivery van   ½

            FYA @ 130%   ½

            Motor car [1]   ½

            WDA   ½

            Motor car [2]   ½

            FYA @ 100%   ½

      Structures and Buildings allowance

            Exclude cost of land   ½

            @ 3%   ½

            Time-apportion   ½

                                            9

(b)   Trading profit   ½

      Bank interest   ½

      Carry back loss relief p/e 31 March 2021   1

      Carry back loss relief in y/e 31 August 2020   1

      Qualifying charitable donations   1

                                            4

(c)   Unrelieved trading loss amount   1

      Carry forward loss relief   1

                                          2

                                        15

ANSWERS

(a) **Trading loss for the year ended 31 March 2022**

	£
Loss before taxation	(80,340)
Gifts to employees	0
Gifts to customers	0
Qualifying charitable donations	1,100
Impairment loss	0
Lease of motor car (4,400 × 15%)	660
Health and safety fine	5,100
Interest payable	0
Capital allowances (working 1)	(50,420)
Structures and Buildings allowance (working 2)	(12,000)
Trading loss	(135,900)

Tutorial notes

1   Gifts to customers are an allowable deduction if they cost less than £50 per recipient per year, are not of food, drink, tobacco or vouchers for exchangeable goods and carry a conspicuous advertisement for the company making the gift. Gifts to employees are an allowable deduction because the gifts will potentially be assessed on the employees as benefits.

2   Interest on a loan used for trading purposes is deductible on an accruals basis.

Working 1: Capital allowances

	FYA £	Main pool £	Allowances £
WDV brought forward		39,300	
Delivery van (£21,769 × 130%)	28,300		
FYA – 130%	(28,300)		28,300
Addition – Motor car [1]		14,700	
		54,000	
WDA – 18%		(9,720)	9,720
Motor car [2]	12,400		
FYA – 100%	(12,400)		12,400
	0		
WDV carried forward		44,280	
Total allowances			50,420

Working 2: Structures and Buildings allowance

(£850,000 − £50,000) × 3% × 6/12 = £12,000

Tutorial notes

1   Motor car [1] has CO_2 emissions between 1 and 50 grams per kilometre, and therefore qualifies for writing down allowances at the rate of 18%.

2   Motor car [2] has zero CO_2 emissions and is new, and therefore qualifies for the 100% first year allowance.

(b)

	Year ended 31 August 2020	Period ended 31 March 2021
	£	£
Trading profit	56,600	47,900
Bank interest	1,300	0
	57,900	47,900
Loss against total profits (working)	(24,125)	(47,900)
	33,775	0
Qualifying charitable donations	(540)	
Taxable total profits	33,235	0

Working: Trading loss

For the year ended 31 August 2020, loss relief is restricted to £24,125 (57,900 × 5/12).

(c)   The amount of unrelieved trading loss at 31 March 2022 is £63,875 (135,900 − 47,900 − 24,125).

The unrelieved trading loss will be carried forward automatically and a claim can be made to set it, wholly or partly, against total profits of the next accounting period and then against total profits of future accounting periods until it is completely relieved.

243 Lucky Ltd

Workbook references. The computation of taxable total profits and the computation of the corporation tax liability are covered in Chapter 19. The adjustment to trading profits is dealt with in Chapter 7 and capital allowances in Chapter 8. National insurance contributions are covered in Chapter 12.

Top tips. Administrative aspects of corporation tax are very likely to be examined so don't omit them from your revision.

Easy marks. There were some easy marks for the adjustment to trading profit and computation of corporation tax in part (b).

Examining team's comments. In part (a), most candidates appreciated that an accounting period starts when a company commences to trade, but many could not provide any other circumstances. For example, an accounting period will also start when a company otherwise becomes liable to corporation tax.

In part (b), the aspect of this question which appeared to cause candidates the most difficulties was the lease premium deduction and the difficulties were largely due to a failure to read the question carefully. Candidates were given the amount of the premium assessed on the landlord as income. However, a lot of candidates misread this figure as being the total premium paid.

Part (c) of the question was reasonably well answered.

[BPP note. Part (d) has been added to this question and there are no relevant examining team's comments.]

Marks

(a)	After end of previous period	1	
	Other situations	<u>1</u>	
			2
(b)	Trading profit		
	Advertising	½	
	Depreciation	½	
	Amortisation	½	
	Lease premium deduction	1½	
	Capital allowances		
	Integral feature addition	½	
	AIA in preference to 50% FYA	½	
	Computer addition	½	
	Office equipment addition	½	
	FYA @ 130%	1	
	WDA	1	
	Car addition	½	
	FYA	½	
	Interest income	½	
	Corporation tax	<u>½</u>	
			9
(c)	Date for retention	1	
	Penalty	<u>1</u>	
			2
(d)	Capital allowances	1	
	National insurance contributions	<u>1</u>	
			<u>2</u>
			<u><u>15</u></u>

(a) An accounting period will normally start immediately after the end of the preceding accounting period.

An accounting period will also start when a company commences to trade, or otherwise becomes liable to corporation tax.

(b) **Lucky Ltd – Corporation tax computation for the four-month period ended 31 March 2022**

	£
Operating profit	716,903
Advertising	0
Depreciation	14,700
Amortisation	9,000
Deduction for lease premium £46,800/12 × 4/12	(1,300)
Capital allowances (W1)	(364,594)
Trading profit	374,709
Interest income	700
Taxable total profits	375,409
Corporation tax £375,409 @ 19%	71,328

Tutorial note

The advertising expenditure incurred during September 2021 is pre-trading, and is treated as incurred on 1 December 2021. It is therefore deductible and no adjustment is required.

Workings

1   *Capital allowances*

	AIA/FYA £	Main pool £	Allowances £
Integral features	291,200		
AIA (W2)	(291,200)		291,200
Computer (6,300 × 130%)	8,190		
Office equipment (49,566 × 130%)	64,436		
	72,626		
FYA @ 130%	(72,626)		72,626
Motor car		12,800	
WDA 18% × 4/12		(768)	768
TWDV carried forward		12,032	
Total allowances			364,594

2   *Annual investment allowances*

The annual investment allowance is reduced to £333,333 (£1,000,000 × 4/12) because Lucky Ltd's accounting period is four months long.

Tutorial notes

1   It is beneficial to claim the annual investment allowance against the integral features expenditure, as it would otherwise only qualify for first year allowance of 50%, with the balance going into the special rate pool.

2   The computer purchased on 19 August 2021 is pre-trading and is treated as incurred on 1 December 2021.

3   The motor car has CO_2 emissions up to 50 grams per kilometre and therefore qualifies for the 18% WDA in the main pool.

BPP
LEARNING
MEDIA

(c)   Lucky Ltd must retain the records used in preparing its self-assessment corporation tax return until six years after the end of the accounting period, which is 31 March 2028.

Afailure to retain records could result in a penalty of up to £3,000 per accounting period. However, the maximum penalty will only be charged in serious cases.

(d)   The cost of the car will be included in Lucky Ltd's capital allowance computation and written down at the appropriate rate each year depending on the car's CO_2 emissions.

Lucky Ltd will also have to pay Class 1A national insurance contributions on the company car. Class 1A is deductible from taxable trading profits.

244 Jump Ltd

Workbook references. The computation of taxable total profits and the corporation tax liability are covered in Chapter 19. Groups of companies are covered in Chapter 22.

Top tips. In part (a), remember to include a zero when an item needs no adjustment; otherwise, you will not be credited for this knowledge.

Easy marks. Most of the adjustments to profit appear regularly in corporation tax questions.

Marking scheme

		Marks
(a)	*Trading loss*	
	Depreciation	½
	Employee training courses	½
	Employee pension contributions	½
	Staff party	½
	Car lease	1
	Accountancy	½
	Legal fees – share capital	½
	Legal fees – renewal of short lease	½
	Entertaining UK customers	½
	Entertaining overseas customers	½
	Political donations	½
	Balancing charge adjustment	½
	Capital allowances	
	Tax written down values b/f	½
	Motor car 1	1
	Motor car 2	½
	Balancing charge	½
	Writing down allowance	1
		10

				Marks
(b)	(i)	Choice of relief		1
	(ii)	Maximum relief claim – 7 m/e 31.12.21	½	
		Maximum relief claim – y/e 31.5.21	1½	
				2
	(iii)	Maximum surrender	1½	
		Skip Ltd	½	
				2
				15

(a) **Jump Ltd – Trading loss for the three-month period ended 31 March 2022**

	£
Loss before taxation	(144,700)
Depreciation	8,100
Employee training courses	0
Employee pension contributions	0
Staff party	0
Lease of motor car £1,200 × 15%	180
Accountancy	0
Legal fees – Issue of share capital	3,800
– Renewal of short lease	0
Entertaining UK customers	1,700
Entertaining overseas customers	790
Political donations	800
Balancing charge (W)	3,330
Trading loss	(126,000)

Working: Capital allowances

	Main pool	Special rate pool	Allowances
	£	£	£
TWDV brought forward	12,100	5,700	
Proceeds – Motor car [1]		(9,300)	
– Motor car [2]	(6,100)		
Balancing charge		3,600	(3,600)
	6,000		
WDA – 18% × 3/12	(270)		270
TWDV carried forward	5,730		
Net balancing charge			(3,330)

Tutorial note

The proceeds for motor car [1] are restricted to the original cost figure of £9,300.

(b) (i) The main factor which will influence Jump Ltd's choice of loss relief or group relief claims is the timing of the relief obtained, with an earlier claim generally being preferable in terms of cash flow (saving tax sooner is beneficial for cash flow).

Tutorial note

The other possible factor is the extent to which relief for qualifying charitable donations will be lost. However, this is not relevant given that Jump Ltd has not made any charitable donations.

(ii) The maximum loss relief claim for the seven-month period to 31 December 2021 is £42,400, being the total profits for this period.

The loss relief claim for the year ended 31 May 2021 is restricted to £33,250 ((78,600 + 1,200) × 5/12).

(iii) The maximum amount of trading loss which can be surrendered to Hop Ltd is £23,625, being the lower of £23,625 (63,000 × 3/8) and £126,000.

Skip Ltd is not a 75% subsidiary of Jump Ltd, so no group relief claim is possible.

245 Online Ltd

Workbook references. Computing taxable total profits is covered in Chapter 19. Chargeable gains for companies is the subject of Chapter 20. The use of losses is dealt with in Chapter 21. Payment of tax by companies is covered in Chapter 22.

Top tips. Don't forget to answer both parts of the question. In part (b) you only needed to make a couple of points in order to gain the marks.

Easy marks. There should have been easy marks for well-known adjustments such as depreciation and amortisation. The capital allowances computation was quite straightforward.

Examining team's comments. Part (a) was well answered. Surprisingly, the one aspect which consistently caused difficulty was the qualifying charitable donation. Many candidates added this back prior to deducting it, with others grossing up the deduction. Also, it is important that candidates know basic tax rules. Even though all of the items included in the capital allowances special rate pool had been sold, there was no balancing allowance because Online Ltd's trade did not cease. This was another computation where candidates needed to think carefully about where to show workings. In this case, the deduction for the lease premium, capital allowances and the chargeable gain warranted separate workings. It was not a good idea for candidates to attempt a short-cut approach to any of these workings. As regards the chargeable gain, quite a few candidates included the gain from the disposal made three years previously. This shows just how much care needs to be taken over dates.

In part (b) many candidates appreciated that acquiring a 51% group company would mean that the profit threshold for establishing whether Online Ltd is a large company would be reduced to £750,000. It would therefore be likely that the company's corporation tax would in future be payable by quarterly instalments. Having established this point, there was no need to then go on and explain quarterly instalments in detail. If such detail was needed, then this would have been made clear in the requirement. For some candidates, this was another example of where they wanted to answer the question that would have preferred had been set – in this case, explaining why the reliefs available with a 75% group relationship were not available with just a 60% shareholding. Few candidates correctly stated that the dividends received from Offline Ltd, being group dividends, would not form part of Online Ltd's profits when establishing its large company status.

		Marks
(a)	Depreciation	½
	Amortisation	½
	Property loss brought forward	1
	Qualifying charitable donations	½
	Lease premium	
	Amount assessed on landlord	1
	Deduction	1
	Capital allowances	
	Tax written down values b/f	½
	Disposal – car	1
	Disposal – pool	½
	WDA @ 18%	½
	WDA @ 6%	1
	Chargeable gain	
	Disposal proceeds	½
	Share pool – original cost	½
	Share pool – indexation to October 2013	½
	Share pool – disposal October 2013	1
	Share pool – indexation to December 2017	½
	Share pool – disposal March 2021	½
	Capital loss brought forward	½
		__
		13
(b)	Profit threshold reduced	1½
	Group dividends	½
		__
		2
		==
		15

(a) **Online Ltd – Corporation tax computation for the year ended 31 March 2022**

	£
Operating profit	896,700
Depreciation	21,660
Amortisation	9,000
Deduction for lease premium (W1)	(7,380)
Capital allowances (W2)	(9,824)

	£
Trading profit	910,156
Chargeable gain (W3)	59,967
	970,123
Property business loss brought forward	(12,500)
Qualifying charitable donations	(6,800)
Taxable total profits	950,823

Workings

1   *Deduction for lease premium*

	£
Premium paid	90,000
Less: 90,000 × 2% × (10 − 1)	(16,200)
Amount assessed on the landlord	73,800
Deduction (73,800/10)	7,380

2   *Capital allowances*

	Main pool £	Special rate pool £	Allowances £
WDV brought forward	56,700	13,433	
Addition – Motor car	13,700		
Disposals – Motor car	(17,200)		
– Pool		(9,300)	
	53,200	4,133	
WDA – 18%	(9,576)		9,576
WDA – 6%		(248)	248
WDV carried forward	43,624	3,885	
Total allowances			9,824

Tutorial notes

1   The motor car purchased has CO_2 emissions between 1 and 50 grams per kilometre, and therefore qualifies for writing down allowances at the rate of 18%.

2   The proceeds for the motor car which was sold are restricted to the original cost figure of £17,200.

3   Although all of the items included in the special rate pool have been sold, there is no balancing allowance because the business has not ceased.

3   *Chargeable gain*

	£
Disposal proceeds	90,600
Less: Indexed cost (W4)	(27,529)
	63,071
Less: Capital loss brought forward	(3,104)
Chargeable gain	59,967

4   *Share pool*

	Number	Indexed cost
		£
Purchase June 2010	40,000	49,300
Indexation to October 2013 (49,300 × 0.124)		6,113
		55,413
Disposal October 2013 (55,413 × 22,000/40,000)	(22,000)	(30,477)
	18,000	24,936
Indexation to December 2017 (24,936 × 0.104)		2,593
		27,529
Disposal March 2022	(18,000)	(27,529)

(b)   The profit threshold for establishing whether Online Ltd is a large company will be reduced to £750,000 (1,500,000/2), so it is likely that the company's corporation tax will have to be paid by quarterly instalments.

The dividends received from Offline Ltd, being group dividends, will not form part of Online Ltd's profits.

246 Last-Orders Ltd

Workbook references. The computation of taxable total profits is covered in Chapter 19. Chargeable gains for companies are covered in Chapter 20. Corporate losses are the subject of Chapter 21 and group relief is dealt with in Chapter 22.

Top tips. When a company ceases to trade, no writing down allowances are given in the final accounting period but there will be a balancing adjustment.

Easy marks. In part (a) there were plenty of easy marks for adjustment to profit items but be careful to identify the effect of each of the adjustments on the trading loss. An item added back, such as depreciation, will reduce the loss, but an item deducted, such as capital allowances, will increase the loss.

Examining team's comments. Although section (a) was very well answered by many candidates, it caused problems for others. The section did not require any detailed workings, with any adjustments easily contained within the single computation. When commencing with a loss figure, candidates should be particularly careful to indicate which adjustments are deductions and which are additions. A single column approach with deductions shown in brackets avoids any confusion. Many candidates did not show those items not requiring any adjustment, despite being instructed

specifically to do so – easy marks thereby being lost. Also, candidates should appreciate that there is no need to adjust for items of income which occur in the statement of profit or loss **after** the figure used to commence the loss adjustment. Last-Orders Ltd had ceased trading, so this meant that there was a balancing allowance. Many candidates missed this point, instead calculating capital allowances for the period.

Section (b) was generally well answered, with a number of perfect answers. However, candidates do not impress if they make basic mistakes such as deducting the annual exempt amount when calculating a corporate chargeable gain. Also, candidates should always be careful to follow the requirements – an easy half-mark was sometimes missed by not showing a figure for the amount of unused trading loss despite this being specifically requested.

In section (c), given that the company had ceased trading, candidates should really have realised that the loss could not be carried forward. Vague answers such as 'claim terminal loss relief' are not sufficient. Instead, candidates should have stated that relief was against total profits, for the previous three years and on a latest year first (LIFO) basis.

Marking scheme

		Marks	
(a)	Depreciation	½	
	Counselling services	½	
	Employee pension contributions	½	
	Employer Class 1 NICs	½	
	Employer Class 1A NICs	½	
	Unpaid bonuses	½	
	Lease of motor car	½	
	Entertaining UK suppliers	½	
	Entertaining overseas customers	½	
	Qualifying charitable donations	½	
	Balancing allowance	<u>1</u>	
			6
(b)	Property business income		
	Rent receivable	1	
	Insurance	1	
	Repairs	½	
	Chargeable gain	1	
	Trading loss	½	
	Qualifying charitable donation	½	
	Unused trading loss	<u>½</u>	
			5
(c)	Terminal loss relief	1½	
	Group relief to Gastro Ltd	2	
	No group relief to Gourmet Ltd	<u>½</u>	
			<u>4</u>
			<u>15</u>

(a) Last-Orders Ltd – Trading loss for the ten-month period ended 31 January 2022

	£
Operating loss	(276,480)
Add Depreciation	9,460
Counselling services	0
Employee pension contributions	0
Employer Class 1 NICs	0
Employer Class 1A NICs	0
Unpaid bonuses	10,400
Lease of motor car	0
Entertaining UK suppliers	1,920
Entertaining overseas customers	440
Employer Class 1A NICs	0
Employer Class 1A NICs	0
Qualifying charitable donations	800
Less Balancing allowance £(24,200 – 13,600)	(10,600)
Trading loss	(264,060)

Tutorial notes

1 No deduction is permitted where earnings are not paid within nine months of the end of the period of account.

2 No adjustment is required where the CO_2 emissions of a leased motor car do not exceed 50 grams per kilometre.

3 All business entertaining is disallowable. The distinction between UK and overseas is only relevant for value added tax (VAT) purposes.

(b) Last-Orders Ltd – Taxable total profits for the ten-month period ended 31 January 2022

	£
Property business income (W)	22,800
Chargeable gain £(126,800 – 79,400 – 12,900)	34,500
Total profits	57,300
Less Trading loss	(57,300)
Qualifying charitable donations	(0)
Taxable total profits	0
Unused trading loss £(264,060 – 57,300)	206,760

Working

	£
Rent receivable £19,200 × 2 × 10/12	32,000
Less Insurance £1,800 × 10/12	(1,500)
Repairs	(7,700)
Property business income	22,800

Tutorial note

The accruals basis is always used by companies in computing property business income.

(c)

The trading loss can be relieved against Last-Orders Ltd's total profits for the previous three years, later years first, because it is a terminal loss.

The trading loss can be surrendered to Gastro Ltd because there is a 75% group relationship. The amount surrendered will be restricted to 10/12ths of Gastro Ltd's taxable total profits for the year ended 31 March 2022.

There is not a 75% group relationship with Gourmet Ltd, so no group relief claim is possible.

247 Solo Ltd

Examining team's comments. Part (a) for 3 marks required candidates to calculate Solo Ltd's revised tax-adjusted trading loss for the year ended 31 March 2022. This section was quite well answered. However, when dealing with a trading loss, candidates need to be very careful that adjustments are correctly added or deducted. Treating the loss as a negative means that there is no need to change the approach from that used for a trading profit. A number of candidates did not appreciate that there was a balancing charge because the disposal proceeds for the plant and machinery main pool exceeded the written down value brought forward.

Part (b) for 8 marks asked candidates to prepare a corporation tax computation for the year ended 31 March 2022 showing taxable total profits. This was on the basis that Solo Ltd claimed relief for its trading loss against its total profits. The requirement meant that candidates had to calculate property business income, calculate a chargeable gain on a share disposal, deduct brought forward capital losses from the gain, and then deduct the trading loss so that taxable total profits were nil. This section was again well answered. One aspect which consistently caused difficulty was candidates not preparing a separate gain calculation for the share purchase made during the preceding nine days. A number of candidates incorrectly restricted the insurance deduction in the property business income calculation to 8/12ths because the building was unoccupied from 1 April to 31 July 2021.

Information was provided in date order, and candidates often tried to use the details provided for the year ended 31 December 2020 and the period ended 31 March 2021 in this section of the question. The only details which were relevant were the capital losses, and these were often omitted in any case.

Part (c) for 4 marks required candidates to calculate Solo Ltd's taxable total profits for the year ended 31 December 2020 and the three-month period ended 31 March 2021. This was on the basis that the company claimed relief for the remainder of its trading loss as early as possible. This section was very well answered, and it was pleasing to see most candidates correctly restricting the trading loss set off for the year ended 31 December 2020 to 9/12ths of the total profits. Candidates should note that where two accounting periods are involved, then a two-column approach avoids the need to type out descriptions twice.

Marking scheme

		Marks
(a)	Deduction for lease premium	
	Premium received	½
	Amount treated as capital	1
	Trading income deduction	½
	Balancing charge	1
		3

(b)   Property business income

        Rent receivable — 1

        Security deposit — ½

        Insurance — 1

    Chargeable gain

        Disposal proceeds on shares purchased in previous 9 days — ½

        Cost of shares purchased in previous 9 days — ½

        Disposal proceeds on shares from share pool — ½

        Share pool

            Original purchase — ½

            Indexation to December 2017 — 1

            Disposal — 1

    Capital losses relieved — 1

    Trading loss relieved — ½

                            8

(c)   Trading profits — ½

    Property business income — ½

    Chargeable gains — ½

    Trading loss relieved — 1½

    Qualifying charitable donations — 1

                            4

                            15

(a)   **Solo Ltd – Trading loss for the year ended 31 March 2022**

	£
Trading loss	(151,300)
Less Deduction for lease premium (W)	(2,150)
Add Balancing charge	4,300
Trading loss	(149,150)

Working

	£
Premium received	20,000
Less £20,000 × 2% × (8 – 1)	(2,800)
Amount assessable on landlord	17,200
Trading income deduction £17,200/8	2,150

(b)   **Solo Ltd – Corporation tax computation for the year ended 31 March 2022**

	£
Property business income (W1)	9,480
Net chargeable gains £(16,198(W2) – 3,300 – 2,100)	10,798
Total profits	20,278
Less Trading loss	(20,278)
Taxable total profits	0

Workings

1   *Property business income*

	£
Rent receivable £(7,800 + (7,800 × 2/6))	10,400
Security deposit	0
Less Insurance	(920)
Property business income	9,480

Tutorial notes

1   The accruals basis is always used by companies in computing property business income.

2   A security deposit is not treated as income when received. It will be treated as income if the landlord uses it, for example to cover unpaid rent at the end of the tenancy. Any amount repaid to the tenant is not treated as an expense.

2   *Chargeable gains*

	£	£
Purchase 8 December 2021		
Disposal proceeds £31,200 × 1,000/6,500	4,800	
Less Cost	(4,600)	
		200
Share pool		
Disposal proceeds £31,200 × 5,500/6,500	26,400	
Less Cost (W3)	(10,402)	
		15,998
Chargeable gains		16,198

3   *Share pool*

	No.	Cost £
Purchase June 2006	20,000	27,000
Indexation to December 2017 £27,000 × 0.401		10,827
		37,827
Disposal December 2021 £37,827 × 5,500/20,000	(5,500)	(10,402)
C/f	14,500	27,425

Tutorial notes

1   The disposal is first matched with the shares purchased in the nine days before the disposal and then against the share pool.

2   Indexation is frozen at December 2017.

(c) **Solo Ltd – Taxable total profits for the periods ended 31 December 2020 and 31 March 2021**

	Year ended 31 December 2020 £	Period ended 31 March 2021 £
Trading profit	35,900	12,300
Property business income	12,100	4,200
Chargeable gains	0	0
Total profits	48,000	16,500
Less Trading loss relief	(36,000) (W)	(16,500)
Qualifying charitable donations	(1,200)	wasted
Taxable total profits	10,800	0

Working

	£
Year ended 31 December 2020 £48,000 × 9/12	36,000

248 Ash Ltd, Beech Ltd and Cedar Ltd

Workbook references. Computing taxable total profits (including residence of companies and accounting periods) and the corporation tax liability are covered in Chapter 19. Chargeable gains for companies is the subject of Chapter 20. Losses for a single company are dealt with in Chapter 21 and group relief in Chapter 22.

Top tips. Take care you answer all three part of the question.

Easy marks. These were available for basic adjustments to profits in part (b).

Examining team's comments. Part (a)(i) was quite well answered. However, when considering accounting periods, it is very important not to confuse the corporate and unincorporated business rules. Applying the unincorporated business opening year rules to a limited company will obviously not achieve many marks.

If asked to identify a company's accounting periods throughout a given period, then candidates should make sure that all relevant periods are stated. It does not create a good impression if there are gaps between the accounting periods stated by a candidate, or if a stated period ends before it has started.

In part (a)(ii), again candidates should be careful not to confuse the rules for companies with those applicable to individuals. If a limited company is incorporated in the UK, then nothing else is relevant. So, as regards the majority of Ash Ltd's director/shareholders moving overseas, candidates should just have stated that this did not have any impact on the company's residence status.

Part (b) was very well answered. When making adjustments to a trading profit, candidates need to be very careful that adjustments are correctly added and not deducted.

Part (c) was again well answered. When calculating chargeable gains for a corporate share disposal, then carefully check the dates that have been given. There was a rights issue which had taken place in the month of purchase, so there was no need to index prior to adding the new shares into the share pool.

Marks

(a) (i) 1st accounting period · · · · · · · · · · · 1
2nd accounting period · · · · · · · · · · · ½
3rd accounting period · · · · · · · · · · · ½

2

(ii) Incorporated in UK · · · · · · · · · · · 1
Move overseas by director/shareholders · · · · · · · · · · · 1

2

(b) Depreciation · · · · · · · · · · · ½
Gifts to customers · · · · · · · · · · · ½
Gifts to staff · · · · · · · · · · · ½
Qualifying charitable donations added back · · · · · · · · · · · ½
Impairment loss · · · · · · · · · · · ½
Lease of motor cars · · · · · · · · · · · 1
Fine · · · · · · · · · · · ½
Legal fees · · · · · · · · · · · ½
Interest payable · · · · · · · · · · · ½
Qualifying charitable donations deducted from total profits · · · · · · · · · · · ½
Corporation tax liability · · · · · · · · · · · ½

6

(c) Disposal proceeds · · · · · · · · · · · ½
Indexed cost
Purchase · · · · · · · · · · · ½
Rights issue · · · · · · · · · · · 1
Indexation allowance · · · · · · · · · · · 1
Capital loss · · · · · · · · · · · 1
Loss relief · · · · · · · · · · · ½
Group relief · · · · · · · · · · · ½

5

15

(a) **Ash Ltd**

(i) *Accounting periods*

1 February 2020 to 31 January 2021

1 February 2021 to 31 March 2021

Year ended 31 March 2022

Tutorial notes

1 The bank account opened by Ash Ltd on 1 December 2019 is not a source of income, and therefore does not trigger the start of an accounting period.

2 An accounting period cannot be longer than 12 months, so the period of account ended 31 March 2021 must be split into two accounting periods.

3 The move overseas of a majority of Ash Ltd's director/shareholders on 1 October 2021 has no impact on the company's accounting periods.

(ii) *Residence status*

1   Ash Ltd was incorporated in the UK, so the company is therefore resident in the UK throughout the period 1 December 2019 to 31 March 2022.

2   The move overseas of a majority of Ash Ltd's director/shareholders on 1 October 2021 does not have any impact on the company's residence status.

(b) **Beech Ltd**

Corporation tax computation for the year ended 31 January 2022

	£
Profit before taxation	305,500
Depreciation	14,700
Gifts to customers	3,500
Gifts to staff	0
Qualifying charitable donations	1,100
Impairment loss	0
Lease of motor cars (12,600 × 15%)	1,890
Data protection fine	6,400
Legal fees – Renewal of short lease	0
Interest payable	0
Trading profit/Total profits	333,090
Less Qualifying charitable donations	(1,100)
Taxable total profits	331,990
Corporation tax	
331,990 at 19%	63,078

Tutorial note

Gifts to customers are only an allowable deduction if they cost less than £50 per recipient per year, are not of food, drink, tobacco or vouchers for exchangeable goods and carry a conspicuous advertisement for the company making the gift. Gifts to staff are allowable.

(c) **Cedar Ltd**

Corporation tax computation for the year ended 31 March 2022

	£
Disposal proceeds (25,000 × 6.00)	150,000
Indexed cost (W)	(38,004)
Chargeable gain	111,996
Capital loss	(8,800)
Loss relief	(19,700)
Group relief	(20,800)
Taxable total profits	62,696

Working – Indexed cost

Share pool

	Number £	Indexed cost £
Purchase July 2010	20,000	24,800
Rights issue July 2010		
20,000 × 1/4 × £1.15	5,000	5,750
	25,000	30,550
Indexation to December 2017 (frozen)		
30,550 × 0.244		7,454
		38,004
Disposal December 2021	(25,000)	(38,004)

Tutorial notes

1   A joint election can be made so that Cedar Ltd is treated as having incurred Timber Ltd's capital loss.

2   Indexation allowance is frozen at December 2017

249 Aoede Ltd, Bianca Ltd and Charon Ltd

Workbook references. Computing taxable total profits is covered in Chapter 19, losses for a single company in Chapter 21 and group relief in Chapter 22. Chargeable gains for companies is the subject of Chapter 20.

Top tips. It is important that you attempt all three parts of this question in order to gain reasonable marks.

Easy marks. There were easy marks for straightforward adjustments to profits in part (b).

Examining team's comments. Although Moon Ltd was often overlooked, part (a)(i) was generally well answered. For the year ended 31 March 2021, many candidates did not appreciate that loss relief was claimed against Aoede Ltd's chargeable gain in priority to offsetting the qualifying charitable donations.

Part (a)(ii) was often not answered. The answer was simply that it was not beneficial for Aoede Ltd to make the loss relief claim against total income for the year ended 31 March 2021 because the income would have otherwise been covered by qualifying charitable donations.

Part (b) was very well answered. Candidates should note that when dealing with straightforward capital allowance computations such as those involved here, it is quicker to include them in the main computation rather than producing a full capital allowances working.

Part (c) was also well answered. However, a few candidates combined the two computations. Where a question involves more than one disposal, then the gain or loss for each disposal must be calculated separately.

Marks

(a) (i) Aoede Ltd y/e 31.3.21
            Total profits   ½
            Current period loss relief   1
            Qualifying charitable donation unrelieved   ½
         Aoede Ltd y/e 31.3.22
            Total profits   ½
            Carry forward loss relief   1
            Qualifying charitable donation   ½
         Moon Ltd y/e 31.3.22
            Trading profit   ½
            Group relief   ½
                                                                       ──
                                                                              5
     (ii) Loss relief claim not beneficial   1

(b) Advertising expenditure   ½
     Lease of motor cars   1½
     Laptops   1
     Motor car [1]   1
     Motor car [2]   1
                                                                       ──
                                                                              5

(c) First property
            Disposal proceeds   ½
            Cost   ½
            Enhancement expenditure   ½
            Indexation allowance   1
         Second property
            Disposal proceeds   ½
            Cost   ½
            Indexation allowance   ½
                                                                       ──
                                                                              4
                                                                             ══
                                                                             15

(a) (i) Aoede Ltd - Taxable total profits

	y/e 31.3.21 £	y/e 31.3.22 £
Trading profit	0	67,800
Property business income	0	23,400
Chargeable gain	5,800	16,200
Total profits	5,800	107,400
Less Current period trading loss relief	(5,800)	(0)
Carry forward trading loss relief	(0)	(100,800)
Qualifying charitable donation	(0)	(6,600)
Taxable total profits	0	0

BPP LEARNING MEDIA

Moon Ltd – Taxable total profits

	y/e 31.3.22 £
Trading profit	19,700
Less Trading loss carry forward group relief	(4,700)
Property business loss carry forward group relief	(15,000)
Taxable total profits	0

Tutorial notes

1   Loss memorandum

	Trading loss £	Property business loss £
Y/e 31.3.21	111,300	26,400
Used in y/e 31.3.21 against own profits	(5,800)	(0)
Used in y/e 31.3.22 against own profits	(100,800)	(0)
Used in y/e 31.3.22 as group relief	(4,700)	(15,000)
Losses c/f	0	11,400

2   There are independent claims for Aoede Ltd's trading loss and property business loss. We have used the trading loss in priority to the property business loss but it would be possible to use the property business loss first – the result for these two accounting periods would be the same.

3   Aoede Ltd's current period loss relief claim must be taken against total profits as far as possible. It is not possible to restrict it to preserve relief on the qualifying charitable donation of £6,000.

4   Aoede Ltd will automatically carry forward its unused losses to y/e 31 March 2022 but can make a partial relief claim to keep sufficient total profits in charge to cover the qualifying charitable donation of £6,600.

5   Aoede Ltd must use its carried forward losses itself before surrendering losses under carry forward group relief.

6   It is not beneficial for Aoede Ltd to make the loss relief claim against total income for the year ended 31 March 2021 because the income would have otherwise been covered by the qualifying charitable donations of £6,000.

(b)   **Bianca Ltd – Tax adjusted trading profit for the year ended 31 March 2022**

	£
Trading profit	256,300
Less Advertising expenditure	(5,800)
Add Lease of motor cars (5,100 × 15%)	765
Less Capital allowances	
Laptops (1,000 × 4 × 130%)	(5,200)
Motor car [1] (12,400 × 18%)	(2,232)
Motor car [2] (13,900 × 6%)	(834)
Revised trading profit	242,999

Tutorial notes

1   The advertising expenditure incurred during January 2020 is pre-trading, and is therefore treated as incurred on 1 April 2021.

2   The original cost of the laptops is irrelevant.

3   Motor car [2] has CO_2 emissions over 50 grams per kilometre and therefore qualifies for writing down allowances at the rate of 6%.

(c) **Charon Ltd – Chargeable gains and capital losses for the year ended 31 March 2022**

First property

	£
Disposal proceeds	368,000
Less Cost	(147,000)
Less Enhancement expenditure	(39,000)
	182,000
Indexation allowance	
147,000 × 0.856	(125,832)
Chargeable gain	56,168

Second property

	£
Disposal proceeds	167,000
Less Cost	(172,000)
Indexation allowance	0
Less Capital loss	(5,000)

Tutorial note

There is no indexation allowance for the first property's enhancement expenditure of £39,000 because this was incurred after December 2017.

OTQ bank – Value added tax 1

250 Deposit 18 August, Balancing payment 2 September

The basic tax point is the date the goods were supplied (26 August). Where payment is received before the basic tax point, then this date becomes the actual tax point. The tax point for the 10% deposit is therefore the date that it is received (18 August). The actual tax point for the balancing payment is the date the invoice was issued (2 September) as this was within 14 days of the basic tax point.

251

	BARRY	CHRIS

Input tax related to zero rated (children's clothing) and standard rated (adult clothing) supplies is recoverable but input tax related to exempt supplies (financial services) is not.

252 £62

	£
Output VAT: £377 × 1/6	63
Less input VAT: £625 × 20%	(125)
VAT due	(62)

Input VAT on the motor car is not recoverable because there is private use. The answer £50 treats the scale charge as VAT-exclusive but recovers the correct amount on the petrol. The answer £75 treats the scale charge as VAT-exclusive and fails to recover the VAT on the actual petrol purchase. The answer £41 treats petrol as inclusive, instead of exclusive, of VAT.

253 Return 7 July 2021, payment 7 July 2021

The time limit for submission of the return and payment is one month plus seven days after the end of the VAT period.

254 VAT quarter ended 30 June 2022

The value added tax (VAT) on an impaired debt may only be reclaimed once the debt has been outstanding for six months from the due date. The due date in this instance is 10 October 2021; therefore the VAT can be reclaimed in the quarter ended 30 June 2022.

OTQ bank – Value added tax 2

255 £1,600

The VAT will be calculated on the actual amount received so is £8,000 × 20% = £1,600.

256 £333

Input tax on the motor car is not recoverable because there is private use. However, since there is some use of the car for business purposes, then any VAT charged on repairs and maintenance costs can be treated as input tax without apportionment for private use. The input VAT recoverable is therefore £2,000 × 1/6 = £333.

257 £2,320

	£
New car for salesman	0
New motor van £10,320 × 1/6	1,720
Entertaining UK customers	0
Entertaining overseas customers £3,600 × 1/6	600
Total input tax recoverable	2,320

The answer £5,360 allows full input tax recovery. The answer £4,192 allows business use recovery of input tax on the car. The answer £3,020 allows recovery of input tax on the entertaining of UK customers.

258 £270

The following rules apply to pre-registration input tax:

Goods: if acquired within four years prior to registration and still held on registration date (so the VAT on the inventory of spare parts is recoverable).

Services: if supplied within six months prior to registration (so the VAT on the accountancy fees is recoverable but not that on the legal fees).

259 1 August 2021

Scott is required to notify HMRC within 30 days of exceeding the £85,000 registration threshold ie 30 July 2021 (30 days after the year to 30 June 2021). He will then be registered from 1 August 2021.

260 £4,925

	£
Output VAT: £35,250 × 1/6	5,875
Less input VAT: £5,700 × 1/6 (UK customer entertaining not recoverable)	(950)
VAT due	4,925

261 0%

Charlie will charge VAT at zero rate because exports of goods to anywhere in the world are zero rated.

262 Date of payment or receipt determines the VAT period in which the transaction is dealt with.

Gives automatic impairment loss relief (bad debt relief).

263 £8,500

	£
Standard rated sales (£50,000 × 120%)	60,000
Zero rated sales	20,000
Exempt sales	5,000
Total VAT inclusive sales	85,000
Value added tax £85,000 × 10%	8,500

264

Join scheme	Tax exclusive annual taxable turnover up to £150,000

Leave scheme	Tax inclusive annual turnover up to £230,000

OT case – Anne

265 £5,600

Cash sales £28,000 (adult clothes standard rated) × 20%	<u>£5,600</u>

266 £2,292

	£
Credit sales with discount £12,000 × 95% × 90% × 20%	2,052
Credit sales without discount £12,000 × 10% × 20%	<u>240</u>
	<u>2,292</u>

The calculation of output VAT on the credit sales only takes into account the discount for prompt payment for the 90% of customers that took it.

The answer £2,052 is just the output VAT on the discounted sales. The answer £2,280 is the output tax if all sales are treated as discounted. The answer £2,400 is the answer if no sales are treated as discounted.

267   £2,400

	£
Purchases and expenses £11,200 × 20%	2,240
Impairment loss £800 × 20%	160
	2,400

Relief for an impairment loss is not given until six months from the time that payment is due. Therefore relief can only be claimed in respect of the invoice due for payment on 10 April 2021. Obviously the customer did not take up the discount for prompt payment.

268   Anne will be permitted to join the scheme if her expected taxable turnover for the next 12 months does not exceed £1,350,000.

If the value of Anne's taxable supplies exceeds £1,600,000 in the 12 months to the end of a VAT period she must leave the scheme immediately.

Anne will be permitted to join the scheme if she is up to date with both her VAT payments and her VAT returns. Payment in nine monthly instalments is a feature of the annual accounting scheme.

269

Reduced amount of output VAT payable		NOT ADVANTAGE
Automatic impairment loss relief (bad debt relief)	ADVANTAGE	
Only one VAT return each year		NOT ADVANTAGE
Output VAT on 10% of credit sales will be accounted for up to 1 month later than at present	ADVANTAGE	

The output VAT payable will remain the same and accounting for VAT will also remain the same.

OT case – Auy and Bim

> **Workbook references.** The tax point and VAT liability are covered in Chapter 24. Special schemes are dealt with in Chapter 25.
>
> **Top tips.** Learn the rules about the tax point – they are often examined! For the basic tax point you need to distinguish between supplies of goods (date goods are removed or made available to the customer) and services (date on which services are completed).
>
> **Easy marks.** There were easy marks in questions 271 and 274 for the computation of the VAT paid or payable by the partnership.

270   If the VAT invoice is issued within 14 days after the basic tax point and payment has not been received before the basic tax point, the invoice date becomes the tax point.

The tax point determines the VAT period in which output tax must be accounted for and credit for input tax will be allowed.

The basic tax point for services is the date that services are completed. If the VAT invoice is issued and payment is received before the basic tax point, the actual tax point is the earlier of those two dates.

271 £25,280

The partnership's output VAT for the year ended 5 April 2022 is £25,600 and its total input VAT for the year is £(180 + 140) = £320.

Therefore VAT of £25,280 (25,600 – 320) will have been paid to HM Revenue & Customs for the year ended 5 April 2022.

272 Businesses using the scheme must still issue VAT invoices to their VAT registered customers.

Businesses using the scheme cannot reclaim any input tax suffered.

Under the scheme, businesses calculate VAT by applying a fixed percentage to all their income (ie including reduced rate, zero rated and exempt income). A 1% reduction off the flat rate percentage can be made by businesses in the first year that they use the flat rate scheme only if it is also the first year of registration.

273 Join: expected taxable turnover (excluding VAT) for the next 12 months does not exceed £150,000, Continue to use: until its total turnover (including VAT) for the previous year exceeds £230,000

274 £23,291

If the partnership had used the flat rate scheme throughout the year ended 5 April 2022 then it would have paid VAT of £(140,762 + 25,600) = £166,362 @ 14% = £23,291.

OT case – Aston

> **Workbook references.** Registration for value added tax is covered in Chapter 24. VAT invoices, penalties and overseas aspects are dealt with in Chapter 25.
>
> **Top tips.** Remember that the common penalty regime for errors applies to a number of taxes, including VAT.
>
> **Easy marks.** There were easy marks for dealing with the registration of Aston in question 275.

275 Liable for registration: 31 January 2022, Date of registration: 1 March 2022

Aston would have been liable to compulsory value added tax (VAT) registration when his taxable supplies during any 12-month period (or the period from commencement of trade, if less) exceeded £85,000.

This happened on 31 January 2022 when taxable supplies amounted to £85,200 (6,300 + 6,400 + 21,900 + 4,800 + 11,700 + 17,100 + 14,800 + 2,200).

Registration is required from the end of the month following the month in which the limit is exceeded, so Aston will have been registered from 1 March 2022 or from an agreed earlier date.

276 Submission: one month and seven days after the end of the VAT period. Payment: one month and seven days after the end of the VAT period.

277 Aston's VAT registration number

An identifying number (invoice number)

278 The transaction is entered on Aston's VAT return as an output and an input.

The service is treated as being supplied in the UK since this is where Aston is situated.

The tax point for a supply of such services is the earlier of the time the service is completed and the time the service is paid for. Supplies of services from VAT registered businesses situated elsewhere within the European Union are categorised in the same way as UK supplies and so are not necessarily zero rated.

279   Maximum penalty 30% of the VAT underpaid, Minimum penalty 0% of the VAT underpaid

HM Revenue & Customs (HMRC) will not charge a penalty if Aston has taken reasonable care, provided he informs them of any errors upon subsequent discovery.

However, applying the incorrect rate of VAT is more likely to be treated as careless, since Aston would be expected to check the VAT classification of his supplies.

The maximum amount of penalty will therefore be 30% of the VAT underpaid, but this penalty could be reduced to 0% as a result of a subsequent unprompted disclosure to HMRC.

OT case – Starfish Ltd

> **Workbook references.** Calculation of value added tax (VAT) and transfer of a business as a going concern are covered in Chapter 24. Default interest is dealt with in Chapter 25.
>
> **Top tips.** In question 284 you need to identify the supplies which will not be subject to VAT as a result of the transfer of going concern rules.
>
> **Easy marks.** There were some easy marks available in the computation of VAT in question 281.

280   £390

	£
Credit sales revenue discount taken up £2,000 × (100 − 4)% × 60% × 20%	230
Credit sales revenue discount not taken up £2,000 × 40% × 20%	160
	390

281   £16,420

	£
Cash sales revenue £38,520 × 20/120	6,420
Sale of inventory on cessation £28,800 × 20/120	4,800
Sale of non-current assets £31,200 × 20/120	5,200
	16,420

There is no VAT charged on the sale of the car, as none was recovered on purchase (owing to private usage).

282   £11,324

	£
Expenses £([69,960 − 4,320] = £65,640) × 20/120	10,940
Impairment loss	384
	11,324

Input VAT on business entertainment for UK customers is not recoverable.

Relief for the impairment loss is available because the claim is made more than six months from the time that payment was due, and the debt has been written off in the company's books.

283 7 May 2022

Default interest will be payable from the reckonable date (7 May 2022) to the date of payment.

284 No output VAT would have been due on the sale of the inventory or the sale of the non-current assets.

A sale of a business as a going concern is outside the scope of VAT, and therefore output VAT would not have been due on either the sale of the inventory or the sale of the non-current assets.

OT case – Greenzone Ltd

Workbook references. All the VAT aspects in this question are dealt with in Chapter 24.

Top tips. Watch out for the difference between entertaining UK customers and overseas customers.

Easy marks. There were easy marks in question 285 for working out the output VAT.

285 £42,540

	£
Output VAT	
Sales	38,210
Group sales	4,330
Output VAT	42,540

The tax point for the deposit is the date of payment, so no adjustment is required to the output VAT figure of £38,210.

The answer £38,210 does not include group sales. The answer £42,140 does not include the deposit. The answer £37,810 does not include either group sales or the deposit.

286 £27 recoverable

	£
Output VAT	
Fuel scale charge £334 × 20/120	56
Input VAT	
Fuel purchased £500 × 20/120	(83)
VAT recoverable	(27)

The answer £23 payable adjusts the input tax for private mileage so the input VAT is £500 × 40% × 20/120 = £33. The answer £33 recoverable treats the amounts as VAT exclusive. The answer £56 payable is just the fuel scale charge.

287   £12,560

	£
Total input VAT	12,770
Entertaining UK customers	(210)
Entertaining overseas customers	0
Repainting office building	0
New reception area	0
	12,560

Input VAT on business entertaining is not recoverable unless it relates to the cost of entertaining overseas customers. There is no distinction between capital and revenue expenditure for VAT so input tax is recoverable on both the repainting of the office building (revenue) and the building of the new reception area (capital).

288

ARE LTD		

Are Ltd can register with Greenzone Ltd as a group for VAT purposes as it is UK resident and controlled by Greenzone Ltd. Be Ltd is not controlled by Greenzone Ltd and Doer Inc is not UK resident and does not have a fixed establishment in the UK.

289   Each VAT group must appoint a representative member which must account for the group's output tax and input tax.

Any supply of goods or services by a member of the group to another member of the group is disregarded for VAT purposes.

All members of the group are jointly and severally liable for any VAT due from the representative member. It is not necessary for each company, which is eligible for group registration, to join a particular VAT group.

OT case – Long Ltd group (B)

> **Workbook references.** Value added tax (VAT) calculation and group registration will be found in Chapter 24.
>
> **Top tips.** It is vital to understand the difference between making exempt supplies and zero rated supplies – think about whether input VAT can be recovered in either case.
>
> **Easy marks.** There were some easy marks for dealing with input VAT in questions 291 and 293.

290   £53,780

	£
Sales £(52,640 – 1,760)	50,880
Group sales £(1,940 + 960)	2,900
	53,780

The tax point for the deposit is the date of payment, so this will have been included in output VAT for the quarter ended 31 December 2021.

291 £15,638

	£
Expenses	14,720
Hire of photocopier	
£18 × [(4 years × 12 = 48 months) + 3 months]	918
	15,638

Refunds of VAT are subject to a four-year time limit so, in addition to the input VAT for the hire of the photocopier incurred during the quarter ended 31 March 2022, Long Ltd can also claim for the input VAT incurred during the period 1 January 2018 to 31 December 2021.

The answer £14,720 does not include the hire of the photocopies. The answer £14,774 includes only three months of the hire of the photocopier. The answer £14,882 includes an additional six months of hire of the photocopier giving nine months in total – this is a confusion between the rules for recovery of goods and of services.

292 £0

Wind Ltd's sales are exempt from VAT, so the company cannot be registered for VAT and thus cannot recover input tax.

293 £3,500

	£
Expenses	3,120
Advertising	380
	3,500

Input VAT on services incurred prior to registration is subject to a 6-month time limit, so the input VAT of £640 in respect of the advertising expenditure incurred during April 2021 cannot be recovered.

The answer £3,120 does not include the advertising at all. The answer £4,140 includes all the advertising. The answer £3,540 includes only the £640 of advertising expenditure.

294 Supplies of goods or services to Road Ltd from outside the group will be treated as a supply to Long Ltd.

The supplies by Long Ltd to Wind Ltd and Road Ltd would be disregarded for VAT purposes.

Two or more companies are eligible to be treated as members of a group if one of them controls each of the others, or one person (which could be an individual or a holding company) controls all of them, or two or more persons carrying on a business in partnership control all of them. The controlling entity therefore does not need to be a company. It is not necessary for each company, which meets the requirements, to join a particular VAT group.

OT case – Zim

Workbook references. Value added tax is dealt with in Chapters 24 and 25.

Top tips. You must make sure you know the thresholds for entering and leaving the flat rate scheme as they are not given in the rates and allowances available in the examination.

Easy marks. Question 295 provided easy marks for working out the net VAT payable.

295   £12,000

		£	£
Sales	– Standard rated £115,200 × 20/120		19,200
	– Zero rated		0
Purchases	– Standard rated £43,200 × 20/120	7,200	
	– Zero rated	0	
			(7,200)
Net VAT payable			12,000

296   £240

Impairment losses £(780 + 660) = 1,440 × 20/120 = £240

Relief for impairment losses is given once six months have expired from the time when payment was due, so relief can be claimed in respect of both impairment losses.

The answer £0 assumes no relief for impairment losses is available. The answer £130 gives relief only on the loss of £780. The answer £110 gives relief only on the loss of £660.

297   Mobile phone £260, Customers £40

Mobile phone £2,600 × 60% (100% – 40%) × 20/120 = £260

An apportionment is made where a service such as the use of a telephone is partly for business purposes and partly for private purposes.

Customer entertainment £240 × 20/120 = £40

Input VAT on business entertainment is not recoverable unless it relates to the cost of entertaining overseas customers.

298

Join	Taxable turnover excluding VAT not more than £150,000 in next 12 months

Leave	Total turnover including VAT more than £230,000 in previous 12 months

299   £15,120

Using the flat rate scheme to calculate his VAT liability, Zim would have paid VAT of £126,000 × 12% = £15,120 for the year ended 31 March 2022.

The answer £13,860 assumes that the 1% reduction is available – be careful of this rule as it only applies in the first year of VAT registration. The answer £13,824 only charges standard rated sales. The answer £9,216 charges the flat rate on sales less expenses.

BPP
LEARNING
MEDIA

OT case – Smart Ltd

300

Register	1 November 2021

Notification	30 November 2021

Smart Ltd was liable to register for VAT from 1 November 2021 because this is the date when it signed the contract valued at £86,000. The company would therefore have known that its taxable supplies for the following 30-day period would have exceeded £85,000. Registration is required from the start of the 30-day period.

Smart Ltd would have had to notify HM Revenue & Customs by 30 November 2021, being the end of the 30-day period.

301

Smart Ltd can file its VAT returns by entering figures manually on HMRC's website		FALSE
Smart Ltd can choose whether to pay the VAT which is due electronically or by cheque.		FALSE
The deadline for paying any VAT which is due is one month after the end of each quarter.		FALSE
The deadline for filing the VAT return is one month and seven days after the end of each quarter.	TRUE	

Smart Ltd must use the Making Tax Digital software to directly submit its VAT returns to HMRC.

Smart Ltd must pay the VAT which is due electronically. The deadline for paying any VAT which is due is one month and seven days after the end of each quarter.

302   The basic tax point is the date on which services are completed.

If a customer pays for services before the basic tax point, the payment date will be the tax point.

303   1 and 4

The scheme will provide automatic relief for an impairment loss should a customer default on the payment of a debt. Output VAT will be accounted for 60 days later than at present, because the scheme will result in the tax point becoming the date when payment is received from customers.

304   Maximum penalty: 30% of the VAT underpaid. Minimum penalty for prompted disclosure: 15% of the VAT underpaid.

OT case – Thidar

305   Month 14

	£	£
Months 1 to 12 Standard rated and Zero rated		84,400
Month 13 Standard rated and Zero rated	3,700	
Less Month 1 Standard rated and Zero rated	(3,400)	
		300
		84,700
Month 14 Standard rated and Zero rated	4,900	
Less Month 2 Standard rated and Zero rated	(1,900)	
		3,000
		87,700

VAT registration threshold of £85,000 exceeded at the end of Month 14.

The answer Month 15 ignores the month where no supplies are made as one of the 12 months. The answer Month 13 uses the first 13-months of trading (ie does not take out Month 1). The answer Not yet exceeded only uses the standard rated supplies.

306   £0

Pre-registration input tax suffered on the supply of services within six months prior to registration can be reclaimed. The supply on 10 June 2020 is earlier than six months before registration on 1 January 2021. The input tax on the supply on 8 December 2020, whilst it is within six months before registration, cannot be reclaimed as Thidar does not have evidence for the supply.

The answer £360 allows reclaim for the 10 June 2020 supply only. The answer £60 allows reclaim for the 8 December 2020 supply only. The answer £420 allows reclaim for both supplies.

307   Option 2

VAT invoices must be issued within 30 days. VAT records (including invoices) must be retained for six years.

308   Because separate disclosure of the VAT underpayment was not required.

Default interest on unpaid VAT as a result of an error is only charged where the limit is exceeded for the error to be corrected on the next VAT return (here £10,000) such that it must be separately disclosed to HM Revenue & Customs.

The 12-month period is not relevant for penalties for errors (it applies to penalties for failure to notify chargeability). There can be a penalty for a careless (ie not deliberate) error. Default interest runs from the date the VAT should have been paid if the error had not been made.

309   Option 3

The input tax of £800 × 20% = £160 on entertaining UK customers is non-deductible (but would be deductible for entertaining overseas customers). The answer £0 permits deduction of input tax on entertaining UK customers.

50% of the input tax is deductible on leased cars where there is some private use so the remaining 50% × £700 × 20% = £70 is non-deductible. The answer £105 is 75% × £700 × 20% = £105 (ie based on the amount of private use).

310 Jogger Ltd (B)

Workbook references. Value added tax default surcharges and special schemes are covered in Chapter 25.

Top tips. In part (b) make sure that you make four points to get the available marks.

Easy marks. The conditions for Jogger Ltd to join the annual accounting scheme in part (b) should have been easy marks.

Marking scheme

		Marks	
(a)	Quarter ended 30 September 2020	2	
	Quarter ended 31 March 2021	2	
	Quarter ended 31 March 2022	2	
			6
(b)	One VAT return	1	
	Payments on account	1	
	Limit	1	
	VAT payments up to date	1	
			4
			10

(a)   The late submission of the VAT return for the quarter ended 30 September 2020 will have resulted in HM Revenue & Customs (HMRC) issuing a surcharge liability notice specifying a surcharge period running to 30 September 2021.

The late payment of VAT for the quarter ended 31 March 2021 will have resulted in a surcharge of £778 (£38,900 × 2%) because this is the first default in the surcharge period. The surcharge period will also have been extended to 31 March 2022.

The late payment of VAT for the quarter ended 31 March 2022 will therefore have resulted in a surcharge of £4,455 (£89,100 × 5%) because this is the second default in the surcharge period. The surcharge period will also have been extended to 31 March 2023.

(b)   The reduced administration from only having to submit one VAT return each year should mean that default surcharges are avoided in respect of the late submission of VAT returns.

In addition, making payments on account based on the previous year's VAT liability will improve both budgeting and possibly cash flow if Jogger Ltd's business is expanding.

Jogger Ltd can apply to use the annual accounting scheme if its expected taxable turnover for the next 12 months does not exceed £1,350,000 exclusive of VAT.

However, the company must be up to date with its VAT payments before it is allowed to use the scheme.

311 Flick

Marking scheme

			Marks
(a)	Flat rate scheme	1	
	Normal basis	1	
	Conclusion	1	
			3
(b)	No recovery of VAT by customers	1	
	Possible need to absorb VAT	1	
	Conclusion	1	
			3
(c)	VAT period	1	
	Basic tax point	1	
	Deposit	1	
	Balance	1	
			4
			10

(a) Using the flat rate scheme to calculate its VAT liability the partnership will have paid VAT of £(59,700 × 12%) = £7,164 for the quarter ended 31 March 2022.

If the partnership had used the normal basis it would have paid VAT of £(59,700 – 27,300 = 32,400 × 20/120) = £5,400.

It was therefore not beneficial to use the flat rate scheme as the additional cost of £(7,164 – 5,400) = £1,764 for the quarter would appear to outweigh the advantage of simplified VAT administration.

(b) The partnership's sales are all to members of the general public, who cannot recover the input VAT.

It may not therefore be possible to pass the output VAT on to customers in the prices charged. To the extent this is not possible the partnership would have had to absorb all or some of this amount itself as a cost.

It was therefore not beneficial for the partnership to have voluntarily registered for VAT from 1 January 2022. For the quarter ended 31 March 2022 voluntary registration reduced the partnership's profits by a maximum of £7,164 (£5,400 if the normal basis had been used).

(c) Output VAT must be accounted for according to the VAT period in which the supply is treated as being made. This is determined by the tax point.

The basic tax point is the date when the service is completed, which will be the date that a film is screened.

Where payment is received before the basic tax point, then this date becomes the actual tax point. The tax point for each 25% deposit is therefore the date that it is received.

Invoices are issued on the same day as the basic tax point, so this is the tax point for the balance of 75%.

BPP
LEARNING
MEDIA

312 Richard

Workbook references. Registration for VAT is covered in Chapter 24 as is VAT administration. VAT invoices are dealt with in Chapter 25. Ethical considerations are covered in Chapter 1.

Top tips. Ethical considerations are an important part of the Taxation (TX – UK) syllabus and you might be asked about them in relation to any tax.

Easy marks. The calculation of the date for registration for VAT in part (a) was straightforward.

Marking scheme

			Marks
(a)	Compulsory registration limit	½	
	Date registration required	1½	
	Date registration effective	1	
	Consequences of non-registration	1	
			4
(b)	Honesty and integrity	½	
	Cease to act and inform HMRC	1	
	Money laundering notification	½	
			2
(c)	Simplified invoice	1	
	Request for invoice	½	
	Details on invoice: ½ mark per item to maximum	2½	
			4
			10

(a) Richard would have been liable to compulsory VAT registration when his taxable supplies during any 12-month period (or from the commencement of trade, if less) exceeded £85,000.

This happened on 31 October 2021 when taxable supplies were £([10,500 × 4] + [15,000 × 3]) = £87,000.

Registration is required from the end of the month following the month in which the limit is exceeded, so Richard should have been registered from 1 December 2021.

If Richard continued to trade after 1 December 2021 without registering for VAT, he would still have to pay the VAT due from the time he should have been registered.

(b) The matter is one of professional judgement and a trainee Chartered Certified Accountant would be expected to act honestly and with integrity.

If Richard refuses to register for VAT, you should cease to act for him. You must notify HM Revenue & Customs (HMRC) that you no longer act for Richard although you should not provide any reason for this.

You would also be obliged to make a report under the money laundering regulations.

(c) A simplified (or less detailed) VAT invoice can be issued by a trader where the VAT inclusive total of the invoice is less than £250.

Such an invoice should be issued when a customer requests a VAT invoice.

A simplified VAT invoice must show the following information:

- The supplier's name and address
- The supplier's registration number
- The date of the supply
- A description of the goods or services supplied
- The rate of VAT chargeable
- The total amount chargeable including VAT

313 Clueless Ltd

Marking scheme

			Marks	
(a)	Eligible for both schemes on turnover	1½		
	Up to date with payments for both schemes	1		
	Up to date with returns for cash accounting scheme	½		
	Output tax under cash accounting scheme	1		
	Input tax under cash accounting scheme	1		
	Annual accounting scheme – one return	1		
			6	
(b)	(i) Payment on importation	1		
	Input tax recovery	1		
	(ii) Output tax on date of acquisition	1		
	Input tax reclaimed on same return	1		
			4	
			10	

(a) **Clueless Ltd can use both schemes because its expected taxable turnover for the next 12 months does not exceed £1,350,000 exclusive of VAT.**

In addition, for both schemes the company is up to date with its VAT payments, and for the cash accounting scheme it is up to date with its VAT returns.

With the cash accounting scheme, output VAT will be accounted for two months later than at present as the date of the cash receipt determines the return in which the transaction is dealt with rather than the invoice date.

The recovery of input VAT on expenses will not be affected as these are dealt with on a cash basis.

With the annual accounting scheme, the reduced administration in only having to file one VAT return each year should save on overtime costs.

(b) (i) **Import without postponed accounting**

Clueless Ltd will have to pay VAT of £22,000 @ 20% = £4,400 to HM Revenue & Customs at the time of importation.

This will then be reclaimed as input VAT on the VAT return for the period during which the machinery is imported.

(ii) **Import with postponed accounting**

Import VAT is declared as output VAT on the VAT return covering the date that the machinery is imported. It is reclaimed as input VAT on the same VAT return, so there is no VAT cost.

314 Garfield

Marking scheme

		Marks
(a)	*Output VAT*	
	Discounted sale	1
	Equipment	1
	Input VAT	
	Equipment	½
	Impairment losses	1
	Entertaining	1
	Motor expenses	1½
	VAT payable (including figures provided in question)	1
		7
(b)	Possible schemes	1
	Identify cash accounting scheme as beneficial	½
	Benefits of cash accounting scheme (½ mark each)	1½
		3
		10

(a) **Garfield – Value added tax (VAT) return for the quarter ended 31 March 2022**

	£
Output VAT	
Sales	22,500*
Discounted sale £4,300 × 90% × 20%	774
Equipment £12,400 × 20%	2,480
Fuel scale charge	414*
Input VAT	
Purchases	(11,200)*
Motor car	0*
Equipment	(2,480)
Impairment losses £1,400 × 20%	(280)
Entertaining – UK customers	0*
– Overseas customers £960 × 20/120	(160)
Motor expenses £1,668 (1,008 + 660) × 20/120	(278)
VAT payable	11,770

*Figures provided in question

Tutorial notes

1   Relief for an impairment loss is only available if the claim is made more than six months from the time when payment was due. Therefore, relief can only be claimed in respect of the invoice due for payment on 29 August 2021.

2   Input VAT on business entertainment is recoverable if it relates to the cost of entertaining overseas customers.

(b)   Given Garfield's current annual turnover of £450,000, he can use the cash accounting scheme and the annual accounting scheme, but not the flat rate scheme.

The cash accounting scheme would appear to be the most beneficial scheme for Garfield to use.

The scheme will provide automatic VAT relief for the impairment losses which he is incurring.

Where credit is given to customers, output VAT could be accounted for later than at present.

The recovery of input VAT on most purchases and expenses will not be affected as Garfield pays for these on a cash basis.

Tutorial notes

1   The annual turnover limit for both the annual accounting scheme and the cash accounting scheme is £1,350,000, but for the flat rate scheme it is £150,000.

2   Although the annual accounting scheme would mean only having to submit one VAT return each year (reducing the risk of late return penalties), payments on account are based on the VAT payable for the previous year. From a cash flow viewpoint, this is not beneficial where turnover is decreasing.

315 Zhi

Workbook references. Self-assessment and payment of tax by individuals is covered in Chapter 17. Capital gains tax business reliefs are the subject of Chapter 15. The VAT tax point is dealt with in Chapter 24. Computation of income tax is covered in Chapter 2 and national insurance contributions in Chapter 12. The PAYE system is dealt with in Chapter 4.

Top tips. If you are asked to calculate a reduction in tax, don't waste time setting out a full tax computation. Just work out the reduction using the marginal rate of tax. This is a similar process to working out additional tax covered in Chapter 2 of the Workbook.

Easy marks. There were some easy marks in part (c) for applying the rules on the tax point.

Examining team's comments. This 10-mark question had a focus on higher skills.

Part (a) was not very well answered and was not attempted by some candidates. Essentially, all that candidates had to do was select the two relevant tax years (out of the three provided), deduct one set of figures from the other, and divide by two.

Part (b) was the only part of the question which was consistently well answered. One particular issue, however, was that some candidates worked out the current capital gains tax liability (prior to the rollover relief claim) despite this being provided. Carefully noting which information has been provided in the question will avoid time being wasted in this manner.

Whether or not candidates did well in part (c) depended on them realising that 1 February 2022 was more than 14 days after 12 December 2021. This being the case, postponing the sales invoice would not affect the basic tax point. Candidates should appreciate that a suggested tax planning strategy might not necessarily be effective, and they need to have the courage to base their answer on this conclusion if led there following the application of basic principles. However, some candidates either did not read the question carefully or chose to answer a question they would have preferred to have been asked, and based their answer on the amount of VAT which could be postponed.

There were some good answers to part (d). However, only a few candidates appreciated that by far the quickest and easiest way to calculate the tax reductions was to work at the margin – rather than producing full before and after tax computations. Of course it was also important to realise that the first employee was a basic rate taxpayer, subject to employee national insurance contributions at 12%, whereas the second employee was a higher rate taxpayer and only subject to employee national insurance contributions at 2%.

			Marks
(a)	No reduction in balancing payment	½	
	Reduction in payment on account	1½	
			2
(b)	Current CGT liability	½	
	Proceeds not reinvested	1	
	Annual exempt amount	1	
	CGT computation	½	
			3
(c)	Basic tax point	½	
	Invoice does not displace	1	
	Cannot reduce VAT payable	½	
			2
(d)	*First employee*		
	PAYE	½	
	NIC – employee	½	
	NIC – employer	½	
	Second employee		
	PAYE	½	
	NIC – employee	½	
	NIC – employer	½	
	Payment date	½	
	Max		3
			10

(a) The balancing payment for 2020/21 due on 31 January 2022 cannot be reduced.

A claim can be made to reduce the payment on account for 2020/21 due on 31 January 2022 by £5,040:

	£
Current POA (27,600 + 4,204) × 50%	15,902
Revised POA (18,000 + 3,724) × 50%	(10,862)
Reduction	5,040

(b)

	£	£
Current CGT liability		12,740
Revised CGT liability		
Proceeds not reinvested (210,000 – 164,000)	46,000	
Annual exempt amount	(12,300)	
	33,700	
CGT: 33,700 at 20%		(6,740)
Reduction		6,000

Tutorial note

Equivalent marks will be awarded if the reduction is alternatively calculated as 30,000 (76,000 – (210,000 – 164,000)) at 20% = £6,000.

(c) The basic tax point for goods is the date when they are made available to the customer, which in the case of Zhi's sale is 12 December 2021.

An invoice date of 1 February 2022 will not affect this because the invoice will not have been issued within 14 days of the basic tax point.

Zhi therefore cannot reduce the amount of VAT payable on 7 February 2022.

(d)

	£
First employee	
PAYE (1,500 at 20%)	300
NIC – Employee (1,500 at 12%)	180
– Employer (1,500 at 13.8%)	207
Second employee	
PAYE (5,000 at 40%)	2,000
NIC – Employee (5,000 at 2%)	100
– Employer (5,000 at 13.8%)	690
Reduction	3,477

The postponed PAYE and NICs of £3,477 will be payable one month later on 22 February 2022.

Mock exams

ACCA Applied Skills

Taxation (TX – UK)

Mock Exam 1 (September 2016 exam updated to FA 2021)

Questions	
Time allowed	**3 hours**
This exam is divided into three sections:	
Section A – ALL 15 questions are compulsory and MUST be attempted.	
Section B – ALL 15 questions are compulsory and MUST be attempted.	
Section C – ALL THREE questions are compulsory and MUST be attempted.	

DO NOT OPEN THIS EXAM UNTIL YOU ARE READY TO START UNDER EXAMINATION CONDITIONS

Section A – ALL 15 questions are compulsory and MUST be attempted

1   On 1 July 2020, Sameer made a cash gift of £2,500 to his sister.

On 1 May 2021, he made a cash gift of £2,000 to a friend.

On 1 June 2021, he made a cash gift of £50,000 to a trust.

Sameer has not made any other lifetime gifts.

In respect of Sameer's cash gift of £50,000 to the trust, what is the lifetime transfer of value for inheritance tax purposes after taking account of all available exemptions?

○   £48,500

○   £44,000

○   £46,000

○   £46,500

(2 marks)

2   On 31 March 2022, Angus sold a house, which he had bought on 31 March 2008.

Angus occupied the house as his main residence until 31 March 2013, when he left for employment abroad.

Angus returned to the UK on 1 April 2015 and lived in the house until 31 March 2016, when he bought a flat in a neighbouring town and made that his private residence.

What is Angus' total number of qualifying months of occupation for private residence relief on the sale of the house?

○   72 months

○   141 months

○   105 months

○   96 months

(2 marks)

3   Abena has made the following gross contributions to her personal pension scheme over the past three tax years:

Tax year	£
2018/19	42,000
2019/20	27,000
2020/21	28,000

Abena is entitled to an annual allowance of £40,000 in all tax years from 2018/19 to 2021/22.

What is the maximum gross contribution which Abena can make to her personal pension scheme for the tax year 2021/22 without giving rise to an annual allowance charge?

○   £63,000

○   £40,000

○   £65,000

○   £35,000

(2 marks)

BPP
LEARNING
MEDIA

4   Triangle Ltd is registered for value added tax (VAT) and uses the annual accounting scheme.

For the year ended 31 December 2021, the net VAT payable by Triangle Ltd was £73,500.

For the year ended 31 December 2020, the net VAT payable by Triangle Ltd was £47,700.

Indicate, by clicking on the relevant boxes in the table below, the number and amount of the monthly payments on account of VAT which Triangle Ltd must make in respect of the year ended 31 December 2021 prior to submitting its VAT return for that year.

Number of monthly payments	NINE	TEN
Monthly payment amount	£4,770	£7,350

(2 marks)

---

5   Lili Ltd commenced trading on 1 January 2021. The company incurred the following expenditure prior to 1 January 2021:

		£
30 November 2013	Initial market research	15,000
6 June 2016	Research into competitors	12,000
31 July 2020	Entertaining potential customers and suppliers	8,000
15 December 2020	Donation to local school fair in exchange for advertising	2,000

What is the amount of Lili Ltd's deductible pre-trading expenditure in respect of the year ended 31 December 2021?

£ [   ]

(2 marks)

---

6   Paloma has been trading for a number of years. Her tax adjusted trading profit for the year ended 31 May 2021 was £53,150 and for the year ended 31 May 2022 was £50,350.

What is the amount of class 4 national insurance contributions (NIC) payable by Paloma for the tax year 2021/22?

○   £3,674

○   £3,922

○   £3,663

○   £3,721

(2 marks)

---

7   Identify, by clicking on the relevant boxes in the table below, whether the following statements are true or false.

Corporation tax is a direct tax on the turnover of companies.	TRUE	FALSE
National insurance is a direct tax suffered by employees, employers and the self-employed on earnings.	TRUE	FALSE
Inheritance tax is a direct tax on transfers of income by individuals.	TRUE	FALSE
Value added tax is a direct tax on the supply of goods and services by businesses.	TRUE	FALSE

(2 marks)

---

8   Which of the following statements concerning self-assessment tax returns for individuals is TRUE?

○   Individuals with tax payable of less than £1,000 for a tax year are not required to file a tax return.

○   Individuals are only required to file a tax return for a tax year if they receive a notice to deliver from HM Revenue & Customs (HMRC).

○   All individuals who submit a tax return on time are able to have their tax payable calculated by HMRC.

○   The tax return for an individual covers income tax, class 1, class 2 and class 4 national insurance contributions and capital gains tax liabilities.

(2 marks)

9   In certain circumstances, an individual is automatically not resident in the UK.

Indicate, by clicking on the relevant boxes in the table below, whether the following two individuals satisfy or do not satisfy the tests to be treated as automatically not resident in the UK for the tax year 2021/22.

Eric, who has never previously been resident in the UK. In the tax year 2021/22, he was in the UK for 40 days.

Fran, who was resident in the UK for the two tax years prior to the tax year 2021/22. In the tax year 2021/22, she was in the UK for 18 days.

Eric	SATISFIES	DOES NOT SATISFY
Fran	SATISFIES	DOES NOT SATISFY

(2 marks)

10   Max is employed by Star Ltd. On 6 April 2020, Star Ltd provided Max with a camera for his personal use. The camera had a market value of £2,000 on 6 April 2020.

On 6 April 2021, Star Ltd gave the camera to Max for free. The camera had a market value of £1,400 on 6 April 2021.

What is Max's taxable benefit in respect of the camera for the tax year 2021/22?

Pull down list

£1,000
£1,400
£2,000
£1,600

(2 marks)

11   Cora made a cash gift of £300,000 to her niece on 30 April 2016.

She then made a cash gift of £500,000 to her nephew on 31 May 2017.

Both of these amounts are stated after deducting available exemptions.

Cora subsequently died on 31 October 2021.

What amount of inheritance tax was payable as a result of Cora's death in respect of the cash gift of £500,000 to her nephew?

- O   £190,000
- O   £110,000
- O   £114,000
- O   £105,000

(2 marks)

---

12   Rajesh is a sole trader. He correctly calculated his self-assessment payments on account for the tax year 2021/22 and paid these on the due dates.

Rajesh paid the correct balancing payment of £1,200 for the tax year 2021/22 on 30 June 2023.

Indicate, by clicking on the relevant boxes in the table below, what penalties and interest Rajesh may be charged as a result of his late balancing payment for the tax year 2021/22.

Penalty	£0	£60
Interest	£13	£31

(2 marks)

---

13   Oblong Ltd has had the following results:

	Year ended 31 March 2021 £	Year ended 31 March 2022 £
Trading profit/(loss)	79,400	(102,800)
Property business income	6,800	10,100
Qualifying charitable donations	(1,600)	(1,300)

If Oblong Ltd makes a claim to relieve its trading loss of £102,800 for the year ended 31 March 2022 against total profits for the year ended 31 March 2021, how much of this loss will remain unrelieved?

- O   £6,500
- O   £16,600
- O   £9,400
- O   £23,400

(2 marks)

14   Putting an asset into joint names with a spouse (or a partner in a registered civil partnership) prior to the asset's disposal can be sensible capital gains tax (CGT) planning.

Which of the following CANNOT be achieved as a direct result of using this type of tax planning?

[▼]

Pull down list

Making the best use of annual exempt amounts
Deferring the CGT due date
Reducing the amount of CGT payable
Making the best use of capital losses

(2 marks)

15   Eva's income tax liability and class 4 national insurance contributions (NIC) for the tax year 2021/22 are £4,840. Her income tax liability and class 4 NICs for the tax year 2020/21 were £6,360.

What is the lowest amount to which Eva could make a claim to reduce each of her payments on account for the tax year 2021/22 without being charged interest?

£ [   ]

(2 marks)

(Total = 30 marks)

Section B – ALL 15 questions are compulsory and MUST be attempted

Adana

The following scenario relates to Questions 16 to 20.

Adana died on 17 March 2022, and inheritance tax (IHT) of £566,000 is payable in respect of her chargeable estate. Under the terms of her will, Adana left her entire estate to her children.

At the date of her death, Adana did not own a main residence. She had the following debts and liabilities:

(1)   An outstanding interest-only mortgage of £220,000
(2)   Income tax of £43,700 payable in respect of the tax year 2021/22
(3)   Legal fees of £4,600 incurred by Adana's sister which Adana had verbally promised to pay

Adana's husband had died on 28 May 2006, and only 20% of his inheritance tax nil rate band was used on his death. The nil rate band for the tax year 2006/07 was £285,000.

On 22 April 2009, Adana had made a chargeable lifetime transfer of shares valued at £500,000 to a trust. Adana paid the lifetime IHT of £52,250 arising from this gift. If Adana had not made this gift, her chargeable estate at the time of her death would have been £650,000 higher than it otherwise was. This was because of the subsequent increase in the value of the gifted shares.

16   What is the maximum nil rate band which will have been available when calculating the IHT of £566,000 payable in respect of Adana's chargeable estate?

[_____ ▼]

Pull down list

£325,000
£553,000
£390,000
£585,000

(2 marks)

---

17   What is the total amount of deductions which would have been permitted in calculating Adana's chargeable estate for IHT purposes?

£ [_____]

(2 marks)

---

18   Indicate, by clicking on the relevant boxes in the table below, who will be responsible for paying the IHT of £566,000 in respect of Adana's chargeable estate, and what is the due date for the payment of this liability.

Responsible persons	BENEFICIARIES OF ADANA'S ESTATE (HER CHILDREN)	PERSONAL RESPRESENTATIVES OF ADANA'S ESTATE
Due date for payment	17 SEPTEMBER 2022	30 SEPTEMBER 2022

(2 marks)

---

19   How much of the IHT payable in respect of Adana's estate would have been saved if, under the terms of her will, Adana had made specific gifts of £400,000 to a trust and £200,000 to her grandchildren, instead of leaving her entire estate to her children?

○   £240,000

○   £160,000

○   £0

○   £80,000

(2 marks)

20   How much IHT did Adana save by making the chargeable lifetime transfer of £500,000 to a trust on 22 April 2009, rather than retaining the gifted investments until her death?

○   £260,000

○   £207,750

○   £147,750

○   £200,000

(2 marks)

(Total = 10 marks)

Kat Ltd and Kitten

The following scenario relates to Questions 21 to 25.

Kitten is the controlling shareholder in Kat Ltd, an unquoted trading company.

Kat Ltd

Kat Ltd sold a freehold factory on 31 May 2022 for £364,000, which resulted in a chargeable gain of £120,700. The factory was purchased on 1 October 2005 for £138,600, and further capital improvements were immediately made at a cost of £23,400 during the month of purchase. Further improvements to the factory were made during the month of disposal. The relevant indexation factor is 0.439.

Kat Ltd is unsure how to reinvest the proceeds from the sale of the factory. The company is considering either purchasing a freehold warehouse for £272,000 or acquiring a leasehold office building on a 40-year lease for a premium of £370,000. If either reinvestment is made, it will take place on 30 September 2022.

All of the above buildings have been, or will be, used for the purposes of Kat Ltd's trade.

Kitten

Kitten sold 20,000 £1 ordinary shares in Kat Ltd on 5 October 2021, which resulted in a chargeable gain of £142,200. This disposal qualified for business asset disposal relief.

Kitten had originally subscribed for 90,000 shares in Kat Ltd on 7 July 2010 at their par value. On 22 September 2013, Kat Ltd made a 2 for 3 rights issue. Kitten took up her allocation under the rights issue in full, paying £6.40 for each new share issued.

Kitten also sold an antique vase on 16 January 2022, which resulted in a chargeable gain of £28,900.

For the tax year 2021/22, Kitten had taxable income of £12,000.

21 What amount of indexation allowance will have been deducted in calculating the chargeable gain of £120,700 on the disposal of Kat Ltd's factory?

£ [   ]   (2 marks)

---

22 If Kat Ltd decides to purchase the freehold warehouse and makes a claim to roll over the chargeable gain on the factory under the rollover relief rules, what will be the base cost of the warehouse for chargeable gains purposes?

○   £243,300

○   £272,000

○   £180,000

○   £151,300   (2 marks)

---

23 If Kat Ltd decides to acquire the leasehold office building and makes a claim to hold over the chargeable gain on the factory under the rollover relief rules, what is the latest date by which the held-over gain will crystallise?

[▼]

Pull down list

10 years from 31 May 2022
The date when the office building is sold
40 years from 30 September 2022
10 years from 30 September 2022

(2 marks)

---

24 What cost figure will have been used in calculating the chargeable gain on Kitten's disposal of 20,000 ordinary shares in Kat Ltd?

○   £12,000

○   £63,200

○   £84,800

○   £20,000   (2 marks)

---

25 What is Kitten's capital gains tax (CGT) liability for the tax year 2021/22?

○   £15,880

○   £20,000

○   £18,770

○   £17,540   (2 marks)

(Total = 10 marks)

Alisa

The following scenario relates to Questions 26 to 30.

Alisa commenced trading on 1 January 2021. Her sales since commencement have been as follows:

January to April 2021	£7,500 per month
May to August 2021	£10,000 per month
September to December 2021	£15,500 per month

The above figures are stated exclusive of value added tax (VAT). Alisa only supplies services, and these are all standard rated for VAT purposes. Alisa notified her liability to compulsorily register for VAT by the appropriate deadline.

For each of the eight months prior to the date on which she registered for VAT, Alisa paid £240 per month (inclusive of VAT) for website design services and £180 per month (exclusive of VAT) for advertising. Both of these supplies are standard rated for VAT purposes and relate to Alisa's business activity after the date from when she registered for VAT.

After registering for VAT, Alisa purchased a motor car on 1 January 2022. The motor car is used 60% for business mileage. During the quarter ended 31 March 2022, Alisa spent £456 on repairs to the motor car and £624 on fuel for both her business and private mileage. The relevant quarterly scale charge is £290. All of these figures are inclusive of VAT.

All of Alisa's customers are registered for VAT, so she appreciates that she has to issue VAT invoices when services are supplied.

26   From what date would Alisa have been required to be compulsorily registered for VAT and therefore have had to charge output VAT on her supplies of services?

[▼]

Pull down list

30 September 2021
1 November 2021
1 October 2021
30 October 2021

(2 marks)

27   What amount of pre-registration input VAT would Alisa have been able to recover in respect of inputs incurred prior to the date on which she registered for VAT?

- ○   £468
- ○   £608
- ○   £536
- ○   £456

(2 marks)

28   What is the maximum amount of input VAT which Alisa can reclaim in respect of her motor expenses for the quarter ended 31 March 2022?

- ○   £108
- ○   £138
- ○   £180
- ○   £125

(2 marks)

29 Complete the following sentence by matching the correct due date and payment method into the relevant target area.

Alisa has to pay any VAT liability for the quarter ended 31 March 2022

by [＿＿＿＿＿＿＿] using [＿＿＿＿＿＿＿] method.

Due date	Payment method
30 April 2022	an electronic
7 May 2022	any payment

(2 marks)

30 Identify, by clicking on the relevant box in the table below, which of the following items of information is NOT required to be included by Alisa on a valid VAT invoice.

THE CUSTOMER'S VAT REGISTRATION NUMBER	THE CUSTOMER'S ADDRESS
AN INVOICE NUMBER	A DESCRIPTION OF THE SERVICES SUPPLIED

(2 marks)

(Total = 10 marks)

Section C – ALL three questions are compulsory and MUST be attempted

31 Joe

Joe is the managing director and 100% shareholder of OK-Joe Ltd. He has always withdrawn the entire profits of the company as director's remuneration but given a recent increase in profitability he wants to know whether this basis of extracting the profits is beneficial.

For the year ended 5 April 2022, OK-Joe Ltd's taxable total profits, before taking account of director's remuneration, are £65,000. After allowing for employer's class 1 national insurance contributions (NIC) of £6,810 Joe's gross director's remuneration is £58,190.

The figure for employer's NIC of £6,810 does not deduct the £4,000 employment allowance as this is not available since Joe is the only employee of OK-Joe Ltd.

Required

Calculate the overall saving of tax and NIC for the year ended 5 April 2022 if Joe had instead paid himself gross director's remuneration of £8,000 and dividends of £46,170.   (10 marks)

Notes

1   You are expected to calculate the income tax payable by Joe, the class 1 NIC payable by both Joe and OK-Joe Ltd, and the corporation tax liability of OK-Joe Ltd for the year ended 5 April 2022.

2   You should assume that the rate of corporation tax remains unchanged.

<hr>

(Total = 10 marks)

32 Ashura

Ashura has been employed by Rift plc since 1 January 2019. She has also been self-employed since 1 July 2021, preparing her first accounts for the nine-month period ended 5 April 2022. The following information is available for the tax year 2021/22:

Employment

(1)   During the tax year 2021/22, Ashura was paid a gross annual salary of £56,600.

(2)   On 1 January 2022, Ashura personally paid two subscriptions. The first was a professional subscription of £320 paid to a professional body. The second was a subscription of £680 to a health club which Ashura regularly uses to meet Rift plc's clients. Ashura was not reimbursed for the costs of either of these subscriptions by Rift plc.

(3)   During the tax year 2021/22, Ashura used her private motor car for business purposes. She drove 3,400 miles in the performance of her duties for Rift plc, for which the company paid her an allowance of 55 pence per mile.

(4)   During the tax year 2021/22, Ashura contributed £2,800 into Rift plc's occupational pension scheme and £3,400 (gross) into a personal pension scheme.

Self-employment

(1)   Ashura's tax adjusted trading loss based on her draft accounts for the nine-month period ended 5 April 2022 is £3,300. This figure is before making any adjustments required for:

   (i)   Advertising expenditure of £800 incurred during January 2021. This expenditure has not been deducted in calculating the loss of £3,300.

   (ii)   The cost of Ashura's office (see note (2) below).

   (iii)   Capital allowances.

(2)   Ashura runs her business using one of the five rooms in her private house as an office. The total running costs of the house for the nine-month period ended 5 April 2022 were £4,350. No deduction has been made for the cost of the office in calculating the loss of £3,300.

(3)   On 10 June 2021, Ashura purchased a laptop computer for £2,600.

        On 1 July 2021, Ashura purchased a motor car for £25,600. The motor car has a CO_2 emission rate of 117 grams per kilometre. During the nine-month period ended 5 April 2022, Ashura drove a total of 8,000 miles, of which 2,500 were for self-employed business journeys.

Other information

Ashura's total income for the previous four tax years is as follows:

Tax year	Total income £
2017/18	11,100
2018/19	10,800
2019/20	48,800
2020/21	54,300

Required

(a)   State **TWO** advantages for Ashura of choosing 5 April as her accounting date rather than a date early in the tax year such as 30 April.   **(2 marks)**

(b)   Calculate Ashura's revised tax adjusted trading loss for the nine-month period ended 5 April 2022.   **(6 marks)**

(c)   Explain why it would not be beneficial for Ashura to claim loss relief under the provisions giving relief to a loss incurred in the early years of trade.

        Note. You should assume that the tax rates and allowances for the tax year 2021/22 also applied in all previous tax years.   **(2 marks)**

(d)   Assuming that Ashura claims loss relief against her total income for the tax year 2021/22, calculate her taxable income for this tax year.   **(5 marks)**

(Total = 15 marks)

33 Mable

Mable is a serial entrepreneur, regularly starting and disposing of businesses. On 31 July 2021, Tenth Ltd, a company owned by Mable, ceased trading. On 1 October 2021, Eleventh Ltd, another company owned by Mable, commenced trading. The following information is available:

Tenth Ltd

(1)   For the final four-month period of trading ended 31 July 2021, Tenth Ltd had a tax adjusted trading profit of £52,400. This figure is **before** taking account of capital allowances.

(2)   On 1 April 2021, the tax written down value of the company's main pool was £12,400. On 3 June 2021, Tenth Ltd purchased a laptop computer for £1,800.

        On 31 July 2021, the company sold all of the items included in the main pool at the start of the period for £28,200 and the laptop computer for £1,300. None of the items included in the main pool was sold for more than its original cost.

(3)   On 31 July 2021, Tenth Ltd sold the company's freehold office building for £180,300. The building was purchased on 3 May 2014 for £151,334, and its indexed cost to December 2017 was £164,500.

(4)   During the four-month period ended 31 July 2021, Tenth Ltd let out one floor of its freehold office building which was always surplus to requirements. The floor was rented at £1,200 per month, but the tenant left owing the rent for July 2021 which Tenth Ltd was unable to

recover. The total running costs of the office building for the four-month period ended 31 July 2021 were £6,300, of which one-third related to the let floor. The other two-thirds of the running costs have been deducted in calculating Tenth Ltd's tax-adjusted trading profit of £52,400.

(5) During the four-month period ended 31 July 2021, Tenth Ltd made qualifying charitable donations of £800.

Eleventh Ltd

(1) Eleventh Ltd's operating profit for the six-month period ended 31 March 2022 is £122,900. Depreciation of £2,580 and amortisation of leasehold property of £2,000 (see note (2) below) have been deducted in arriving at this figure.

(2) On 1 October 2021, Eleventh Ltd acquired a leasehold office building, paying a premium of £60,000 for the grant of a 15-year lease. The office building was used for business purposes by Eleventh Ltd throughout the six-month period ended 31 March 2022.

(3) On 1 October 2021, Eleventh Ltd purchased two new motor cars. The first motor car cost £12,600 and has a CO_2 emission rate of 40 grams per kilometre. This motor car is used as a pool car by the company's employees. The second motor car cost £13,200 and has a zero CO_2 emission rate per kilometre. This motor car is used by Mable, and 45% of the mileage is for private journeys.

(4) On 1 October 2021, Mable made a loan of £100,000 to Eleventh Ltd at an annual interest rate of 5%. This is a commercial rate of interest, and no loan repayments were made during the period ended 31 March 2022. The loan was used to finance the company's trading activities.

Required

(a) Calculate Tenth Ltd's taxable total profits for the four-month period ended 31 July 2021.

(7 marks)

(b) Calculate Eleventh Ltd's tax adjusted trading profit for the six-month period ended 31 March 2022.

(8 marks)

(Total = 15 marks)

Answers

A plan of attack

If this were the real Taxation (TX – UK) exam and you had been told to turn over and begin, what would be going through your mind?

Perhaps you're having a panic. You've spent most of your study time on income tax and corporation tax computations (because that's what your tutor/BPP Workbook told you to do), plus a selection of other topics, and you're really not sure that you know enough. So calm down. Spend the first few moments or so **looking at the exam**, and develop a **plan of attack**.

Looking through the exam.

Section A contains **15 Objective Test (OT) questions** each worth **2 marks**. These will cover all sections of the syllabus. Some you may find easy and some more difficult. In Question 8, where you are asked to identify the true statement about self-assessment tax returns for individuals, read the possible answers at least twice before you decide which one to select. Don't spend a lot of time on anything you really don't know. For multiple choice questions you are not penalised for wrong answers, so you should answer all of them. If all else fails – guess!

Section B contains **three OT Case** scenarios. These each have **five questions** each worth **2 marks**. Make sure you read the scenario carefully before you start to answer the OTQs.

- **Questions 16 to 20** test your knowledge of inheritance tax (IHT). Question 18 is a quick question as you only need to select two answers, one is the persons responsible for payment of tax and the other is the date for payment.

- **Questions 21 to 25** concern chargeable gains for a company and for an individual. Make sure to double check your calculations to avoid losing marks for simple mistakes. This is particularly applicable to Question 25.

- **Questions 26 to 30** are about value added tax (VAT). Read the questions carefully to make sure you answer the question set. For example, in Question 26 you need to identify the date from which Alisa would have been required to be compulsorily registered, not the date on which the registration limit was exceeded.

In **Section C** you have **three constructed response (long) questions**:

- **Question 31** for **10 marks** is about whether there is an overall tax saving by taking a mixture of dividends and remuneration from a company rather than just remuneration. You need to work out the individual's income tax, the national insurance contributions for an employee and corporation tax.

- **Question 32** for **15 marks** is an income tax computation and also deals with choice of accounting date.

- **Question 33** for **15 marks** is a corporation tax question dealing with a company ceasing to trade and one commencing to trade.

Allocating your time

BPP's advice is always allocate your time **according to the marks for the question** in total and for the parts of the question. But **use common sense**. If you're confronted by an OTQ on a topic of which you know nothing, pick an answer and move on. Use the time to pick up marks elsewhere.

After the exam...**Forget about it!**

And don't worry if you found the exam difficult. More than likely other candidates will too. If this were the real thing you would need to **forget** the exam the minute you left the exam hall and **think about the next one**. Or, if it's the last one, **celebrate!**

Section A

1   £48,500

	£
Gift 1 June 2021	50,000
Less: AE 2021/22 £(3,000 – 2,000 PET 1 May 2021)	(1,000)
AE 2020/21 b/f £(3,000 – 2,500 PET 1 July 2020)	(500)
Chargeable lifetime transfer	48,500

Note that the current tax year annual exemption is used first (against the PET on 1 May 2021 and then against the CLT on 1 June 2021) and then the balance brought forward from the previous tax year.

2   105 months

Qualifying period		Months
31.3.08–31.3.13	Actual occupation	60
1.4.13–31.3.15	Employed abroad (any length with reoccupation)	24
1.4.15–31.3.16	Actual occupation	12
1.7.21–31.3.22	Last 9 months ownership	9
Qualifying months		105

Check: non-qualifying months 1.4.16–30.6.21 = 63 months, total period of ownership 31.3.08–31.3.22 = 168 months = (105 + 63) months.

3   £65,000

	£
2021/22	40,000
2018/19 £(40,000 – 42,000) = £(2,000) excess	0
2019/20 £(40,000 – 27,000)	13,000
2020/21 £(40,000 – 28,000)	12,000
Available annual allowance	65,000

Use the current tax year allowance first and then starting working forwards from the earliest available tax year (maximum three tax years before current year).

4

Number of monthly payments	NINE	
Monthly payment amount	£4,770	

$$\frac{90\% \times £47,700 \, (\text{previous year VAT payable})}{9} \qquad £4,770$$

5   £14,000

		£
30.11.13	More than seven years before commencement	0
6.6.16	Research deductible	12,000
31.7.20	Entertaining not deductible under general rules	0
15.12.20	Donation for trade purposes deductible	2,000
Deductible pre-trading expenditure	14,000

6   £3,721

	£
£(53,150 − 50,270) = 2,880 @ 2%	58
£(50,270 − 9,568) = 40,702 @ 9%	3,663
Class 4 NIC payable	3,721

The answer £3,674 uses the accruals basis rather than the profits for the year ended 31 May 2021. The answer £3,922 uses a rate of 9% throughout. The answer £3,663 is just the amount chargeable at 9%.

7

Corporation tax is a direct tax on the turnover of companies.		FALSE
National insurance is a direct tax suffered by employees, employers and the self-employed on earnings.	TRUE	
Inheritance tax is a direct tax on transfers of income by individuals.		FALSE
Value added tax is a direct tax on the supply of goods and services by businesses.		FALSE

Corporation tax is a direct tax on profits (not turnover).

National insurance is a direct tax (collected directly from taxpayer either through PAYE or by self-assessment) suffered by employees (Class 1 employee's), employers (Class 1 employer's) and the self-employed (Classes 2 and 4).

Inheritance tax is a direct tax on transfers of capital (not income) by individuals.

Value added tax is an indirect tax (collected by businesses not customers) on the supply of goods and services by businesses.

8   All individuals who submit a tax return on time are able to have their tax payable calculated by HMRC.

> **Examining team's comments.** This question tested candidates' knowledge of various aspects of the income tax self-assessment system. The majority of candidates appreciated that there can be a requirement to file a tax return despite not receiving a notice to do so from HMRC. However, a significant number of candidates chose the last option, despite class 1 national insurance contributions (NIC) not being part of the self-assessment system. Many candidates chose the first option, not remembering that the de minimis limit of £1,000 instead relates to payments on account. All individuals who submit a tax return on time (either a paper return or electronically) are able to have the tax payable calculated by HMRC therefore the third option was the correct answer.
>
> This should have been a fairly straightforward question and it demonstrates the need to carefully read and consider each alternative – not just quickly jump to the first one that seems to fit.

9

Eric	SATISFIES	
Fran		DOES NOT SATISFY

Eric was not previously UK resident and was present in the UK for between 16 and 45 days (see table in Tax Rates and Allowances). He is therefore automatically not UK resident in the tax year 2021/22.

Fran was previously UK resident and was present in the UK for between 16 and 45 days (again, see table in Tax Rates and Allowances). Her residence status is therefore determined by the number of her UK ties so she is not automatically not UK resident in the tax year 2021/22.

10   £1,600

		£	£
2020/21	Use benefit £2,000 × 20%	400	
2021/22	Gift		
	Greater of:		
	(1) Market value at gift	1,400	
	(2) Original cost	2,000	
	Less: use benefit	(400)	
		1,600	
			1,600

11   £114,000

	£	£
31.5.17 PET now chargeable		500,000
Nil rate band at death	325,000	
Less: 30.4.16 PET now chargeable	(300,000)	
		(25,000)
Transfer chargeable to IHT @ 40%		475,000
£475,000 @ 40%		190,000
Less: taper relief (4 to 5 years) @ 40%		(76,000)
IHT payable as a result of Cora's death		114,000

12

Penalty		£60
Interest	£13	

The due date for payment of the balancing payment was 31 January 2023.

Interest is due for the period February 2023 to June 2023 (working in whole months) so is £1,200 × 2.6% × 5/12 = £13. The answer £31 is the interest for a 12-month period.

The penalty date was 30 days after the due date and so payment was less than five months after the penalty date. The penalty due is £1,200 × 5% = £60.

13   £6,500

	Y/e 31.3.21	Y/e 31.3.22
	£	£
Trading income	79,400	0
Property business income	6,800	10,100
Total profits	86,200	10,100
Less: loss against total profits	(86,200)	(10,100)
Taxable trading profits	0	0

Loss memorandum

	£
Trading loss incurred in y/e 31.3.22	102,800
Less: used in y/e 31.3.22	(10,100)
used in y/e 31.3.21	(86,200)
Loss unrelieved	6,500

The qualifying charitable donations are unrelieved.

14   Deferring the CGT due date

The CGT due date will be 31 January following the end of the tax year of the disposal for both spouses/civil partners.

Note the three ways in which tax planning for spouses can be used: making the best use of annual exempt amounts; reducing the amount of CGT payable (eg if one spouse has unused basic rate band); and making best use of capital losses.

15   £2,420

2021/22 Relevant amount $\dfrac{£4,840}{2}$ £2,420

Section B

Adana

16   £585,000

	£
Adana: own nil rate band (lifetime transfer more than 7 years before death)	325,000
Adana's husband: 80% × £325,000 (use 2021/22 nil rate band)	260,000
Maximum nil rate band available	585,000

17   £263,700

	£
Mortgage (debt incurred for consideration)	220,000
Income tax (statutory debt)	43,700
Total deductions	263,700

The legal fees are not deductible as the agreement to pay them is not legally enforceable because no consideration is received.

18

Responsible persons		PERSONNAL RESPRESENTATIVES OF ADANA'S ESTATE
Due date for payment		30 SEPTEMBER 2022

The beneficiaries of Adana's estate will bear the IHT, as it will reduce the amount due to them from the estate, but it is her personal representatives (the executors of her will) who are responsible for making the payment. The IHT on a death estate is due by the end of six months from the end of the month of death.

19   £0

There would be no IHT saving by making either of these gifts as both are chargeable in the same way as gifting the entire estate to Adana's children. The only exempt transfer in relation to the death estate for Taxation (TX – UK) purposes is a gift to a spouse/civil partner.

20   £207,750

	£
Extra IHT on death estate: £650,000 × 40%	260,000
Less: lifetime IHT paid	(52,250)
IHT saving	207,750

Kat Ltd and Kitten

Workbook references. Chargeable gains for companies is dealt with in Chapter 20. Computation of CGT is covered in Chapter 13 and business reliefs in Chapter 15.

Top tips. Double check your computations! Just because your answer is one of those given, it does not necessarily mean that it is correct.

Easy marks. The indexation allowance in Question 21 was made easier by both the cost and the enhancement expenditure being incurred in the same month.

Examining team's report. Questions involving the indexation allowance, the crystallisation date for a heldover gain and the base cost of shares following a rights issue were well answered.

One of the questions asked for the base cost of an asset against which a rollover relief claim had been made. Although the correct answer was the most popular (with candidates appreciating that the amount of proceeds not reinvested could not be rolled over), a significant number of candidates ignored the amount of proceeds not reinvested and rolled over the full amount of gain.

Another question asked for the taxpayer's CGT liability. Again, the correct answer (the disposal qualifying for business asset disposal relief utilised the available basic rate tax band, with the other gain therefore taxed at [20]%) was marginally the most popular. However, many candidates ignored the impact of business asset disposal' relief on the basic rate band or did not deduct the annual exempt amount.

These two less well answered questions demonstrate the need to be very careful with all aspects of a calculation. One simple mistake means the loss of the two marks available.

21   £71,118

	£
0.439 × £162,000 (138,600 + 23,400)	71,118

22 £243,300

	£
Gain	120,700
Immediately chargeable = amount not reinvested £(364,000 − 272,000)	(92,000)
Deduction from base cost of new warehouse	28,700

The base cost of the new warehouse is £(272,000 −28,700) = £243,300.

23 Ten years from 30 September 2022

The gain will become chargeable on the latest of: the date of disposal of the replacement asset; the date it ceases to be used in the trade; and ten years from its acquisition.

24 £63,200

Date	Transaction	No. of shares	Cost £
7 July 2010	Acquisition at par £1 cost for each £1 share bought	90,000	90,000
22 September 2013	Rights issue 2 new shares for every 3 original shares held @ £6.40	60,000	384,000
		150,000	474,000
5 October 2021	Sale	(20,000)	(63,200)
c/f		130,000	410,800

25 £17,540

	BADR gain £	Non-BADR gain £
Gains	142,200	28,900
Less: annual exempt amount (best use)		(12,300)
Taxable gains	142,200	16,600
Tax @ 10%/20%	14,220	3,320
Total CGT payable		£17,540

The basic rate band is treated as being used first by the gain qualifying for business asset disposal relief. This means that the band is entirely used up and so the tax on the gain not qualifying for business asset disposal relief is taxable at 20%.

The answer £15,880 uses the basic rate of 10% on the gain not qualifying for business asset disposal relief. The answer £20,000 does not deduct the annual exempt amount. The answer £18,770 sets the annual exempt amount against the gain qualifying for business asset disposal relief.

Alisa

Workbook references. Value added tax is covered in Chapters 24 and 25.

Top tips. For Question 28 note that the fuel scale charge is the basis for **output** tax charged in relation to private use fuel. You were asked to identify the **input** tax which could be reclaimed.

Easy marks. There were easy marks in Question 26 for identifying the date from which the trader would have been required to be compulsorily registered for VAT. However, it was important to read the question carefully to see exactly what was being asked – it was **not** the date on which the registration threshold was reached.

Examining team's comments. Generally, this case question was not as well answered as the previous two. However, candidates made reasonable attempts at questions on the recovery of pre-registration input VAT, how and by when the VAT liability would be paid, and the information included on a valid VAT invoice.

A further question asked for the date of compulsory VAT registration. Although the correct answer was the most popular, many candidates opted for the end of the month in which the registration limit was exceeded.

One of the questions asked for the maximum amount of input VAT which could be reclaimed in respect of motor expenses. The correct answer (ignoring private use) was by a long way the most popular, but a significant number of candidates either adjusted for private use or used the fuel scale charge instead of the actual fuel figure.

26   1 November 2021

	£
January to April: 4 × £7,500	30,000
May to August: 4 × £10,000	40,000
September	15,500
	85,500

The registration threshold of £85,000 is met by 30 September 2021. Alisa should therefore have notified HMRC by 30 October 2021, with registration effective from 1 November 2021.

27   £456

	£
Website design service: £240 × 6 × 1/6	240
Advertising: £180 × 6 × 20%	216
Input tax reclaimable	456

Pre-registration input tax is recoverable on services which are supplied within six months prior to registration. Note the different calculations for VAT-inclusive and VAT-exclusive amounts.

28   £180

	£
Repairs	456
Fuel	624
	1,080
Input tax reclaimable £1,080 × 1/6	180

Full input tax can be reclaimed on the repairs to the car - the private use of the car is not relevant.

All the input tax will be reclaimed on fuel and the adjustment to private use will be made by charging output tax based on the fuel scale charge.

29   Alisa has to pay any VAT liability for the quarter ended 31 March 2022

by | 7 May 2022 | using | an electronic | method.

30

THE CUSTOMER'S VAT REGISTRATION NUMBER	

Section C

31 Joe

Marking scheme

	Marks
Profits withdrawn as director's remuneration	
Income tax	1½
Class 1 employee's NIC	1½
Corporation tax	½
Profits withdrawn as a mix of director's remuneration and dividends	
Income tax	3
Class 1 NIC	1
Corporation tax	1½
Overall tax saving	1
	10

Joe – Income tax liability 2021/22 if just remuneration

	Non-savings income £
Director's remuneration/Net income	58,190
Less personal allowance	(12,570)
Taxable income	45,620
Tax	
£37,700 @ 20%	7,540
£(45,620 – 37,700) = 7,920 @ 40%	3,168
Income tax payable	10,708

Joe – National insurance contributions 2021/22 if just remuneration

	£
£(58,190 − 50,270) = 7,920 @ 2%	158
£(50,270 − 9,568) = 40,702 @ 12%	4,884
Class 1 employee's NIC payable	5,042

There will be no corporation tax payable since the profits are entirely withdrawn as director's remuneration (including Class 1 employer's NIC).

Joe – Income tax liability 2021/22 if mix of remuneration and dividends

	Non-savings income £	Dividend income £	Total income £
Director's remuneration	8,000		
Dividends		46,170	
Net income	8,000	46,170	54,170
Less personal allowance	(8,000)	(4,570)	
Taxable income	0	41,600	41,600

Tax

	£
£2,000 @ 0% (dividend nil rate band)	0
£(37,700 − 2,000) = 35,700 @ 7.5%	2,678
£(41,600 − 37,700) = 3,900 @ 32.5%	1,268
Income tax payable	3,946

There will be no Class 1 NIC for either OK-Joe Ltd or Joe as the earnings are below the NIC employee's and employer's thresholds.

Corporation tax liability of OK-Joe Ltd for the year ended 5 April 2022 if mix of remuneration and dividends

	£
Trading profit	65,000
Less director's remuneration	(8,000)
Taxable trading profit	57,000
Corporation tax £57,000 @ 19%	10,830

Summary of tax and NIC liabilities

	Remuneration only £	Mix of remuneration and dividends £
Income tax	10,708	3,946
Class 1 NIC employee's	5,042	0
Class 1 NIC employer's (given in question)	6,810	0
Corporation tax	0	10,830
Total tax and NIC	22,560	14,776

Therefore the overall tax and NIC saving if Joe extracts profits using a mix of director's remuneration and dividends is £(22,560 − 14,776) = £7,784.

32 Ashura

Workbook references. Assessable trading income is dealt with in Chapter 9, capital allowances in Chapter 8 and losses in Chapter 10. Employment income is dealt with in Chapters 3 and 4. Taxable income is covered in Chapter 2.

Top tips. In part (d), note the difference between the tax treatment of occupational pension contributions (paid gross and deducted in the income computation giving tax relief at all rates) and personal pension contributions (basic rate relief given by being paid net and further tax relief being given by increasing the basic rate limit so not relevant to this question which only required a calculation of taxable income).

Easy marks. There were some easy marks in part (b) for straightforward adjustments to profit. Part (d) had some easy marks for dealing with the mileage allowance and subscriptions.

Examining team's comments. For part (a), the requirement was to state two advantages of the taxpayer choosing 5 April as an accounting date rather than a date early in the tax year such as 30 April. There were three obvious advantages, and many candidates correctly explained that the application of the basis period rules is more straightforward and that there will be no overlap profits. Less well prepared candidates instead covered the advantages of a 30 April accounting date, so not surprisingly did not achieve high marks.

Part (b) required a calculation of the taxpayer's revised tax adjusted trading loss for the first period of account. This meant adjusting for pre-trading expenditure, use of one of the five rooms in the taxpayer's private house as an office, and capital allowances. There were many good answers to this section, although a common mistake was to not appreciate that each of the three adjustments increased (not decreased) the trading loss.

For part (c), candidates had to explain why it was not beneficial for the taxpayer to claim loss relief under the provisions giving relief to a loss incurred in the early years of trade. It should have been fairly obvious that such a claim would have wasted the personal allowance and not resulted in any tax saving. This section was not as well answered, with many candidates not appreciating that the loss could only be carried back for three years. Some candidates actually explained why a claim would be beneficial.

Part (d) required a calculation of the taxpayer's taxable income (on the basis that loss relief was claimed against total income). This meant taking account of two subscriptions (only one of which was deductible), a mileage allowance deduction for the use of a private motor car for business purposes, and pension contributions (both to an occupational scheme and a personal pension scheme). This section was generally well answered, although many candidates wasted time by calculating the tax liability. The occupational pension scheme contribution was often grossed up (such contributions are not paid net of tax). Many candidates made things more difficult than they needed to be by attempting this section before section (b).

		Marks
(a)	Two advantages of basis period ending on 5 April (one mark for each)	2
(b)	Trading loss	2½
	Capital allowances	3½
		6
(c)	Early years loss relief	2
(d)	Salary	½
	Mileage	1
	Pension	1
	Subscriptions	1
	Loss	1
	Personal allowance	½
		5
		15

(a) **Advantages of choosing 5 April as accounting date rather than earlier date in tax year**

Any **two** of:

The basis period rules are more straightforward.

On commencement, there will be no overlap profits.

On cessation, the final basis period will be a maximum of 12 months. If a date earlier in the tax year is chosen, the final basis period will be longer, up to 23 months with a 30 April year end.

(b) **Ashura – Trading loss for the nine-month period ended 5 April 2022**

	£
Trading loss	(3,300)
Less: pre-trading expenditure	(800)
use of office £4,350 × 1/5	(870)
capital allowance (W)	(2,960)
Adjusted trading loss	(7,930)

Working – Capital allowances

9 months to 5 April 2022	AIA £	Main pool £	Motor car £	Allowances £
Additions				
Laptop	2,600			
AIA	(2,600)			2,600
Transfer to pool	0	0		
Motor car			25,600	
WDA @ 6% × 9/12			(1,152) × 2,500/8,000	360
WDA c/f		0	24,448	
Allowances				2,960

Tutorial notes

1   The advertising expenditure incurred in January 2021 is pre-trading expenditure which is treated as incurred on the first day of trading. An adjustment is therefore required.

2   Ashura's motor car has CO_2 emissions over 50g/km and therefore only qualifies for writing down allowance at the rate of 6%.

3   The laptop computer purchased on 10 June 2021 is pre-trading capital expenditure and is therefore treated as incurred on the first day of trading.

BPP
LEARNING
MEDIA

(c) **Early years trading loss relief**

Under early years trading loss relief, the loss of £7,930 in 2021/22 would be relieved against her total income of £10,800 in 2018/19 since this is the earliest of the three years 2018/19, 2019/20 and 2020/21.

However, since Ashura's total income for 2018/19 is covered by her personal allowance of £12,570 (assumed), there would be no tax saving by making an early years loss relief claim.

(d) **Ashura – Taxable income 2021/22**

		£
Salary		56,600
Mileage allowance 3,400 × 10p (55p – 45p)		340
Pension contributions	Occupational	(2,800)
	Personal	(0)
Subscriptions	Professional	(320)
	Health club	(0)
Total income		53,820
Less: loss relief against total income		(7,930)
Net income		45,890
Less: personal allowance		(12,570)
Taxable income		33,320

Tutorial notes

1 The personal pension scheme contribution does not affect the calculation of taxable income, but will instead increase Ashura's basic rate limit by the gross contribution of £3,400.

2 The health club subscription is not an allowable deduction because membership is not a necessary expense for Ashura to carry out the duties of her employment.

3 The loss relief cap does not apply because Ashura's trading loss is less than the greater of £50,000 and 25% of her total income.

33 Mable

Workbook references. The computation of taxable total profits is covered in Chapter 19. The adjustment to trading profits is dealt with in Chapter 7 and capital allowances in Chapter 8. Property business income is covered in Chapter 5.

Top tips. Be careful when working with short accounting periods. For example, in part (b) you needed to adjust the writing down allowance so that only six months of allowances were given.

Easy marks. There were some easy marks in part (b) for adjustments to profits which should have been well-known.

Examining team's comments. Part (a) was generally very well answered, requiring a calculation of the first company's taxable total profits for the final period of trading. This involved calculating the balancing charge on cessation (all of the items included in the company's main pool being sold), the chargeable gain on the sale of the company's freehold office building and the property business income in respect of one floor of the office building which had been let out. The company has also made qualifying charitable donations. The only consistent problem here was the capital allowances, with many candidates not appreciating that neither the annual investment allowance (a laptop computer had been purchased during the period) nor writing down allowances are given in the period of cessation. A few candidates ignored the cessation altogether and therefore did not calculate a balancing charge.

Part (b) was also well answered on the whole, requiring a calculation of the second company's tax adjusted trading profit for the initial period of trading. This involved adjusting for depreciation and amortisation, calculating the deduction in respect of a lease premium, calculating capital allowances for two motor cars (one car was used as a pool car by the company's employees, with the other having private use by a director) and deducting loan interest in respect of a loan made to the company by a director/owner. Some candidates attempted to calculate benefits in respect of the motor cars and loan which, although correct as regards the motor cars, had no relevance to the requirement. Perhaps not surprisingly, the deduction for the lease premium caused quite a few problems.

Marking scheme

		Marks
(a)	Taxable total profits	2½
	Balancing charge	3
	Property business income	1½
		7
(b)	Profit and add-backs	1½
	Interest payable	1
	Lease premium	2½
	Capital allowances	3
		8
		15

(a) **Tenth Ltd – Taxable total profits for the four-month period ended 31 July 2021**

	£
Trading profits	52,400
Balancing charge (W1)	15,300
Adjusted trading profits	67,700
Property business income (W2)	1,500
Chargeable gain £(180,300 – 164,500)	15,800
Total profits	85,000
Less qualifying charitable donations	(800)
Taxable total profits	84,200

Workings

1 *Capital allowances*

	Main pool £	Allowances £
TWDV brought forward	12,400	
Addition		
Laptop computer	1,800	
Disposal		
Main pool items £(28,200 + 1,300)	(29,500)	
Balancing charge	15,300	(15,300)

2   *Property business income*

		£
Rent receivable £1,200 × 4		4,800
Less: Impairment loss		(1,200)
	Running costs £6,300 × 1/3	(2,100)
Property business income		1,500

(b)   **Eleventh Ltd – Tax adjusted trading profit for the six-month period ended 31 March 2022**

		£
Operating profit		122,900
Add:	depreciation	2,580
	amortisation	2,000
Less:	deduction for lease premium (W1)	(1,440)
	interest payable £100,000 × 5% × 6/12	(2,500)
	capital allowances (W2)	(14,334)
Tax adjusted trading profit		109,206

Workings

1   *Deduction for lease premium*

	£
Premium paid	60,000
Less: £60,000 × 2% × (15 −1)	(16,800)
Amount taxable on landlord as property business income	43,200

Deduction $\dfrac{£43,200}{15} \times 6/12$

	1,440

2   *Capital allowances*

	FYA £	Main pool £	Allowances £
Addition not qualifying for FYA			
Motor car [1]		12,600	
WDA @ 18% × 6/12		(1,134)	1,134
Addition qualifying for FYA			
Motor car [2]	13,200		
FYA @ 100%	(13,200)		13,200
Transfer to pool	0	0	
TWDV carried forward		11,466	
Allowances			14,334

Tutorial notes

1   Motor car [1] has CO_2 emissions of below 50g/km. It therefore goes into the main pool and has writing down allowances at 18% scaled down for the short accounting period.

2   Motor car [2] is new and has zero CO_2 emissions so therefore qualifies for the 100% first year allowance. This is not scaled down for the short accounting period. The private use of the motor car is not relevant for the company.

ACCA Applied Skills

Taxation (TX – UK)

Mock Exam 2
(Specimen exam updated to FA 2021)

Questions	
Time allowed	**3 hours**
This exam is divided into three sections:	
Section A – ALL 15 questions are compulsory and MUST be attempted.	
Section B – ALL 15 questions are compulsory and MUST be attempted.	
Section C – ALL THREE questions are compulsory and MUST be attempted.	

DO NOT OPEN THIS EXAM UNTIL YOU ARE READY TO START UNDER EXAMINATION CONDITIONS

Section A – ALL 15 questions are compulsory and MUST be attempted

1   William is self-employed, and his tax adjusted trading profit for the year ended 5 April 2022 was £84,050. During the tax year 2021/22, William contributed £5,400 (gross) into a personal pension scheme.

What amount of Class 4 national insurance contributions (NIC) will William pay for the tax year 2021/22?

   ○   £4,498

   ○   £6,703

   ○   £4,339

   ○   £3,663

                                                                                    (2 marks)

2   You are a trainee Chartered Certified Accountant and your firm has a client who has refused to disclose a chargeable gain to HM Revenue & Customs (HMRC).

From an ethical viewpoint, which TWO of the following actions could be expected of your firm?

   ☐   Reporting under the money laundering regulations

   ☐   Advising the client to make disclosure

   ☐   Informing HMRC of the non-disclosure

   ☐   Warning the client that your firm will be reporting the non-disclosure   (2 marks)

3   Martin is self-employed and for the year ended 5 April 2022 his trading profit was £109,400. During the tax year 2021/22, Martin made a gift aid donation of £800 (gross) to a national charity.

What amount of personal allowance will Martin be entitled to for the tax year 2021/22?

   £ [   ]

                                                                                    (2 marks)

4   For the year ended 31 March 2022, Halo Ltd made a trading loss of £180,000.

Halo Ltd has owned 100% of the ordinary share capital of Shallow Ltd since it began trading on 1 July 2021. For the year ended 30 June 2022, Shallow Ltd will make a trading profit of £224,000.

Neither company has any other taxable profits or allowable losses.

What is the maximum amount of group relief which Shallow Ltd can claim from Halo Ltd in respect of the trading loss of £180,000 for the year ended 31 March 2022?

   ○   £180,000

   ○   £168,000

   ○   £45,000

   ○   £135,000

                                                                                    (2 marks)

5   For the year ended 31 March 2021, Sizeable Ltd had taxable total profits of £820,000, and for the year ended 31 March 2022 had taxable total profits of £970,000. The profits accrue evenly throughout the year.

Sizeable Ltd has had one 51% group company for many years.

How will Sizeable Ltd pay its corporation tax liability for the year ended 31 March 2022?

- ◯   Nine instalments of £15,580 and a balancing payment of £28,500
- ◯   Four instalments of £46,075
- ◯   Four instalments of £38,950 and a balancing payment of £28,500
- ◯   One payment of £184,300   (2 marks)

---

6   For the year ended 31 December 2021, Lateness Ltd had a corporation tax liability of £60,000, which it did not pay until 31 March 2023. Lateness Ltd is not a large company.

How much interest will Lateness Ltd be charged by HM Revenue & Customs (HMRC) in respect of the late payment of its corporation tax liability for the year ended 31 December 2021?

[▼]

Pull down list:

£780
£1,950
£260
£390   (2 marks)

---

7   On 26 November 2021 Alice sold an antique table for £8,700. The antique table had been purchased on 16 May 2014 for £3,800.

What is Alice's chargeable gain in respect of the disposal of the antique table?

- ◯   £4,500
- ◯   £1,620
- ◯   £4,900
- ◯   £0   (2 marks)

---

8   On 14 November 2021, Jane made a cash gift to a trust of £800,000 (after deducting all available exemptions). Jane paid the inheritance tax arising from this gift. Jane has not made any other lifetime gifts.

What amount of lifetime inheritance tax would have been payable in respect of Jane's gift to the trust?

[£   ]   (2 marks)

---

9   During the tax year 2021/22, Mildred made four cash gifts to her grandchildren.

For each of the gifts listed below, click in the box to indicate whether the gift will be exempt or not exempt from inheritance tax under the small gifts exemption.

£400 to Alfred	EXEMPT	NOT EXEMPT
£140 to Minnie	EXEMPT	NOT EXEMPT
A further £280 to Minnie	EXEMPT	NOT EXEMPT
£175 to Winifred	EXEMPT	NOT EXEMPT

(2 marks)

---

10   For the quarter ended 31 March 2022, Faro had standard rated sales of £49,750 and standard rated expenses of £22,750. Both figures are exclusive of value added tax (VAT).

Faro uses the flat rate scheme to calculate the amount of VAT payable, with the relevant scheme percentage for her trade being 12%. The percentage reduction for the first year of VAT registration is not available.

How much VAT will Faro have to pay to HM Revenue & Customs (HMRC) for the quarter ended 31 March 2022?

○   £5,970

○   £3,888

○   £5,400

○   £7,164   (2 marks)

---

11   **Which TWO of the following assets will ALWAYS be exempt from capital gains tax?**

☐   A motor car suitable for private use

☐   A chattel

☐   A UK government security (gilt)

☐   A house   (2 marks)

---

12   Winston invested £8,000 into a cash individual savings account (ISA) during the tax year 2021/22. He now wants to invest into a stocks and shares ISA.

What is the maximum possible amount which Winston can invest into a stocks and shares ISA for the tax year 2021/22?

○   £20,000

○   £12,000

○   £0

○   £10,000   (2 marks)

13 Ming is self-employed.

For each of the types of records listed below, click in the box to indicate the date until which Ming must retain the records used in preparing her self-assessment tax return for the tax year 2021/22.

Business records	31 JANUARY 2024	31 JANUARY 2028
Non-business records	31 JANUARY 2024	31 JANUARY 2028

(2 marks)

14 Moon Ltd has had the following tax adjusted trading profits and losses:

Period	Profit/(loss) £
Year ended 31 December 2021	(105,000)
Four-month period ended 31 December 2020	43,000
Year ended 31 August 2020	96,000

The company does not have any other income.

How much of Moon Ltd's trading loss for the year ended 31 December 2021 can be relieved against its total profits of £96,000 for the year ended 31 August 2020?

○ £64,000

○ £96,000

○ £70,000

○ £62,000

(2 marks)

15 Nigel has not previously been resident in the UK, being in the UK for less than 20 days each tax year. For the tax year 2021/22, he has three ties with the UK.

What is the maximum number of days which Nigel could spend in the UK during the tax year 2021/22 without being treated as resident in the UK for that year?

○ 90 days

○ 182 days

○ 45 days

○ 120 days

(2 marks)

(Total = 30 marks)

Section B – ALL 15 questions are compulsory and MUST be attempted

Delroy and Marlon

The following scenario relates to Questions 16 to 20.

Delroy and Grant

On 10 January 2022, Delroy made a gift of 25,000 £1 ordinary shares in Dub Ltd, an unquoted trading company, to his son, Grant. The market value of the shares on that date was £240,000. Delroy had subscribed for the 25,000 shares in Dub Ltd at par on 1 July 2008. Delroy and Grant have elected to claim gift holdover relief.

Grant sold the 25,000 shares in Dub Ltd on 18 March 2022 for £240,000.

Dub Ltd has a share capital of 100,000 £1 ordinary shares. Delroy was the sales director of the company from its incorporation on 1 July 2008 until 10 January 2022. Grant has never been an employee or a director of Dub Ltd.

For the tax year 2021/22 Delroy and Grant are both higher rate taxpayers. They have each made other disposals of assets during the tax year 2021/22, and therefore they have both already utilised their annual exempt amounts for this year.

Marlon and Alvita

On 28 March 2022, Marlon sold a residential property for £497,000, which he had owned individually. The property had been purchased on 22 October 2004 for £152,600.

Throughout the period of ownership the property was occupied by Marlon and his wife, Alvita, as their main residence. One-third of the property was always used exclusively for business purposes by the couple. Business asset disposal relief is not available in respect of this disposal.

For the tax year 2021/22, Marlon is a higher rate taxpayer, but Alvita did not have any taxable income. This will remain the case for the tax year 2022/23. Neither of them has made any other disposals of assets during the year.

16   What is Grant's capital gains tax (CGT) liability for the tax year 2021/22 in respect of the disposal of the shares in Dub Ltd?

   ○   £43,000

   ○   £21,500

   ○   £0

   ○   £40,540

   (2 marks)

17   Which TWO of the following statements would have been true in relation to the CGT implications if Delroy had instead sold the 25,000 shares in Dub Ltd himself for £240,000 on 10 January 2022, and then gifted the cash proceeds to Grant?

   ☐   Business asset disposal relief would have been available.

   ☐   The CGT liability would have been paid later.

   ☐   The cash gift would not have been a chargeable disposal.

   ☐   The cash gift would have qualified for gift holdover relief.

   (2 marks)

18   What is Marlon's chargeable gain for the tax year 2021/22?

○   £229,600

○   £0

○   £114,800

○   £344,400   (2 marks)

---

19   What is the amount of CGT which could have been saved if Marlon had transferred 50% ownership of the residential property to Alvita prior to its disposal?

○   £3,444

○   £7,214

○   £3,770

○   £14,000   (2 marks)

---

20   What is the payment date for the capital gains tax payable on the disposal of the residential property on 28 March 2022?

[▼]

Pull down list:

31 January 2023
31 January 2024
30 April 2022
27 April 2022   (2 marks)

(Total = 10 marks)

Opal

The following scenario relates to Questions 21 to 25.

You should assume that today's date is 15 March 2022.

Opal is aged 71 and has a chargeable estate for inheritance tax (IHT) purposes valued at £950,000.

She owns two investment properties respectively valued at £374,000 and £442,000. The first property has an outstanding repayment mortgage of £160,000, and the second property is owned outright with no mortgage.

Opal owes £22,400 in respect of a personal loan from a bank, and she has also verbally promised to pay legal fees of £4,600 incurred by her nephew. Opal expects the cost of her funeral to be £5,200, and this cost will be covered by the £6,000 she has invested in an individual savings account (ISA).

Under the terms of her will, Opal has left all of her estate to her children. Opal's husband is still alive.

On 14 August 2012, Opal had made a gift of £100,000 to her daughter, and on 7 November 2021, she made a gift of £220,000 to her son. Both these figures are after deducting all available exemptions.

The nil rate band for the tax year 2012/13 is £325,000.

You should assume that both the value of Opal's estate and the nil rate band will remain unchanged for future years.

21   What is the net value for the two properties, and related mortgages, which will have been included in the calculation of Opal's chargeable estate of £950,000?

○   £816,000

○   £564,000

○   £656,000

○   £724,000

(2 marks)

22   Which TWO of the following amounts will have been deducted in calculating Opal's chargeable estate of £950,000?

☐   Personal loan from a bank of £22,400

☐   Promise to pay legal fees of £4,600

☐   Funeral cost of £5,200

☐   ISA investment of £6,000

(2 marks)

23   What amount of IHT will be payable in respect of Opal's chargeable estate valued at £950,000 were she to die on 20 March 2022?

○   £250,000

○   £338,000

○   £378,000

○   £335,600

(2 marks)

24   By how much would the IHT payable on Opal's death be reduced if she were to live for another seven years until 20 March 2029, compared to if she were to die on 20 March 2022?

[▼]

Pull down list:

£88,000
£40,000
£128,000
£0

(2 marks)

25   Which TWO of the following conditions must be met if Opal wants to make gifts out of her income, so that these gifts are exempt from IHT?

☐   The gifts cannot exceed 10% of income.

☐   The gifts must be habitual.

☐   Opal must have enough remaining income to maintain her normal standard of living.

☐   Opal must make the gifts monthly or quarterly.

(2 marks)

(Total = 10 marks)

Glacier Ltd

The following scenario relates to Questions 26 to 30.

The following information is available in respect of Glacier Ltd's value added tax (VAT) for the quarter ended 31 March 2022:

(1) Invoices were issued for sales of £44,600 to VAT registered customers. Of this figure, £35,200 was in respect of exempt sales and the balance in respect of standard rated sales. The standard rated sales figure is exclusive of VAT.

(2) In addition to the above, on 1 March 2022 Glacier Ltd issued a VAT invoice for £8,000 plus VAT of £1,600 to a VAT registered customer in respect of a contract which will be completed on 15 April 2022. The customer paid for the contract in two instalments of £4,800 on 31 March 2022 and 30 April 2022.

(3) The managing director of Glacier Ltd is provided with free fuel for private mileage driven in her company motor car. During the quarter ended 31 March 2022, the total cost of fuel for business and private mileage was £720, of which £270 was for private mileage. The relevant quarterly scale charge is £406. All of these figures are inclusive of VAT.

For the quarters ended 30 September 2020 and 30 June 2021, Glacier Ltd was one month late in submitting its VAT returns and in paying the related VAT liabilities. All of the company's other VAT returns have been submitted on time.

26   **What is the amount of output VAT payable by Glacier Ltd in respect of its sales for the quarter ended 31 March 2022?**

[dropdown ▼]

Pull down list:

£2,680
£3,480
£10,520
£1,880   (2 marks)

27   **Calculate the amounts required to complete the following sentence:**

Glacier Ltd will include output VAT of

£ [   ]

and input VAT of

£ [   ]

on its VAT return for the quarter ended 31 March 2022 in respect of the managing director's company motor car.   (2 marks)

28   **What surcharge penalty could Glacier Ltd be charged if the company is one month late in paying its VAT liability for the quarter ended 31 March 2022?**

○   5% of the VAT liability

○   2% of the VAT liability

○   There will be no penalty

○   10% of the VAT liability   (2 marks)

29   What is the minimum requirement which Glacier Ltd needs to meet in order to revert to a
      clean default surcharge record?

      ○   Submit four consecutive VAT returns on time

      ○   Submit any four VAT returns on time and also pay the related VAT liabilities on time

      ○   Pay four consecutive VAT liabilities on time

      ○   Submit four consecutive VAT returns on time and also pay the related VAT liabilities
           on time
                                                                                    (2 marks)

30   Complete the following sentence by matching one of the 'types of supply' and one of the
      'types of customer' into each target area.

      Glacier Ltd will be required to issue a VAT invoice when [   ]

      is made to [   ] .

Types of supply	Types of customer
a standard rated supply	a VAT registered
any type of supply	any customer

                                                                                    (2 marks)

                                                                         (Total = 10 marks)

Section C – ALL three questions are compulsory and MUST be attempted

31 Sarah

You should assume that today's date is 1 March 2021.

Sarah is currently self-employed. If she continues to trade on a self-employed basis, her total income tax liability and national insurance contributions (NIC) for the tax year 2021/22 will be £11,304.

However, Sarah is considering incorporating her business on 6 April 2021. The forecast taxable total profits of the new limited company for the year ended 5 April 2022 will be £50,000 (before taking account of any director's remuneration). Sarah will pay herself gross director's remuneration of £30,000 and dividends of £10,000. The balance of the profits will remain undrawn within the new company.

Required

(a) Determine whether or not there will be an overall saving of tax and national insurance contributions (NIC) for the year ended 5 April 2022 if Sarah incorporates her business on 6 April 2022.

   Notes

   1   You are expected to calculate the income tax payable by Sarah, the Class 1 NIC payable by Sarah and the new limited company, and the corporation tax liability of the new limited company for the year ended 5 April 2022.

   2   The new limited company will not be entitled to the NIC annual employment allowance.

   3   You should assume that the rates of corporation tax remain unchanged.   **(8 marks)**

(b) Advise Sarah as to why her proposed basis of extracting profits from the new limited company is not optimum for tax purposes, and suggest how the mix of director's remuneration and dividends could therefore be improved.

   Note. You are not expected to calculate any revised tax or NIC figures.   **(2 marks)**

   (Total = 10 marks)

32 Simon

On 6 April 2021, Simon commenced employment with Echo Ltd. On 1 January 2022, he commenced in partnership with Art, preparing accounts to 30 April. The following information is available for the tax year 2021/22:

Employment

(1)   During the tax year 2021/22, Simon was paid a gross annual salary of £23,940.

(2)   Throughout the tax year 2021/22, Echo Ltd provided Simon with living accommodation. The company had purchased the property in 2009 for £89,000, and it was valued at £143,000 on 6 April 2021. The annual value of the property is £4,600. The property was furnished by Echo Ltd during March 2021 at a cost of £9,400. The living accommodation is not job related.

(3)   On 1 December 2021, Echo Ltd provided Simon with an interest-free loan of £84,000, which he used to purchase a holiday cottage.

Partnership

(1) The partnership's tax adjusted trading profit for the four-month period ended 30 April 2022 is £29,700. This figure is before taking account of capital allowances.

(2) The only item of plant and machinery owned by the partnership is a motor car which cost £25,000 on 1 February 2022. The motor car has a CO2 emission rate of 75 grams per kilometre. It is used by Art, and 40% of the mileage is for private journeys.

(3) Profits are shared 40% to Simon and 60% to Art. This is after paying an annual salary of £6,000 to Art.

Property income

(1) Simon owns a freehold house which is let out furnished. The property was let throughout the tax year 2021/22 at a monthly rent of £660, all of which was received during the tax year.

(2) During the tax year 2021/22, Simon paid council tax and water rates totalling £1,320 in respect of the property. He also replaced the property's washing machine during March 2022. The old washing machine was sold for £70, being replaced by a washer-dryer costing £970. The cost of a similar washing machine would have been £730.

Required

(a) Calculate Simon's taxable income for the tax year 2021/22. **(13 marks)**

(b) State **TWO** advantages for the partnership of choosing 30 April as its accounting date rather than 5 April. **(2 marks)**

(Total = 15 marks)

33 Naive Ltd

(a) You are a trainee accountant and your manager has asked you to correct a corporation tax computation which has been prepared by the managing director of Naive Ltd. The corporation tax computation is for the year ended 31 March 2022 and contains a significant number of errors:

Naive Ltd – Corporation tax computation for the year ended 31 March 2022

	£
Trading profit (working 1)	372,900
Loan interest received (working 2)	32,100
	405,000
Corporation tax (405,000 at 19%)	76,950

Workings

1 *Trading profit*

	£
Operating profit before interest and taxation	287,220
Depreciation	15,740
Donations to political parties	400
Qualifying charitable donations	900
Accountancy	2,300
Legal fees in connection with the issue of loan notes (the loan was used to finance the company's trading activities)	5,700

		£
Entertaining suppliers		3,600
Entertaining employees		1,700
Gifts to customers (pens costing £40 each and displaying Naive Ltd's name)		920
Gifts to customers (food hampers costing £45 each and displaying Naive Ltd's name)		1,650
Capital allowances (working 3)		65,460
Trading profit		385,590

2   *Loan interest received*

	£
Loan interest receivable	32,800
Accrued at 1 April 2021	10,600
Accrued at 31 March 2022	(11,300)
Loan interest received	32,100

The loan was made for non-trading purposes.

3   *Capital allowances*

	Main pool £	Motor car £	Special rate pool £	Allowances £
Written down value (WDV) brought forward	12,400		13,600	
Additions				
Machinery	42,300			
Motor car [1]	13,800			
Motor car [2]		14,000		
	68,500			
Annual investment allowance (AIA)	(68,500)			68,500
Disposal proceeds			(9,300)	
			4,300	
Balancing allowance			(4,300)	(4,300)
Writing down allowance (WDA) – 18%		(2,520) × 50%		1,260
WDV carried forward	0	11,480		
Total allowances				65,460

(1)   Motor car [1] has a CO_2 emission rate of 40 grams per kilometre.

(2)   Motor car [2] has a CO_2 emission rate of 125 grams per kilometre. This motor car is used by the sales manager and 50% of the mileage is for private journeys.

(3)   All of the items included in the special rate pool at 1 April 2021 were sold for £9,300 during the year ended 31 March 2022. The original cost of these items was £16,200.

Required

Prepare a corrected version of Naive Ltd's corporation tax computation for the year ended 31 March 2022.

Note. Your calculations should commence with the operating profit before interest and taxation figure of £287,220, and you should indicate by the use of zero (0) any items in the computation of the trading profit for which no adjustment is required.

(12 marks)

(b) The managing director of Naive Ltd understands that the company will have to file its self-assessment corporation tax returns online, and that the supporting accounts and tax computations will have to be filed using the inline eXtensible Business Reporting Language (iXBRL). The managing director is concerned with how the company will be able to produce the documents in this format.

Required

Explain the options available to Naive Ltd regarding the production of accounts and tax computations in the iXBRL format. (3 marks)

(Total = 15 marks)

Answers

A plan of attack

If this were the real Taxation (TX – UK) exam and you had been told to turn over and begin, what would be going through your mind?

Perhaps you're having a panic. You've spent most of your study time on income tax and corporation tax computations (because that's what your tutor/BPP Workbook told you to do), plus a selection of other topics, and you're really not sure that you know enough. So calm down. Spend the first few moments or so **looking at the exam**, and develop a **plan of attack**.

Looking through the exam.

Section A contains **15 Objective Test (OT) questions** each worth **2 marks**. These will cover all sections of the syllabus. Some you may find easy and some more difficult. For example, Question 13 on keeping records for tax should be easy marks and you just need to pick the right answers from the table. Don't spend a lot of time on anything you really don't know. For multiple choice questions you are not penalised for wrong answers, so you should answer all of them. If all else fails – guess!

Section B contains **three OT Case** scenarios. These each have **five questions** each worth 2 **marks**. Make sure you read the scenario carefully before you start to answer the OTQs.

- **Questions 16 to 20** are about chargeable gains for individuals. In Question 19, note that you are asked for the amount of CGT which could have been **saved** if Marlon had transferred 50% ownership of the residential property to Alvita prior to its disposal so you need to think about how CGT is computed for Alvita bearing in mind that she has no taxable income or other disposals in the year.

- **Questions 21 to 25** concern inheritance tax (IHT). In Question 24, you need to consider how the seven year accumulation period works.

- **Questions 26 to 30** test topics in value added tax (VAT). For Question 26, you need to think about the tax point for the contract in part (2).

In **Section C** you have **three constructed response (long) questions**:

- **Question 31** for **10 marks** is about the potential tax saving by incorporating a sole trader business. You need to work out the individual's income tax, the national insurance contributions for an employee and corporation tax.

- **Question 32** for **15 marks** is an income tax computation and also deals with choice of accounting date.

- **Question 33** for **15 marks** is a corporation tax question and includes capital allowances. Part (b) is about how a company files its corporation tax return and supporting accounts.

Allocating your time

BPP's advice is always allocate your time **according to the marks for the question** in total and for the parts of the question. But **use common sense**. If you're confronted by an OTQ on a topic of which you know nothing, pick an answer and move on. Use the time to pick up marks elsewhere.

After the exam...**Forget about it!**

And don't worry if you found the exam difficult. More than likely other candidates will too. If this were the real thing you would need to **forget** the exam the minute you left the exam hall and **think about the next one**. Or, if it's the last one, **celebrate!**

Section A

1   £4,339

		£
£(50,270 – 9,568) = £40,702 × 9%		3,663
£(84,050 – 50,270) = £33,780 × 2%		676
Class 4 NICs		4,339

The answer £4,498 includes Class 2 NIC. The answer £6,703 uses 9% throughout. The answer £3,663 is just the 9% band liability.

2   Reporting under the money laundering regulations

Advising the client to make disclosure

Your firm should advise the client to make disclosure. Your firm should make a report under the money laundering regulations.

You should not inform HMRC of the non-disclosure. Your firm also should not warn the client that it will be reporting the non-disclosure as this might constitute the criminal offence of 'tipping-off'.

3   £8,270

		£
Personal allowance		12,570
Less restriction £(109,400 – 800 – 100,000) = £8,600/2		(4,300)
Restricted personal allowance		8,270

4   £135,000

The lower of:		£
Taxable total profits of Shallow Ltd for the corresponding accounting period (1.7.21 – 31.3.22)		
£224,000 × 9/12		168,000
Losses of Halo Ltd for the corresponding accounting period		
£180,000 × 9/12		135,000

5   Four instalments of £46,075

Profits threshold £1,500,000/2 (related 51% company)		£750,000

Sizeable Ltd was therefore a large company in both years.

| Each instalment for the year to 31 March 2022 is | | £46,075 |
| £(970,000 @ 19%) = 184,300/4 | | |

The answer nine instalments of £15,580 and a balancing payment of £28,500 is based on the previous accounting period's profits with each of the instalments being 10% of the liability. This is the VAT annual accounting schedule of payments. The answer instalments of £38,950 and a balancing payment of £28,500 again is based on the previous year's profits, similar to self-assessment for individuals. The answer £184,300 is the full amount of corporation tax which would be payable if Sizeable Ltd was not a large company.

6   £780

Interest runs from due date (1 October 2022) to the date of payment (31 March 2023) which is six months.

£60,000 × 2.6% × 6/12		£780

The answer £1,950 is for a 15-month period from 31 January 2022 to 31 March 2023.
The answer £260 is for a two-month period from 31 January 2023 to 31 March 2023.
The answer £390 is for a three-month period from the filing date of 1 January 2023 to 31 March 2023.

7   £4,500

	£
Proceeds	8,700
Less cost	(3,800)
Gain	4,900

The maximum gain is $5/3 \times £(8,700 - 6,000) = £4,500$.

The chargeable gain is the lower of £4,900 and £4,500, so it is £4,500.

The answer £0 assumes that this is an exempt chattel.

8   £118,750

	£
Net chargeable transfer	800,000
Less nil rate band	(325,000)
	475,000

IHT £475,000 × 20/80 (donor paid tax)   118,750

9

£400 to Alfred	NOT EXEMPT
£140 to Minnie	NOT EXEMPT
A further £280 to Minnie	NOT EXEMPT
£175 to Winifred	EXEMPT

Outright gifts to individuals totalling £250 or less per donee in any one tax year are exempt under the small gifts exemption. The £400 gift to Alfred is therefore not exempt under the small gifts exemption. If gifts total more than £250 the whole amount is chargeable. Therefore neither of the gifts to Minnie which total £(140 + 280) = £420 are exempt under the small gifts exemption. The gift of £175 to Winifred is exempt under the small gifts exemption.

10   £7,164

£(49,750 × 120/100) = 59,700 × 12%   £7,164

Under the flat rate scheme, a business calculates VAT by applying a fixed percentage to its tax inclusive turnover. However, the business cannot reclaim any input tax suffered.

11   A motor car suitable for private use

A UK government security (gilt)

A wasting chattel is exempt, as is a chattel sold for gross proceeds of £6,000 or less. Other chattels are chargeable assets. A house may be exempt if private residence relief applies, but is otherwise a chargeable asset.

12   £12,000

£(20,000 – 8,000)   £12,000

The answer £20,000 is the full ISA allowance. The answer £0 assumes that only one ISA can be opened in a tax year and so Winston cannot invest into a stocks and shares ISA having invested in a cash ISA. The answer £10,000 assumes that the ISA limit is divided equally between the two accounts.

13

Business records		31 JANUARY 2028
Non-business records		31 JANUARY 2028

Records must be retained until five years after the 31 January following the tax year where the taxpayer is in business. This applies to all of the records, not only the business records.

14   £62,000

	£
Loss incurred in y/e 31.12.21	105,000
p/e 31.12.20	(43,000)
	62,000
y/e 31.8.20	
Lower of £96,000 × 8/12 = £64,000 and unused loss	(62,000)
C/f	0

Loss relief by deduction from total profits may be given by deduction from current period profits and from the previous 12 months. Therefore relief can be given in the four-month period ended 31 December 2020 and for eight months of the year ended 31 August 2020.

The answer £64,000 is the time apportioned amount of profits. The answer £96,000 assumes that the earlier accounting period profits can be relieved first.

15   90 days

Nigel was not previously resident in the UK. He will be UK resident for 2021/22 with three UK ties if he spends at least 91 days in the UK during that tax year. Therefore the maximum number of days that Nigel could spend in the UK during the tax year 2021/22 without being treated as UK resident for that year is 90 days.

Section B

Delroy and Marlon

16   £43,000

	£
Ordinary shares in Dub Ltd	
Proceeds	240,000
Less cost	(25,000)
Gain	215,000
Less annual exempt amount (already used as stated in question)	(0)
Taxable gain	215,000
CGT: £215,000 × 20%	43,000

Tutorial notes

1   The effect of the gift holdover relief election is that Grant effectively took over Delroy's original cost of £25,000.

2   The disposal does not qualify for business asset disposal relief as Grant was neither an officer nor an employee of Dub Ltd and, in any case, had only owned the shares for just over two months (the minimum period for the conditions for the relief to be satisfied is two years).

The answer £21,500 assumes that business asset disposal relief applies to the disposal so the rate of tax is 10%. The answer £0 assumes this is an exempt disposal. The answer £40,540 deducts the annual exempt amount – read the question carefully!

17   Business asset disposal relief would have been available.

The cash gift would not have been a chargeable disposal.

Delroy's disposal would have qualified for business asset disposal relief because for at least two years prior to the disposal:

- Dub Ltd was Delroy's personal company as he owned at least 5% of the ordinary share capital

- Dub Ltd was a trading company

- Delroy was an officer or employee of Dub Ltd

There are no capital gains tax implications of a gift of cash.

18   £114,800

Residential property	£
Proceeds	497,000
Less cost	(152,600)
Gain before PRR	344,400
Less PRR (W)	(229,600)
Gain after PRR	114,800

Working

One-third of the residential property was always used exclusively for business purposes, so the private residence relief exemption is restricted to £(344,400 × 2/3) = £229,600.

The answer £229,600 is the PRR. The answer £0 assumes this is an exempt disposal. The answer £344,400 is the gain before PRR.

19   £7,214

		£
Annual exempt amount	£12,300 × 28%	3,444
Basic rate band	£37,700 × (28 – 18)%	3,770
Total tax saving		7,214

The 50% ownership of the house would have been transferred from Marlon to Alvita on a no gain, no loss basis. The effect of this is that 50% of the gain on disposal would accrue to Marlon and 50% to Alvita.

Transferring 50% ownership of the house to Alvita prior to its disposal would have enabled her annual exempt amount and basic rate tax band for 2021/22 to be utilised.

The answer £3,444 is just the annual exempt amount saving. The answer £3,770 is just the basic rate band saving. The answer £14,000 is the annual exempt amount and the basic rate band, all at 28%.

20   27 April 2022

The CGT on disposal of a residential property is due within 30 days of the disposal.

Opal

Workbook references. Inheritance tax is covered in Chapter 18.

Top tips. Try drawing a timeline and mark on it the date of Opal's death and the lifetime transfers. Then mark the date which is seven years before Opal's death. It will be clear that the lifetime transfer in 2010 falls more than seven years before Opal's death and is therefore exempt.

Easy marks. There were some easy marks for working out the IHT on the death estate in Question 23.

21   £656,000

	£	£
Property one	374,000	
Less repayment mortgage	(160,000)	
		214,000
Property two	442,000	
Less endowment mortgage	0	442,000
Net value of two properties		656,000

There is no deduction in respect of the endowment mortgage as this will be repaid upon death by the life assurance element of the mortgage.

The answer £816,000 does not deduct the repayment mortgage. The answer £564,000 deducts the endowment mortgage. The answer £724,000 deducts the endowment mortgage but not the repayment mortgage.

22   Personal loan from a bank of £22,400

Funeral cost of £5,200

The promise to pay the nephew's legal fees is not deductible as it is not legally enforceable.

23   £338,000

	£
Chargeable estate	950,000
105,000 (W) × 0%	0
845,000 × 40%	338,000
950,000	
IHT on death estate	338,000

Working

	£
Nil rate band at death	325,000
Less: PET 14 August 2012	(0)
PET 7 November 2021	(220,000)
Available nil rate band	105,000

The potentially exempt transfer on 14 August 2012 is exempt from inheritance tax as it was made more than seven years before 20 March 2022.

The answer £250,000 has an unrestricted nil rate band. The answer £378,000 assumes that the PET in 2012 becomes chargeable on Opal's death. The answer £335,600 deducts two annual exemptions from the gift in 2021.

24   £88,000

If Opal were to live for another seven years, then the potentially exempt transfer on 7 November 2021 would become exempt.

The inheritance tax payable in respect of her estate would therefore decrease by £(220,000 × 40%) = £88,000.

25   The gifts must be habitual

Opal must have enough remaining income to maintain her usual standard of living

Glacier Ltd

> **Workbook references.** Value added tax is covered in Chapters 24 and 25.
>
> **Top tips.** The tax point is frequently examined and is relevant in Question 26. The basic tax point for a supply of services is the date when they are completed, but if a VAT invoice is issued or payment received before the basic tax point, then this becomes the actual tax point.
>
> **Easy marks.** There were easy marks in Questions 28 and 29 concerning the default surcharge penalty.

26   £3,480

	£
Sales	
VAT registered customers £(44,600 − 35,200) = £9,400 × 20%	1,880
Additional contract (1 March 2022)	1,600
Output VAT	3,480

The tax point for the contract is when the VAT invoice was issued on 1 March 2022, which is earlier than both the basic tax point of 15 April and the receipt of cash on 31 March.

27   Glacier Ltd will include output VAT of **£68** and input VAT of **£120** on its VAT return for the
      quarter ended 31 March 2022 in respect of the managing director's company motor car.

      Output VAT £406 × 20/120   £68

      Input VAT £720 × 20/120   £120

28   5% of the VAT liability

      Glacier Ltd was late in submitting VAT returns and paying the related VAT liability for two
      previous quarters. The late payment of VAT for the quarter ended 31 March 2022 will
      therefore result in a surcharge of 5% of the VAT liability for that period since this is the
      second default during the surcharge period.

29   Submit four consecutive VAT returns on time and also pay the related VAT liabilities on time

30   Glacier Ltd will be required to issue a VAT invoice when   a standard rated supply

      is made to   a VAT registered customer   .

Section C

31 Sarah

> **Workbook references.** Employment income is covered in Chapter 3. The income tax computation is the subject of Chapter 2. National insurance contributions are dealt with in Chapter 12. Corporation tax is covered in Chapter 19.
>
> **Top tips.** Note 1 outlines the steps that you need to take to complete the question.
>
> **Easy marks.** There were some easy marks for basic income tax and corporation tax computations.

Marking scheme

		Marks	
(a)	*Income tax liability*		
	Director's remuneration	½	
	Dividends	½	
	Personal allowance	½	
	Basic rate on earnings	½	
	Nil rate on dividends	½	
	Basic rate on dividends	½	
	National insurance contributions		
	Class 1 employee	1	
	Class 1 employer	1	
	Corporation tax		
	Trading profit	½	
	Director's remuneration	½	
	Employer's Class 1 NIC	½	
	Corporation tax	½	
	Total tax cost if incorporates	½	
	Additional tax	½	
			8
(b)	Salary attracting NICs	1	
	Restrict salary, take more dividends	1	2
			10

(a)   **Sarah – Income tax liability 2021/22**

	Non-savings income £	Dividend income £	Total income £
Director's remuneration	30,000		
Dividends		10,000	
Net income	30,000	10,000	40,000
Less personal allowance	(12,570)		
Taxable income	17,430	10,000	27,430

Tax
Non-savings income

	£
£17,430 @ 20%	3,486
Dividend income	
£2,000 @ 0%	0
£8,000 (10,000 – 2,000) @ 7.5%	600
Income tax liability	4,086

Sarah – National insurance contributions 2021/22

	£
Employee Class 1 £(30,000 – 9,568) = 20,432 @ 12%	2,452
Employer Class 1 £(30,000 – 8,840) = 21,160 @ 13.8%	2,920

Corporation tax liability of the new limited company for the year ended 5 April 2022

	£
Trading profit	50,000
Less: director's remuneration	(30,000)
employer's Class 1 NIC	(2,920)
Taxable trading profit	17,080
Corporation tax £17,080 @ 19%	3,245

The total tax and NIC cost if Sarah incorporates her business is £12,703 (4,086 + 2,452 + 2,920 + 3,245).

Therefore, if Sarah incorporated her business there would be additional tax and NIC payable as there would be an increase of £1,399 (12,703 – 11,304) compared to continuing on a self-employed basis.

(b)   The relatively high tax cost of Sarah incorporating her business arises because of her salary attracting both employee and employer NICs.

Restricting the salary to around £8,000 and taxing a correspondingly higher amount of dividends, would significantly reduce her overall tax cost.

32 Simon

Marking scheme

			Marks
(a)	Employment income		
	Salary		½
	Living accommodation	annual value	½
		additional benefit – market value	1
		additional benefit – limit	½
		additional benefit – benefit	½
		furniture	1
	Loan benefit		1
	Trading income		
	Accounts profit		½
	Capital allowances – addition		½
	Capital allowances – WDA		1½
	Salary paid to Art		1
	Profit share		½
	Trading income 2021/22		1
	Property business income		
	Rent receivable		½
	Council tax		½
	Furniture		1½
	Personal allowance		½
			13
(b)	Payment of tax delayed		1
	Calculation of profits in advance of end of tax year		1
			2
			15

(a)   **Simon – Taxable income 2021/22**

	£
Employment income	
Salary	23,940
Living accommodation – annual value	4,600
Living accommodation – additional benefit (W1)	1,360
Living accommodation – furniture £9,400 × 20%	1,880
Loan benefit £84,000 × 2.0% × 4/12	560
	32,340
Trading income (W2)	8,220
Property business income (W4)	5,940
Net income	46,500
Less personal allowance	(12,570)
Taxable income	33,930

Workings

1   *Living accommodation – additional benefit*

	£
Market value when first provided to Simon	143,000
Less limit	(75,000)
	68,000
Additional benefit £68,000 × 2.0%	1,360

Tutorial note

Where the property was acquired by the employer more than six years before first being provided to the employee, the market value when first so provided is used as the cost of providing the living accommodation.

2   *Trading income*

Simon's share of the partnership's trading profit for the period ended 30 April 2022 is £10,960 calculated as follows:

	£
Trading profit	29,700
Less capital allowances (W3)	(300)
	29,400
Less salary paid to Art £6,000 × 4/12	(2,000)
	27,400
Profit share £27,400 × 40%	10,960
Simon's trading income 2021/22 £10,960 × 3/4	8,220

Tutorial note

Simon's trading income for 2021/22 is for the period 1 January 2022 to 5 April 2022 as this is his first year of trading and the actual basis applies.

3   *Capital allowances*

	Motor car		Allowances
Four-month period to 30 April 2022	£		£
Addition	25,000		
WDA @ 6% × 4/12	(500)	× 60%	300
WDA c/f	24,500		

Tutorial note

The partnership's motor car has CO_2 emissions over 50 grams per kilometre and therefore qualifies for writing down allowances at the rate of 6%.

4   *Property business income*

	£	£
Rent received £660 × 12		7,920
Council tax and water rates	1,320	
Replacement furniture relief		
Washing machine £(730 − 70)	660	
		(1,980)
Property business income		5,940

Tutorial note

No relief is given for that part of the cost of the washer-dryer which represents an improvement over the original washing machine. Relief is therefore restricted to the cost of a similar washing machine. This figure is then reduced by the proceeds from the sale of the original washing machine.

(b)   The interval between earning profits and paying the related tax liability will be 11 months longer. This can be particularly beneficial where profits are rising.

It will be possible to calculate taxable profits well in advance of the end of the tax year, making it much easier to implement tax planning and make pension contributions.

33 Naive Ltd

> **Workbook references.** The computation of taxable total profits and the computation of the corporation tax liability are covered in Chapter 19. The adjustment to trading profits is dealt with in Chapter 7 and capital allowances in Chapter 8.
>
> **Top tips.** The best approach to this style of question is to start new computations using the information given in the question, rather than trying to correct the wrong computations.
>
> **Easy marks.** There were some easy marks for the adjustment to trading profit and computation of corporation tax in part (a).

			Marks
(a)	Trading profit		
		Depreciation	½
		Donations to political parties	½
		Qualifying charitable donations	½
		Accountancy	½
		Legal fees	½
		Entertaining suppliers	½
		Entertaining employees	½
		Gift to customers – pens	½
		Gift to customers – food hampers	½
		Capital allowances brought from working	½
	Capital allowances		
		WDV brought forward	1
		Annual investment allowance	1
		Addition – motor car [1]	½
		Addition – motor car [2]	½
		Disposal	½
		WDA @ 18%	½
		WDA @ 6%	1
	Loan interest		1
	Qualifying charitable donations		½
	Corporation tax		½
			12
(b)	HMRC software automatically to produce in iXBRL		1
	Other software automatically to produce in iXBRL		1
	Tagging services and software used by Naive Ltd to tag		1
			3
			15

(a) **Naive Ltd – Corporation tax computation for the year ended 31 March 2022**

	£
Trading profit (W1)	248,706
Loan interest	32,800
Total profits	281,506
Less qualifying charitable donations	(900)
Taxable total profits	280,606
Corporation tax	
£280,606 × 19%	53,315

Workings

1   Trading profit for the year ended 31 March 2022

	£
Operating profit before interest and taxation	287,220
Add: depreciation	15,740
donations to political parties	400
qualifying charitable donations	900
accountancy	0
legal fees	0
entertaining suppliers	3,600
entertaining employees	0
gifts to customers – pens	0
gifts to customers – food hampers	1,650
	309,510
Less capital allowances (W2)	(60,804)
Adjusted trading profit	248,706

2 Capital allowances

	FYA	Main pool	Special rate pool	Allowances
	£	£	£	£
WDV brought forward		12,400	13,600	
AIA additions				
Machinery (£42,300 × 130%)	54,990			
FYA @ 130%	(54,990)			54,990
Transfer to pool	0	0		
Non-AIA additions				
Motor car [1]		13,800		
Motor car [2]			14,000	
Disposal				
Special rate pool items			(9,300)	
		26,200	18,300	
WDA @ 18%		(4,716)		4,716
WDA @ 6%			(1,098)	1,098
WDV carried forward		21,484	17,202	
Allowances				60,804

Tutorial notes

1. Motor car [1] has CO_2 emissions between 1 and 50 grams per kilometre and therefore qualifies for writing down allowances at the rate of 18%. Cars do not qualify for the AIA.

2. Motor car [2] has CO_2 emissions over 50 grams per kilometre and therefore qualifies for writing down allowances at the rate of 6%. The private use of the motor car is irrelevant, since such usage will be assessed on the employee as a benefit.

(b) If Naive Ltd has straightforward accounts, it could use the software provided by HM Revenue & Customs. This automatically produces accounts and tax computations in the iXBRL format.

Alternatively, other software which automatically produces iXBRL accounts and computations could be used.

A tagging service could be used to apply the appropriate tags to the accounts and tax computations, or Naive Ltd could use software to tag documents itself.

ACCA Applied Skills

Taxation (TX – UK)

Mock Exam 3 (December 2016 exam updated to FA 2021)

Questions	
Time allowed	3 hours
This exam is divided into three sections:	
Section A – ALL 15 questions are compulsory and MUST be attempted.	
Section B – ALL 15 questions are compulsory and MUST be attempted.	
Section C – ALL THREE questions are compulsory and MUST be attempted.	

DO NOT OPEN THIS EXAM UNTIL YOU ARE READY TO START UNDER EXAMINATION CONDITIONS

Section A – ALL 15 questions are compulsory and MUST be attempted

1   Emil is registered for value added tax (VAT). For the quarter ended 31 March 2022, the input VAT incurred on his purchases and expenses included the following:

	£
Entertaining overseas customers	320
Purchase of new office equipment	1,250
Purchase of a new motor car for business and private use by one of Emil's employees	3,000

What is the amount of input VAT recoverable by Emil in the quarter ended 31 March 2022 in respect of the entertaining, office equipment and motor car?

£ [   ]

(2 marks)

2   Acasta Ltd owns 75% of the ordinary share capital of Barge Ltd and 100% of the ordinary share capital of Coracle Ltd. Barge Ltd owns 75% of the ordinary share capital of Dhow Ltd. Coracle Ltd owns 51% of the ordinary share capital of Eight Ltd.

Which companies, along with Coracle Ltd, are within Acasta Ltd's chargeable gains group?

○   Barge Ltd, Dhow Ltd and Eight Ltd

○   Barge Ltd only

○   Barge Ltd and Dhow Ltd only

○   None of the other companies

(2 marks)

3   Nadia died on 13 February 2004, leaving an estate valued at £275,400 for inheritance tax purposes. Nadia left 50% of her estate to her son and 50% to her husband, Tareq.

Tareq subsequently died on 17 January 2022. Tareq did not own a main residence at the date of his death.

Neither Nadia nor Tareq made any lifetime gifts.

The inheritance nil rate band for the tax year 2003/04 was £255,000.

What is the maximum available nil rate band which can be used when calculating the inheritance tax payable in respect of Tareq's estate?

○   £500,500

○   £474,500

○   £442,300

○   £462,700

(2 marks)

4   Habib purchased a copyright on 30 April 2005 for £31,320. The remaining life of the copyright at the date of purchase was 30 years. On 30 April 2021, Habib sold the copyright for £27,900.

What is Habib's chargeable gain or allowable loss for the tax year 2021/22 in respect of the disposal of the copyright?

○   (£3,420)

○   £11,196

○   £0

○   £13,284   (2 marks)

---

5   **Which of the following is the correct definition of an extra-statutory concession?**

○   A provision for the relaxation of the strict application of the law where it would lead to anomalies or cause hardship

○   Supplementary information providing additional detail in relation to the general principles set out in legislation

○   HM Revenue & Customs' interpretation of tax legislation

○   Guidance provided to HM Revenue & Customs' staff in interpreting and applying tax legislation   (2 marks)

---

6   **Complete the following sentence relating to the length of time a sole trader is required to keep their accounting records after the end of a tax year in which a self-assessment tax return has been completed.**

A sole trader is required to keep their accounting records for | Number of |

months after the | Period |

Number of months	Period
12	End of the tax year
60	31 January that follows the end of the tax year

(2 marks)

---

7   Sanjay commenced trading on 1 January 2021 and prepared his first set of accounts for the six-month period ended 30 June 2021. His second set of accounts were prepared for the year ended 30 June 2022.

Sanjay's tax-adjusted trading profits were:

Six-month period ended 30 June 2021   £10,500
Year ended 30 June 2022   £24,400

What are the class 4 national insurance contributions (NICs) which Sanjay should pay in respect of the tax year 2021/22?

○   £84

○   £1,182

○   £1,258

○   £1,335   (2 marks)

8   Modal Ltd lets out an unfurnished investment property.

During the year ended 31 December 2021, the company received rental income of £3,000 per month and paid electricity (relating to the rental property) of £200 per month. The electricity payment for December 2021 was not paid until 30 January 2022.

Modal Ltd also paid interest of £1,200 per month on a loan taken out to finance the purchase of the rental property.

What amount of property business income will be included in Modal Ltd's corporation tax computation for the year ended 31 December 2021?

○   £33,600

○   £19,200

○   £33,800

○   £19,400

(2 marks)

---

9   **Which of the following will NOT cause Harper to be treated as automatically UK resident for the tax year 2021/22?**

○   Harper spending 192 days in the UK during the tax year 2021/22

○   Harper renting a house in the UK to live in and then occupying it (as her only home) throughout the tax year 2021/22

○   Harper accepting a 15-month contract for a full-time job in the UK on 6 April 2021

○   Harper's husband living in the UK throughout the tax year 2021/22 and Harper staying with him when she visits the UK

(2 marks)

---

10 Somily Ltd filed its self-assessment corporation tax return for the year ended 31 December 2021 on 15 March 2023.

What is the deadline for HM Revenue & Customs (HMRC) to start a compliance check enquiry into Somily Ltd's corporation tax return for the year ended 31 December 2021?

31 December 2023   31 January 2024   15 March 2024   30 April 2024

(2 marks)

---

11 On 6 April 2021, Melinda rented out a furnished room in her house to Jenny at a rent of £720 a month. Jenny continued to rent the room on the same terms until 5 July 2022.

Melinda continued to live in the house and paid for all of the living expenses, of which £175 a month related to the room rented out to Jenny.

What is Melinda's property income for the tax year 2021/22, assuming that any beneficial elections are made?

○   £1,140

○   £0

○   £6,540

○   £2,760

(2 marks)

12   Three unconnected companies have the following results for corporation tax purposes:

Company	Current accounting period	Number of 51% group companies	Taxable total profits (TTP) £	TTP for previous 12-month period £
Asher Ltd	Year ended 31 March 2022	3	700,000	600,000
Barton Ltd	Four-month period ended 31 December 2021	0	600,000	1,600,000
Chelfry Ltd	Year ended 30 November 2021	0	1,600,000	1,400,000

All the companies have had the same number of 51% group companies for many years. None of the companies have received any dividends.

Which of the three companies will NOT have to pay corporation tax by quarterly instalments for the current accounting period?

○   Asher Ltd only

○   Barton Ltd only

○   Chelfry Ltd only

○   Barton Ltd and Chelfry Ltd only   (2 marks)

---

13   David had the following taxable income (after deduction of his personal allowance) for the tax year 2021/22:

Non-savings income	£8,500
Savings income	£2,400
Dividend income	£4,250

What is David's total income tax liability for the tax year 2021/22?

Pull down list:

£2,149
£2,299
£2,349
£2,499   (2 marks)

14   Gita died on 17 May 2021. At the date of her death she owned the following assets:

	£
Investment property	390,000
Chattels and cash	70,000
Shares held in an individual savings account (ISA)	60,000

At the date of her death, Gita owed income tax of £25,000 in respect of the tax year 2021/22.

Gita left £100,000 of her estate to her husband, with the remainder of the estate left to her daughter.

What is Gita's chargeable estate for inheritance tax purposes?

Pull down list:

£335,000
£395,000
£495,000
£420,000

(2 marks)

15   Anika sold her entire holding of 3,000 £1 ordinary shares in Distribo Ltd, a trading company, to her son, Hemi, for £53,000 on 14 July 2021. The market value of the shares on that date was £98,000. Anika had purchased the 3,000 shares on 28 October 2007 for £41,500. She has never worked for Distribo Ltd.

Identify, by clicking on the relevant boxes in the table below, the amount of gift holdover relief (if any) that could be claimed in respect of the disposal of these shares, and Anika's chargeable gain for the tax year 2021/22 after taking account of any available relief.

	Amount			
Gift holdover relief	£0	£11,500	£45,000	£56,500
Gain	£0	£11,500		

(2 marks)

(Total = 30 marks)

Section B – ALL 15 questions are compulsory and MUST be attempted

Zoyla

The following scenario relates to Questions 16 to 20.

Zoyla's capital gains tax (CGT) liability for the tax year 2021/22 is calculated as follows:

	Gain £
Ordinary shares in Minor Ltd	98,800
Ordinary shares in Major plc	44,400
Annual exempt amount	(12,300)
	130,900
CGT: 10,600 at 10%	1,060
120,300 at 20%	24,060
	25,120

Minor Ltd is an unquoted trading company with an issued share capital of 200,000 £1 ordinary shares. Zoyla has been a director of this company since 1 April 2014. On 20 June 2021, Zoyla sold 20,000 of her holding of 45,000 ordinary shares in Minor Ltd. She had originally purchased 22,500 shares on 15 August 2020 for £117,000. On 12 December 2020, Minor Ltd made a 1 for 1 rights issue. Zoyla took up her allocation under the rights issue in full, paying £7.40 for each new share issued.

Major plc is a quoted trading company with an issued share capital of 2,000,000 £1 ordinary shares. Zoyla has been an employee of Major plc since 1 November 2020 when she acquired 16,000 ordinary shares in the company. On 6 March 2022, Zoyla sold her entire holding of ordinary shares in Major plc to her son for £152,000. On that date, shares in Major plc were quoted on the stock exchange at £9.62–£9.74.

Zoyla will not make any other disposals in the foreseeable future, and her taxable income will remain unchanged.

16 **Complete the following sentences to explain why neither of Zoyla's share disposals during the tax year 2021/22 qualified for business asset disposal relief.**

The disposal of shares in Minor Ltd did not qualifying for business asset disposal relief in the tax year 2021/22 due to

Minor Ltd

The disposal of shares in Major plc did not qualifying for business asset disposal relief in the tax year 2021/22 due to

Major Ltd

Minor Ltd	Minor Ltd
Holding period	Holding period
Size of shareholding	Size of shareholding

(2 marks)

17   What cost figure will have been used in calculating the chargeable gain on Zoyla's disposal of 20,000 ordinary shares in Minor Ltd?

    ○   £126,000

    ○   £104,000

    ○   £148,000

    ○   £252,000   (2 marks)

---

18   What proceeds figure will have been used in calculating the chargeable gain on Zoyla's disposal of 16,000 ordinary shares in Major plc?

    ○   £152,000

    ○   £154,400

    ○   £153,920

    ○   £154,880   (2 marks)

---

19   If Zoyla had delayed the sale of her 16,000 ordinary shares in Major plc until 6 April 2022, by how long would the related CGT liability have been deferred?

[▼]

Pull down list

11 months
12 months
1 month
6 months   (2 marks)

---

20   Assuming that the tax rates and allowances for the tax year 2021/22 continue to apply, how much CGT would Zoyla have saved if she had delayed the sale of her 16,000 ordinary shares in Major plc until the following tax year?

    ○   £1,060

    ○   £4,580

    ○   £3,520

    ○   £2,460   (2 marks)

                                           (Total = 10 marks)

Roman and Paris

The following scenario relates to Questions 21 to 25.

Roman died on 7 August 2021, and his wife, Paris, died on 18 February 2022.

The couple had attempted to mitigate their inheritance tax (IHT) liabilities when they both made substantial gifts during 2019. These gifts made full use of their respective nil rate bands of £325,000, but unfortunately neither Roman nor Paris then survived long enough for any of the gifts to benefit from taper relief. Neither Roman nor Paris had made any previous lifetime gifts.

Roman

On 4 March 2019, Roman made a cash gift of £210,000 to his daughter. On 26 August 2019, he made a cash gift of £190,000 to a trust. No lifetime IHT arose in respect of the gift to the trust.

Roman's estate for IHT purposes was valued at £560,000. He did not own a main residence at the date of his death. Under the terms of his will, Roman left £300,000 to Paris (his wife) and the residue of his estate to his daughter.

Paris

On 12 December 2019, Paris made a gift of 75,000 £1 ordinary shares in Capital Ltd, an unquoted investment company, to her son. Before the transfer, Paris owned 100,000 of Capital Ltd's 250,000 ordinary shares. The market value of Capital Ltd's ordinary shares on 12 December 2019 was as follows:

Holding	Market value per share
10%	£5
30%	£6
40%	£8

Paris also made cash gifts of £80, £210, £195 and £460 to various friends during February 2020. The gifts of £80 and £195 were to the same friend.

Paris's estate for IHT purposes was valued at £840,000, including the inheritance from Roman (her husband). She did not own a main residence at the date of her death. Under the terms of her will, Paris left a specific legacy of £20,000 to a friend and the residue of her estate to her grandchildren.

21 **How much IHT will be payable in respect of the gift made to the trust by Roman as a result of his death?**

  ○ £26,400

  ○ £30,000

  ○ £27,600

  ○ £13,200   (2 marks)

22 **Who will be responsible for paying the IHT arising from Roman's gift to the trust as a result of his death, and when will the tax be due?**

  ○ The personal representatives of Roman's estate on 30 April 2022

  ○ The personal representatives of Roman's estate on 28 February 2022

  ○ The trustees of the trust on 30 April 2022

  ○ The trustees of the trust on 28 February 2022   (2 marks)

23 For IHT purposes, what was the amount of the transfer of value as a result of Paris's gift of 75,000 ordinary shares in Capital Ltd?

○ £450,000

○ £600,000

○ £675,000

○ £425,000   (2 marks)

---

24 What is the amount of the cash gifts made by Paris to her friends during February 2020 NOT covered by the small gifts exemption?

○ £735

○ £460

○ £670

○ £0   (2 marks)

---

25 What is the amount of IHT payable in respect of Roman's and Paris's estates on death?

	Roman's estate	Paris's estate
○	£224,000	£336,000
○	£104,000	£336,000
○	£104,000	£328,000
○	£224,000	£328,000

                                                                              (2 marks)

(Total = 10 marks)

Ardent Ltd

The following scenario relates to Questions 26 to 30.

Ardent Ltd was incorporated on 1 April 2021 and commenced trading on 1 January 2022. The company voluntarily registered for valued added tax (VAT) on 1 January 2022, preparing its first VAT return for the quarter ended 31 March 2022. Ardent Ltd's sales have been as follows:

		Standard rated	Zero-rated
		£	£
2022	January	24,800	30,100
	February	42,600	28,700
	March	58,300	22,700
		125,700	81,500

Where applicable, the above figures are stated exclusive of VAT.

During the period 1 April to 31 December 2021, Ardent Ltd incurred input VAT of £120 each month in respect of payments made for advertising services. The company also incurred input VAT totalling £400 (£200 each) in respect of the purchase of two laptop computers on 10 July 2021. One of the laptop computers was scrapped on 30 November 2021 at a nil value, and the other laptop was not used until Ardent Ltd commenced trading on 1 January 2022.

During the quarter ended 31 March 2022, Ardent Ltd received standard rated invoices totalling £56,400 (inclusive of VAT) in respect of purchases and expenses. As at 31 March 2022, £11,400 (inclusive of VAT) of the purchases were unsold and therefore included in inventory.

Ardent Ltd was late in submitting its VAT return for the quarter ended 31 March 2022, and in paying the related VAT liability. The company currently does not use either the VAT cash accounting scheme or the annual accounting scheme.

26 **From what date would Ardent Ltd have been required to be compulsorily registered for VAT?**

[▼]

Pull down list

1 February 2022
1 March 2022
1 April 2022
1 May 2022

(2 marks)

27 **What amount of pre-registration input VAT was Ardent Ltd able to recover in respect of the inputs incurred prior to it registering for VAT on 1 January 2022?**

☐ £920

☐ £1,120

☐ £1,480

☐ £1,280

(2 marks)

28 **Ignoring pre-registration input VAT, what amount of VAT should Ardent Ltd have paid to HM Revenue & Customs in respect of the quarter ended 31 March 2022?**

○ £17,640

○ £32,040

○ £13,860

○ £15,740

(2 marks)

29   How and by when should Ardent Ltd have filed its VAT return for the quarter ended 31 March 2022?

○   Either on the HMRC website or by using Making Tax Digital software by 30 April 2022

○   Using Making Tax Digital software by 7 May 2022

○   Using Making Tax Digital software by 30 April 2022

○   Either on the HMRC website or by using Making Tax Digital software by 7 May 2022

(2 marks)

30   Drag and drop the correct period and VAT scheme from the options below to correctly identify for which period after 31 March 2022 Ardent Ltd will need to avoid further defaults in order to revert to a clean default surcharge record, and which VAT scheme may help in avoiding such further defaults.

Period	Period after 31 March 2022	VAT scheme
6 months	Period	Scheme
12 months		

VAT scheme

Cash accounting scheme

Annual accounting scheme

(2 marks)

(Total = 10 marks)

Section C – ALL three questions are compulsory and MUST be attempted

31 Jack

You should assume that today's date is 15 March 2022 and that the tax rates and allowances for the tax year 2021/22 continue to apply.

Jack, aged 44, is a widower following the recent death of his wife. He has just cashed in a substantial share portfolio and is now considering what to do with the proceeds.

Gift to a trust

The value of Jack's estate is in excess of £1,000,000, and he is worried about the amount of inheritance tax which will be payable should he die. His wife's nil rate band was fully used when she died.

Jack is therefore planning to make an immediate lifetime cash gift of £300,000 to a trust with the funds then being held for the benefit of his two children aged 10 and 12. Jack has not made any previous lifetime gifts.

Personal pension contribution

The only pension contributions which Jack has made previously is the gross amount of £500 per month which he saves into a personal pension scheme. Jack has continued to make these contributions throughout the tax year 2021/22. Although Jack has been saving into this scheme for the previous 15 years, he is concerned that he is not saving enough for his retirement. Jack therefore wants to make the maximum possible amount of additional gross personal pension contribution for the tax year 2021/22, but only to the extent that the contribution will attract tax relief at the higher rate of income tax.

Jack is self-employed, and his trading profit for the tax year 2021/22 is £100,000. He does not have any other income and expects to make the same level of profit in future years.

Individual savings account (ISA)

Jack has never invested any amounts in ISAs. During the next 30 days he would like to invest the maximum possible amounts into stocks and shares ISAs.

Required

(a) Explain, with supporting calculations where necessary, why it is good inheritance tax planning for Jack to make the immediate lifetime cash gift of £300,000 to a trust.

   Note. You are not expected to consider taper relief.   (3 marks)

(b) (i)   Advise Jack of the amount of additional gross personal pension contribution he can make for the tax year 2021/22 which will benefit from tax relief at the higher rate of income tax, and explain why this is a tax efficient approach to pension saving.
                                                                    (4 marks)

   (ii) Calculate the amount of unused pension annual allowances which Jack will be able to carry forward to the tax year 2022/23 if the contribution in (i) above is made.
                                                                    (1 mark)

(c) Advise Jack as to the maximum possible amount which he can invest into stocks and shares ISAs during the next 30 days.   (2 marks)

_____

(Total = 10 marks)

32 Array Ltd

Array Ltd provides its employees with various benefits. It does not payroll benefits.

The benefits were all provided throughout the tax year 2021/22 unless otherwise stated.

Alice

Alice was provided with a brand new petrol-powered motor car which has a list price of £24,600. The motor car has an official CO_2 emissions rate of 107 grams per kilometre. Alice made a capital contribution of £5,600 towards the cost of the motor car when it was first provided to her by Array Ltd.

Alice was also provided with fuel for her private journeys. The total cost to Array Ltd of fuel for the motor car during the tax year 2021/22 was £1,500.

During the tax year 2021/22, Alice drove a total of 12,000 miles, of which 8,000 were for business journeys.

Buma

Buma was provided with a loan of £48,000 on 1 October 2019, which she used to renovate her main residence. Buma repays £1,000 of the capital of the loan to Array Ltd each month, and by 6 April 2021 the amount of the loan outstanding had been reduced to £30,000. In addition, Buma paid loan interest of £180 to Array Ltd during the tax year 2021/22.

The taxable benefit in respect of this loan is calculated using the average method.

Claude

On 6 July 2021, Claude was provided with a mobile telephone. The telephone is a smartphone which is mainly used by Claude for personal internet access. It was purchased by Array Ltd on 6 July 2021 for £600.

On 6 January 2022, Claude was provided with a home entertainment system for his personal use. This was purchased by Array Ltd on 6 January 2022 for £3,200. The market value of the home entertainment system on 5 April 2022 was £2,400.

Denise

During May 2021, Array Ltd paid £10,400 towards the cost of Denise's removal expenses when she permanently moved to take up her new employment with Array Ltd, as she did not live within a reasonable commuting distance. The £10,400 covered both her removal expenses and the legal costs of acquiring a new main residence.

During February 2022, Array Ltd paid for £340 of Denise's medical costs. She had been away from work for three months due to an injury, and the medical treatment (as recommended by a doctor) was to assist her return to work.

Required

(a) State how employers are required to report details of employees' taxable benefits to HM Revenue & Customs following the end of the tax year, and the deadline for submitting this information for the tax year 2021/22. **(2 marks)**

(b) Calculate the taxable benefits which Array Ltd will have to report to HM Revenue & Customs in respect of each of its employees for the tax year 2021/22.

   Note. Your answer should include an explanation for any benefits which are exempt or partially exempt. **(11 marks)**

(c) Calculate the class 1A national insurance contributions which Array Ltd would have had to pay in respect of its employees' taxable benefits for the tax year 2021/22, and state when this would have been due if paid electronically. **(2 marks)**

(Total = 15 marks)

33 Wretched Ltd

Wretched Ltd commenced trading on 1 August 2021, preparing its first accounts for the eight-month period ended 31 March 2022.

Wretched Ltd is incorporated in the United Kingdom, but its three directors are all non-resident in the United Kingdom. Board meetings are always held overseas.

The following information is available:

Trading loss

The trading loss based on the draft accounts for the eight-month period ended 31 March 2022 is £140,840. This figure is **before** making any adjustments required for:

(1)   Advertising expenditure of £7,990 incurred during April 2021. This expenditure has not been deducted in arriving at the trading loss for the eight-month period ended 31 March 2022 of £141,200.

(2)   The premium which was paid to acquire a leasehold office building on a ten-year lease.

(3)   Capital allowances.

Premium paid to acquire a leasehold office building

On 1 August 2021, Wretched Ltd paid a premium to acquire a leasehold office building on a ten-year lease. The amount of premium assessed on the landlord as income was £34,440. The office building was used for business purposes by Wretched Ltd throughout the eight-month period ended 31 March 2022.

Plant and machinery

On 1 August 2021, Wretched Ltd purchased three laptop computers at a discounted cost of £400 per laptop. The original price of each laptop was £850, but they were sold at the discounted price because they were ex-display.

Wretched Ltd also purchased three second-hand motor cars on 1 August 2021. Details are:

	Cost £	CO_2 emissions rate
Motor car [1]	8,300	0 grams per kilometre
Motor car [2]	12,300	40 grams per kilometre
Motor car [3]	18,800	125 grams per kilometre

Property business income

Wretched Ltd lets out a warehouse which is surplus to requirements. The warehouse was let out from 1 August to 31 October 2021 at a rent of £1,400 per month. The tenant left on 31 October 2021, and the warehouse was not re-let before 31 March 2022.

During the eight-month period ended 31 March 2022, Wretched Ltd spent £2,100 on advertising for tenants.

Due to a serious flood, Wretched Ltd spent £5,900 on repairs during January 2022. The damage was not covered by insurance.

Loss on the disposal of shares

On 20 March 2022, Wretched Ltd sold its entire 1% shareholding of £1 ordinary shares in Worthless plc for £21,400. Wretched Ltd had purchased these shares on 5 August 2016 for £26,200.

The indexation factor from August 2016 to December 2017 is 0.052.

Other information

Wretched Ltd does not have any 51% group companies.

Wretched Ltd will continue to trade for the foreseeable future.

Required

(a) State, giving reasons, whether Wretched Ltd is resident or not resident in the United Kingdom for corporation tax purposes.

(1 mark)

(b) Assuming that Wretched Ltd is resident in the United Kingdom, calculate the company's trading loss, property business loss and capital loss for the eight-month period ended 31 March 2022.

Note. You should assume that the company claims the maximum available capital allowances.

(11 marks)

(c) Explain how Wretched Ltd will be able to relieve its trading loss, property business loss and capital loss for the eight-month period ended 31 March 2022.

(3 marks)

(Total = 15 marks)

Answers

A plan of attack

If this were the real Taxation (TX – UK) exam and you had been told to turn over and begin, what would be going through your mind?

Perhaps you're having a panic. You've spent most of your study time on income tax and corporation tax computations (because that's what your tutor/BPP Workbook told you to do), plus a selection of other topics, and you're really not sure that you know enough. So calm down. Spend the first few moments or so **looking at the exam**, and develop a **plan of attack**.

Looking through the exam.

Section A contains **15 Objective Test (OT) questions** each worth **2 marks**. These will cover all sections of the syllabus. Some you may find easy and some more difficult. For Question 5, make sure you carefully consider each statement about extra-statutory concessions before making your choice. Don't spend a lot of time on anything you really don't know. For multiple choice questions you are not penalised for wrong answers, so you should answer all of them. If all else fails – guess!

Section B contains **three OT Case** scenarios. These each have **five questions** each worth **2 marks**. Make sure you read the scenario carefully before you start to answer the OTQs.

- Questions 16 to 20 are about chargeable gains for an individual. In Question 18, do you know how quoted shares are valued if there is an element of a gift?

- Questions 21 to 25 tests your knowledge of inheritance tax (IHT). Don't forget to double check your calculations especially in Question 21.

- Questions 26 to 30 concerns value added tax (VAT). Question 29 should be easy marks about payment of VAT.

In **Section C** you have **three constructed response (long) questions**:

- Question 31 for **10 marks** covers a number of areas of tax planning. These are inheritance tax lifetime gifts, pensions and individual savings accounts.

- Question 32 for **15 marks** is an income tax computation which also tests national insurance contributions. The scenario involves the provision of employment benefits.

- Question 33 for **15 marks** is a corporation tax question. The test for UK residence is examined, the calculation of losses for companies and the use of those losses.

All of these questions are compulsory.

This means that you do not have to waste time wondering which questions to answer.

Allocating your time

BPP's advice is always allocate your time **according to the marks for the question** in total and for the parts of the question. But **use common sense**. If you're confronted by an OTQ on a topic of which you know nothing, pick an answer and move on. Use the time to pick up marks elsewhere.

After the exam…**Forget about it!**

And don't worry if you found the exam difficult. More than likely other candidates will too. If this were the real thing you would need to **forget** the exam the minute you left the exam hall and **think about the next one**. Or, if it's the last one, **celebrate!**

Section A

1   £1,570

	£
Entertaining overseas customers	320
Purchase of new office equipment	1,250
Input tax recoverable	1,570

Note the difference between entertaining overseas customers (input tax recoverable) and UK customers (input tax not recoverable). Input tax is not usually recoverable on cars with any private use – this could be by the owner of the business or an employee.

2   Barge Ltd and Dhow Ltd only

Companies are in a chargeable gains group if at each level there is a 75% holding and the top company has an effective interest of over 50% in the group companies.

There is a 75% holding of Barge Ltd by the top company Acasta Ltd so this is in Acasta Ltd's chargeable gains group.

There is a 75% holding of Dhow Ltd by Barge Ltd and an effective interest of over 50% (75% × 75% = 56.25%) by Acasta Ltd in Dhow Ltd so Dhow Ltd is also in Acasta Ltd's chargeable gains group.

Coracle Ltd is in Acasta Ltd's chargeable gains group (given in question). However, there is no 75% holding between Coracle Ltd and Eight Ltd so Eight Ltd cannot be in Acasta Ltd's chargeable gains group.

> **Examining team's comments.** This question tested candidates' knowledge of the group relationship which is necessary for chargeable gains purposes. The most popular answer was the second option, with candidates appreciating that Barge Ltd was included because of the 75% group relationship with Acasta Ltd (and that Eight Ltd was correspondingly excluded). However, Dhow Ltd is also included in the chargeable gains group because the 75% group relationship need only be met at each level, subject to Acasta Ltd having an effective interest of over 50% (and 75% of 75% is 56.25%). So the correct answer was the third option.
>
> This demonstrates the need to carefully consider each alternative – not just quickly jumping to the most obvious one.

3   £474,500

	£
Nil rate band (NRB) at Nadia's death in 2003/04	255,000
NRB used at Nadia's death	(137,700)
Unused NRB available for transfer	117,300
Tareq's NRB 2021/22	325,000
Nadia's transferred NRB adjusted for 2021/22 rate	
£117,300 × $\dfrac{325,000}{255,000}$	149,500
Total NRB available for Tareq's estate	474,500

4   £13,284

	£
Proceeds	27,900
Less cost £31,320 × $\frac{14}{30}$	(14,616)
Gain	13,284

5   A provision for the relaxation of the strict application of the law where it would lead to anomalies or cause hardship

6   A sole trader is required to keep their accounting records for [**60**] months after the [**31 January that follows the end of the tax year**]

7   £1,182

	£
2021/22	
Second year: basis period first 12 months of trading	
1.1.21 to 30.6.21	10,500
1.7.21 to 31.12.21 6/12 × £24,400	12,200
Taxable profit	22,700
Class 4 NICs £(22,700 − 9,568) = 13,132 @ 9%	1,182

The answer £84 uses £10,500 as the taxable profit. The answer £1,258 uses the accruals basis to give £23,550 as the taxable profits. The answer £1,335 uses £24,400 as the taxable profit.

8   £33,600

	£
Rent receivable £3,000 × 12	36,000
Less electricity payable £200 × 12	(2,400)
Property business income	33,600

The electricity expense is deductible on an accruals basis (companies always use this basis) so the late payment for December 2021 does not affect the deduction. Finance costs for a company are a loan relationship and so not deducted in computing the property business income. They are also not subject to the finance cost restriction which only applies to individuals.

9   Harper's husband living in the UK throughout the tax year 2021/22 and Harper staying with him when she visits the UK

The first three answers are automatic UK residency tests. The last answer is a combination of two of the sufficient ties tests and so is not an automatic UK residency test.

10   30 April 2024

The corporation tax return should have been filed by 31 December 2022. It was therefore filed late. The deadline for HM Revenue & Customs (HMRC) to start a compliance check enquiry is therefore the quarter day following the first anniversary of the actual filing date of 15 March 2023 so is 30 April 2024.

BPP
LEARNING
MEDIA

11   £1,140

	£
Rent receivable £720 × 12	8,640
Less rent a room limit	(7,500)
Property business income	1,140

This is less than the normal basis of assessment which would be £8,640 – (175 × 12) = £6,540.

12   Chelfry Ltd only

Asher Ltd was a large company in the current period and the previous period as its TTP exceeded the limit of £1,500,000/(3 + 1) = £375,000 in both periods and so will have to pay corporation tax by quarterly instalments for the current period.

Barton Ltd was a large company in the current period and the previous period as its TTP exceeded the limit of £1,500,000 in the previous period and £1,500,000 × 4/12 = £500,000 in the current period and so will have to pay corporation tax by quarterly instalments for the current period.

Chelfry Ltd was a large company in the current period as its TTP exceeded the limit of £1,500,000, but was not a large company in the previous period as its TTP did not exceed the limit. It is therefore not required to pay corporation tax by quarterly instalments for the current period.

13   £2,149

	£
Non-savings income	
£8,500 @ 20%	1,700
Savings income	
£1,000 @ 0%	0
£1,400 (2,400 – 1,000) @ 20%	280
Dividend income	
£2,000 @ 0%	0
£2,250 (4,250 – 2,000) @ 7.5%	169
Income tax liability	2,149

The answer £2,299 omits the dividend nil rate band. The answer £2,349 omits the savings income nil rate band. The answer £2,499 omits both the savings income nil rate band and the dividend nil rate band.

14   £395,000

	£
Investment property	390,000
Chattels and cash	70,000
Shares in an ISA	60,000
Income tax owed	(25,000)
Total estate	495,000
Less spouse exemption	(100,000)
Chargeable estate	395,000

Remember that the ISA exemptions only apply for income tax and capital gains tax.

15

			Amount	
Gift holdover relief			£45,000	
Gain		£11,500		

	£
Proceeds (MV)	98,000
Less cost	(41,500)
Gain before relief	56,500
Gift holdover relief (balancing figure)	(45,000)
Gain = actual proceeds minus original cost £(53,000 − 41,500)	11,500

Section B

Zoyla

16   The disposal of shares in Minor Ltd did not qualifying for business asset disposal relief in the tax year 2021/22 due to

> Holding period

The disposal of shares in Major plc did not qualifying for business asset disposal relief in the tax year 2021/22 due to

> Size of shareholding

A disposal of shares in a company qualifies for business asset disposal relief if the company is the individual's personal company, which is one where the shareholder owns at least 5% of the ordinary share capital of the company, the company is a trading company and the shareholder is an officer or employee of the company. These conditions must be satisfied for at least two years prior to the disposal of the shares.

The shares in Minor Ltd were acquired on 15 August 2020 and disposed of on 20 June 2021 and so the conditions were not satisfied for at least two years.

The shares in Major Ltd were a shareholding of (16,000/2,000,000 × 100) = 0.8% and so Major Ltd was not Zoyla's personal company due to the size of the shareholding.

17   £126,000

Date	Transaction	No. of shares	Cost
			£
15 August 2020	Acquisition	22,500	117,000
12 December 2020	Rights issue 1 new share for every 1 original share held @ £7.40	22,500	166,500
		45,000	283,500
20 June 2021	Sale	(20,000)	(126,000)
c/f		25,000	157,500

18   £154,880

The actual proceeds are £152,000 but this must be compared with the market value of the shares to see if this is a sale at an undervalue. The market value per share is £9.62 + 1/2(9.74 – 9.62) = £9.68. The total market value is therefore £9.68 × 16,000 = £154,880 which is used as the proceeds for capital gains tax purposes.

19   12 months

The date of the CGT liability on the sale of Major Ltd shares on 6 March 2022 (tax year 2021/22) was 31 January 2023. If Zoyla had delayed the sale until 6 April 2022 the disposal would have been in the tax year 2022/23 and so the CGT liability would have been due on 31 January 2024 thus deferring the payment by 12 months.

20   £3,520

	£
Tax saved due to availability of another annual exempt amount: £12,300 × 20%	2,460
Tax saved due to part of the gain being taxed at basic rate instead of higher rate:	
£10,600 × (20% – 10%)	1,060
Total CGT saving	3,520

The answer £1,060 is just the higher rate tax saving. The answer £4,580 uses 20% for both calculations. The answer £2,460 is just the annual exempt amount saving.

Roman and Paris

Workbook references. Inheritance tax is the subject of Chapter 18.

Top tips. A gift of shares in an unquoted company will usually involve a computation of the amount by which the donor's estate decreases as in Question 23. You need to compare the value of the shareholding before the gift and after the gift.

Easy marks. There were easy marks in Question 22 for identifying the persons responsible for paying the inheritance tax on death on the chargeable lifetime transfer and the date of payment.

21   £26,400

		£	£
4 March 2019	Gift	210,000	
	Less: annual exemption 2018/19	(3,000)	
	annual exemption 2017/18 b/f	(3,000)	
	Potentially exempt transfer		204,000
26 August 2019	Gift	190,000	
	Less: annual exemption 2019/20	(3,000)	
	annual exemption 2018/19 b/f	(0)	
	Chargeable lifetime transfer		187,000
7 August 2021	Nil rate band at death	325,000	
	Less PET now chargeable and within seven years of CLT	(204,000)	
	Available nil rate band for CLT	121,000	

	£	£
IHT on CLT:		
£121,000 @ 0%		0
£66,000 @ 40%		26,400
£187,000		26,400

The calculation above is for teaching purposes to show in detail how the computation works. In the exam you could simplify it to:

£((190,000 – 3,000) – (325,000 – (210,000 – 3,000 – 3,000))) @ 40% = £26,400

> **Examining team's comments.** This question caused particular problems. The requirement was to establish how much inheritance tax was payable in respect of a chargeable lifetime transfer as a result of the donor's death. The chargeable lifetime transfer had been preceded by a potentially exempt transfer. In selecting the most popular alternative, candidates failed to take account of the £3,000 annual exemptions which were available. In selecting the second most popular alternative, candidates did not appreciate that the two gifts were made in consecutive tax years, meaning that three annual exemptions were available rather than the two used in this option.
>
> This demonstrates just how careful candidates need to be in using each piece of information given, be it a date, number or fact.

22   The trustees of the trust on 28 February 2022

23   £675,000

	£
Before: 100,000 @ £8	800,000
After: 25,000 @ £5	(125,000)
Transfer of value	675,000

Before the transfer, Paris owned a 100,000/250,000 × 100 = 40% shareholding and after the transfer she owned a 25,000/250,000 × 100 = 10% shareholding.

24   £735

	£
Gifts to same friend exceeding £250 in tax year £(80 + 195)	275
Gift exceeding £250	460
Gifts not covered by small gifts exemption	735

25   Roman's estate £104,000, Paris's estate £336,000

Roman's estate

	£
Death estate	560,000
Less spouse exemption	(300,000)
Chargeable death estate	260,000
Nil rate band used by lifetime transfers	
£260,000 @ 40%	104,000

Paris's estate

	£
Chargeable death estate	840,000
Nil rate band used by lifetime transfer	
£840,000 @ 40%	336,000

There is no exemption for legacies on death to another person other than a spouse or civil partner.

Ardent Ltd

Workbook references. Value added tax is covered in Chapters 24 and 25.

Top tips. In Question 27, note the different time limits for pre-registration input tax to be recovered. The time limit for services is six months before registration but for goods it is four years before registration.

Easy marks. There were easy marks in Question 29 for the filing requirement and date.

26   1 April 2022

	£
January 2022 £(24,800 + 30,100)	54,900
February 2022 £(42,600 + 28,700)	71,300
	126,200

Note that all taxable supplies (here standard rated and zero rated) are taken into account when working out whether the registration threshold has been exceeded.

The registration threshold of £85,000 is exceeded by 28 February 2022. Ardent Ltd should therefore have notified HMRC by 30 March 2022, with registration effective from 1 April 2022.

27   £920

	£
Advertising: £120 × 6 months (max) before registration	720
Computer acquired in four years before registration and still held at registration	200
Input tax reclaimable	920

28   £15,740

	£
Output tax £125,700 @ 20%	25,140
Less input tax £56,400 × 1/6	(9,400)
VAT payable to HMRC	15,740

It is not relevant whether the purchases are still held in inventory.

29   Using Making Tax Digital software by 7 May 2022

30

Period after 31 March 2022	VAT scheme
12 months	Annual accounting

A trader must submit one year's returns on time and pay the VAT shown on them on time in order to break out of the surcharge liability period and the escalation of surcharge percentages.

The annual accounting scheme may help because only one VAT return is required each year so there are fewer occasions to trigger a default surcharge.

Section C

31 Jack

Workbook references. Inheritance tax is the subject of Chapter 18. Pension contributions are covered in Chapter 5. The ISA limits are dealt with in Chapter 2.

Top tips. There are three marks for part (a) so you should be making three relevant points to obtain these marks. It is important to attempt all three parts of the question to gain a reasonable overall mark.

Easy marks. There were some easy marks in part (b)(i) for working out the available annual allowances and in
part (c) for identifying the ISA limits. The basic information required is in the tax rates and allowances provided in the examination.

Examining team's comments. This question proved difficult for many candidates, with some aspects consistently causing problems:

(a)   As regards part (a), long, detailed, computations were often provided when the answer was quite straightforward. For example, the gift would have reduced the taxpayer's death estate by £300,000, so the inheritance tax saving was simply £120,000 (£300,000 at 40%). There was no need for before and after computations.

(b)   As regards part (b), few candidates appreciated that restricting the amount of personal pension contributions to the amount qualifying for tax relief at the higher rate minimises the cost of pension saving because each £100 saved effectively only costs £60 (£100 less 40% tax relief).

(c)   As regards part (c), very few candidates realised that the 30-day period fell into two tax years, so the taxpayer could invest £20,000 by 5 April 2022, and then another £20,000 (using the tax year 2022/23 limit) on or after 6 April 2022.

Marking scheme

			Marks	
(a)	Chargeable lifetime transfer		1	
	No inheritance tax		1	
	Inheritance tax saving		1	
				3
(b)	(i)	Higher rate income	1	
		Available annual allowances	2	
		Minimising cost of pension saving	1	
				4
	(ii)	Unused annual allowances		1
(c)	ISA limits		1	
	Maximum investments		1	
				2
				10

(a)   The gift will be a chargeable lifetime transfer of £294,000 (£300,000 less annual exemptions of £3,000 for 2021/22 and 2020/21).

No lifetime inheritance tax will be payable because this is less than the nil rate band, and if Jack survives for seven years, there will be no additional inheritance tax liability either.

The value of Jack's estate will therefore be reduced by £300,000, which will mean an eventual inheritance tax saving of £120,000 (£300,000 at 40%).

Tutorial note

Although it might itself be fully exempt, the chargeable lifetime transfer will have to be taken into account when calculating any inheritance tax liability arising on any further lifetime transfers which may be made within the following seven years. After seven years, a further gift can be made to a trust.

(b) (i) For 2021/22, £(100,000 – 12,570 – (37,700 + (500 × 12))) = £43,730 of Jack's income is currently taxable at the higher rate of income tax.

This is less than the available annual allowances of £(40,000 × 4 – ((500 × 12) × 4)) = £136,000 for 2021/22.

Restricting the amount of personal pension contributions to the amount qualifying for tax relief at the higher rate will minimise the cost of pension saving because each £100 saved will effectively only cost £60 (£100 less 40% tax relief).

Tutorial notes

1 Unused annual allowances can be carried forward for up to three years.

2 Although Jack's approach to pension saving will maximise the available tax relief, it will mean that some carried forward annual allowances are wasted.

(ii) Jack will have unused allowances of £68,000 being £(40,000 – 6,000) = £34,000 from 2019/20 and the same amount for 2020/21 to carry forward to 2022/23.

Where an annual allowance is exceeded with contributions made in a tax year the current year AA is used first and then the unused AA from the previous three years can be used on a first-in, first out basis. The £44,000 contribution would therefore be set against the 2021/22 AA first and then £10,000 would be used from 2018/19, leaving £34,000 from each of 2019/20 and 2020/21 to carry forward as follows.

Tax year	Annual allowance	Already used (£500 x 12)	Additional contribution in 2021/22	Carry forward to 2022/23
2018/19	£40,000	(£6,000)	(£10,000)	0
2019/20	£40,000	(£6,000)		£34,000
2020/21	£40,000	(£6,000)		£34,000
2021/22	£40,000	(£6,000)	(£34,000)	

(c) Jack can invest in an ISA for 2021/22 by 5 April 2022, and another ISA for 2022/23 between 6 April 2022 and 5 April 2023.

The maximum possible amount which he can invest into stocks and shares ISAs during the next 30 days is therefore £20,000 × 2 = £40,000.

32 Array Ltd

Marking scheme

			Marks
(a)	Form P11D	1	
	Submission deadline	1	
			2
(b)	*Alice*		
	Car benefit percentage	1	
	Car use taxable benefit	2	
	Fuel taxable benefit	1	
	Buma		
	Interest benefit	2	
	Deduction for interest paid by employee	½	
	Claude		
	Mobile phone	1	
	Home entertainment system	1½	
	Denise		
	Relocation costs	1	
	Medical costs	1	
			11
(c)	Class 1A NIC	1	
	Payment date	1	
			2
			15

(a)   Details of employees' taxable benefits are reported to HM Revenue & Customs (HMRC) using a form P11D for each employee.

The P11D submission deadline for 2021/22 is 6 July 2022.

(b)   **Alice**

The relevant percentage for the car benefit is 15% + 10% ((105 − 55)/5) = 25%.

The motor car was available throughout 2021/22, so the taxable benefit is £(24,600 − 5,000) × 25% = £4,900.

The fuel benefit is £(24,600 × 25%) = £6,150.

Tutorial notes

1   The amount of capital contribution which can be used to reduce the list price when calculating a car benefit is restricted to £5,000.

2   The proportion of business mileage is not relevant to the calculation of the car benefit.

Buma

	£
$\dfrac{30,000 + (30,000 - (1,000 \times 12))}{2} \times 2.0\%$	480
Less interest paid	(180)
Taxable benefit	300

Claude

The provision of one mobile telephone does not give rise to a taxable benefit even if the telephone is a smartphone.

The taxable benefit for the use of the home entertainment system is £(3,200 × 20% × 3/12) = £160.

Tutorial note

The home entertainment system has not been given to Claude, so the market value on 5 April 2022 is irrelevant.

Denise

Only £8,000 of the relocation costs is exempt, so the taxable benefit is £(10,400 − 8,000) = £2,400.

The payment of medical costs of up to £500 does not result in a taxable benefit provided the medical treatment is recommended in writing by a medical professional to assist an employee to return to work following a period of absence due to ill-health or injury lasting at least 28 days.

(c)   The employer's Class 1A NIC payable by Array Ltd for 2021/22 is £(4,900 + 6,150 + 300 + 160 + 2,400) = 13,910 @ 13.8%) = £1,920.

If paid electronically, this would have been payable by 22 July 2022.

33 Wretched Ltd

Marking scheme

			Marks
(a)	Company residence		1
(b)	*Trading loss*		
	Pre-trading expenditure	1	
	Deduction for lease premium	1½	
	Capital allowances		
	Additions qualifying for AIA	1	
	AIA	½	
	Motor car [1]	1	
	Motor car [2]	½	
	Motor car [3]	½	
	WDA main pool	1	
	WDA special rate pool	1	
	Property business loss		
	Rent receivable	½	
	Advertising	½	
	Repairs	½	
	Capital loss		
	Proceeds	½	
	Cost	½	
	Indexation allowance	½	
			11

		Marks
(c)	Trading loss relief	1
	Property business loss relief	1
	Capital loss relief	1
		3
		15

(a) Companies which are incorporated in the UK such as Wretched Ltd are resident in the UK regardless of where their central management and control is exercised.

(b) **Wretched Ltd – period ended 31 March 2022**

Trading loss

	£
Trading loss	(140,840)
Advertising expenditure	(7,990)
Deduction for lease premium £(34,440/10) × 8/12	(2,296)
Capital allowances (W)	(4,784)
Revised trading loss	(155,910)

Tutorial note

The advertising expenditure incurred during April 2021 is pre-trading and is treated as incurred on 1 August 2021. It is therefore deductible, and an adjustment is required.

Working

Capital allowances

	FYA	Main pool	Special rate pool	Allowances
	£	£	£	£
Additions qualifying for AIA				
Laptops ((£400 × 3) × 130%	1,560			
FYA @ 130%	(1,560)			1,560
Transfer to pool	0	0		
Additions not qualifying for AIA				
Motor car [1]		8,300		
Motor car [2]		12,300		
Motor car [3]			18,800	
		20,600		
WDA @ 18% × 8/12		(2,472)		2,472
WDA @ 6% × 8/12			(752)	752
TWDVs carried forward		18,128	18,048	
Allowances				4,784

Tutorial notes

1   The original cost of the laptops is irrelevant.

2   Although motor car [1] has zero CO_2 emissions, it is second hand and therefore does not qualify for the 100% first year allowance. It instead qualifies for writing down allowances at the rate of 18%.

3   Motor car [2] has CO_2 emissions between 1 and 50 grams per kilometre and therefore qualifies for writing down allowances at the rate of 18%.

4   Motor car [3] has CO_2 emissions over 50 grams per kilometre and therefore qualifies for writing down allowances at the rate of 6%.

Property business loss

	£
Rent receivable £1,400 × 3	4,200
Less: advertising	(2,100)
repairs	(5,900)
Property business loss	(3,800)

Capital loss

	£
Disposal proceeds	21,400
Less: cost	(26,200)
indexation allowance	(0)
Capital loss	(4,800)

Tutorial note

Where a company makes a capital loss, then no indexation allowance is available because it cannot be used to increase a loss.

(c)   The trading loss of £155,910 will be carried forward and relieved against the total profits of the next accounting period (and then subsequent accounting periods if there is any unrelieved loss). The company can decide how much of the loss is to be relieved in each accounting period.

The property business loss of £3,800 will be carried forward and relieved against total profits in the same way as the trading loss.

The capital loss of £4,800 will be carried forward and relieved against the first available chargeable gains.

BPP
LEARNING
MEDIA

ACCA Applied Skills

Taxation (TX – UK)

Mock Exam 4 (March/June 2021 amended)

Questions	
Time allowed	**3 hours**
This exam is divided into three sections:	
Section A – ALL 15 questions are compulsory and MUST be attempted.	
Section B – ALL 15 questions are compulsory and MUST be attempted.	
Section C – ALL THREE questions are compulsory and MUST be attempted.	

DO NOT OPEN THIS EXAM UNTIL YOU ARE READY TO START UNDER EXAMINATION CONDITIONS

BPP LEARNING MEDIA

Section A – ALL 15 questions are compulsory and MUST be attempted

1   Simon has been a sole trader since 2012, preparing accounts to 30 June each year. In the year to 30 June 2021 he had trading profits of £60,000 and in the year to 30 June 2022 he had trading profits of £66,000.

What is the amount of Class 4 National Insurance Contributions (NIC) that Simon will have to pay for the tax year 2021/22?

£ [   ]

(2 marks)

2   **Which TWO of the following statements about tax appeals are correct?**

☐   The First Tier Tribunal deals with straightforward cases such as the imposition of fixed filing penalties

☐   The Crown Prosecution Service (CPS) conducts tax appeals against taxpayers

☐   The taxpayer must apply for an internal review by HM Revenue and Customs (HMRC) before making an appeal to the Tax Tribunal

☐   The Upper Tribunal hears appeals against decisions of the First Tier Tribunal

(2 marks)

3   Kate sold a flat in November 2021, realising a gain of £31,800. The flat had always been rented out to tenants and was the only chargeable asset that Kate owned. Kate had taxable income of £31,500 in the tax year 2021/22. She made a gross Gift Aid donation of £800 in December 2021.

What is Kate's capital gains tax liability for the tax year 2021/22?

○   £4,840

○   £8,204

○   £3,200

○   £4,760

(2 marks)

4   Melton plc prepared accounts for the 12-month period to 31 July 2021. There will not be a compliance check into this accounting period.

Complete the following sentence about the retention of records for Melton plc by matching the date of retention and the maximum penalty into the relevant target area.

Melton plc will be liable for a penalty of up to [   ] if it does not retain its records until [   ] .

Date of retention	Maximum penalty
31 July 2023	£1,000
31 July 2027	£3,000

(2 marks)

5   Nicola bought a residential property on 6 April 2021. She let it out immediately at an annual rent of £2,000 per month, all of which was received in the tax year 2021/22. Nicola had bought the property using an interest-only mortgage. The interest paid in the tax year 2021/22 was £9,500. She paid £2,400 in the year to a managing agent.

For many years Nicola's only income has been employment income of £60,000.

What is Nicola's additional income tax liability in respect of her property business income in the tax year 2021/22?

○   £8,640

○   £7,700

○   £6,740

○   £4,840   (2 marks)

---

6   Shona had always been resident in the UK before the tax year 2021/22. She spent more than 90 days in the UK in every tax year up to 2021/22.

Shona's only relative is her father who is UK resident in 2021/22. Shona owns a house in the UK which is available to her for the whole of 2021/22. On 6 April 2021, Shona bought an overseas house where she spent 260 days during 2021/22. She lived in her UK house for the remaining 105 days. Shona is neither employed nor self-employed.

How many ties does Shona have with the UK for the tax year 2021/22 for the purposes of the sufficient ties test for UK residence?

[▼]

Pull down list:

One
Two
Three   (2 marks)
Four

---

7   Ronald is self-employed. He purchased a house and lived in it for two years. The house was then unoccupied for five years because Ronald went to work outside the UK. He then lived in the house for three years. Ronald then went to live with his mother and the house was unoccupied for six and a half years. Finally, Ronald lived in the house for the last six months of his ownership.

How many months of Ronald's 17-year period of ownership of the house will be exempt for the purposes of private residence relief?

○   66 months

○   150 months

○   153 months

○   165 months   (2 marks)

8   Charlotte's tax payable for the tax years 2020/21 and 2021/22 is as follows:

	2020/21	2021/22
	£	£
Income tax on trading income	9,000	10,600
Class 2 NIC	159	159
Class 4 NIC	1,350	1,800
Capital gains tax	1,750	4,970

Charlotte made the appropriate payments on account on 31 January 2022 and 31 July 2022.

What is the amount payable due on 31 January 2023 in respect of the tax year 2021/22?

○   £2,050

○   £7,179

○   £7,020

○   £5,270   (2 marks)

---

9   On 1 December 2022, Devonte was issued by HM Revenue & Customs (HMRC) with a notice to file his tax return for the tax year 2021/22. Devonte submitted his return online on 20 February 2023. HMRC wishes to conduct a compliance check into this return.

Complete the following sentence about the submission of the online return and the date by which HMRC will have to notify Devonte of a compliance check into the return by matching the date of submission of the tax return and the date of notification of the compliance check into the relevant target area.

The due date for the submission of the return was [   ] and HMRC must

notify Devonte by [   ] of a compliance check into the return.

20 February 2024	28 February 2023
31 January 2023	28 February 2024
31 January 2024	30 April 2023

                                                                        (2 marks)

---

10   Caster plc sold the whole of its 4% shareholding in Antics Ltd on 15 November 2021. Caster plc had purchased 10,000 shares in Antics Ltd on 16 July 2010 for £20,000. There was a 1 for 2 rights issue at £2.50 per share in December 2017 and Caster plc took up all its rights.

The indexation factor between July 2010 and December 2017 was 0.190.

What is the indexed cost of the shares sold in November 2021?

£ [   ]   (2 marks)

11 On 12 August 2017, Patience made a gross chargeable transfer (after all exemptions) of £175,000. On 24 November 2021 she gave £180,000 to a trust. Patience agreed to pay any lifetime inheritance tax (IHT) due.

How much IHT will be payable by Patience on the November 2021 transfer of value?

○   £6,000

○   £4,800

○   £7,500

○   £4,500   (2 marks)

---

12 Alberto died on 3 September 2021. His only asset was his main residence valued at £525,000 which he left to his daughter. Alberto had made a potentially exempt transfer (after all exemptions) of £40,000 in July 2019. He had been divorced for several years.

What is the inheritance tax (IHT) liability on Alberto's death estate?

○   £26,000

○   £10,000

○   £96,000

○   £0   (2 marks)

---

13 Rebecca started trading on 1 January 2020 and her taxable turnover for the first 12 months of trading was £5,500 a month.

For the first seven months of 2021 her taxable turnover was as follows:

	£
January 2021	8,100
February 2021	8,300
March 2021	8,400
April 2021	9,200
May 2021	9,500
June 2021	10,300
July 2021	10,600

What was the date by which Rebecca must have notified HM Revenue & Customs (HMRC) that she was liable to be registered for value added tax (VAT)?

[▼]

Pull down list:

30 June 2021
30 July 2021
30 August 2021
30 September 2021   (2 marks)

---

14 **Which TWO of the following are required for a full value added tax (VAT) invoice to be valid?**

☐ Customer's VAT registration number

☐ Supplier's email address

☐ Date of invoice

☐ Total invoice price excluding VAT   (2 marks)

15 Wogan Ltd started trading on 1 April 2020 and made a trading loss of £70,000 in the year ended 31 March 2021. It had no other income or gains in the accounting period and made no qualifying charitable donations.

In the year ended 31 March 2022, Wogan Ltd had the following taxable total profits:

	£
Trading profits	50,000
Chargeable gain	1,800
Total profits	51,800
Less: qualifying charitable donation	(1,500)
Taxable total profits	50,300

Assuming that Wogan Ltd uses its trading loss in the most tax efficient manner, what is the company's unused trading loss carried forward at 1 April 2022?

○ £19,700

○ £20,000

○ £21,500

○ £18,200   (2 marks)

                                                          (Total = 30 marks)

Section B – ALL 15 questions are compulsory and MUST be attempted

Jaquetta

The following scenario relates to Questions 16 to 20.

Jaquetta started in business as a sole trader on 1 February 2007. She prepared accounts to 30 September each year and had overlap profits on commencement of £1,800.

On 31 December 2021, Jaquetta sold her business to Richard. Her results to the date of cessation **after** capital allowances were as follows:

	£
Year ended 30 September 2020	48,000
Year ended 30 September 2021	36,000
Period ended 31 December 2021	6,000

Jaquetta had a main pool for capital allowances with a tax written-down value of £8,600 at 1 October 2021. She purchased a car with emissions of 35g CO_2/km on 15 October 2021 at a cost of £900.

Jaquetta sold the following assets of her business to Richard on 31 December 2021:

	Proceeds	Cost
	£	£
Goodwill	15,000	0
Plant and machinery in main pool	7,800	13,690
Freehold shop	50,000	43,000

Jaquetta had no other chargeable assets and had property business income in addition to her trading income such that she was a higher rate taxpayer in 2021/22.

Richard commenced trading on 1 January 2022 and will prepare accounts to 30 June each year, the first accounts being prepared for the 18-month period to 30 June 2023.

Richard anticipates that he will have a trading loss for the tax year 2022/23. He was previously employed with employment income of at least £50,000 each tax year since 2013/14.

16 **What is the amount of trading income assessable on Jaquetta for the tax year 2021/22?**

£ _____

(2 marks)

17 **What balancing allowance was deducted from Jaquetta's trading profits for the period ended 31 December 2021?**

○ £656

○ £1,700

○ £764

○ £1,624

(2 marks)

18   What is Jaquetta's capital gains tax liability for the tax year 2021/22?

    ○   £1,940

    ○   £381

    ○   £970

    ○   £2,200   (2 marks)

---

19   Complete the following sentence about Richard's basis period for the tax year 2022/23 by matching the start date of the basis period and the end date of the basis period into the relevant target area.

Richard's basis period for the tax year 2022/23 will start on [   ] and end

on [   ] .

1 January 2022	6 April 2022
1 July 2022	31 December 2022
5 April 2023	30 June 2023

(2 marks)

---

20   **Which TWO of the following are possible uses by Richard of his trading loss for the tax year 2022/23?**

    ☐   Early years loss relief against general income in 2019/20, 2020/21 and 2021/22 in that order

    ☐   Carry forward against general income in 2023/24

    ☐   Early years loss relief against general income in 2021/22, 2020/21 and 2019/20 in that order

    ☐   Against general income in 2021/22 and/or 2022/23   (2 marks)

(Total = 10 marks)

Diggory Ltd

The following scenario relates to Questions 21 to 25.

Diggory Ltd is a manufacturing company which owns 78% of another manufacturing company, Chang Ltd. Both companies have been registered for value added tax (VAT) for many years. The companies do not currently have a group registration. Both only make standard-rated supplies.

The following information is available in respect of Diggory Ltd's value added tax (VAT) for the quarter ended 31 December 2021:

(1)   Output VAT of £36,500 has been charged in respect of sales. This figure includes output VAT of £700 where an invoice was issued on 2 January 2022 for goods supplied on 29 December 2021 and output VAT of £500 where an invoice was issued on 24 December 2021 for goods supplied on 5 January 2022.

(2)   In addition to the above, Diggory Ltd also charged output VAT of £460 on sales to Chang Ltd.

(3)   Input VAT included the following:

	£
Entertaining UK customers	210
Entertaining overseas customers	330
Redecorating a room in the managing director's house	500
Building a wall around Diggory Ltd's car park	2,300

In the quarter to 31 March 2022, Diggory Ltd supplied goods to a customer in another country which operates a valued added tax on certain goods. The goods had a VAT-exclusive price of £1,200. The rate of VAT in the other country on the goods supplied is 15%. Diggory Ltd has evidence of the export in the form required by HM Revenue and Customs.

Diggory Ltd is considering expanding its business. It will either acquire part of the business of a sole trader, John, or will acquire 100% of the shares in Downs Ltd. Both John and Downs Ltd are registered for VAT. Downs Ltd makes largely zero-rated supplies.

If Diggory Ltd acquires part of the business of John, this will satisfy the requirements to be a transfer of a going concern. John will continue to run the remainder of his business.

Diggory Ltd is considering entering into a group registration.

21   **What is the amount of output VAT should be charged on the sales in (1) and (2) for the quarter to 31 December 2021?**

○   £36,960

○   £36,260

○   £35,300

○   £35,760   (2 marks)

---

22   **What is the amount of input VAT recoverable on the expenses in (3) for the quarter to 31 December 2021?**

○   £2,300

○   £330

○   £2,630

○   £3,130   (2 marks)

---

23   What is the amount of VAT that Diggory Ltd will charge on the sale of the goods to the customer in another country?

○   £180

○   £0

○   £240

○   £200   (2 marks)

24   Which TWO of the following statements about Diggory Ltd's acquisition of part of the business of John as a transfer of a going concern are correct?

☐   Diggory Ltd will automatically be liable for any outstanding VAT penalties incurred by John in respect of the part of the business acquired

☐   The acquisition of the part of the business of John is outside the scope of VAT

☐   If the VAT chargeable on the acquisition is less than £1,000 it need not be paid

☐   John will not need to register again for VAT   (2 marks)

25   Which TWO of the following statements about Diggory Ltd group's possible VAT group registration are correct?

☐   The Diggory Ltd group must appoint one of the group companies to be a representative member which is solely liable for paying the group VAT liability

☐   Downs Ltd should not be included in the group registration because it is largely making zero-rated supplies

☐   Supplies of services by Diggory Ltd to Chang Ltd will be disregarded for VAT purposes if they are both within the group registration

☐   Each of the companies in the Diggory Ltd group will have to make separate VAT returns   (2 marks)

(Total = 10 marks)

Christophe

The following scenario relates to Questions 26 to 30.

You should assume that the current date is 22 April 2022.

On 10 December 2018, Christophe was appointed as a director of an investment company, Custard Ltd, and he acquired a 3% shareholding of the company at a cost of £10 per share. On 5 April 2021, he acquired a further 48% shareholding in Custard Ltd at a cost of £80 per share.

Due to unexpected ill-health, Christophe wished to reduce his involvement in Custard Ltd and on 1 April 2022, he resigned his directorship and gave a 49% shareholding in Custard Ltd to his son, Dexter.

The values of the shares on 1 April 2022 were as follows:

Shareholding	Value per share
%	£
51 – 75	120
26 – 50	90
1 – 25	30

Custard Ltd has always had 10,000 shares in issue. Christophe has no other chargeable assets.

Christophe has been told by a friend that he ought to have waited until 6 April 2022 to make the gift of the Custard Ltd shares to Dexter as this would have been beneficial for capital gains tax (CGT). If Christophe had delayed the gift until 6 April 2022, the values of the shares in Custard Ltd would have been the same as on 1 April 2022.

Christophe is considering making regular payments of £250 to his granddaughter each month, starting on 30 April 2022, to cover some of her living costs while she is at university. He will not make any other gifts in the tax year 2022/23. You have advised Christophe that the gifts to his granddaughter will be exempt from inheritance tax (IHT).

The following information is available about the income and expenses of Christophe:

Tax year	Gross income	Expenses
	£	£
2021/22	60,000	25,000
2022/23	20,000	18,000

Christophe was married to Leah for many years. Leah died in March 2009 and in her will she left her estate of £250,000 to Christophe. The IHT nil rate band in 2008/09 was £312,000. Leah had made a potentially exempt transfer of £20,000 (after all exemptions) to her sister in August 2005.

Assume the tax rates and allowances in 2021/22 also apply in future years.

26 **What is the IHT transfer of value made by Christophe on 1 April 2022?**

£ _____

(2 marks)

27   What is Christophe's gain chargeable to CGT on 1 April 2022?

    ○   £216,176

    ○   £56,000

    ○   £70,000

    ○   £69,176

(2 marks)

28   Which TWO of the following statements about the CGT advantages of Christophe delaying his gift until 6 April 2022 are correct?

    ☐   He would have been able to set the annual exempt amounts for both 2021/22 and 2022/23 against the chargeable gain

    ☐   Payment of the CGT liability would have been postponed for 12 months

    ☐   He would have been chargeable to CGT at 10% instead of 20% on some of the taxable gain

    ☐   He would have been entitled to business asset disposal relief on the disposal

(2 marks)

29   Which one of the following IHT exemptions applies to the gifts made by Christophe to his granddaughter?

    ○   Normal expenditure out of income exemption

    ○   Small gifts exemption

    ○   Annual exemption 2022/23

    ○   Annual exemption 2021/22

(2 marks)

30   What amount of Leah's unused nil rate band can Christophe's personal representatives claim to reduce the IHT payable on his death?

    ○   £260,417

    ○   £292,000

    ○   £304,167

    ○   £308,333

(2 marks)

(Total = 10 marks)

Section C – ALL three questions are compulsory and MUST be attempted

31 (September/December 2019)

This scenario relates to four requirements.

You should assume that today's date is 4 April 2021.

On 2 April 2021, Kagan inherited some quoted ordinary shares valued at £510,000 following the death of his aunt. Kagan is unsure whether to retain the shares or sell some of them in order to make some alternative investments.

Kagan is aged 61 and is an additional rate taxpayer. Prior to the inheritance, his taxable income, consisting entirely of employment income, for the tax year 2021/22 would have been £400,000. The income tax liability on this income for the tax year 2021/22 would have been £165,000.

Prior to receiving the inheritance, Kagan's chargeable estate for inheritance tax (IHT) purposes was valued at £1,700,000. IHT of £550,000 would be payable were he to die in the near future.

Retain the inherited shares

If Kagan simply retains the inherited shares, then he will receive dividend income of £15,300 during the tax year 2021/22. This is in addition to his employment income of £400,000.

Sell some inherited shares and make four alternative investments

Kagan is considering selling some of his inherited shares (for which there has only been a minimal increase in value since he inherited them) to fund the following four investments, all of which will be made at the start of the tax year 2021/22:

(1)   Kagan will make a gross personal pension contribution of £100,000. Kagan is a member of a pension scheme but has not made any contributions in recent years because his income has been substantially lower than it is for the tax year 2021/22. Kagan will immediately withdraw £25,000 of the pension fund tax free. This is the permitted 25% tax-free lump sum. However, no pension will be taken during the tax year 2021/22.

(2)   Kagan will invest £50,000 in premium bonds. The expected amount of premium bond prizes which will be received during the tax year 2021/22 is £700.

(3)   Kagan will invest the maximum permitted amount of £20,000 in a cash individual savings account (ISA). This ISA will pay interest of £400 during the tax year 2021/22.

(4)   Kagan will purchase a freehold property for £295,000 (including all costs of purchase). The property will be let out unfurnished, with Kagan receiving property income of £9,600 during the tax year 2021/22.

After making these four investments, Kagan will be left with £65,000 of inherited shares, on which he will receive dividend income of £1,950 during the tax year 2021/22. He will also have his employment income of £400,000.

Kagan will not make any other disposals during the tax year 2021/22.

Required

(a)   Calculate Kagan's revised income tax liability for the tax year 2021/22 if he retains the inherited shares.

(1 mark)

(b)   (i)   Explain why little or no capital gains tax (CGT) will be payable if Kagan sells some of his inherited shares.

(1 mark)

        (ii)   Calculate Kagan's revised income tax liability for the tax year 2021/22 if he sells some of his inherited shares and makes the four alternative investments.

Notes

1 For this part of the question, you are expected to produce a full income tax computation.

2 You should indicate by use of zero (0) any items which are not taxable. **(6 marks)**

(c) For each of the four alternative investments (pension contribution, premium bonds, ISA and freehold property) state whether the investment will reduce Kagan's potential IHT liability compared to him retaining the inherited shares.

Note. For this part of the question, no computations are required. **(2 marks)**

(Total = 10 marks)

32 Robinette (September/December 2019)

This scenario relates to three requirements.

Robinette ceased self-employment on 30 June 2021. She was then employed by Bird plc for the six-month period from 1 August 2021 to 31 January 2022. Robinette commenced self-employment again, in a new business, on 1 February 2022.

Self-employment ceasing on 30 June 2021

(1) Robinette's trading profit for the final 14-month period of trading from 1 May 2020 to 30 June 2021 was £106,900. This figure is **before** taking account of capital allowances.

(2) The tax written down value of the capital allowances main pool at 1 May 2020 was £15,300. On 11 June 2020 Robinette purchased a laptop computer for £2,600.

On the cessation of trading, Robinette personally retained the laptop computer. Its value on 30 June 2021 was £1,750. The remaining items included in the main pool were sold for £7,300 on 30 June 2021.

(3) Robinette had unused overlap profits brought forward of £22,700.

Employment from 1 August 2021 to 31 January 2022

(1) During the six-month period from 1 August 2021 to 31 January 2022, Robinette was paid a gross monthly salary of £10,600 in respect of her employment with Bird plc.

(2) Throughout the period from 1 August 2021 to 31 January 2022, Bird plc provided Robinette with living accommodation. The property was rented by Bird plc at a cost of £690 per month (this is higher than the annual value of the property). Bird plc also paid for the running costs relating to the property, and for the period 1 August 2021 to 31 January 2022 these amounted to £1,440.

(3) Throughout the period from 1 August 2021 to 31 January 2022, Robinette's two-year old son was provided with a place at Bird plc's workplace nursery. The total cost to the company of providing this nursery place was £4,800 (120 days at £40 per day).

(4) Robinette used her private motor car for business purposes. During the period from 1 August 2021 to 31 January 2022, she drove 5,200 miles in the performance of her duties for Bird plc, for which the company paid an allowance of 35 pence per mile.

Self-employment from 1 February 2022

(1) Robinette's trading profit for the first five-month period of trading from 1 February to 30 June 2022 was £55,700. This figure is **before** taking account of capital allowances.

(2) The only item of plant and machinery owned by Robinette, and used in this business, is office equipment which was purchased for £26,200 on 1 February 2022.

Property income

(1) During the period 1 August 2021 to 31 January 2022, Robinette let out her main residence at a monthly rent of £1,100. Robinette lived in this property up to 31 July 2021 and then again from 1 February 2022 onwards.

(2) The only expenditure incurred by Robinette in respect of the letting was property insurance, which cost £624 for the year ended 5 April 2022.

(3) Robinette has opted to calculate her property income using the accruals basis. Rent-a-room relief is not available in respect of the letting.

Self-assessment tax return

Robinette filed for her self-assessment tax return for the tax year 2021/22 on 14 August 2022. She is quite confident that all of her income for the tax year 2021/22 was correctly declared and that no deductions were incorrectly claimed.

Required

(a)   Calculate Robinette's taxable income for the tax year 2021/22.   **(12 marks)**

Note. You should indicate by the use of zero (0) any items which are not taxable or deductible.

(b)   (i)   State the period during which HM Revenue and Customs (HMRC) will have to notify Robinette if they intend to carry out a compliance check in respect of her self-assessment tax return for the tax year 2021/22, and the likely reason why such a check would be made.   **(2 marks)**

        (ii)   Advise Robinette as to how long she must retain the records used in preparing her self- assessment tax return for the tax year 2021/22.   **(1 mark)**

(Total = 15 marks)

33 Maison Ltd

This scenario relates to one requirement.

You are a trainee Chartered Certified Accountant dealing with the tax affairs of Maison Ltd.

Your assistant has prepared a partly completed draft corporation tax computation for the year ended 31 March 2022. All of your assistant's workings for the figures provided are correct, but there are four uncompleted sections, all related to property, which your assistant does not know how to deal with.

The assistant's corporation tax computation, along with references to the uncompleted sections (with missing figures indicated by a question mark (?)), is shown below:

Maison Ltd – Corporation tax computation for the year ended 31 March 2022

	Uncompleted section	£
Operating profit		892,900
Non-deductible expenditure		22,340
Deduction for lease premium	1	?
Capital allowances	2	?
Trading profit		?
Property business income	3	?
Loan interest receivable		1,460
Chargeable gains	4	?
Taxable total profits		?
Corporation tax		?

Uncompleted section 1 – Deduction for lease premium

Your assistant has identified that on 1 January 2022, Maison Ltd acquired a leasehold office building, paying a premium of £44,000 for the grant of a 12-year lease. The office building was used for business purposes by Maison Ltd throughout the period 1 January to 31 March 2022.

Uncompleted section 2 – Capital allowances

Your assistant has correctly calculated that capital allowances of £12,037 are available on the main pool. However, she is unsure of the amounts of capital allowance and structures and buildings allowance which are available in respect of the £140,000 spent by Maison Ltd during November 2021 constructing an extension which is adjacent to the company's existing freehold office building. The extension is used by the company's employees as a staff room and was ready for use on 1 December 2021. The total cost of £140,000 is made up as follows:

Integral to the building	£
Building costs of extension	93,300
Ventilation system	6,700
Heating system	3,900
Not integral to the building	
Furniture and furnishings	33,500
Refrigerator and microwave cooker	2,600
Total cost	140,000

Uncompleted section 3 – Property business income

On 1 July 2021, Maison Ltd purchased a freehold warehouse. The warehouse is currently surplus to requirements, so it was let out from 1 November 2021. However, the warehouse was purchased in a dilapidated state and could not be let until repair work was carried out during August 2021. This fact was represented by a reduced purchase price. Your assistant has listed any income and expenditure that is potentially relevant:

Date received/(paid)		£
1 July 2021	Insurance for the period to 31 March 2022	(1,035)
August 2021	Initial repairs	(17,680)
28 September 2021	Advertising for tenants	(780)
1 November 2021	Security deposit of two months' rent	12,200
1 November 2021	Rent for the quarter ended 31 January 2022	18,300
1 February 2022	Rent for the quarter ended 30 April 2022	18,300

Uncompleted section 4 – Chargeable gains

Maison Ltd disposed of two investment properties during August 2021, both resulting in gains. Your assistant has correctly calculated the gains but is unsure of the amount of indexation allowance available. The assistant's workings are as follows:

	Date	First property £	Second property £
Disposal proceeds	August 2021	237,000	143,000
Cost	April 2009	(101,000)	(117,000)
Enhancement expenditure	May 2018	(26,200)	0
Gain		109,800	26,000

Indexation factors are:

April 2009 to December 2017	0.315

No rollover relief claim is possible in respect of these gains.

Required

Prepare a completed version of Maison Ltd's corporation tax computation for the year ended 31 March 2022 after dealing with the sections uncompleted by your assistant.

Notes

1   Your computation should commence with the operating profit figure of £892,900, and you should indicate by the use of zero (0) any items which are not included in your calculation.

2   In calculating the operating profit figure of £892,900, no deduction has been made for the lease premium (uncompleted section 1) or any capital allowances (uncompleted section 2). It also does not include any income or expenditure in relation to property business income (uncompleted section 3) or any chargeable gains in relation to the disposal of the two investment properties (uncompleted section 4).

(Total = 15 marks)

Answers

A plan of attack

If this were the real Taxation (TX – UK) exam and you had been told to turn over and begin, what would be going through your mind?

Perhaps you're having a panic. You've spent most of your study time on income tax and corporation tax computations (because that's what your tutor/BPP Workbook told you to do), plus a selection of other topics, and you're really not sure that you know enough. So, calm down. Spend the first few moments or so **looking at the exam** and develop a **plan of attack**.

Looking through the exam.

Section A contains **15 Objective Test (OT) questions** each worth **2 marks**. These will cover all sections of the syllabus. Some you may find easy and some more difficult. In Question 2, where you are asked to identify the true statement, read the possible answers at least twice before you decide which one to select. Don't spend a lot of time on anything you really don't know. For multiple choice questions you are not penalised for wrong answers, so you should answer all of them. If all else fails – guess!

Section B contains **three OT Case** scenarios. These each have **five questions** each worth **2 marks**. Make sure you read the scenario carefully before you start to answer the OTQs.

- **Questions 16 to 20** test your knowledge of trading income taking in basis periods, balancing adjustments and losses. Question 20 is a relatively quick question as you don't need to do any calculations.

- **Questions 21 to 25** concern VAT for companies in a small group. Make sure to double check your calculations to avoid losing marks for simple mistakes. A couple of knowledge questions with no calculations should save you some time here.

- **Questions 26 to 30** are about inheritance tax (IHT). Read the questions carefully to make sure you answer the question set. For example, in Question 26 you are considering IHT and in Q27 CGT on the same gift.

In **Section C** you have **three constructed response (long) questions**:

- **Question 31** for **10 marks** is about the income tax implications of making various investments. The question demonstrates that sometimes you can quickly identify the extra income tax due without the need for a whole computation, whereas in other situations the whole computation is required.

- **Question 32** for **15 marks** looks at taxable income and also deals with trading and employment income. In a large computation like this there will always be some harder areas - you must focus on getting the easier marks and not worry too much about the more complicated bits.

- **Question 33** for **15 marks** is a corporation tax question dealing with an incomplete draft computation.

Allocating your time

BPP's advice is always allocate your time **according to the marks for the question** in total and for the parts of the question. But **use common sense**. If you're confronted by an OTQ on a topic of which you know nothing, pick an answer and move on. Use the time to pick up marks elsewhere.

After the exam…**Forget about it!**

And don't worry if you found the exam difficult. More than likely other candidates will too. If this were the real thing you would need to **forget** the exam the minute you left the exam hall and **think about the next one**. Or, if it's the last one, **celebrate!**

Section A

1   £3,858

	£
£(60,000 − 50,270) = 9,730 × 2%	195
£(50,270 − 9,568) = 40,702 × 9%	3,663
Class 4 contributions	3,858

Class 4 NICs are based on the trading profits for the period of account ending in the tax year.

2   The First Tier Tribunal deals with straightforward cases such as the imposition of fixed filing penalties

The Upper Tribunal hears appeals against decisions of the First Tier Tribunal

HMRC conducts tax appeals against taxpayers. The CPS provides legal advice and institutes and conducts criminal prosecutions in England and Wales where there has been an investigation by HMRC.

The taxpayer does not have to use the internal review procedure before making an appeal to the Tax Tribunal.

3   £4,760

	£
Chargeable gain	31,800
Less annual exempt amount	(12,300)
Taxable gains	19,500
Tax	
£((37,700 + 800) − 31,500) = 7,000 × 18%	1,260
£(19,500 − 7,000) = 12,500 × 28%	3,500
Total capital gains tax	4,760

The residential property rates apply.

The answer £4,840 does not adjust for Gift Aid. The answer £8,204 does not deduct the annual exempt amount. The answer £3,200 uses the rates of 10% and 20% which apply to other assets.

4   Melton plc will be liable for a penalty of up to £3,000 if it does not retain its records until 31 July 2027 .

5   £6,740

	£
Rent received	24,000
Less: Agent's fees	(2,400)
Property business income	21,600

	£
£21,600 × 40%	8,640
Less: finance costs tax reducer £9,500 × 20%	(1,900)
Income tax liability on property business income	6,740

The answer £8,640 does not make any adjustment for the finance costs. The answer £7,700 does not deduct the agent's fees in the computation of property business income. The answer £4,840 allows full deduction of the finance costs in the property business income computation.

6   Two

The two ties are: available accommodation in the UK, in which she spends at least one night in the tax year, and more than 90 days spent in the UK in either or both of the previous two tax years.

Shona's father is not treated as close family (not a spouse/civil partner or child under the age of 18) so that tie does not apply. She does not have substantive UK work. She is not present in the UK at midnight for at least an equal number of days in the tax year as in any other country.

7   153 months

	Exempt months	Chargeable months	Total months
Actual occupation	24		24
Deemed occupation – up to 4 years self-employed overseas, plus 1 year any reason	60		60
Actual occupation	36		36
Deemed occupation – remaining 2 years up to 3 years any reason	24		24
Unoccupied		51	51
Last 9 months of ownership	9	—	9
Totals	153	51	204

The answer 66 months is the actual occupation. The answer 150 months ignores the last 9 months of ownership rule and only gives 6 months of actual occupation. The answer 165 months treats the overseas period as fully exempt – this only applies if the taxpayer is employed (rather than self-employed) outside the UK.

8   £7,179

	£
Income tax £(10,600 – 9,000 payments on account)	1,600
Class 2 NIC	159
Class 4 NIC £(1,800 – 1,350 payments on account)	450
Capital gains tax	4,970
Amount payable on 31 January 2023 for 2021/22	7,179

There are no payments on account for Class 2 NIC or capital gains tax.

The answer £2,050 is just the income tax and the Class 4 NIC. The answer £7,020 ignores the Class 2 NIC. The answer £5,270 treats the Class 2 NIC and the capital gains tax as having payments on account.

9   The due date for the submission of the return was [28 February 2023] and HMRC must

notify Devonte by [20 February 2024] of a compliance check into the return.

The notice to file a return was issued after 31 October 2022 so the due filing date was the last day of the three-month period starting with the issue. Because the return was made on or before the due date, the date for notification of the compliance check is the first anniversary of the actual filing date.

10   £36,300

	£
July 2010 shares	20,000
Add: indexation to December 2017	
0.190 × £20,000	3,800
December 2017 shares	
10,000/2 × £2.50	12,500
Total indexed cost	36,300

Indexation is frozen at December 2017 so there is no further indexation allowance on either the original shares or the rights issue shares.

11   £6,000

	£
Gift	180,000
Less AE × 2 (2021/22 and 2020/21 b/f)	(6,000)
	174,000
Less nil rate band available £(325,000 − 175,000)	(150,000)
	24,000
IHT @ $^{20}/_{80}$	6,000

The answer £4,800 uses the rate of 20%. The answer £7,500 does not deduct the annual exemptions. The answer £4,500 deducts annual exemptions again from the brought forward transfer.

12   £26,000

	£
£175,000 @ 0% (residence nil rate band)	0
£285,000 @ 0% (£(325,000 − 40,000) nil rate band)	0
£ 65,000 @ 40%	26,000
£525,000	26,000

The residence nil rate band is the lower of the maximum (2021/22) of £175,000 and the value of the main residence.

The answer £10,000 applies the full nil rate band. The answer £96,000 does not apply the residence nil rate band. The answer £0 assumes that the residence nil rate band is £525,000 and so there is no liability on the estate.

Since Alberto was divorced there can be no transfer of the residence nil rate band nor the nil rate band between spouses.

13 30 July 2021

Rebecca was required to notify HMRC within 30 days of exceeding the £85,000 registration threshold ie 30 July 2021 (30 days after the year to 30 June 2021 when her cumulative 12-month turnover was £86,800).

14 Date of invoice

Total invoice price excluding VAT

The customer's VAT registration number is not required, only the supplier's VAT registration number. The supplier must give a business name and address but is not required to give an email address.

15 £19,700

	£
Loss brought forward	70,000
Used in y/e 31.3.22	(50,300)
Loss carried forward at 1.4.22	19,700

The loss brought forward is set against total profits but the claim can be restricted to leave total profits of £1,500 in charge to preserve tax relief on the qualifying charitable donation.

The answer £20,000 sets the brought forward loss against trading profits only. The answer £21,500 sets the brought forward loss against trading profits only but restricts the loss used to leave trading profits in charge to cover the qualifying charitable donation. The answer £18,200 does not restrict the claim to leave total profits in charge to cover the qualifying charitable donation.

Section B

Jaquetta

16   £40,200

	£
Y/e 30.9.21	36,000
P/e 31.12.21	6,000
Less overlap profits	(1,800)
Trading income	40,200

17   £1,700

	Main pool
	£
TWDV b/f	8,600
Addition	900
	9,500
Disposal	(7,800)
Balancing allowance	1,700

There is no annual investment allowance or writing down allowance in the period to cessation.

The answer £656 gives an annual investment allowance of £900 and 12-month writing down allowance of £144 so the balance of the pool is £656. The answer £764 gives an annual investment allowance of £900 and 3-month writing down allowance of £36 so the balance of the pool is £764. The answer £1,624 gives just a 3-month writing down allowance of £76 so the balance of the pool is £1,624.

18   £970

	£
Goodwill £(15,000 − 0)	15,000
Plant and machinery	0
Freehold shop £(50,000 − 43,000)	7,000
	22,000
Less annual exempt amount	(12,300)
Taxable gains	9,700
CGT @ 10% (business asset disposal relief applies)	970

As the plant and machinery on which capital allowances have been obtained are sold at a loss, the result is no gain and no loss. This is because relief for the loss has already been given through the capital allowances computation.

The answer £1,940 uses the 20% rate. The answer £381 deducts the loss on the plant and machinery. The answer £2,200 does not deduct the annual exempt amount.

19   Richard's basis period for the tax year 2022/23 will start on [6 April 2022] and end

on [5 April 2023].

The tax year 2022/23 is Richard's second year of trading. There is no period of account ending in that tax year so the basis period is the tax year itself.

20   Early years loss relief against general income in 2019/20, 2020/21 and 2021/22 in that order

Against general income in 2021/22 and/or 2022/23

Carry forward loss relief is against trading income of the same trade.

Early years loss relief is against earlier years before later years.

Diggory Ltd

21   £36,260

	£
Output VAT	
Sales £(36,500 – 700)	35,800
Sale to Chang Ltd (no group registration)	460
Output VAT	36,260

The tax point for the goods supplied on 29 December 2021 is 2 January 2022 (invoice within 14 days) and so the output tax is not due for payment in the 31 December 2021 quarter. However, the tax point for the goods supplied on 5 January 2022 is the issue of the invoice on 24 December 2021 and so no adjustment is needed for this supply.

The answer £36,960 does not adjust for the 29 December 2021 supply. The answer £35,300 omits the sales to Chang Ltd and adjusts for both the 24 and 29 December 2021 supplies. The answer £35,760 adjusts for the 24 and 29 December 2021 supplies.

22   £2,630

	£
Entertaining UK customers	0
Entertaining overseas customers	330
Redecoration	0
Wall	2,300
	2,630

Input VAT on business entertaining is only recoverable if it relates to the cost of entertaining overseas customers. No input tax is recoverable on expenditure on domestic accommodation for directors. There is no distinction between capital and revenue expenditure for VAT so input tax is recoverable on the building of the new wall (capital).

The answer £2,300 disallows all the input VAT except on the wall. The answer £330 disallows all the input VAT except on the overseas entertaining. The answer £3,130 disallows UK customer entertaining only.

23   £0

Diggory Ltd will charge VAT at zero rate because there is general zero-rating where a UK VAT registered trader exports goods.

The answer £180 charges VAT at the rate in the other country – this is not relevant for UK VAT. The answer £240 charges the supply at the UK standard rate. The answer £200 treats the supply as VAT-inclusive and charges the supply at the UK standard rate.

24   The acquisition of the business of John is outside the scope of VAT

John will not need to register again for VAT

Diggory Ltd is not taking over the registration of John and so is not liable for his VAT penalties and John will not have to re-register for VAT.

The rule that if the VAT chargeable is less than £1,000 it need not be paid applies on deregistration.

25   Downs Ltd should not be included in the group registration because it is largely making zero-rated supplies.

This is because Downs Ltd is in a repayment position and will continue to benefit from cash flow repayments by completing monthly VAT returns.

Supplies of services by Diggory Ltd to Chang Ltd will be disregarded for VAT purposes if they are both within the group registration.

All members of the Diggory Ltd group will be jointly and severally liable for any VAT due from the representative member.

The Diggory Ltd group will make one VAT return.

Christophe

26   £606,000

	£
Before: (3% + 48%) = 51% 5,100 shares @ £120	612,000
After: (51% – 49%) = 2% 200 shares @ £30	(6,000)
Transfer of value	606,000

27   £69,176

	£
Proceeds (49%) 4,900 shares @ £90 per share	441,000
Less cost (W)	(371,824)
Gain	69,176

Working

	No. of shares	Cost
		£
10 December 2018 @ £10 per share	300	3,000
5 April 2021 @ £80 per share	4,800	384,000
	5,100	387,000
1 April 2022 disposal	(4,900)	(371,824)
	200	15,176

The answer £216,176 uses £120 per share as the proceeds. The answer £56,000 does not pool the shares and treats the 5 April 2021 shares as sold first. The answer £70,000 does not pool the shares and treats the 10 December 2018 shares as sold first.

28   Payment of the CGT liability would have been postponed for 12 months

The payment date for the disposal on 1 April 2022 (2021/22) is 31 January 2023 and on a disposal on 6 April 2022 (2022/23) would be 31 January 2024

He would have been chargeable to CGT at 10% instead of 20% on some of the taxable gain

Christophe is a higher rate taxpayer in 2021/22 since his income exceeds the total of the personal allowance and the basic rate band £(12,570 + 37,700) = £50,270. In 2022/23 (assuming 2021/22 rates and allowances) his income is within that total, so some of the taxable gain would have been chargeable at 10% instead of 20%.

Christophe would only have been able to set the annual exempt amount for 2022/23 against the chargeable gain on 6 April 2022. It is not possible to carry forward CGT unused annual exempt amounts, unlike IHT annual exemptions.

He would not have been entitled to business asset disposal relief on the disposal because Custard Ltd is an investment company. Business asset disposal relief for shares only applies to those in trading companies.

29   Annual exemption 2022/23

The normal expenditure out of income exemption cannot apply because Christophe only has excess income of £(20,000 − 18,000) = £2,000 which is insufficient to cover the gifts of £(250 × 12) = £3,000. The small gifts exemption only applies to gifts up to £250 per donee in a tax year; once exceeded all of the gifts to the same donee are chargeable. The annual exemption for 2021/22 has been used against the gift on 1 April 2022 and, in any case, the current year exemption is used first.

30   £304,167

$$\frac{£(312,000 - 20,000)}{312,000} \times £325,000 = £304,167$$

The answer £260,417 treats the exempt estate passing to Christophe as the unused nil rate band. The answer £292,000 does not deal with the increase in the nil rate band. The answer £308,333 treats the PET as being reduced by 20% taper relief. Remember that taper relief reduces death tax on a lifetime transfer, not the transfer itself.

Section C

31 (September/December 2019)

				Marks
(a)		Revised income tax liability		1
(b)	(i)	Base cost value inherited		1
	(ii)	Employment income	½	
		Pension lump sum	½	
		Premium bond prizes	½	
		Interest from ISA	½	
		Property income	½	
		Dividend income	½	
		Personal allowance	½	
		Income tax liability	2½	
				6
(c)	(1)	Pension fund outside estate	½	
	(2)	Other investments	1½	
				2
				10

(a) Kagan's revised income tax liability for 2021/22 will be £170,067 (165,000 + ((15,300 − 2,000) at 38.1%)).

(b) (i) The base cost of the shares will be their value at the time of the aunt's death (£510,000), so the minimal increase in value is likely to be covered by Kagan's annual exempt amount of £12,300.

(ii) **Kagan – Income tax liability 2021/22**

	£
Employment income	400,000
Pension lump sum	0
Premium bond prizes	0
Interest from ISA	0
Property income	9,600
Dividend income	1,950
	411,550
Personal allowance	0
Taxable income	411,550

Income tax

	£
37,700 at 20%	7,540
100,000 at 20%	20,000
112,300 at 40%	44,920
159,600 (411,550 – 1,950 – 100,000 – 150,000) at 45%	71,820
1,950 at 0%	0
411,550	
Income tax liability	144,280

(c) (1) The amount invested in the pension fund (and not withdrawn) will be outside of Kagan's estate, reducing the potential IHT liability.

(2) The investments in premium bonds, the ISA and the freehold property will not affect Kagan's potential IHT liability because one asset is simply being replaced with another of equivalent value.

This question involved Kagan who had inherited quoted ordinary shares valued at £510,000. Kagan was unsure whether to retain the shares or sell some of them in order to make four alternative investments.

Retain the inherited shares: Kagan would have received dividend income of £15,300 in addition to his employment income of £400,000 (for which the income tax liability was given) for the tax year 2021/22.

Four alternative investments: These consisted of:

(1) A personal pension contribution of £100,000, with Kagan having sufficient unused annual allowances to cover the pension contribution. He would immediately have withdrawn £25,000 of the pension fund tax-free.

(2) Investing £50,000 in premium bonds.

(3) Investing £20,000 in a cash individual savings account (ISA).

(4) Purchasing a freehold property for £295,000, with the property then let out unfurnished.

After making the four investments, Kagan would have been left with £65,000 of inherited shares, on which he would have received dividend income of £1,950 for the tax year 2021/22.

Part (a) for 1 mark required candidates to calculate Kagan's revised income tax liability for the tax year 2021/22 if he retained the inherited shares. Although fairly well answered, many candidates used valuable time doing full before and after tax computations. Kagan was clearly an additional rate taxpayer, so all that was required was to calculate the additional rate tax due on the dividend income and then add it to the provided figure of tax on the employment income.

Part (b)(i) for 1 mark required an explanation as to why little or no capital gains tax would have been payable if Kagan had sold some of his inherited shares. This was because assets are inherited at the value at the time of the deceased's death. If these assets are sold soon after being inherited, there will generally be a minimal increase in value (this fact was stated in the question), so any gain is likely to be covered by the annual exempt amount. It was pleasing to see that this part was well answered by those candidates who appreciated the tax treatment.

Part (b)(ii) for 6 marks required a calculation of Kagan's revised income tax liability for the tax year 2021/22 if he sold some of his inherited shares and made the four alternative investments. This section was reasonably well answered, but several points should be noted:

• The question stated that a full tax computation was required, so exempt items (pension lump sum, premium bond prizes and the interest from the ISA) should simply have been listed within the main computation and indicated as such by the use of zero (0) – not by an explanation.

- The non-availability of the personal allowance should have been indicated in the same manner. There was no need to justify the non-availability given the level of Kagan's income.

- Although there might only be a ½ mark available for recognising an exemption, it is important to know the various exemptions so that time is not spent producing unnecessary, and more complicated workings – such as applying the savings income nil rate band where the interest from the ISA was included as savings income.

Part (c) for 2 marks required candidates to state for each of the four alternative investments whether the investment would reduce Kagan's potential inheritance tax liability compared to him retaining the inherited shares. Unfortunately, this section was not well answered. Candidates need to remember, that unlike other taxes, there are few exemptions from inheritance tax. Therefore, the replacement of the quoted shares with either premium bonds, an ISA or freehold property would not have changed the value of Kagan's chargeable estate. However, the investment in the pension fund (which is not withdrawn) would have been outside of Kagan's estate, thereby reducing his potential IHT liability.

32 Robinette (September/December 2019)

			Marks
(a)	(i)	Salary	½
		Living accommodation	1
		Running costs	½
		Workplace nursery	½
		Mileage allowance	1
		Personal allowance	½
		(W1) Trading profit old business	3½
		(W2) Trading profit new business	2½
		(W3) Property income	2
			12
(b)	(i)	(1) 12 months from receipt	1
		(2) Random basis	1
			2
	(ii)	5 years from 31 January after tax year	1
			15

(a) Robinette – Taxable income 2021/22

	£
Employment income	
Salary (10,600 × 6)	63,600
Living accommodation – Rent paid (690 × 6)	4,140
Running costs	1,440
Workplace nursery	0
Mileage allowance (5,200 at 10p (45p – 35p))	(520)
	68,660
Trading profit – Old business (working 1)	75,350
– New business (working 2)	11,800
	155,810
Property income (working 3)	6,288
	162,098
Personal allowance	(0)
Taxable income	162,098

Tutorial notes

1   The provision of a workplace nursery is an exempt benefit regardless of the cost to the employer.

2   No personal allowance is available because Robinette's adjusted net income of £162,098 exceeds £125,140.

Working 1 – Trading profit (old business)

	£
14-month period ended 30 June 2021	106,900
Balancing allowance	
(15,300 + 2,600 − 1,750 − 7,300)	(8,850)
	98,050
Relief for overlap profits	(22,700)
	75,350

Working 2 – Trading profit (new business)

		£
Five-month period ended 30 June 2020		55,700
Capital allowances (26,200 × 100% AIA)		(26,200)
		29,500
Assessed in 2021/22	29,500 × 2/5 =	11,800
1 February - 5 April 2022		

Working 3 – Property income

	£
Rent receivable (1,100 × 6)	6,600
Insurance (624 × 6/12)	(312)
Property income	6,288

(b) (i) (1) If HMRC intend to carry out a compliance check into Robinette's self-assessment tax return for 2021/22, then they will have to notify her by 14 August 2023 (12 months after they received her tax return).

(2) If Robinette is confident that her return is complete and accurate, then the likely reason for HMRC carrying out a compliance check is because the return has been selected on a random basis.

(ii) Robinette was in business during 2021/22, so all of her records (both business and non-business) must be retained until five years after 31 January following the tax year, which is 31 January 2028.

The income tax question involved Robinette.

- She had ceased self-employment on 30 June 2021, preparing accounts for the 14-month period from 1 May 2020 to 30 June 2021. The trading profit figure was given (before taking account of capital allowances).

- From 1 August 2021 to 31 January 2022, Robinette was employed by Bird plc, who provided her with living accommodation and a place in the company's workplace nursery for Robinette's son. Robinette used her private motor car for business purposes.

- Robinette commenced self-employment again, in a new business, on 1 February 2022. She prepared accounts for the five-month period from 1 February to 30 June 2022. The trading profit figure was again given (before taking account of capital allowances).

- In addition, Robinette received property income from letting out her main residence during the period she was employed by Bird plc.

Part (a) for 12 marks required candidates to calculate Robinette's taxable income for the tax year 2021/22. This section was generally very well answered.

However, candidates should always read the question carefully to ensure they understand what needs to be done before starting their answers. Where only taxable income is required, as in this part, candidates should never spend valuable time in also calculating the income tax liability.

However, taxable income is after deducting the personal allowance, and this should have been shown by the use of zero (0) (Robinette's level of income meant that the personal allowance was reduced to nil).

Given that the question involved various changes in Robinette's sources of income, candidates needed to be very careful in regard to time-apportionment and basis periods. Common problems included:

- Time-apportioning profits for the period of cessation.

- Not appreciating that WDAs, the AIA and FYAs are not given for the period of cessation.

- Time-apportioning the trading profits on commencement before capital allowances have been deducted.

With this type of question, candidates should think carefully about which workings can be included as one-line calculations within the main computation, and which need their own separate working. For example, the mileage allowance working of 5,200 at 10p (45p − 35p) = £520 should have been included within the main computation.

Part (b) for 3 marks required candidates to (1) state the period during which HM Revenue and Customs (HMRC) would have to notify Robinette if they intended to carry out a compliance check in respect of her self-assessment tax return for the tax year 2021/22, and the likely reason why such a check would be made, and (2) to advise Robinette as to how long she must retain the records used in preparing her self-assessment tax return for the tax year 2021/22. Although there were a number of good answers, in general this section was not so well answered as part (a). Candidates should note:

- The fact that the requirement was for a total of just three marks should have been a good indication that only a few brief points needed to be made, and not a much longer discussion.

- Where a question asks for dates, then these dates need to be precise – including the year relevant to the question.

- Answers should always be related to the information provided. The question made it clear that Robinette's self-assessment tax return was complete and accurate, so the likely reason for HMRC carrying out a compliance check was because her tax return was selected on a random basis.

33 Maison Ltd

Marks

(W1)	Deduction for lease premium		
		Premium paid	½
		Deduction	1
		Per annum and time apportioned	1
(W2)	Capital allowances		
		Main pool	½
		AIA on integral features	1
		130% FYA on P&M	1
		SBA on building costs	1
(W3)	Property income		
		Rent receivable	1
		Security deposit	½
		Insurance	1
		Initial repairs	1
		Advertising	½
(W4)	Chargeable gains		
		First property	
		Gain	½
		Indexation allowance	1
		Enhancement expenditure	½
		Second property	
		Gain	½
		Indexation allowance	1
Corporation Tax			½
Figures provided in question			1
			15
			15

Maison Ltd – Corporation tax computation for the year ended 31 March 2022

	£
Operating profit	892,900*
Non-deductible expenditure	22,340*
Deduction for lease premium (working 1)	(715)
Capital allowances (working 2)	(70,500)
Trading profit	844,025
Property business income (working 3)	28,685
Loan interest receivable	1,460*
Chargeable gains (working 4)	77,985
Taxable total profits	952,155
Corporation tax (952,155 at 19%)	180,909

*Figures provided in question

Working 1 – Deduction for lease premium

	£
Premium paid	44,000
Less: 44,000 × 2% × (12 – 1)	(9,680)
Amount assessed on the landlord as income	34,320
Deduction (34,320/12 years × 3/12)	715

Working 2 – Capital allowances

	£	£
Main pool		12,037
Capital allowances		
Building costs	0	
Ventilation system - AIA preferable to 50% FYA	6,700	
Heating system - AIA preferable to 50% FYA	3,900	
Furniture and furnishings - 130% FYA (£33,500 × 130%)	43,550	
Refrigerator and microwave cooker- 130% FYA (£2,600 × 130%)	3,380	
		57,530
Structures and buildings allowance (£93,300 × 3% × 4/12)		933
Total allowances		70,500

Working 3 – Property business income

	£
Rent receivable (18,300 + (18,300 × 2/3))	30,500
Security deposit	0
Insurance	(1,035)
Initial repairs	0
Advertising	(780)
Property business income	28,685

Tutorial notes

1   A security deposit, less the cost of making good any damage, is returned to the tenant on the cessation of a letting. It is therefore initially not treated as income.

2   The cost of insurance for the period 1 July to 1 November 2021 is deductible as pre-trading expenditure.

3   The cost of the initial repairs to the warehouse are disallowable capital expenditure as the warehouse could not be let out in its original state and this was reflected in the purchase price paid.

Working 4 – Chargeable gains

	£
First property	
Gain	109,800
Indexation allowance	
Cost (101,000 × 0.315)	(31,815)
Enhancement expenditure	0
Chargeable gain	77,985
Second property	
Gain	26,000
Indexation allowance	
Cost (117,000 × 0.315) – Restricted	(26,000)
Chargeable gain	0

Tutorial notes

1   There is no indexation allowance for the first property's enhancement expenditure of £26,200 because this was incurred after December 2017.

2   For the second property, the indexation allowance cannot create a capital loss.

The corporation tax question involved Maison Ltd, for which a partly completed draft corporation tax computation had been prepared for the year ended 31 March 2022. The figures provided were correct, but there were four uncompleted sections, all related to property. These were:

*   A deduction for the payment of a lease premium.

*   Capital allowances in respect of the construction of an extension adjacent to the company's existing freehold office building.

*   Property business income from the letting of a warehouse which was purchased in a dilapidated state.

*   Chargeable gains on the disposal of two investment properties.

The sole requirement for 15 marks was to prepare a completed version of Maison Ltd's corporation tax computation for the year ended 31 March 2022 after dealing with the uncompleted sections. The question was generally very well answered.

As regards layout, candidates should again include as many workings as possible within the main computation. Given that a draft layout was provided, then this layout should have been followed by candidates in their answers, thereby allowing candidates to achieve as many of the available marks as possible.

Lease premium: A number of candidates did not appreciate that this was a deduction rather than an addition.

Capital allowances: This part of the question has been amended due to changes in the Finance Act so the examining team's comments are no longer relevant.

Property business income: Many candidates were not aware that the cost of initial repairs was disallowable capital expenditure because the property could not have been let out in its original state and this was reflected in the purchase price paid.

Chargeable gains: Figures for the two chargeable gains were given, so candidates should not have recalculated them. The reason for giving more information (proceeds and expenditure) was so that the indexation allowance could be calculated. Candidates should always deal with each gain separately, and not combine the figures.

Tax tables

SUPPLEMENTARY INFORMATION

(a)   Calculations and workings need only be made to the nearest £.
(b)   All apportionments should be made to the nearest month.
(c)   All workings should be shown in Section C.

TAX RATES AND ALLOWANCES

The following tax rates and allowances are to be used in answering the questions.

Income tax

		Normal rates	Dividend rates
Basic rate	£1 – £37,700	20%	7.5%
Higher rate	£37,701 – £150,000	40%	32.5%
Additional rate	£150,001 and over	45%	38.1%

Savings income nil rate band	– Basic rate taxpayers	£1,000
	– Higher rate taxpayers	£500
Dividend nil rate band		£2,000

A starting rate of 0% applies to savings income where it falls within the first £5,000 of taxable income.

Personal allowance

	£
Personal allowance	12,570
Transferable amount	1,260
Income limit	100,000

Where adjusted net income is £125,140 or more, the personal allowance is reduced to zero.

Residence status

Days in UK	Previously resident	Not previously resident
Less than 16	Automatically not resident	Automatically not resident
16 to 45	Resident if 4 UK ties (or more)	Automatically not resident
46 to 90	Resident if 3 UK ties (or more)	Resident if 4 UK ties
91 to 120	Resident if 2 UK ties (or more)	Resident if 3 UK ties (or more)
121 to 182	Resident if 1 UK tie (or more)	Resident if 2 UK ties (or more)
183 or more	Automatically resident	Automatically resident

Child benefit income tax charge

Where income is between £50,000 and £60,000, the charge is 1% of the amount of child benefit received for every £100 of income over £50,000.

Car benefit percentage

The relevant base level of CO_2 emissions is 55 grams per kilometre.

The percentage rates applying to petrol-powered motor cars (and diesel-powered motor cars meeting the RDE2 standard) with CO_2 emissions up to this level are:

51 grams to 54 grams per kilometre	14%
55 grams per kilometre	15%

The percentage for electric-powered motor cars with zero CO_2 emissions is 1%.

For hybrid-electric motor cars with CO_2 emissions between 1 and 50 grams per kilometre, the electric range of a motor car is relevant:

Electric range

130 miles or more	1%
70 to 129 miles	4%
40 to 69 miles	7%
30 to 39 miles	11%
Less than 30 miles	13%

Car fuel benefit

The base figure for calculating the car fuel benefit is £24,600.

Company van benefits

The company van benefit scale charge is £3,500, and the van fuel benefit is £669.

Vans producing zero CO_2 emissions (zero emission vans) have a zero benefit charge.

Individual savings accounts (ISAs)

The overall investment limit is £20,000.

Property income

Basic rate restriction applies to 100% of finance costs relating to residential properties.

Pension scheme limits

Annual allowance	£40,000
Minimum allowance	£4,000
Income limit	£240,000
Lifetime allowance	£1,073,100

The maximum contribution which can qualify for tax relief without any earnings is £3,600.

Approved mileage allowances: cars

Up to 10,000 miles	45p
Over 10,000 miles	25p

Capital allowances: rates of allowance

Plant and machinery

Main pool	18%
Special rate pool	6%

Motor cars

New cars with zero CO_2 emissions	100%
CO_2 emissions between 1 and 50 grams per kilometre	18%
CO_2 emissions over 50 grams per kilometre	6%

Annual investment allowance

Rate of allowance	100%
Expenditure limit	£1,000,000

Enhanced capital allowances for companies

Main pool super deduction 130%
Special rate pool first year allowance 50%

Commercial structures and buildings

Straight-line allowance 3%

Cash basis accounting

Revenue limit £150,000

Cap on income tax reliefs

Unless otherwise restricted, reliefs are capped at the higher of £50,000 or 25% of income.

Corporation tax

Rate of tax: Financial year 2021	19%
Financial year 2020	19%
Financial year 2019	19%
Profit threshold	£1,500,000

Value added tax (VAT)

Standard rate	20%
Registration limit	£85,000
Deregistration limit	£83,000

Inheritance tax: nil rate bands and tax rates

	£
Nil rate band	325,000
Residence nil rate band	175,000
Rate of tax on excess over nil rate band – Lifetime rate	20%
– Death rate	40%

Inheritance tax: taper relief

Years before death	Percentage reduction
More than 3 but less than 4 years	20%
More than 4 but less than 5 years	40%
More than 5 but less than 6 years	60%
More than 6 but less than 7 years	80%

Capital gains tax

	Normal rates	Residential property
Rates of tax: Lower rate	10%	18%
Higher rate	20%	28%
Annual exempt amount		£12,300

Capital gains tax: business asset disposal relief (formerly entrepreneurs' relief) and investors' relief

Lifetime limit – business asset disposal relief	£1,000,000
– investors' relief	£10,000,000
Rate of tax	10%

National insurance contributions

Class 1 Employee	£1 to £9,568 per year	Nil
	£9,569 to £50,270 per year	12%
	£50,271 and above per year	2%
Class 1 Employer	£1 – £8,840 per year	Nil
	£8,841 and above per year	13.8%
	Employment allowance	£4,000
Class 1A		13.8%
Class 2	£3.05 per week	
	Small profits threshold	£6,515
Class 4	£1 to £9,568 per year	Nil
	£9,569 to £50,270 per year	9%
	£50,271 and above per year	2%

Rates of interest (assumed)

Official rate of interest	2%
Rate of interest on underpaid tax	2.60%
Rate of interest on overpaid tax	0.50%

Standard penalties for errors

Taxpayer behaviour	Maximum penalty	Minimum penalty – unprompted disclosure	Minimum penalty – prompted disclosure
Deliberate and concealed	100%	30%	50%
Deliberate but not concealed	70%	20%	35%
Careless	30%	0%	15%

Review Form – Taxation (TX – UK)

Name: _____   **Address**: _____

_____

_____

How have you used this Kit?
(Tick one box only)

☐ On its own (book only)

☐ On a BPP in-centre course_____

☐ On a BPP online course

☐ On a course with another college

☐ Other _____

Why did you decide to purchase this Kit?
(Tick one box only)

☐ Have used the Workbook

☐ Have used other BPP products in the past

☐ Recommendation by friend/colleague

☐ Recommendation by a lecturer at college

☐ Saw advertising

☐ Other _____

Which BPP products have you used?

Workbook   *Other*

Practice & Revision Kit   ☑

During the past six months do you recall seeing/receiving any of the following?
(Tick as many boxes as are relevant)

☐ Our advertisement in *Student Accountant*

☐ Our advertisement in *Pass*

☐ Our advertisement in *PQ*

☐ Our brochure with a letter through the post

☐ Our website www.bpp.com

Which (if any) aspects of our advertising do you find useful?
(Tick as many boxes as are relevant)

☐ Prices and publication dates of new editions

☐ Information on product content

☐ Facility to order books

☐ None of the above

☐

Your ratings, comments and suggestions would be appreciated on the following areas.

	Very useful	Useful	Not useful
Passing Taxation (TX – UK)	☐	☐	☐
Questions	☐	☐	☐
Top Tips etc in answers	☐	☐	☐
Content and structure of answers	☐	☐	☐
Mock exam answers	☐	☐	☐

Overall opinion of this Practice & Revision Kit   Excellent ☐   Good ☐   Adequate ☐   Poor ☐

Do you intend to continue using BPP products?   Yes ☐   No ☐

The BPP author of this edition can be emailed at: learningmedia@bpp.com

Review Form (continued)

TELL US WHAT YOU THINK

Please note any further comments and suggestions/errors below.